Inventing the Israelite

STANFORD STUDIES IN JEWISH HISTORY AND CULTURE

EDITED BY *Aron Rodrigue and Steven J. Zipperstein*

Inventing the Israelite

Jewish Fiction in
Nineteenth-Century France

Maurice Samuels

STANFORD UNIVERSITY PRESS

STANFORD, CALIFORNIA

Stanford University Press
Stanford, California

Published with the assistance of the Frederick W. Hilles
Publication Fund of Yale University.

Portions of Chapter 2 and the Conclusion will appear in the
forthcoming book *A Global Approach to French Literary History*,
edited by Christie McDonald and Susan Suleiman (Columbia
University Press). Reprinted with permission of the publisher.

Library of Congress Cataloging-in-Publication Data
Samuels, Maurice.
    Inventing the Israelite : Jewish fiction in nineteenth-century
France / Maurice Samuels.
        p.   cm.—(Stanford studies in Jewish history and culture)
    Includes bibliographical references and index.
    ISBN 978-0-8047-6384-4 (cloth : alk. paper)
        1. French fiction—Jewish authors—History and criticism.
    2. French fiction—19th century—History and criticism.
    3. Judaism and literature—France—History—19th century.
    4. Jews in literature. I. Title. II. Series: Stanford studies in
Jewish history and culture.
    PQ637.J4S26 2010
    843'.7098924044—dc22
                                                    2009023661

Typeset by Motto Publishing Services in 10.5/14 Galliard

Contents

Acknowledgments

This book speaks across the disciplines of French studies and Jewish studies. As a scholar trained in the former, I had much to learn about the latter. I therefore wish to thank all the colleagues who facilitated my education and welcomed me into the field with generosity and patience.

I began the project while teaching at the University of Pennsylvania, and the book bears the stamp of the dynamic scholarly community there. A grant from the Penn Research Foundation enabled me to undertake initial research in Paris, and the Gruss Fellowship at Penn's Center for Advanced Judaic Studies provided a stimulating forum to begin writing. I thank David Ruderman and the staff of the CAJS for their encouragement and support. The other fellows at the CAJS offered important guidance as I launched the project. John Pollack and Arthur Kiron from the Penn library went above and beyond to help me locate texts and images. David Stern, Beth Wenger, and the other members of the Jewish Studies faculty at Penn made me feel part of an exciting team. My sorely missed writing group at Penn—Barbara Fuchs, Kevin Platt, and Emily Steiner—helped me shape the project and were my first readers. Other colleagues in Philadelphia, especially Gerald and Ellen Prince, Michèle Richman, Jerome Singerman and Liliane Weissberg, Jacob Soll and Ellen Wayland-Smith, and the late Frank Bowman, shared their wisdom in memorable ways.

My move to Yale may have slowed the book down a bit, but it also made it better. I'm very grateful to my colleagues in the French Department at Yale, as well as in the university as a whole, for creating such a supportive working environment. Conversations with Ora Avni,

Howard Bloch, Peter Brooks, Edwin Duval, Steven Fraade, Paula Hyman, Alice Kaplan, Thomas Kavanagh, Ivan Marcus, Millicent Marcus, Maria Rosa Menocal, John Merriman, Christopher Miller, Julia Prest, Marci Shore, and Francesca Trivellato have taught me a great deal. Agnès Bolton and Brenda Crocker supplied much-appreciated administrative support. The students in my undergraduate seminars on Jewish identity and French culture, both at Penn and Yale, provided a challenging sounding board. The graduate students at both institutions have been some of my best interlocutors.

Sections of this book appeared as articles, and I wish to thank all the editors who helped me refine my arguments and prose. Sheila Jelen, Michael Kramer, and Scott Lerner have continued to offer valuable advice even after the editing process ended. Invitations to present material related to this project at Colby College, Columbia, Dartmouth, Johns Hopkins, Harvard, NYU, and Stanford, as well as Penn and Yale, helped me to imagine an audience for the book when such a thing still seemed distant. I thank the colleagues who invited me, as well as those who listened to me, at all those institutions. I gave many papers from the project at the Nineteenth-Century French Studies Colloquium and am deeply thankful for the wonderful feedback I received from colleagues there. Emily Apter, Dorian Bell, Margaret Cohen, Elisabeth Ladenson, Bettina Lerner, Marshall Olds, and Lawrence Schehr deserve special thanks for engaging with this project over the years.

Although Naomi Schor died before I started this book, her work on French universalism helped me finish it. Susan Suleiman has taught me about both French and Jewish subjects since I was an undergraduate, and I value our continued discussions of these issues tremendously. I owe a great debt to friends and colleagues who have supplied much-needed help at various stages of the project: Evelyne Bloch-Dano, Brian Cheyette, Alain Créhange, Elisabeth Franck, Chuck Goldblum, Carine Hazan, Elisabeth Hodges, Elana Kay, Aaron Kuhn, Philippe Landau, Elisabeth-Christine Muelsch, Yves Niquil, Gisèle Sapiro, Sarah Sasson, Ronald Schechter, Nelson Schwartz, Alyssa Sepinwall, Jennifer Siegel, Jonathan Skolnick, Elliot Thomson, Melissa Toth, Karen Underhill, Nicolas Weill, Patrick Weill, and Steven Zipperstein.

The librarians and archivists at the Bibliothèque Nationale de France, the Alliance Israélite Universelle, and the Archives Nationales deserve my very special thanks. Sara Phenix and Chapman Wing provided extremely valuable research assistance. I am grateful for all the help I received at Stanford University Press. I could not have asked for a better editor than Norris Pope.

The support of Aron Rodrigue has been vital to me from the beginning of this project. His encouragement helped me conceive the book, and his advice all along the way made it immeasurably better. I am also deeply grateful to Olga Borovaya for her careful reading and her excellent suggestions at every stage, as well as for organizing an inspiring conference on Franco-Jewish writers at Stanford. Pierre Birnbaum, Jonathan Hess, and Lisa Moses Leff all gave wonderful advice on sections of the manuscript. Lawrence Kritzman deserves my deepest thanks for his incisive reading and excellent suggestions. As always, Jann Matlock has been generous with her advice, her editorial expertise, and her friendship. Other close friends—David Geller, Valerie Steiker, and Caroline Weber—provided much-needed feedback on parts of the manuscript. Ghita Schwarz heroically read the entire thing and has more than anyone supported me through the project's ups and downs. I thank them, along with all my other friends, for listening to me complain about the book for so long.

I am grateful, finally, to my family for their love and for showing me just how complex Jewish identity can be. Barbara Samuels has, as always, been a source of inspiration. I dedicate this book to my father, Richard Samuels, for once again making everything possible.

Inventing the Israelite

Introduction: Out of the Archive

Nineteenth-century French Jews have often received bad press. Victims of some of the most virulent attacks in the history of modern antisemitism, they were pilloried in their time by foes on both the left and the right. In the 1840s, socialist firebrands denounced them as lords of a new financial feudalism.[1] In the 1880s, Édouard Drumont's best-selling *La France juive* [Jewish France] cast them as nefarious agents of revolution and as rootless invaders intent on taking over the nation.[2] By the time of the Dreyfus affair in the 1890s, antisemitic mobs in both metropolitan France and colonial Algeria accused them of high treason. However, more potentially damning condemnations—because less preposterous—have come from other Jews.

Certain historians of Judaism fault nineteenth-century French Jews for having made the least of the most. When I began this project, a librarian at a major American Jewish research center, to whom I had turned for help in locating some nineteenth-century periodicals, asked me why the French Jews in this period had contributed nothing to Jewish culture despite having more freedom than Jews in any other country in Europe. According to her, there were no nineteenth-century French Jewish religious thinkers worth mentioning, no biblical scholars or philosophers of Judaism, no fiction writers who described the Jewish experience before Marcel Proust—and he was baptized. How different from the German Jews!

Alongside this cultural critique, political critics have portrayed nineteenth-century French Jews as misguided apostles of assimilation.[3] Writing in the aftermath of the Nazi genocide, Hannah Arendt devotes a large portion of her section on antisemitism in *The Origins of Totalitarianism* to the French case and specifically to the French Jews' inability to meet the challenge of the Dreyfus affair. For Arendt, nineteenth-century French Jews were parvenus who failed to see their true status as pariahs. "When the Dreyfus Affair broke out to warn them that their security was menaced, they were deep in the process of a disintegrating assimilation,"[4] Arendt maintains, describing how French Jews at the time of the affair refused to speak out against anti-semitism for fear of jeopardizing their own social integration. According to Arendt, this explains "why so few wholehearted supporters of Dreyfus were to be found in the ranks of French Jewry."[5]

These are serious charges, for they paint a picture of a deluded community—or lack of community—that failed to act in politically responsible ways. The legacy of these nineteenth-century delusions, Arendt implies, led the French Jews into the snare of Auschwitz.[6] Even if we avoid the error of viewing the nineteenth century through the lens of twentieth-century catastrophe, the critiques of both Arendt and the librarian raise serious questions. Were nineteenth-century French Jews really so politically and culturally deficient? Did they contribute nothing to Jewish culture? Did their embrace of French citizenship blind them to menacing realities and inhibit communal solidarity? Did their desire to become French preclude their remaining Jews? Or have our own ideologies, our own assumptions about the nature of assimilation—or about the nature of France—blinded us to the historical reality of the French Jewish experience?

I began this project on the hunch that fiction produced by these nineteenth-century French Jews—were it to exist—would help answer these questions. What kinds of stories, I wondered, did French Jews tell about their situation in the century after the Revolution of 1789, when France became the first modern country to emancipate the Jews? How did nineteenth-century French Jews imagine their place in the nation and the world? How did they conceive of their past and their future? How did they view their relation to other Jews? Increasingly, scholars have come to view fiction as a place where such existential questions are asked with particular urgency and where ideologies become manifest in particularly telling ways. Moreover, literary publication, by definition, represents a form of public expression. The mere existence of nineteenth-century French Jewish fiction—which I define as fiction by and about Jews, published in French[7]—would thus constitute a refutation of charges that French Jews completely abandoned their communal affiliations or made their Judaism a matter of private confession only.[8]

But have we even bothered to look for such literature, let alone tried to understand what it has to say about the dynamics of Jewish emancipation and assimilation?[9] The answer is clearly no. The reasons for this lacuna are partly ideological; until recently, literary critics in France, and to a lesser extent in the United States, have tended to avoid categorizing fiction through reference to a writer's ethnic or religious background. This is no doubt partly a reaction to the overt antisemitism of certain literary critics before World War II.[10] Even if this taboo has been lifted, leading to a number of fine studies of French Jewish fiction of the twentieth century, the case of the nineteenth century remains almost totally unexplored.[11]

Indeed, historians of French Jewish literature have denied that Jews wrote fiction in French before 1900. Armand Lunel (1892–1977), for example, maintained that until the end of the nineteenth century "there was not yet in France a literature that one could call specifically and exclusively Jewish. . . . It is in vain that one would look for a Jew who had manifested himself as such in Belles-Lettres."[12] A recent textbook on French Jewish history echoes this view, arguing that nineteenth-century French Jews were too preoccupied with material concerns and with the struggle to integrate into French society to write fiction: "But, in the 1890s, an intellectual generation succeeded the economic and social emancipation generation."[13] It was in response to the virulent antisemitism of the Dreyfus affair, according to this source, that a small handful of writers—including André Spire (1868–1966), Edmond Fleg (1874–1963), Jean-Richard Bloch (1884–1947), and most significantly Marcel Proust (1871–1922)—began to confront the difficult realities facing modern French Jews in fiction as well as poetry.[14]

And yet, while researching my last book, on historical representation in nineteenth-century France, I came across the historical novel *La juive* [The Jewess], published in 1835 by a Jewish woman from Bordeaux named Eugénie Foa. Written in the descriptive style of Walter Scott, this melodramatic page-turner, set in eighteenth-century Paris, tells the story of a Jewish woman who falls in love with a handsome Christian nobleman and dies as a result of her illicit passion. When I started to become interested in the question of Jewish literature a few years later, I went back to Foa and discovered that, beginning in 1830, she wrote a series of novels and stories about Jews and Judaism. These works fascinated me because of the way they used the popular generic forms of the day—including those of the historical and sentimental novel—to confront the central problems of Jewish modernity, including intermarriage, conversion, and the conflict between personal freedom and Jewish tradition. It seemed that this was evidence that a French Jew of the early nineteenth century in fact had made an attempt at writing fiction. But was Foa a lone case?

I knew that a few popular French writers of the nineteenth century were Jews, including Léon Gozlan (1803–1866), the prolific novelist, playwright, and biographer of Balzac, and Adolphe d'Ennery (1811–1899), the equally prolific playwright, librettist, and novelist.[15] They did not, however, write about Jews.[16] Although they might shed light on, or rather epitomize, the process of assimilation precisely through their failure to represent Jews or Judaism, their writing does not offer the kind of rich insight into the French Jewish experience that I found in Foa. Then I turned to the archive, or rather to *Les Archives*. I began to read the new French Jewish press of the period, especially the two major monthly Jewish newspapers founded in the early 1840s, *Les Archives Israélites* and *L'Univers Israélite*. These journals, which continued to thrive until World War II, published a great deal of writing in many genres, including fiction, and all of it depicted Jews. These journals also published reviews of other works, including much fiction that I was able to locate at the Bibliothèque Nationale in Paris, which finally convinced me that Foa had in fact inaugurated a trend.

This book represents my attempt to recover the forgotten tradition of nineteenth-century French Jewish fiction and to interpret it in light of both Jewish and French history. I focus on the novels and short stories produced in the period 1830–1870 by the first generation of Jews born as French citizens. This span, covering the July Monarchy (1830–1848), the Second Republic (1848–1852), and the Second Empire (1852–1870), represents the point at which Jewish faith in the path of emancipation was at its highest level, following the fall of the conservative Restoration monarchy (1815–1830) and before the outbreak of fin de siècle antisemitism. I ask what the fiction produced by French Jews at this moment of greatest confidence in their social integration has to tell us about the nature of Jewish modernity, about the processes of acculturation and assimilation, and about the role of literature, specifically French literature, in theorizing this struggle. I also ask what this fiction tells us about the place of minority groups in France and about the possibilities for forging particular identities within the French universalist tradition, which, as Naomi Schor has noted, grants rights not to groups but only to individuals, conceived as abstract, neutral subjects.[17] Might French Jewish fiction lead us to revise our assumptions not only about the failure of nineteenth-century French Jews to contribute to Jewish culture but also about the French Republican hostility to all public manifestations of group identification?

In *Inventing the Israelite* I argue that fictional narrative served French Jews as a unique kind of laboratory for experimenting with new identities.[18] Because of its imaginative nature, fiction provided nineteenth-century French Jews with a way to envision situations that had not necessarily presented themselves in the world but that could present themselves. It let them test possibilities, imagine scenarios, and work out their implications. And because narrative always unfolds in a time sequence—with a beginning, middle, and end—it provided a particularly apt way to explore what might happen to a given social actor in a given situation.[19] Fictional narrative, I suggest, offered a way for French Jews to think through their new historical situation.

I intend this book to speak to those interested in French literature and history as well as to those interested in Jewish literature and history. I enter the conversations in each of these areas while simultaneously speaking across disciplinary boundaries by showing what each field has to offer the other. By revealing the existence of a specifically *French* Jewish literature in the nineteenth century, I contribute to the ongoing effort to correct the myopia in Jewish studies resulting from a traditional focus on the German case—emblematized by Jacob Katz's *Out of the Ghetto*—as the paradigm for Jewish modernity.[20] Similarly, by bringing to light a uniquely *Jewish* brand of French fiction, I show how minority difference has inhabited modern French literature from the start. Literary analysis, then, becomes a vehicle for historical analysis, just as historiographic debates provide the necessary framework for making sense of these little-known novels and short stories. And although I draw throughout this book on literary and historical theorists, my goal is to reveal how these fiction writers were themselves theorists of the modern French Jewish experience.

In the remainder of this introduction, I sketch out some of the more specific contributions I see this book making. First, however, I present a bit of background on the history of Jews in modern France. I begin this survey with the French Revolution, the great turning point in the history of France's Jews—indeed, in the history of all Jews—the moment at which they first became full and equal citizens of a modern nation. My goal in this introduction, as throughout the book, is to make this material both accessible to those who know little about Jewish or French history and interesting to those who know a lot. Accordingly, I have tried to emphasize the ways in which the history of France's Jews sheds new light on familiar topics in French historiography. I have also tried to call attention to the features that make the French case unique in modern Jewish history.[21]

Modern French Jews in Historical Perspective

Although France expelled the Jews definitively in 1394, several Jewish communities had taken root on French soil by the eighteenth century. At the time of the Revolution of 1789, approximately 40,000 Jews lived in France.[22] These included the roughly 5,000 Sephardim (Jews from Spain and Portugal) who had fled the Inquisition to settle in southwestern France, in Bordeaux and nearby Bayonne, beginning in the fifteenth century.[23] Roughly 30,000 Ashkenazim (Jews of German origin) lived in the northeastern provinces of Alsace and Lorraine, which became part of France in the seventeenth century. The papal states in and around Avignon in the south, which became part of France in 1791, were home to several thousand Jews who lived in ghettos, called *carrières*, into the eighteenth century. In addition, about 500 to 800 Jews lived in Paris, where they were technically not allowed before the Revolution. Most of these clandestine Parisian Jews originated from the three other poles of French Jewish settlement.[24]

By the time of the Revolution, the Sephardic Jews of southwestern France had achieved a certain amount of integration into French society, although they retained their Jewish communal ties. They spoke French, owned land, and participated actively in the economic and political life of the region.[25] The same was not true for the Ashkenazic Jews in Alsace and Lorraine. These Jews more closely resembled their coreligionists in eastern Europe. Forbidden from inhabiting most large towns or cities and prevented from engaging in most trades and professions, they lived dispersed in small rural villages, spoke Western Yiddish, and eked out meager livings in petty trade, especially peddling, horse trading, and money lending.[26] Largely despised by their Christian neighbors, they retained a high degree of communal autonomy, with their own legal and governance structures. Whereas the Sephardim of Bordeaux were generally open to Enlightenment ideas, the Ashkenazim of Alsace and Lorraine remained bound to Orthodoxy, practicing traditional rabbinic Judaism. Although small pockets of Maskilim (Jewish Enlighteners) formed among the Jews allowed to live in Metz and although these eastern communities did begin to modernize slightly by the eighteenth century, the vast majority of France's eastern Jews lived much as they had since the Middle Ages.[27]

The Revolution radically altered the fate of all of France's Jews and for the first time cast their lots together. Despite their tiny numbers (0.14 percent of a country of about 28 million), the Jews attracted a surprising amount of attention from the revolutionaries. The *cahiers de doléances*, or books of complaint compiled by the government on the eve of the Revolution, contained numerous gripes against Jewish business practices in Alsace and Lorraine, where the Jews, although poor themselves, often offered the only credit available to the local peasantry. But a desire to ameliorate this situation alone does not explain why the revolutionary legislature took up the question of the status of the Jews in nearly thirty sessions between 1789 and 1791, despite more pressing concerns, including famine and war.

Ronald Schechter has argued that the Jews offered eighteenth-century reformers a test case for Enlightenment: If even this most backward of peoples could be made into productive citizens, then anybody could.[28] Voltaire held both the ancient Jews and their modern descendants to be retrograde fanatics, inherently inferior moral beings deserving of their degraded state.[29] But to many of his fellow philosophes, the Jews were capable of transformation. Treat the Jews fairly, provide them with secular education and economic opportunity, and their negative characteristics, the product of centuries of persecution, would fade away. So went the liberal argument of the Abbé Henri Grégoire, the revolutionary priest from Lorraine, who argued first in a prizewinning pamphlet and then before the Constituent Assembly that Jews should be made citizens.[30]

The decision to grant the Jews citizenship seemed to follow naturally from the Declaration of the Rights of Man and the Citizen, promulgated on August 26, 1789, which stated that "all men are born, and remain, free and equal in rights." The implications of this universalist statement did not apply to all in practice, however. The revolutionaries at first denied all non-Catholics the right to hold office, restricted the vote to those who paid a substantial tax, delayed emancipating slaves until 1794, and never allowed women to vote.[31] The revolutionaries nevertheless eventually decided to grant citizenship to Protestants and Jews as part of a general move to dissolve corporations and dismantle the structures of communal autonomy that threatened to intervene between the individual and the new revolutionary state.

Arguing before the Constituent Assembly, the liberal Count Stanislas de Clermont-Tonnerre linked the granting of citizenship to the Jews to the renunciation of their corporate status: "To the Jews as a Nation, nothing; to the Jews as individuals, everything," he proclaimed.[32] For Clermont-Tonnerre, individual Jews could become citizens but must give up their communal political structures—their local governance and legal systems—in exchange. However, the situation was complicated by the fact that the Jews continued to adhere to distinct groups. The Jewish communities of Paris, Bordeaux, and Alsace-

Lorraine all petitioned separately for citizenship, and the Sephardim were especially desirous to avoid what they considered an abasement of their status through inclusion with their less acculturated coreligionists from eastern France.

The revolutionary Constituent Assembly eventually granted citizenship to (male) Jews in two separate decrees. First, the Sephardic Jews of the southwest became citizens in January 1790, and then the mass of Ashkenazic Jews followed in September 1791. The Jews in the papal states were included with the Sephardic Jews in the first decree and became citizens when these territories joined France in 1791.[33] This revolutionary gesture marks the first time a modern nation specifically and deliberately emancipated the Jews, removing all legal obstacles to their civil equality. By contrast, Jews in England could not vote until 1835 and could not sit in Parliament until 1858, and many German Jews did not gain citizenship until German unification in 1870. In the United States, Jews had civil rights from colonial times but were never singled out for emancipation. After American independence and despite the First Amendment to the U.S. Constitution, which prohibited national laws establishing religion, Jews in some states could not hold office and faced other legal restrictions until late in the nineteenth century.[34]

As Napoleon conquered Europe, he brought emancipation to the Italian, Dutch, and German Jews.[35] In France, however, Napoleon's policies toward the Jews were mixed. On the one hand, he established Judaism as an official religion, on a par with Catholicism and Protestantism, through the creation of the Jewish Consistory, a governmental committee elected by Jewish notables, which tightly controlled all aspects of Jewish religious practice and subjected them to the scrutiny of the state. He also convened a body of Jewish notables and rabbis from France and Italy, which he dubbed "the Grand Sanhedrin" in reference to a legal body from ancient Israel, as a means of gaining religious sanction for Jewish social integration. On the other hand, he issued a number of discriminatory decrees regulating Jewish business practices in Alsace.[36]

Following Napoleon's downfall, the government of the Bourbon Restoration was generally liberal in its policies concerning Jews even as it reinstated Catholicism as the state religion. When Napoleon's discriminatory decrees expired in 1818, the Restoration did not renew them. Louis-Philippe, who replaced the Bourbons after the Revolution of 1830, took a giant step forward by instituting official parity between the three major religions. In 1831, he put rabbis on the state payroll (like Catholic priests and Protestant pastors). This gesture—the first time Judaism became a state-subsidized religion in any modern nation—had the paradoxical effect of problematizing Jewish group affiliation in France. Before 1831, French Jews had paid a special tax to support their synagogues; after 1831 the government picked up the tab. The state had cut one of the last tangible cords that tied many Jews to their community.

Freed from the struggle over emancipation that occupied Jews in other European countries and freed from the restrictions that excluded them from schools and professions, individual French Jews achieved unparalleled success in the nineteenth century. As in other countries, Jews particularly excelled in business and the arts. Only in France, however, did unconverted Jews reach the highest levels of government, beginning in the 1830s.[37] In the 1840s, three Jews were elected to the Chamber of Deputies.[38] Following the Revolution of 1848, Jews occupied two of eight ministerial positions in the provisional government and continued to hold high ministerial posts in the Second Empire (1852–1870).[39] Jewish participation in government would accelerate under the Third Republic (1870–1940), despite an increase in antisemitism during this period.[40] In the twentieth century, France had five prime ministers of Jewish origin.[41] And unlike in most other European countries, the French army promoted Jews to officer ranks from the beginning of the nineteenth century. The fact that the Dreyfus affair took place in France can be traced not only to the residual antisemitism of the French army but also to that institution's democratic openness, for Dreyfus had achieved the rank of captain despite practicing Judaism. According to Pierre Birnbaum, the army represented a privileged vector of social integration for French Jews in the nineteenth century, especially for Alsatian Jews.[42]

But although individual Jews achieved remarkable success in a variety of fields in the nineteenth century, a large percentage of France's Jews remained quite poor and only partly acculturated. This is true for many of those Jews who stayed behind in rural villages in Alsace and Lorraine as well as for the constantly increasing numbers of Jews who moved to large towns and cities. Christine Piette estimates that in 1840, 16.6 percent of the Jewish population of Paris was bourgeois, about the same as in the general population.[43] She further estimates that roughly 20 percent lived in poverty, with those in between engaged mostly in small trade. Throughout the century, however, increasing numbers of Jews throughout France began to adopt bourgeois occupations and comportments. This transformation can be traced through the disappearance of the Jewish peddler, the sign of Jewish economic and social backwardness and a figure of opprobrium for both antisemites and acculturating Jews. According to Paula Hyman, in Lyon the percentage of peddlers among the Jews declined from 75 percent in 1810 to roughly 50 percent in 1830 to only 13 percent in 1860.[44]

As the Jews joined the bourgeoisie, they shed many of the trappings of traditional Jewish life, such as the use of Yiddish, and often ceased to attend synagogue as well. However, although numerous voices among both the Reform and the Orthodox complained about the rising tide of religious indifference in the Jewish community, relatively few French Jews chose to convert in the nineteenth century, perhaps because they had little to gain from it. According to Philippe-E. Landau, who consulted church archives, there were only 74 conversions in Paris during the July Monarchy and 222 during the Second Empire.[45] This is another feature that sets the French case apart from the German, for in Germany conversion remained the essential "admission ticket" (the phrase is attributed to Heinrich Heine) to many universities and liberal professions before 1870. Unlike in England, where Protestant conversion societies flourished in the nineteenth century, the French Catholic Church made few concerted efforts to convert the Jews after the July Monarchy.[46] Historians have also estimated that intermarriage rates in France were likewise comparatively low, with acculturated Jews often marrying other acculturated Jews in the nineteenth century.[47] This suggests that communal affiliation and ethnic ties outlasted religious practice.

France's Jewish population grew rapidly throughout the first half of the nineteenth century. There were 70,000–80,000 Jews out of a total French population of 33 million in 1840.[48] By 1861 this number had risen to 95,881, only to fall by 45 percent following the loss of Alsace and Lorraine to Germany in 1870.[49] Paris saw the most significant growth in its Jewish population throughout the nineteenth century.[50] Whereas only 500 to 800 Jews lived in the capital in 1789, the official census of the Consistory in 1809 put the Jewish population of the capital at 2,908. By 1840, this number had risen to roughly 9,000.[51] And by 1880, following the loss of Alsace and Lorraine, which prompted many Jews to move to the French capital from the eastern provinces, the Jewish population of Paris had grown to 40,000, a nearly hundredfold increase in less than a century.

Although some of this increase was the natural result of high birthrates, the Jewish population explosion in Paris also resulted from immigration. Jews came to Paris from not only Alsace-Lorraine but also other European countries in the mid-nineteenth century, especially Germany. These German migrants shared cultural, religious, linguistic, business, and familial ties with the Jews of Alsace-Lorraine and integrated into their communities. Although some Jews also came to France from eastern Europe in the mid-nineteenth century, it was not until after 1880 that France saw a large influx of *Ostjuden* (Jews from eastern Europe), who were on the whole much more Orthodox, traditionalist, and working class than the Jews from Alsace-Lorraine and Germany. These Jews tended to congregate in certain neighborhoods (the Marais as well as the eighteenth and twentieth arrondissements of Paris) and retained the use of Yiddish to a much greater extent than the Jews from Alsace-Lorraine and Germany.

In many ways the cultural and class differences between these two groups of Ashkenazic Jews at the end of the nineteenth century anticipated the divide between the Ashkenazic Jews and the Jews who arrived from North Africa (Algeria, Morocco, Tunisia, and Egypt) following decolonization in the 1950s and 1960s. In the period I am considering (1830–1870), however, the Jewish community of France was more cohesive. The main distinction at the start of the period lay between the Ashkenazic Jews from Alsace-Lorraine and Germany on the one side and the less numerous Sephardic Jews of Bordeaux (and the Jews of the former papal states), who were relatively more acculturated and whose religious rite was slightly different, on the other. But even these differences gradually ceased to signify in the nineteenth century, as the two groups increasingly intermarried and developed close social and economic ties.

In the following sections I take a step back from this rapid survey of the history of Jews in modern France to examine four key issues in greater detail. These four issues bring into focus the features that make nineteenth-century French Jews unique in both French and Jewish history: their struggle to assert their Jewish particularity within the French universalist tradition, their status as representative modern subjects, their special relation to French culture, and their position in debates over religion and state secularism. I provide a sense of the scholarly debates around these issues in order to isolate the ways in which this book makes new contributions. My goal is to reveal how the forgotten fiction produced by Jews in nineteenth-century France sheds important light on their history.

Negotiating the Universal and the Particular

Perhaps the most central question concerning nineteenth-century French Jews is whether or not, or to what extent, they abandoned their Jewish specificity by becoming French citizens. To many, the emancipation bargain presented to the Jews during the French Revolution seemed to be a zero-sum game; their transformation from Jews into Israelites—as the acculturated French citizens of the Mosaic persuasion preferred to call themselves—required the exchange of Jewish specificity for the universal rights of the French Republican tradition. As Birnbaum puts it, "Their entry into the public sphere, which transforms them into citizens, embodies the logic of a State in which universalist principles imply the disappearance of all particularisms: in this sense, the fate of the Jews is a product of that top-down emancipation, which is hostile to all communitarian forms of social or political organization."[52] In other words, the French revolutionary tradition's universalizing logic, the same logic that provided the

Jews with citizenship, also seemed to demand of them the surrender of their identity as Jews.

Because of their rapid and comparatively easy path to emancipation, French Jews developed a unique confidence in the French state as the guarantor of their universal rights. This confidence increased to the extent that France offered the example of one of the world's oldest, strongest, and most centralized state structures. Birnbaum has argued that as a result, French Jews in the nineteenth century came to identify closely with the state and its universalizing ideology, transforming from the Old Regime "court Jew" into the modern "state Jew" (*juif d'état*). It is this "statist model" that Birnbaum sees as defining the specificity of Franco-Judaism, especially after the advent of the Third Republic in 1870, when Jews increasingly sought careers in the army and civil administration, becoming what Birnbaum calls "crazy for the Republic" (*fous de la République*).[53] For Arendt, as well as for later historians of French Judaism, including most notably Michael Marrus, this close identification with the state left the French Jews unable to meet the challenges of the Dreyfus affair and later the Vichy government, when the state and its institutions suddenly turned against them.[54] Having supposedly surrendered their Jewish identity and having disbanded their community, French Jews had few resources to fall back on.

Recently, Birnbaum and other historians have complicated this picture by questioning to what extent French Jews in the mid-nineteenth century actually surrendered all forms of Jewish identity as they became citizens. Did accepting the universal really result in a loss of the particular? As we have seen, even the most highly acculturated French Jews by and large did not convert or intermarry in this period, suggesting a survival of ethnic affiliation.[55] As Phyllis Cohen Albert maintains, "Even while adopting the French language, identifying with the history and values of France, and turning into French patriots, the Jews retained a sense of belonging to their own culture, which makes them an ethnic sub-group."[56] But if Jews retained their Judaism in private, did they also express their affiliation in public? And if so, in what ways? These are key questions bearing not only on the status of Jews in France but also on the relation of minority groups to the French

Republican tradition more generally. To what extent did the universalizing ideology of the French Revolution necessitate the surrender of ethnic or religious affiliation?

Clearly, Jewish communal organization changed radically as a result of the Revolution: French Jews did surrender the special courts and autonomous government that had structured the community in the Old Regime. But they also developed new forms of communal organization, new ways of bringing their Judaism into the public sphere. The Jewish newspapers that began in the early nineteenth century and flourished beginning in the 1840s are one example of a public expression of minority identity.[57] The creation of state-sponsored Jewish schools is another.[58] And if writers in the Jewish press lamented that synagogue attendance had fallen, the mid-nineteenth century also saw the construction of monumental synagogues throughout France, financed partly at government expense, which forcefully announced the presence of Judaism within the public sphere.[59] French Jews, it has become clear, most certainly did not become invisible in the period leading up to the Dreyfus affair.

They did not even eschew what we would properly consider communitarian forms of political action. Michael Graetz, Aron Rodrigue, and Lisa Moses Leff have called attention to the politics behind the founding of the Alliance Israélite Universelle, the international Jewish aid organization, by French Jews in 1860.[60] This organization is a conundrum for historians attempting to understand why French Jews, at the moment when their place in France seemed most secure, would risk their position by reaching out to their less assimilated coreligionists abroad. This effort, which required them to lobby French politicians and intervene with foreign governments in the name of international Jewish solidarity, contradicts what we thought we knew about Franco-Judaism and its relegation of all forms of Jewish particularity to the private sphere. Certain French Jews in the mid-nineteenth century do seem to have worked within the universalist tradition to advance their interests as a group.

French Jews, then, did in fact continue to think and act as Jews, even in the public and political realm, in the decades leading up to the Dreyfus affair. As Leff argues, it was the affair itself and the outpouring of antisemitism that surrounded it that forced French Jews, including the leaders of the Alliance, to become more circumspect.[61] To a certain extent, it seems that scholars such as Arendt and Marrus have anachronistically projected this fin de siècle circumspection back onto the mid-nineteenth century.[62] In fact, contrary to what is commonly assumed, the French Republican tradition of universalism did not require a relegation of all Jewish particularism to the private sphere, at least before the Third Republic. As Aron Rodrigue has demonstrated, the Alliance Israélite Universelle even saw its mission as the export of French universalism to Jews abroad.

In the chapters that follow I demonstrate that fiction played a key role in helping French Jews negotiate these thorny issues. The very act of publishing fiction *about* Jews and *as* Jews indicates the extent to which authors willingly asserted their Jewish particularity in public ways. But more than this, fiction provided a space for working through the implications of the emancipation bargain for the writers themselves and for their readers. I show how, during the crucial years between the Restoration and the Third Republic, when France was struggling with the legacy of liberalism and universalism inherited from the Revolution, Jewish writers used their novels and short stories to imagine new forms of identification, both individual and collective, and to experiment with possibilities for speaking and acting as Jews. The conflict between the universal and the particular is certainly one of their main concerns. It is in fiction that the new ideology of solidarity binding French Jews to each other and to Jews abroad first makes its appearance. It is likewise in fiction that French Jews make some of their most audacious attempts to reconcile the particular and the universal, indeed to offer a Jewish universal in place of the Christian one they saw lurking behind the supposedly secular Republican tradition.[63]

The struggle between universalism and particularism continues to define French political life today. Because the French revolutionary tradition recognizes the individual alone as the bearer of universal rights, it has been reluctant to acknowledge the political claims of minority groups. The French have only recently begun to allow for "affirmative action," or what they term *la discrimination positive*. However, the perception that these universalist principles have clashed with the ugly realities of racism and with the fact that certain minorities in France—especially those of Arab or African descent today—have experienced disadvantages as a group and not only as individuals has led to a crisis of French universalism in recent years. Those who feel excluded from political, economic, and social life in France because of their belonging to a certain group have found few outlets in the political sphere and at times have turned to violence to express their dissatisfaction.

In this book I suggest that nineteenth-century Jewish fiction sheds light on these persistent concerns. By investigating the strategies developed by Jews to assert their particularity within the universalist framework, I point to a range of options for minorities attempting to assert themselves without sacrificing the advantages offered by the French universalist system. This is not to argue that the nineteenth-century Jews were a "model minority" or an example to follow but rather to note that they confronted the problem of how to reconcile minority affiliation with the demands of French universalism earlier than other groups, and in a paradigmatic way.

I also suggest that nineteenth-century French Jewish fiction can therefore provide a useful point of reference for minority writers in France today. Indeed, the writers I discuss here might be said to have invented the category of ethnic fiction in French, by which I mean fiction by a member of a minority group that represents that group's relation to the dominant culture. Certainly, the Jewish writers I discuss here thematize many of the same concerns faced by more recent immigrant writers, or writers who are the children and grandchildren of immigrants.[64] These concerns include the struggle over religious practice, language use, generational conflict, pressures to succeed and conform, and the omnipresent struggle against prejudice that were as acute in the nineteenth century as they are today. And like contemporary writers, nineteenth-century Jewish writers adapted existing generic forms—such as the sentimental novel—for new purposes, in the process inflecting universalizing codes with ethnic particularity. Once again, my goal is not to argue that these nineteenth-century Jewish writers offer a model for others to follow but rather to insist on a long-standing but hitherto invisible tradition of ethnic writing in French that might help us historicize current literary debates.

At the Forefront of Modernity

The case of nineteenth-century French Jews also offers telling insights into debates about the modernization process. By modernization I mean the adoption of new modes of thought, including a rational and scientific worldview; new kinds of economic activity, including participation in the nascent industrial economy; and new ways of conceiving of the self in relation to the world, including the valorization of the individual. Once again, I want to suggest that the modernization of the French Jews in the nineteenth century was paradigmatic both in Jewish history and in French history.

Although Jewish historians have traditionally seen the Germans as the modernizing vanguard among Europe's Jews, it was really in France that the changes associated with modernization were felt most intensely. This is largely because France, and particularly Paris, confronted its citizens with earlier and more rapid political, technological, economic, and social change than other countries. When most European capitals were still sleepy backwaters, Paris became the "capital of the nineteenth century," in Walter Benjamin's words, the place where modernity—by which I mean the cultural and social effects of industrial capitalism—made itself felt most acutely.[65]

Even though France experienced the transition to industrial capitalism later than England, by the 1830s Paris had become the world's center of consumer culture. The density of Paris made for a unique kind of metropolitan experience that we now identify with the creation of a new kind of modern subject, for whom the fast pace of urban life produced a sensorial overload of which Baudelaire became the bard.[66] The introduction of omnibuses, railways, and gas lamps by midcentury profoundly changed the relation of urban subjects to their milieu. It was in Paris that the arcades, the first urban shopping malls described memorably by Benjamin, helped transform the commodity into a spectacle.[67] During the Second Empire, Napoleon III and his

prefect of the Seine, Baron Haussmann, undertook an enormous re-
building project that completed this process, razing the remainder of
the old medieval city to make way for grand new boulevards, department stores, train stations, palaces for international exhibitions, and
other settings for the worship of capital in all its forms.[68]

French Jews found themselves at the forefront of these changes. If
Voltaire denounced the Jews as the most backward of peoples before
the Revolution and criticized them for their adherence to outdated
customs, by the 1840s the Jews had become synonymous with change
in all its forms. In fact, certain highly visible Jews pioneered many
of the changes associated with the transition to modernity in France.
The Rothschild banking house as well as the Péreire brothers' Crédit
Mobilier revolutionized France's banking system.[69] Beginning in the
1830s, these two rival Jewish families also competed to put in place
France's first railway lines, arguably the most significant technological
innovation of the first half of the nineteenth century. Jews took a leading role not just in modernizing the French economy and infrastruc-
ture but in modernizing French culture as well. Jacques Offenbach
and his new light operettas provided a sound track to the bustling life
of the boulevards, just as publishers like Arthur Meyer helped create
the first mass-circulation newspapers.[70]

The Jewishness of these pioneers did not go unnoticed, especially
by the first wave of socialist pamphleteers, who by the 1840s had begun denouncing the Jews as agents of a nefarious modernity. In *Les
juifs, rois de l'époque* [The Jews, Kings of the Age] (1845), one of the
master texts of a new socialist antisemitism, the Fourierist journalist
Alphonse Toussenel denounced the Rothschilds and their coreligionists for creating a new, modern form of "financial feudalism." Following a deadly accident on the Rothschilds' Northern Railway Line in
1846, a spate of viciously antisemitic pamphlets held the Jews responsible for this frightening new technology.[71] French fiction likewise associated the Jews with the economic as well as the social and cultural
changes that had transformed France. The novels of Stendhal, Balzac,
Sand, Murger, Flaubert, the Goncourts, and Maupassant abound in
mostly unsympathetic Jewish characters—bankers, art dealers, prostitutes, and newspaper publishers. In Zola's *L'argent* [Money] (1891),

his novel about the stock exchange, Jewish characters represent both a new kind of international capitalism as well as the frightening specter of Communist revolution.

Paula Hyman has characterized Jewish modernity in France as "uneven," with great changes taking place in the Parisian Jewish community by the 1830s and the mass of Jews who remained behind in the Alsatian countryside retaining traditional ways late into the nineteenth century.[72] As I show in the chapters that follow, however, this traditional way of life was perceived—by modernizing Parisian Jews—as already endangered by the 1840s. Indeed, it seems that French Jews as a whole were more likely to embrace modernizing trends than their Christian contemporaries. According to Albert, by 1851, 45.1 percent of French Jews lived in large towns or cities versus only 17.9 percent for the total French population. This is a significant change for a population that was overwhelmingly rural—in fact, forbidden from living in most urban centers—only a little more than sixty years before.[73] And French Jews were far more likely to engage in "modern" occupations, such as banking and, after midcentury, the liberal professions, than in the more traditional occupations of farming and artisanal labor.[74]

Parisian Jews, in other words, were canaries in the coal mine of modernity: at the forefront of change in the country and in the cities, which were themselves at the forefront of change. Thus they offer not only Jewish historians but also French historians a unique perspective on the modernization process. French Jews confronted modernity in an especially self-conscious way, in part to take advantage of the new opportunities offered to them and in part to prove themselves worthy of these opportunities in the first place. Watched by a nation that held them as backward fanatics in need of regeneration and also increasingly as the opposite, as avatars of a terrifying new world order, French Jews developed keen insights into the stakes of modernity and its social and psychological effects.

If any one theme dominates their literature, it is this. The fiction I discuss, produced by Jews living in Paris between 1830 and 1870, theorizes the implications of the modernization process and provides a point of view not expressed in literature by Jews in other countries at the time. What did it mean for a French Jew in the 1840s to leave his village in Alsace and find himself on the Parisian boulevards? Or to leave the bustling metropolis and arrive, by train, back in his ancestral village in just a few hours? The novels and stories I analyze describe precisely these shocks of temporality and culture that Jews in other countries did not feel in the same way. The German Jews who wrote about similar issues—for example, Heinrich Heine or Karl Marx—had to come to Paris to feel modern.[75]

French Jewish fiction also provides insights into modernity not found in other French writing of the nineteenth century. Although it is true that non-Jewish fiction writers of the period, such as Balzac, used Jewish characters to frame their vision of modernity, they did so in stereotypical ways. Balzac's Baron Nucingen, who surfaces throughout the *Comédie humaine* [Human Comedy] as the archcapitalist, is described alternately as an Alsatian or German Jew and as the son of a convert from Judaism. In *Splendeurs et misères des courtisanes* [A Harlot High and Low] (1838–1847), Balzac shows how this master financial manipulator gives way to his passion for a beautiful prostitute, Esther, who is also described as Jewish. But the radical otherness of Nucingen—rendered through an opaque, phonetically transcribed Germanic accent, which Balzac's narrator describes as his "awful Polish Jew's jargon"—inhibits our identification with him.[76] The same might be said of Balzac's other Jews—the moneylender Gobseck in the novel *Gobseck* (1830), the art dealer Magus in *Le cousin Pons* (1847), or the beautiful prostitute Esther herself—who, although less linguistically marked, nevertheless betray a kind of all-encompassing difference that blocks the reader's identification. In the Jewish writers of the period, on the other hand, we find Jewish characters viewed from the inside. Balzac's modern Jewish types appear refracted in the fiction of his Jewish contemporaries, transformed from objects of scorn or envy or lust into subjects of social processes who reveal what it meant to become modern.

The Question of Culture

Historians have remarked on the ways that the culture of a given country affects the ways that the Jews in that country modernized.

Michael Meyer, for example, has shown how the movement for Jewish religious reform differed in different national contexts, taking on either the trappings of Catholicism or Protestantism according to the dominant religion in a given region.[77] Literary acculturation provides another, and I would argue highly revealing, example of this process. French Jewish writers developed not only a different language and different literary styles from their coreligionists in other countries but also different perceptual grids for encountering the world and making sense of it. But how exactly did this difference manifest itself?

Much has been made of the way in which German Jews assimilated not only German language and culture but also a specifically German ideal, or ideology, of culture itself. German Jews devoted themselves to the process of *Bildung*, the cultural formation of the individual, as a means of proving their worthiness for citizenship.[78] This idealization of culture outgrew its initial political purpose, coming to define the entire German Jewish self-conception.[79] Some highly educated Jews of the nineteenth and early twentieth centuries even came to see themselves as the fullest emblems of German culture, as the rightful inheritors of the German cultural tradition, at a time when belonging to the German nation was increasingly being defined along racial lines. The Nazi attempt to purge the Jews from the social and economic life of the country also had a strong cultural component, with great effort devoted to ridding the country of decadent—which is to say Jewish—artists, writers, and teachers, who were thought to represent modernity. Jonathan Freedman has traced the way related dynamics played out in the Anglo-American context in a later period, with English-speaking Jews forging their entry into the establishment through an appropriation of the terms of cultural and literary discourse during the twentieth century.[80]

Once again, the French case displays certain parallels with but also definite differences from these other national models. In general, the French in the nineteenth century idealized their nation's culture no less than the Germans or the Anglo-Americans did theirs, but the French did not restrict access to it based on race or religion, just as they did not restrict citizenship along racial lines. Certainly by the end of the nineteenth century, in Maurice Barrès's *Scènes et doctrines du nationalisme* [Scenes and Doctrines of Nationalism] (1902), for example, one begins to see a deterministic conception of culture and the nation linked to territorial or ancestral belonging. This logic would reach its grotesque end point during World War II, when antisemitic writers, including Paul de Man in Belgium, denounced the Jewish influence on French culture as a foreign corruption and the Vichy government stripped Jews of their civil rights.[81] But in the mid-nineteenth century a much more open attitude prevailed, the positive legacy of the liberal Republican universalist tradition in which anyone in theory could participate fully in French cultural life, just as anyone could participate fully in French political life. In other words, the unique way in which the French conceived of the nation as an ideological rather than an organic construct in the nineteenth century helped determine the unique way in which Jews participated in French cultural life.

In the 1830s and 1840s, the actress known as Rachel (Élisa-Rachel Félix, 1821–1858), who was from a poor Jewish family, helped to revive the French classical theater tradition through her interpretation of Racine's heroines—many of them biblical Jews—at the Comédie Française.[82] Commentators at the time remarked on her Jewishness. They were fascinated by it in ways that presage the darker moments of fin de siècle antisemitism, but most did not see it as an impediment to her "genius" or to her becoming the embodiment of an ideal of French culture.[83] Also in the 1830s, the Jewish composer Fromental Halévy exploited Jewish subject matter to create one of the classic works in the French grand opera tradition, *La juive* [The Jewess] (1835).[84] As scholars have argued, such public performances of Jewishness were calculated to appeal to a cultivated, liberal French audience that saw Jewish artists as exotic but did not relegate them to the margins.[85] Significantly, the French imagination of the period conceived of Jews not only as the manipulators of culture but also as its producers. Balzac not only describes his art dealer—Magus—as Jewish but also makes his most significant and admirable writer character—Raoul Nathan in *Illusions perdues* [Lost Illusions] (1837–1843)—a Jew.

French Jewish writers of the mid-nineteenth century thus entered a cultural landscape in which Jewishness often counted as an asset. Advertisements in the mainstream press in 1830 for Foa's first novel billed it erroneously as "translated from the Hebrew," no doubt to capitalize on the author's "exotic" origins (she was actually born in Bordeaux and wrote only in French).[86] By giving it the provocatively opaque title *Le kidouschim* [The Kiddushim] with its French definite article and mysterious Hebrew substantive, Foa clearly participated in this marketing ruse aimed at exploiting her difference to a public fascinated by the Romantic, oriental other. Foa and some of her mid-century followers thus claimed their place in French letters precisely by presenting themselves as Jews. But others, such as Gozlan (possibly the model for Balzac's Nathan) and d'Ennery, neither hid nor advertised their Jewishness and were also accepted into the literary world. Once again, the situation became more fraught for Jews in the late nineteenth century and early twentieth century, when antisemites began to police the borders of French literature.

What interests me, however, is less the location of Jewish writers in French culture than the location of French culture for Jewish writers.[87] How did the specificity of the French literary tradition determine the ways in which Jewish writing in French took shape? How did nineteenth-century Jewish writers negotiate the maze of style and genre choices within the horizon of nineteenth-century French literary culture? To what extent did they inflect these styles or genres or make use of these conventional forms to address specifically Jewish concerns? And how does their appropriation by Jews allow us to see these forms in a new light?

I am interested in the ways in which Jewish writers in France made use of some of the same generic forms as their coreligionists in Germany or England, including the historical novel, which gained international popularity beginning in the 1820s. But I am also interested in the way that French Jews pursued a unique path, in part because of the uniqueness of French literary culture. Nineteenth-century French writers inherited a strong tradition from the Enlightenment, but the period under consideration here, 1830 to 1870, was an especially fertile one for French literature. In 1830, Balzac initiated a way of describing contemporary life that subsequent critics would label realist. In the 1850s and 1860s, Gustave Flaubert would take this mode in new directions, wielding irony as a tool for social criticism in a biting attack on the hypocrisy and banality of the bourgeoisie. At the same time, Victor Hugo and George Sand addressed the era's social questions in a more sentimental manner, calling attention to injustice but also suggesting possible solutions in novels that critics labeled idealist.

French Jewish writers from the period explicitly positioned themselves in relation to these literary trends and debates. Thus we find one of the main features that set French Jewish literature apart from contemporary writing by Jews in other national contexts. Although Jews writing in other languages—Yiddish, for example—used Enlightenment satire as a tool for social critique, the French writers I discuss explicitly parodied classics from the French canon to make their points. Other French Jewish writers sought creative ways to blend the prevailing forms of realism and idealism to address dilemmas specific to French Jews. These French literary forms helped to shape the way French Jewish writers conceived of social and political issues. They determined the ways in which they framed problems and proposed solutions. In other words, Jewish modernity in France was imagined in the forms of the French literary tradition.

French writers at this time were also experimenting with new ways of producing and disseminating literature. With the rapidly expanding literacy that followed the Revolution, new classes of readers emerged who had different literary tastes from the largely aristocratic consumers of literature in the preceding centuries. To meet this increased demand, writers and publishers vastly increased their offerings and sought new ways to make their product available to the masses. One of the most significant of these innovations was the serial novel, or *roman feuilleton*, which began to appear in the era's rapidly expanding periodical press beginning in the 1830s. Many of the Jewish writers I discuss in this book published their works serially in the new Jewish newspapers beginning in the 1840s. They also aimed at new classes of readers by using the new literary codes that had helped make the *roman feuilleton* such a success; the melodramas and adventure stories I discuss were clearly intended as ways to speak to a broad public.

Comparing French Jewish literature with the fiction produced

by Jews in other countries reveals that in many key areas the French
writers were innovators. It was a French Jewish woman—Eugénie
Foa—who most likely wrote the first Jewish historical novel, a form
that would become one of the dominant vehicles for Jewish novelistic
production in Germany, England, and the United States in the mid-
nineteenth century. Because the new mode of nineteenth-century realism was invented in France, French Jews were also the first to use
modern realist codes—as early as the early 1840s—to criticize the
manners of the assimilating Jewish bourgeoisie. It was a French Jew
who claimed to have invented the genre of the village tale. And it was
also a French Jewish writer who initiated the genre of ghetto nostalgia
that would go on to play an important role in Jewish belles lettres in
western Europe beginning in the 1850s and in eastern Europe and the
United States well into the twentieth century.

Throughout *Inventing the Israelite*, I make references to contemporaneous German Jewish literature, drawing heavily on the work of
Jonathan Hess.[88] Although the German case offers the most points
of comparison with the development of Jewish literature in French,
numerous parallels could also be drawn to Jewish fiction in other linguistic and national contexts in the nineteenth century. Jewish newspapers in Russian published fiction serially, for example, beginning
in the 1860s.[89] Other eastern European Jews began to experiment
with Yiddish as a language for fiction at around the same time that
Jews began to write fiction in French. Two of the first Yiddish novelists, Yisroel Aksenfeld (1787–1866) and Yosef Perl (1773–1839), wrote
Enlightenment-inspired, anti-Hasidic satires in the first half of the
nineteenth century.[90] Yiddish writers would also make use of the serial
format to publish fiction in the 1860s, with the creation in Odessa of
Kol-Mevasser, a Yiddish supplement to a Hebrew weekly newspaper.[91]
In such works as *The Travels and Adventures of Benjamin the Third*
(1879), S. Y. Abramovitsh (1836–1917), considered the "grandfather
of Yiddish literature," adopted the traditionalist literary persona of
Mendele Moykher-Sforim (Mendele the book seller), which resembles
the literary alter egos of many of the French Jewish writers I discuss
here, to satirize eastern European Jewish life. As Dan Miron explains,

Abramovitsh/Mendele would later be lionized by the great Yiddish writers of the late nineteenth century in search of a tradition.[92]

American Jewish fiction did not develop as early as in France and Germany, but it eventually followed along a similar path. In the first half of the nineteenth century, fewer than 10,000 Jews lived in the United States and they produced little in the way of fiction. By 1860, however, with the arrival of Jewish immigrants from Germany, the community had grown to 150,000, and the first American Jewish novels began to appear. In 1854, Isaac Mayer Wise (1819–1900), a rabbi in Cincinnati of Bohemian origin, founded *The Israelite* (later *The American Israelite*), a weekly newspaper that would publish dozens of serialized works of fiction in English, mostly historical stories and novellas. These included Wise's own fiction and works by Nathan Mayer (1838–1912), an immigrant from Alsace. Jewish literature in America really took off, however, with the arrival of the large numbers of immigrants from eastern Europe, beginning in the 1880s.[93]

In other parts of the world, the production of Jewish fiction also occurred later than it did in France. In the Ottoman Empire, the first works of fiction in Ladino (Judeo-Spanish) appeared in the Sephardic press in the 1870s, although these periodicals had themselves begun as early as the 1840s. As Olga Borovaya has shown, this new genre of secular fiction involved the adaptation of an original work from another language—often serial novels by the likes of such non-Jewish French writers as Eugène Sue, Victor Hugo, and Alexandre Dumas père and fils, as well as classic English writers. Adaptation could involve simple translation but more often was a complete transformation of the original text to conform to Sephardic cultural norms and to inculcate the modernizing values that the rewriters wished to impart to the masses. Often these "rewritings" appeared without acknowledgment of the original text, its author, or the rewriter.[94]

In all these literary contexts, language played a key role in determining how Jews negotiated their identities in fiction. In the German states and Austria, the German language offered Jewish writers a chance to display their acculturation and to prove their worthiness for citizenship. The choice of Yiddish by novelists in eastern Europe in the nineteenth century reflected a different set of goals. Not considered a literary language at first, Yiddish seemed to offer, at least potentially, a way to spread a message of Enlightenment and reform to the Jewish masses.[95] By the end of the nineteenth century, however, writers began to use Yiddish as a way to define themselves in a secular Jewish culture.

French fiction writers in the nineteenth century wrote almost exclusively in French. Although some of these writers were familiar with Western Yiddish and many continued to study Hebrew as a liturgical language, French Jews did not write fiction in these languages. Alexandre Weill, one of the writers I discuss, who grew up bilingually in Alsace and who lived in Germany for a time, began his literary career by writing in German but switched to French early on. Just as the use of German by German Jewish writers served to signal their belonging in their native land, so too did the use of French become a way that French Jews in the nineteenth century made clear that they were at home in France. This was more of an issue in the first half of the nineteenth century, when large numbers of Jews remained unacculturated and reformers urged rabbis to deliver their sermons in French. By the middle decades of the nineteenth century, however, these debates had largely subsided. For most of the writers I discuss here, French was quite simply their native language and the only language in which they could have written fiction.

I should state at the outset that I resist all essentialist claims about a linguistic specificity of Jewish fiction in French. Jewish writers may have adopted certain literary codes or chosen to blend codes from the Jewish tradition with those of the French tradition in unique ways, but race or religion does not mark their turns of phrase in French. The written French of these writers is unremarkable even when they spoke it with an accent (as in the case of Alexandre Weill). Some of the writers I discuss occasionally used Yiddish or Hebrew words or phrases, but these were always translated immediately into French. Much of the fiction I describe thematizes the importance of speaking and writing good French as a key stage in the acculturation process. But the authors themselves do not display evidence of struggling for linguistic mastery.

The Role of Religion

So far I have described my interest in nineteenth-century French Jewish writers as primarily sociological and literary. I am interested in the ways in which these writers made use of literary and philosophical models inherited from the past, as well as more contemporary French literary genres and styles, to come to terms with their unique historical situation as members of a minority group attempting to redefine itself in the aftermath of the French Revolution. But what place does this leave for the Jewish religion as such? What role does Judaism itself play in this literature and in this struggle to create modern forms of Jewish identity? What did Judaism mean in nineteenth-century France? And how did religious belief change as a result of the radical transformation in both the lives of individual French Jews and in the structure of the community as a whole in the nineteenth century? Once again, these are questions that intersect in important ways with historical debates concerning secularism—or *laïcité*—in the French context today.[96]

To understand these debates, however, it is necessary to return to the Revolution of 1789, one of the main targets of which was Catholicism. Churches were ransacked, and priests who did not swear an oath of loyalty to the Republic were persecuted. The revolutionaries sought to replace the Christian God with an Enlightenment deity and substituted festivals dedicated to the Supreme Being for Sunday mass. This effort to rid the nation of its traditional religious culture never proved entirely successful, especially among the peasantry in remote rural regions. Napoleon's decision to make peace with the Catholic Church by signing the Concordat in 1801 had populist as well as political overtones. And when the Restoration government once again made Catholicism a state religion, it responded to a growing sense that the anticlericalism of the revolutionaries had gone too far.

The Restoration—the regime that immediately preceded the period under consideration in this book—saw a Catholic revival in France. Caroline Ford describes the clerical resurgence engineered by the Restoration authorities, culminating in the 1825 law against sacrilege, which made blasphemy against Christianity punishable by death.[97] Huge amounts of state money flowed into church coffers, and dozens of religious societies sprang up to encourage the spread of religion among the people during this period. The Restoration, however, also witnessed the origin of the modern anticlerical movement, which would come to exert increasing political pressure as liberals struggled to establish a secular republic. According to Theodore Zeldin, the fight over religion represented the most fundamental political division in France during the nineteenth century.[98] The official separation of church and state under the Third Republic, ratified in 1905, represented the culmination of more than a century of conflict.

French Jews had a complicated relation to this battle over religion in the nineteenth century. During the Revolution of 1789, synagogues shared the fate of churches, and Jewish worshippers braved the same dangers as their Christian neighbors. During the Revolution of 1848, writers in the Jewish press worried that the newest wave of antireligious sentiment would result in cuts to the budgets of all of France's official *cultes*.[99] At the same time, French Jewish leaders supported the secularization of the state, which for them meant not that the church and state should be separated but that the state should support the three major religions equally. During the Restoration, they allied themselves strategically with liberal opponents of the regime to oppose the trend toward state Catholicism.[100] Even if certain Orthodox Jews might have had more in common with traditional Catholics than with atheistic freethinkers, they still saw in state secularism the best guarantee of their religious and political liberty.

However, the meaning of religious faith for individual Jews in the nineteenth century is harder to determine than the political alliances of the community's leadership. I have tried to give a sense of the great variety of attitudes toward the religion that prevailed at the time, even as the Consistory managed to keep French Judaism officially unified. In each chapter I focus on a specific opinion or point on the period's religious spectrum. These include strict Orthodoxy, religious reform, and outright apostasy or conversion. I also describe more individual interpretations of Judaism, including calls for rejecting the Talmud in favor of a return to Mosaic monotheism and a secular approach to the religion based on nostalgia for a sentimentalized past. Often these different approaches defined themselves in relation to—or more accurately, in opposition to—each other, and I have tried to give a sense of the urgency of the debates that sprung up among partisans of the different religious approaches.

What emerges is a picture of a community that avoided the schism between Orthodoxy and Reform Judaism that splintered the Jews in Germany but that nevertheless remained divided over fundamental as well as more superficial elements of Judaism. The question of which laws to follow is central for these Jewish writers. But if *practice* emerges as a clear subject of debate, *belief* remains more elusive. Indeed, these authors rarely, if ever, discuss belief at all. They obsess over the relevance of even arcane religious laws but almost never analyze what it means to have faith in God in the first place. This does not mean, of course, that they did not think about such fundamental questions. But by and large their fiction avoids them, as does most of their nonfiction writing (in the press, pamphlets, etc.).

This lacuna is in itself significant. According to Arnold Eisen, there is something specifically Jewish in the tendency to privilege practice over belief: "Abstract matters like God and revelation have almost always remained inchoate and of decidedly secondary importance to the decisions that Jews have made about observance of communal commandments."[101] This became increasingly true in the modern period, when Jews assigned a range of new meanings to old rituals. Jews may have continued to attend synagogue on Yom Kippur out of a fidelity to their ancestors rather than out of a need to seek God's forgiveness. (And perhaps this is why some Jews before the modern period attended Yom Kippur services as well.) This does not mean that their belief in the ritual had vanished or become less "Jewish," only that it had mutated. As Eisen maintains, religious historians intent on tracing the decline of religion in modernity have tended to impose a notion of what constitutes belief and what motivates ritual performance that is derived from Christianity. But this notion effectively negates much of what constitutes Judaism in the modern period.

Accordingly, I have avoided attempts to determine the "real" religious beliefs of the authors in question and give a great deal of attention to their debates over ritual and practice. This is a historically and religiously accurate way of understanding how French Jews viewed matters of religion. What emerges from this study is a more nuanced view of the role of religion in nineteenth-century French life, one that leaves behind the false dichotomies between Orthodoxy and secularism, between faith and practice, between tradition and modernity. The French Jews I describe sought out ways to be religious even while fighting for a secular state, and in the process they redefined what it meant to practice Judaism.

The so-called return of religion in recent years has made these issues newly topical. Despite the "disenchantment of the world" that Max Weber identified as one of the key components of modernity, religious affiliations and beliefs, including fundamentalisms, have staged a comeback across the world.[102] And France has recently seen some of the fiercest clashes over the role of religion in contemporary society. Although France, like other European countries, has witnessed a general "exit from religion," to borrow the term of Marcel Gauchet, it has also struggled to accommodate the religious demands of its minorities.[103] The 1989 *Affaire des foulards*, or head scarf controversy, in which French Muslim girls fought unsuccessfully for the right to wear head coverings in public schools, demonstrates how fraught the question of *laïcisation* continues to be in France. I do not address such recent issues here, but it is my hope that the nineteenth-century debates about Jews and Judaism will provide a useful historical context for understanding current controversies.

In each of the chapters, I focus on the work of a single author but incorporate references to a wide variety of contemporaneous texts by both Jews and non-Jews. Although some of the authors, such as Foa and Daniel Stauben, have begun to receive some scholarly attention, none has amassed a substantial critical literature. Because these writers thus range from the totally unknown to the extremely obscure, I provide basic biographical facts, gleaned from a variety of published and archival sources, to aid in situating their literary production more precisely in its milieu. Issues of regional origin, religious and educational background, gender, and class status shed light on the way these writers envision the past, present, and future of French Jews and French Judaism.

In each case I analyze their writing about Jews and largely leave to the side their writing that does not thematize specifically Jewish concerns. The sampling of writers I describe does not provide a comprehensive view of all the French Jews who wrote fiction in the period. I have left out perhaps dozens of writers—such as Gozlan—who did not thematize Jewish issues as well as dozens more who did in ways I consider less compelling or exemplary than the writers under consideration here. But if my sampling is not comprehensive, it is representative. Each writer, and hence each chapter, marks a different point on the spectrum of approaches to Jewish identity in the mid-nineteenth century. Ranging from apostasy to Orthodoxy, from total assimilation to strict observance of Jewish law and tradition, these writers suggest different possibilities for being a Jew in modern France, for redefining the nature of Jewish affiliation. Taken together, they present the full range of options open to French Jews in the period from 1830 to 1870.

Chapter 1 presents the novels and short stories by the woman I believe was the first Jew to write fiction in French and perhaps the first modern Jewish woman to write fiction in any language. Born to one of the most prominent Sephardic families in Bordeaux, Eugénie Foa (née Rodrigues Henriques, 1796–1853) recast the popular generic forms of the sentimental and historical novel in Jewish terms, tackling issues of central importance to her elite milieu, including the clash between individual freedom and traditional authority. As I show, her interest in these questions remains constant while her opinions shift radically. Her own conversion to Catholicism mirrors the transition in her fiction from Orthodoxy toward a position advocating an extreme form of assimilation. But even though her fiction sanctions conversion and intermarriage as solutions to the problem of Jewish particularity, her own literary example exploits Jewish difference to carve out an identity in the crowded literary marketplace. This identity was also influenced by her gender. I pay especially close attention to the way her fiction analyzes the specific dilemmas faced by women within Jewish families and the Jewish religious tradition.

Ben-Lévi (Godchaux Baruch Weil, 1806–1878), the subject of Chapter 2, hailed from a family of wealthy Parisian Jews of Alsatian origin. Writing in *Les Archives Israélites* in the 1840s, he used the new literary codes that critics at the time were beginning to label realist in order to make the case for religious reform. Witty, urbane, and politically engaged, Ben-Lévi used his short stories to frame the dilemmas faced by the assimilating Jewish bourgeoisie and to attempt to theorize a new form of Judaism that even acculturated French Israelites could embrace, all the while chiding them for abandoning elements of tradition. He also displayed a deep concern for Jewish solidarity across class and national boundaries, and it is in his writings that we see the ideological groundwork for the Alliance Israélite Universelle take shape.

His rival at the Orthodox *Univers Israélite*, Alexandre Créhange (1791–1872), who wrote under the pseudonym Ben Baruch, comes into focus in Chapter 3.[104] Born into a more modest family in Lorraine, Ben Baruch appointed himself the champion of the capital's poor Orthodox workers and put his fiction in service of their struggle against the power structures of the French Jewish community, including the Consistory and the elite reformers of *Les Archives Israélites*. His itinerary as a writer represents a struggle to find the right literary form to express his populist and traditionalist vision of Judaism, shifting from Enlightenment satire to a unique mix of melodrama and Talmudic parable that he published in his own popular almanac. Despite his call to uphold tradition, however, Ben Baruch's Orthodoxy will reveal itself as no less modern than Ben-Lévi's reformist vision.

Alexandre Weill (1811–1899), the subject of Chapter 4, followed his own path, rejecting both Orthodox and Reform Judaism. Raised in a highly observant family in a small Alsatian village, he turned his back on his early training as a Talmudist to pursue a career in journalism in Paris. Vacillating between extreme left-wing and extreme right-wing politics, he eventually returned to Judaism during the Second Empire in order to transform it from within. His tales of life in France's eastern provinces dramatize the conflicts faced by poor rural Jews in their confrontation with modernity and advocate an anti-Talmudic brand of Judaism as a solution to Jewish, as well as French, political and social dilemmas. A tireless political agitator, Weill had no reticence about advocating for Judaism in the public sphere or about criticizing his fellow Jews in public, and he advanced his religious vision as a Jewish recasting of French universalism.

In the final chapter I explore a series of texts published in the 1840s through 1860s that look to the past as a model for the Jewish future. The fictionalized narratives of Daniel Stauben (born Auguste Widal, 1822–1875), which describe journeys from Paris to his native village in Alsace, invent a new form of Jewish nostalgia, whereas the historical fiction of David Schornstein (1826–1879) uses memory as a binding force for a community whose traditional center no longer holds. These texts turn backward as a way of cementing Jewish loyalty in the present and in the process advance literature itself, and especially fiction, as the sacred text of this distinctly modern form of Judaism. In the Conclusion, I look forward to the renaissance in Jewish fiction that occurred after the Dreyfus affair, specifically to the example of Marcel Proust (1871–1922), who I argue inherits the legacy of these nineteenth-century French Jewish writers. I also suggest that the efforts of these nineteenth-century Jewish authors constitute the first attempt at what might be called ethnic fiction in French.

Throughout this book I largely avoid references to the dark years to come (the Dreyfus affair and later the Vichy government) in order to take the Jewish literature of the mid-nineteenth century—with its faith in France and in the future—on its own terms. I wish to avoid the false perspective produced by historical hindsight and more specifically the "tragic" reading of French Jewish history that views the nineteenth century through the lens of the Holocaust.[105] I prefer to believe that the optimism of nineteenth-century French Jews was as justified at the time as its contrary, if not more so. Beyond a belief that Jews were not inherently wrong to believe that they had a future in France, I have tried to suppress, as much as possible, the ideological investments that might lead me to favor one solution to the problem of Jewish modernity over another. I have tried to give all points of view expressed by these nineteenth-century French Jewish writers—from Orthodoxy to apostasy—a fair hearing.

To conclude this introduction, I want to address one final concern, a question I have heard frequently since I began this project more than five years ago: Were these writers any good? I may have shown nineteenth-century Jewish fiction to exist—thus proving the Jewish librarian quoted at the start of this essay wrong. But have I proved that this fiction is worth reading? This is a familiar question for me, one that I heard asked many times in relation to my last book as well, in which I analyzed hundreds of obscure plays, historical texts, and historical novels. I once responded to such a questioner that I had read these texts so that others did not have to. I am not so sure I would answer similarly now. Literary quality is a vexed issue, one that depends on historically determined assumptions and practices. I do not believe it is universal or transhistorical. Certainly texts that were overlooked in a certain period can gain cultural currency in the next, just as texts often see their reputations deflate for reasons of fashion or critical repositioning.

Do these fictional works by nineteenth-century French Jewish writers possess the style and substance that will have today's readers devouring them in droves or that will launch them onto Ph.D. reading lists? Surely not. The questions they ask and the solutions they propose, both political and literary, are too firmly tied to the concerns of a specific minority group in a specific time and place. This is a minor, or more precisely a minority, literature, and one that knows itself as such.[106] But are these works worth reading precisely because they so clearly translate a set of specific historical concerns? Are they worth the investment of time and energy necessary to appreciate their unique, intelligent, often poignant, and frequently witty approaches to issues that, while resolutely historical, have a curious relevance for us today? This book is built on the gamble that they are.

One Romantic Exoticism: Eugénie Foa and the Dilemmas of Assimilation

Jewish fiction in French emerged in 1830, shortly after Jews began to surface as common subjects in fiction by non-Jewish writers. The first French Jewish writers entered the literary field by writing back to their Romantic contemporaries. They countered negative portrayals of Jews and offered a more positive vision of Jewish life in response to hostile attacks. At the same time, Jewish writers were not above trading in exotic stereotypes and indulging in vaguely held notions of racial difference. But even though they exploited Jewish subject matter to intrigue a public fascinated by the foreign, Jewish writers tended to provide a vision of Jewish life from within. Their representations drew on Romantic oriental stereotypes and appropriated the forms and features of literary convention, but they did so to frame issues of relevance to the nineteenth-century French Jewish community.

Perhaps more than any other work of literature or art, Walter Scott's *Ivanhoe* (1819) shaped the way the nineteenth century imagined the Jew. Scott's historical novel, which became a best seller in France, describes the trials and tribulations of the beautiful Jewish woman Rebecca and her father, the moneylender Isaac of York, in twelfth-century England.[1] Scott's novel recast ancient prejudices in liberal garb, foregrounding the Jew's negative traits but encouraging readers to see them as the product of prejudice. It also helped imprint on the Romantic imagination a Jewish gender dichotomy: The male Jew hoards and schemes, whereas the female Jew seduces all who see her with exotic allure. The *belle juive*, or "beautiful Jewess," along with her usurious male counterpart would provide Romantic novelists—and historians, artists, and composers—with a way of registering a fundamental ambivalence toward Jews just as they were beginning to enter the social and economic mainstream in the early decades of the nineteenth century.[2]

Scott's novel provided a framework for thinking through political and cultural dilemmas in racial terms. Although he excuses the Jew's faults, Scott asks the reader to see the Jew as irreconcilably different. Indeed, in *Ivanhoe* the persecution of Jews serves as the premise on which the early modern English state is founded. The only thing linking the rival Normans and Saxons in Scott's novel is their antipathy for the Jew—an antipathy that, in the case of Rebecca, is no less violent for its lustful overtones.[3] Published in the aftermath of Waterloo, Scott's Romantic historical novel looked to the past as a means of forecasting the future.[4] Its reflection on national identity, and particularly on the place of Jews within the European state, resonated across a continent in which nationalisms were gaining force and Jewish emancipation was being debated.[5]

In this chapter I explore what happens when a Jewish woman writes fiction in the Romantic period. How does she depict the relation of the Jew to emerging forms of national identity? How does she imagine the racial identity of the Jew? And what becomes of the long-suffering *belle juive* in her hands?[6] My discussion focuses on Eugénie Foa, the author of a series of fictional works about Jews published in the 1830s and 1840s, many of which explicitly engage with Scott's model. To my knowledge, Foa was the first Jew of either sex to write fiction in French. In what follows I argue that she was not only a pioneering author but also a pioneering theorist of Jewish identity in the post-emancipation period.

In both her historical fiction and her stories set in the present day, Foa tackles problems faced by Jews in nineteenth-century France, such as the clash between the authority of Jewish law and the modern forces of materialism and individualism. Like Scott, Foa uses the past to reflect on the future, but the solutions she devises to the problems of Jewish modernity differ from the Scottian model. They also differ from the solutions of the Jewish writers who followed her. Whereas both Scott and the other Jewish writers I discuss in this book privilege the integrity of Judaism and refuse calls for its dissolution, Foa eventually goes so far as to suggest that Jews may be better off by ceasing to be Jews. Foa oscillates between extreme end points on the French Jewish ideological spectrum in the nineteenth century—a trajectory conditioned, I argue, by her unique position in the social and literary fields.

In her fiction Foa moves from fidelity to Jewish law and tradition to an acceptance of conversion as a solution to the problems of Jewish modernity. And yet, even while calling for the transcendence of Jewish particularity, Foa did more than any other writer to invent a new way of writing about Jews and to forge a path for the Jewish writer in nineteenth-century France. It will be my task to unravel these and other paradoxes in Foa's fiction in order to shed light on both the complex itinerary of Jews in modern France and literature's role in making sense of this history.

A Jewish Writer?

Born Esther Rebecca Eugénie Rodrigues Henriques in 1796, Foa (Figure 1) descended from two of the most illustrious Sephardic families in Bordeaux. According to Arthur Hertzberg, Foa's maternal ancestors, members of the Gradis family, sat at the apex of international Jewish society in the eighteenth century.[7] Eugénie's maternal great-great-great grandfather, Diego Gradis, established himself as a cloth merchant in Bordeaux around 1685. His son, David Gradis (1665–1751), moved into overseas shipping, founding the Gradis firm, which came to dominate France's maritime commerce with its colonies in the Caribbean and Canada. David's son Abraham (1699–1780), Eugénie's uncle, founded the Société du Canada in 1748 and greatly expanded the family's wealth and influence.[8] Family legend maintained that when Louis XVI offered the Gradis family a noble title, they refused to accept it on the grounds that they could not swear on a Catholic bible.[9] The Gradis family did, however, accept special permission to own land in France's Caribbean colonies at a time when Jews were explicitly forbidden from doing so.[10] Slave rebellions in Martinique and Saint-Domingue during the French Revolution devastated the family's West Indian estates and nearly brought about the collapse of the firm.[11]

Figure 1. Portrait of Eugénie Foa. Courtesy of the Bibliothèque Nationale de France.

The family's fortunes had declined by the time of Eugénie's birth, but individual family members continued to enjoy prestige and exert influence, in both the Bordeaux Jewish community and French society at large. During the Revolution of 1789, a maternal relative, David Gradis (1742–1811), was chosen as one of the ninety electors of the Third Estate in Bordeaux, along with a fellow Jew, Abraham Furtado. Gradis missed election to the Estates General by a few votes but became one of Bordeaux's municipal governors.[12] Eugénie's father, Isaac Rodrigues Henriques (1765–1834), who was from a prominent Bordeaux banking family, represented the Jews of Bordeaux at the Assembly of Notables convened by Napoleon in advance of the Grand

Sanhedrin, which set the limits of Jewish religious law and helped pave the way for Jewish assimilation in France.[13]

Eugénie moved to Paris with her family, probably in the late 1820s. In the 1830s, Eugénie's widowed mother, née Esther Gradis (1780–1859), and unmarried siblings would live in the same building on the rue Montholon where their cousins, Olinde and Édouard Rodrigues, who played a leading role in the Saint-Simonian movement, resided.[14] A center of the elite Parisian Jewish social world in the first decades of the century, this building also housed the Halévy family of renowned musicians and writers. Although of Alsatian and hence Ashkenazic origin, Fromental Halévy (1799–1862), the composer of the popular opera *La juive* [The Jewess] (1835), married in 1842 Eugénie's younger sister, Hanna Léonie (1820–1884), who later became a noted sculptor.[15] The couple entertained the leading artistic and political figures of the day. Their daughter, Geneviève Halévy Bizet Straus (1849–1926), ran one of the most famous salons of fin de siècle Paris.[16]

Eugénie came from an extraordinarily talented family. Her younger brother, (Jacob) Hippolyte Rodrigues (1812–1898), retired in 1855 from a successful career as a stockbroker to pursue scholarship and the arts.[17] A founding member of the Société Littéraire-Scientifique Israélite (Israelite Literary-Scientific Society), he wrote a number of religious treatises as well as fiction, plays, humor pieces, and poetry, much of it on Jewish themes. He also composed music for the four-act opera *David Rizzio* in 1873. The painter Eugène Delacroix was a friend, correspondent, and visitor to Hippolyte's chateau at Fromont (Essonne). Hippolyte's son, Edgar Rodrigues (1837–1892), wrote military histories, and another of Eugénie's nephews, William Busnach (1832–1907), the son of her younger sister, Élisa Esther, was an extremely prolific Boulevard dramatist.[18] Eugénie's maternal uncle, Benjamin Gradis (1789–1858), who married her younger sister, Laure Sarah, wrote a number of political treatises, as well as an "oriental novel" titled *Zeïdouna*.[19] Their son, Henri Gradis, was a historian.[20]

Despite her alliances with Paris's Jewish intellectual and financial elite, Eugénie led a difficult life. In 1814, she married Joseph Eugène Foa, a Jewish merchant of Italian origin about whom little is known, and had two children. The marriage ended in separation. Although the sparse biographical accounts of Foa's life dispute whether she left her husband or was abandoned by him, the theme of the unhappily married Jewish woman, abandoned by her husband but unable to procure a divorce, recurs in much of Foa's fiction.[21] In the short story "Rachel, ou l'héritage" [Rachel, or the Inheritance] (1833), which I discuss later in this chapter, the eponymous heroine tells how her repressive Jewish father forced her into an unhappy marriage with a man who soon left her. "While Rachel told me that story that was at once so sad and at the same time so typical of the lives of certain of us weak women whom relatives often sacrifice for money or propriety, I looked at that poor victim of marriage," comments the sympathetic female narrator.[22] Despite the mockery and discouragement of her friends and family, who scorn her as a "woman writer," Rachel turns to writing in the hope of gaining financial independence.[23]

Foa herself turned to writing in 1830, following her separation, to support herself and her children.[24] Although historians have estimated that close to 50 percent of the writers in the July Monarchy were women,[25] female authors in the period still faced social reprobation and encountered numerous material and legal obstacles.[26] That a literary career nevertheless beckoned to a woman such as Foa in a difficult financial situation testifies both to the lack of other career options open to bourgeois women and to the changing economics of book publishing in nineteenth-century France.[27] Growing numbers of readers allowed a growing cadre of authors to live by their pens, and the expansion of newspaper publishing following the July Revolution, along with the creation of the serial novel, the *roman feuilleton*, in the 1830s, provided another venue for enterprising writers of fiction, including many women.[28]

Foa's varied literary output is typical of the professional writer of the period. In addition to contributing articles regularly to a number of newspapers and journals, under her own name and various pseudonyms (including Maria Fitz-Clarence), Foa published a great deal of fiction in a variety of genres. Between 1830 and 1835 alone, she published seven novels and collections of short stories, none of which went through more than one edition.[29] In the 1840s, however, Foa finally found a degree of success as an author of children's literature, founding her own journal for children in 1843, *Le livre de la jeunesse* [The Book of Youth]. Dozens of her moralizing tales for young readers continued to be published throughout the nineteenth century and beyond; her most famous work, *Le petit Robinson de Paris* [The Little Robinson of Paris] was re-edited as late as 1945. As Elisabeth-Christine Muelsch has documented, Foa also took an active interest in the economics of publishing and in promoting female artists and writers. She helped found the Société des Gens de Lettres, dedicated to protecting the property rights of authors,[30] and the Institut des Femmes.[31]

Foa concerned herself with less self-interested causes as well. A collaborator on the newspapers *Le Journal des Femmes* in the 1830s and *La Gazette des Femmes* and *La Voix des Femmes* in the 1840s, she advocated on behalf of the incipient French feminist movement in both her journalism and her fiction as well as through direct political action. During the Revolution of 1848, she founded L'Oeuvre de Bon Secours, a charitable aid society, to provide work to unemployed women.[32] Contracting with a clothing retailer, Foa's charity employed 150 female seamstresses in a shop on the rue de Rivoli, in which Foa read edifying literature to the women as they sewed. "I made sure that their work was well done, but at the same time I took it upon myself to moralize them," Foa proudly maintained in a request for financial support to the minister of public education in December 1848.[33] The charity would close its doors shortly thereafter, when the Ministry of War requisitioned the workshop as a barracks.[34]

Foa's activism clearly shocked some of her contemporaries. Traces of their enmity can be found in exceptionally cruel biographical sketches written about her after her death, which paint her as the archetypical *bas-bleu* (bluestocking). One writer comments on her "masculine physiognomy corresponding to her manners" and notes that her writing contains "a communicative sensibility entirely lacking from her character."[35] By contrast, more favorably disposed contemporaries make reference to her renowned beauty, although most refrain from serious engagement with the subject or style of her writing.[36] Both types of biographies, the openly misogynistic and the lewdly dismissive, testify to the threat that an outspoken woman writer such as Foa posed in nineteenth-century France and to the sexist strategies used by male critics to counter it. Interestingly, however, not a single one of the contemporary biographers comments on her Jewishness, reflecting the lack of overt antisemitism in literary circles of the period.

Jewishness was central to Foa's life and work, although her relationship to the religion itself proved highly ambivalent. A notice in *L'Univers Israélite*, the organ of Orthodox Judaism, recommends Foa's *Livre de jeunesse* by "our famous coreligionist" in 1844, despite the fact that she had begun to be drawn to Christianity several years earlier.[37] In 1841, Foa began writing saints' lives, and in early 1846, she converted to Catholicism under the tutelage of the Abbé Ratisbonne, who himself had come from a prominent Jewish family.[38] The Bibliothèque Marguerite Durand possesses an undated letter by Foa, which I verified, bearing the Catholicized signature "Marie Eugénie Foa," indicating that she intended to make her conversion public.[39] According to Muelsch, Foa received a Catholic burial,[40] and I did not find an obituary for her in either of the two main Jewish newspapers when she died in 1853.

Foa's conversion sets her apart from the other writers I consider in this book. Unlike Germany and Austria, France had no major waves of conversion in the nineteenth century.[41] Foa's circle of elite Parisian Jews, however, did see a relatively small number of high-profile conversions to Catholicism, as well as to Saint-Simonianism, in the early decades of the nineteenth century. Even some of those most closely identified with the Jewish community converted in this period, including the son and son-in-law of the grand rabbi of the Central Consistory and the wife and children of Adolphe Crémieux, France's leading Jewish jurist.[42] These apostasies can partly be explained by the unofficial antisemitism that prevailed in the upper echelons of Parisian society and by the pressures of social assimilation. But conversion was still rare enough in France in the early nineteenth century that the Catholic and Jewish press sparred over individual cases.

Whether Foa converted out of religious conviction or as a means of promoting herself as a Christian author remains in doubt. We have no record of the reasons for her conversion or of her family's reaction to it, although when the granddaughter of Foa's brother Hippolyte— Foa lived with this brother for a time—threatened to convert in the

1880s, so that she could marry a Catholic, Hippolyte published a series of letters denouncing her action and describing the history of their family and the meaning of Judaism. "We live amid a family ravaged by idiotic renegades and by shameless apostates," he complained bitterly to another relative, perhaps referring to Eugénie. "I intend for my granddaughter to marry only an Israelite, and for all her children to be Israelites."[43] Other members of the family had a weaker link to their ancestral faith. At the end of the nineteenth century, when Foa's niece, Geneviève Bizet Straus, was asked why she remained Jewish, she reportedly quipped that she had too little religion to bother changing.[44]

And yet, despite her ambivalent relationship to Judaism, it was by writing about Jews that Foa first sought entry into the literary field. Her first published work, *Le kidouschim* [The Kiddushim] (1830), which I discuss later in this chapter, sought to capture readers' attention with its Hebraic title, and advertisements in the mainstream French press falsely represented it as a translation from the Hebrew (it was composed in French).[45] In both this work and in most of the stories collected in the volume *Rachel*, which she subtitled "Scenes of Hebraic Manners," Foa weaves sentimental plots around Jewish customs or rituals. Foa's early forays into historical fiction—including two more works I discuss later, the novel *La juive* [The Jewess] (1835) and the novella "Billette, ou la fille du juif Jonathas" [Billette, or the Daughter of the Jew Jonathas] (1845)—also focus on the sentimental struggles of Jewish women seeking to marry outside the fold.

During her first decade as an author, then, and before taking up children's literature and saints' lives after 1840, Foa kept returning to Jewish themes, adapting the popular literary forms and subgenres of the day—the Scottian historical novel, the Balzacian "scene of manners"—for Jewish ends. At a time when Romantic orientalism was at its height and the Jewish exotic in particular had captured the French public's imagination—one thinks not only of Scott's *Ivanhoe*, still a best seller in the July Monarchy, but also of the wildly popular Scribe and Halévy opera *La juive* of 1835 and of Delacroix's Moroccan Jewish-themed paintings and drawings of the 1830s—Foa sought to capitalize on her Jewish legacy. Exploiting the recondite and picturesque elements of Jewish life for all their narrative potential, she attempted to carve out a space for herself in a crowded literary marketplace as France's first Jewish author.

Foa and her publisher clearly intended these Jewish-themed works to reach a mainstream public. According to the printers' declarations, which I consulted at the Archives Nationales, the initial print run of *Le kidouschim* in 1830 was 1,000 copies and that of *Rachel* in 1833 was 750 — not enormous but not tiny either at a time when the most popular authors, for example, Victor Hugo and Paul de Kock, hoped to sell only 2,500 copies.[46] Clearly, Foa and her publisher imagined that *Le kidouschim* would sell not just to Jews. During the 1830s, the Jewish population of France was less than 70,000 and Paris had fewer than 9,000 Jews, of whom 2,000 (about 20 percent) lived in poverty.[47] The vast majority of these could not read French and could not afford to purchase a book. That Foa's imaginary readership consisted of gentiles also becomes evident, I will show, in the way she exoticizes her Jewish characters.[48]

But Foa's Jewish fictional works do not merely exoticize. Unlike Scott, Scribe, and Delacroix, Foa grapples with the issues faced by France's Jews as they struggled to make sense of France's unprecedented but not uncomplicated gesture of emancipation. Foa views her Jewish characters through an orientalizing lens in order to appeal to the literary taste of the era. At the same time, she grapples with issues affecting the Jewish community. For Foa, Jewishness represents not merely local color or a screen for the projection of Christian fantasies and anxieties but rather a problem to be struggled with, a series of questions to be answered. In Foa's fiction, Romantic codes cloak specifically Jewish dilemmas. The result is unique in both French and Jewish literary history.

Le Kidouschim

Foa's first published work, *Le kidouschim*, is a deliberately strange novel; the Hebrew substantive of the title, although domesticated by the French definite article, retains its foreignness, its *étrangeté*, and no doubt served to make the novel stand out in publishing catalogues and on booksellers' shelves. And yet the real strangeness of the work has to do less with its exotic trappings than with the novel's conventionality, its investment in the form and logic of French sentimental fiction, including a central conflict involving a romantic love triangle. Foa deploys sentimental conventions in unconventional ways, appropriating them to frame problems facing the Jewish community of postrevolutionary France.[49] This novel, which scholars had not been able to locate previously, contains important keys to understanding both the trajectory of Foa's career and the evolution of her attitudes toward Judaism.[50]

Following not one but two prefaces, in which Foa elaborately performs her anxiety over publishing her first novel but makes no reference to its Jewish content, the story opens at the port of Bordeaux.[51] A ship arrives from Trieste carrying Kesil, son of the rich rabbi Hamminadad, returning home to Paris from a journey to Jerusalem. Kesil remains in Bordeaux long enough to fall in love with Alaï Misaël, a beautiful young woman who has been abandoned by her husband and who turns out to be his cousin. Complications arise when we discover that Kesil, before leaving for Jerusalem, was forced by his scheming Aunt Abida into an engagement with her daughter Elizama. Bound by what the novel explains as a Jewish custom dictating that once a ring—the "kidouschim" of the title—has been given, the engagement cannot be broken, Kesil agrees to marry Elizama despite his love for Alaï, but he faints at the altar before pronouncing his final vow.[52] In a gothic twist, the jealous Elizama then attempts to murder the innocent Alaï by throwing her off the Pont-Neuf. At the end of this 800-page tome, however, it is Elizama who drowns in the Seine and Alaï who is pulled to safety.

Le kidouschim, as we have seen, was advertised in the mainstream French press in terms designed to arouse the orientalist interest of a non-Jewish reading public. And on the surface, the novel does seem to exploit its Jewish subject matter in an exoticizing manner. In addition to the *recherché* ritual of the *kidouschim*, the oriental names of the characters—which bear little relation to the standard French names typically borne by members of the Bordeaux Jewish community, including Foa herself—render the Jewish characters as strange, exotic beings.[53] But on closer inspection, the novel subverts its own exoticizing effort.

Foa makes little attempt to describe her characters physically, and the descriptions she includes do not conform to the Jewish racial traits elaborated by Scott and other Romantic writers. Alaï, for instance, has the blond hair typical of the innocent heroines of sentimental fiction and popular melodrama, not the sable tresses of stereotype. Nor do the clothing and furniture reflect the orientalizing touches Foa would liberally apply in her later work. Indeed, aside from their names and the fact that they go to temple rather than church, little distinguishes the Jewish characters in *Le kidouschim* from the aristocratic Christian protagonists found in other French sentimental novels of the period. Whether going to house parties in the country, where they hunt and flirt, or for rides in the Bois de Boulogne, so they can see and be seen, these characters speak a polished and courtly French with no exotic traces.[54]

The novel's failure to live up to its own exoticizing premise may in part be explained by its generic affiliations. The sentimental novel is a faulty vehicle for exoticism because it focuses on the common interior struggles shared by human beings across time and space and as a result reduces the physical and sociological distinctiveness of its characters to a minimum.[55] Foa's realization of the limits of the genre no doubt motivated her entry into the Scott fold five years later. But Foa's ultimate refusal to present the Jews as exotic specimens in *Le kidouschim* has an ideological explanation as well, deriving from the fact that the novel ignores the problem of Jewish difference. Unlike Foa's later works, which analyze the difficulties faced by Jews in their effort to assimilate into a Christian culture, *Le kidouschim* seems entirely unconcerned with the issue of minority relations in modern society. Rather, the novel explores the effects of modernity as a dynamic *internal* to Judaism.

To analyze the effect of such forces as the rise of materialism and the decline of religious observance on the French Jewish community, Foa eliminates all external factors from the world of her novel, including the interfering presence of the dominant culture. Even though Foa's characters may act like Christian aristocrats, few actual Christians inhabit her fictional France. Whether walking in the countryside or the Bois de Boulogne, on the streets of Bordeaux or Paris, the characters in *Le kidouschim* meet only fellow Jews. Neither the characters nor the narrator even mentions the existence of other religions or social groups. In one of the novel's subplots, told to dramatize the tragic force of the *kidouschim* custom, a young Jewish girl named Esther runs away from home because her father has betrothed her to a man she has never met. In the coach on the way from Paris to Bordeaux, Esther begs for help from a woman who introduces herself as Noëmi Lemuel. "I believe that we profess the same religion," declares Esther in the novel's only acknowledgment that not everybody in France does (3: 208).[56] The sole—one presumes by their names—Christian characters appear in the novel's final paragraph, when Old Bertrand and Mother Baptiste, part of a crowd of onlookers who watch as Alaï is pulled alive from the river's torrents, comment on events of the story's denouement.

Even the novel's geography reflects this cultural homogeneity as Foa moves her characters between the capitals of French Jewish settlement—Bordeaux, Paris, and Alsace—and erases all points in between. Such social segregation is typical of Jewish travel writing dating back to the Middle Ages, which often features Jews moving between Jewish communities and paying scant regard to non-Jews. In Foa's novel, however, the elision of anything pertaining to Christianity is striking and provides an extremely distorted view of Jewish life in 1830s France—or for that matter the reality of what it means to be a minority group in any time or place. The characters in *Le kidouschim* experience no prejudice, either overt or subtle. How can they, when they do not come into contact with or even seem conscious of the existence of anyone not like themselves?

In *Le kidouschim* the threats to traditional Judaism come from within the Jewish community itself. The catalyst for this conflict is the atheistic Abida, the villain of the piece, who plots to marry her daughter, Elizama, to the son of her rich brother-in-law, the rabbi Hamminadad, although he detests her for reasons that the reader suspects go beyond her lack of piety. Abida knows that Hamminadad will feel bound to enforce the law of the *kidouschim*, despite his hatred of her, so she manipulates his innocent son into offering her daughter the sacred engagement ring. These two parental figures embody fundamentally opposed moral viewpoints, which lend the novel the antithetical structure typical of melodrama. Although Hamminadad is a stern traditionalist, Abida is a modern Parisian Jew, unbound by tradition or religious law but capable of manipulating it to her own advantage.

This difference manifests itself most clearly in a discussion between Abida and her daughter over the nature of Jewish religious law early on in the novel. "Why . . . don't you follow exactly the laws of Moses, like my Uncle Hamminadad?" Elizama naïvely asks her mother, before she has taken up her mother's plan to trap Kesil. Abida's candid response echoes the cynicism and materialism that observers at the time feared represented the attitude of a growing number of Jews in the capital.

> "Because I don't believe in them," responded Abida with a solemn air.
> "What do you believe in then, mother?" retorted the young girl.
> "Nothing," said Abida.
> "Nothing. . . . But you must believe in something."
> "All of that is prejudice," she said shrugging her shoulders. (2: 97)

Despite her claim to believe nothing, Abida in fact believes deeply in the power of money and social prestige, and it is this belief that motivates her single-minded quest to find a rich husband for her daughter. Through the mouthpiece of her villain, Foa raises the specter of a loss of religious observance in the Parisian Jewish community, testifying not only to the decline of traditional authority among modern French Jews but also to a more disturbing rise of materialism that would undermine the very basis of moral action.

Putting an end to her daughter's religious questioning, Abida declares that they will go for a ride in the Bois de Boulogne, but this leads her further into religious debate. The gallant Nephtali ("a tall young blond man, with an elegant figure," 2: 101), one of Elizama's suitors, offers to accompany them in his carriage. Despite his fashionable attire, Nephtali proves to be a traditionalist, vexing Abida with his insistence that they return by sundown because it is Friday, the eve of the Sabbath.

> "There wouldn't be any great harm," responded Abida laughing, in beginning the holiday in a coach. That would hardly be a great crime.

"Ah! madame," responded Nephtali seriously, "We must follow the laws of our fathers without discussion and never expose ourselves to public scorn."

"I beg your pardon," Abida added, in a mocking tone. "I thought M. Nephtali was too much of a philosopher to believe in all those prejudices; I thought he had more wit than that."

"Allow me," the latter said blushing, "to observe to you that wit is not in the heart, and in matters of religion, it's the soul that believes."

"We will finish this dissertation in the coach," retorted Abida.

"With your permission," responded Nepthali, "we will leave it there. I'm not smart enough to convince you, and you, madame, are too incredulous to persuade me." (2: 103)

Surely this is the first time that an argument over the details of Jewish religious law makes an appearance in French literature, and this scene must have perplexed Foa's non-Jewish readers. The fact that the novel does not attempt to explain why riding is prohibited on the Jewish Sabbath but rather assumes the reader's familiarity with the intricacies of such religious regulations suggests that *Le kidouschim* is thus not only a novel about Jews—like *Ivanhoe*—but a novel *for* Jews, at least in part.[57]

Foa uses her novel to respond to pressing religious and social questions for French Jews in the 1830s; unlike the relative obscurity of the *kidouschim* custom, Sabbath prohibitions were a crucial feature of Jewish life and would have been the subject of much debate in Jewish circles at the time. Foa's novel appeared just as the movement for Jewish religious reform, which argued for reducing the number of Jewish religious obligations, was beginning to make itself felt in France. In 1821, Olry Terquem (1782–1862) published his first *Letter from a French Israelite to His Coreligionists*, under the pseudonym Tsarphati (meaning "French Jew"), which included calls for modifying Sabbath regulations. In the two decades that followed, in a series of twenty-seven letters, Terquem continued to advocate relaxing the observance of Jewish religious laws in order to make Judaism easier for modern Jews to practice.[58]

Despite the notorious religious laxity of certain members of Foa's own family, the attitude toward Jewish religious law places *Le kidou-*

schim on the conservative end of the spectrum of opinions found in the period.[59] The novel censures Abida's disregard of the law through the explicit reproaches of the other characters, including Nephtali and, at the beginning, Elizama herself, who points out to her mother that her observant uncle Hamminadad not only seems happy but also enjoys the respect of the community. More significantly, the unfolding of the novel's plot reveals how deviation from Orthodoxy ultimately leads to tragedy. Driving on the Sabbath is merely the first stage in a process that will lead Elizama down the path to murder. Abida has already killed—we discover later that she killed Kesil's mother years before out of jealous love for Hamminadad, which explains why the rabbi hates her so passionately. But Elizama is a murderess in training, seduced by her mother's lessons in impiety to attempt the murder-suicide on the bridge over the Seine in the novel's last chapter that will end in her own death but her victim's survival.

The story's central conflict, however, centers on Kesil's choice of marriage partner. As Margaret Cohen has shown, early nineteenth-century French sentimental novels tend to revolve around the protagonist's struggle between "conflicting duties," in which romantic love, associated with individual freedom, is opposed to familial loyalty and communal obligation. Cohen reads this conflict as a reflection on opposing notions of rights in a liberal democracy—the clash between negative freedom (liberty) and positive freedom (active citizenship)—which dominated postrevolutionary political theory.[60] In *Le kidouschim*, Foa appropriates this framework to explore specifically Jewish questions. Kesil must choose not only between his two cousins but also between fidelity to Jewish tradition—symbolized here by the custom of the *kidouschim*—and personal freedom. Through Kesil's dilemma the novel asks to what extent can and should modern French Jews assert their individuality, their independence from the community, family responsibility, and the weight of the past.

The French Revolution had sought unsuccessfully to resolve this question. Inherent in the Jacobin revolutionary program was a radical attempt to divorce individuals from the kinds of group affiliations that defined life under the Old Regime; the Le Chapelier law dissolving corporations and guilds (1791) and the efforts of the Abbé Grégoire to suppress provincial languages reveal how a certain strain of revolutionary sought the creation of a universal state composed of abstract citizens, divorced from all particular or local ties.[61] The fact that Grégoire was also the most vocal advocate of Jewish emancipation signals the extent to which the offer of citizenship in the universal republic entailed, in theory, a renouncing of Jewish particularity. Clermont-Tonnerre's famous speech to the National Assembly in favor of Jewish emancipation—"To the Jews as a Nation, nothing; to the Jews as individuals, everything"[62]—has been seen to state the revolutionary case succinctly: The Jews must trade their group affiliation for individual rights as citizens.

In practice, however, French Jews accepted this bargain on their own terms. Although they did surrender certain forms of communal affiliation—such as the legal autonomy of their communities—they continued after the Revolution to associate mostly with other Jews, as witnessed by their low intermarriage rates and their concentration in certain neighborhoods and professions. Indeed, Napoleon's perception that Jews had retained their "national" bond and continued to represent a "nation within the nation"—along with his desire to respond to complaints about Jewish money lending in Alsace—motivated him to convene the Grand Sanhedrin, in order to solicit official sanction for Jewish social integration. But even though they mostly followed Napoleon's script, the rabbis and notables who made up the Grand Sanhedrin risked the emperor's wrath by refusing to condone marriages between Jews and non-Jews.[63] In other words, Jewish social integration had its limits.

During the Restoration, Jewish community leaders struggled to balance the rights of the Jews as individuals with their obligations to the community. Until the July Monarchy, the state required the Jewish consistories—unlike the Protestant consistories—to identify and tax Jewish members to pay for Jewish institutions. Lisa Moses Leff describes how Jewish community leaders fought against this policy, which they perceived as discriminatory, and also militated to free Jews from debts contracted by the Jewish communities of the Old Regime. The great Jewish lawyer Adolphe Crémieux, who took on the case, argued that because Jews became citizens as individuals, they should not bear responsibility for—or in the legal language of the 1804 civil code, "solidarity with"—the debts of a dissolved corporate body.[64] Inherent in this argument was a new notion of the Jew as individual, free from obligatory ties to the Jewish community or to the Jewish past. Louis-Philippe eventually ended the practice of taxing the Jews separately, but the Jewish community leaders did not succeed in the battle over the community debts, which dragged on into the 1840s.

And yet, even though community leaders sought to redefine the Jew as an individual in legal terms, they also advocated for new forms of Jewish communal solidarity.[65] This included the founding of Jewish schools, hospitals, and other social organizations, beginning in the 1820s; many of these institutions would be funded by the state. Community leaders saw no contradiction here; their vision of state secularism was not one in which all forms of religious identification were relegated to the private sphere but one in which the state had the responsibility to treat the three major religions equally. Thus if the state funded Christian institutions, it should fund Jewish ones as well. For these Jewish leaders, becoming a French citizen did not mean renouncing Jewish specificity or forms of Jewish solidarity in the public sphere. As Leff points out, the Jews were not alone in seeking ways to retain forms of communal identity even as they became citizens. Regional identities and languages, which had been the target of the revolutionary desire for standardization, persisted or were revived in the nineteenth century, just as workers created new forms of solidarity.[66]

But even though Jewish community leaders negotiated a balance between allowing for social integration and maintaining a sense of Jewish difference, individual French Jews struggled with these issues in acute ways. With the possibility of entering French culture came the temptation to leave behind a Jewish tradition that many perceived as onerous, outdated, and inhibiting. The ideology of individualism that accompanied the rise of the bourgeois class to political dominance in the nineteenth century further encouraged a liberation from the ancient ties to the Jewish community—indeed from all sorts of ties to the past. Many in the generation that came of age in 1830, born as French citizens, came to associate Judaism with the limitations that stifled the generations of their parents and grandparents. The freedom from political despotism that the Revolution heralded seemed to some within the Jewish community as a call to liberation from all forms of restriction. And Judaism as a religion and as a cultural system imposed restrictions everywhere.

These issues surfaced with particular vehemence for the elite Jews of Foa's milieu. Certain prominent families, such as the parents of the mathematician and Saint-Simonian Olinde Rodrigues (1795–1851), chose to send their children to French lycées and abandoned most forms of Jewish ritual by the 1820s.[67] As we have seen, a small number among the most prominent Jews converted to Catholicism—or to the new Saint-Simonian "religion"—during this period. This disaffection did not confine itself to the Sephardim. Gustave d'Eichthal (1804–1886), whose mother descended from one of the most prominent families of Alsatian Jews and whose father came from a German Jewish family, attended the prestigious Lycée Henri IV and received baptism in 1817. He also became involved with the Saint-Simonians.

French Jews, especially the wealthier ones, found themselves torn in the early nineteenth century between particularity and universality, between the claims of tradition on the one hand and the aspirations of republican citizenship, and with it bourgeois individualism, on the other. Foa's sentimental novel brings this political and existential conflict to the fore, cast in the garb of a romantic dilemma in which the choice of partner involves deciding whether to remain bound by Jewish tradition. The *kidouschim* contract, which prevents Kesil from marrying the woman he loves, stands in here for a much larger debate over the limits of individual freedom in postrevolutionary French society.

Although the narrative ultimately resolves in such a way as to leave Kesil free to follow his heart, it pointedly does not condone the violation of Jewish religious law. Indeed, Kesil never really considers rebelling against the *kidouschim*; his body might betray him by fainting, by asserting through hysterical symptoms the independence that his will lacks the courage to demand, but he remains an observant Jew, bound to the tradition epitomized by his stern father. That the novel rewards his steadfastness by freeing him from his bonds does not mitigate its message that a Jew must obey the rules. Nor does the fact that the atheistic Abida demands obedience to the *kidouschim* for purely cynical reasons lessen the hold it has over Kesil.[68]

In her first novel, Foa thus raises doubts about the authority of traditional Judaism and even expresses sympathy for Kesil's desire for romantic freedom, but these sentiments are suppressed. The fact that the *kidouschim* represents a rather arcane Jewish law—and appears outmoded even to the characters in the novel—underscores the novel's hard line. Judaism may be archaic, but it still commands obedience. The individual's claim to freedom appears justified by the intolerance and hypocrisy of the forces arrayed against it. But this does not mitigate responsibility to the community or allegiance to Jewish law and tradition. Such, at any rate, is the conclusion arrived at in *Le kidouschim*. In her subsequent fictional works, Foa continued to explore these questions but arrived at a series of very different answers.

Scenes of Hebraic Manners

Foa's next exploration of the conflict between individual autonomy and Jewish tradition occurs in a series of short stories published in the collection *Rachel* in 1833, which followed several sentimental and political novels on non-Jewish themes.[69] *Rachel* actually contains a mix of stories, some on Jewish themes and some not. Those that do focus on Jewish characters and subject matter once again tend to describe closed Jewish worlds, in which Jewish characters confront religious and moral dilemmas largely in the absence of interference from the outside. Almost all these tales, like *Le kidouschim*, derive their plots from arcane aspects of Jewish law or tradition.

"Le rachat du premier né" [Redeeming the Firstborn Son], subtitled "Scène de moeurs hébraïques" [Scene of Hebraic Manners], begins with seven letters. The first is a birth announcement, dated January 2, 1833, announcing that Mme. Hozny has had a son.[70] There follows a series of letters between the new mother and her former lover, Élie Cohenne, in which he receives confirmation of his paternity. We learn that her father ended their romance by forcing her to marry a wealthy older man (Hozny) whom she did not love in order to save the family from financial ruin. On the night before her wedding, however, Élie slipped into her room and fathered the child she has now delivered. Her husband suspects nothing and proudly invites the whole community to attend the traditional ceremony of the Redemption of the Firstborn Son. Some guests explain that the origin of the ceremony dates back to the Exodus of the Jews from Egypt, when God claimed the firstborn sons but allowed them to be bought back or redeemed. A member of the priestly class of Cohenim must act as God's surrogate in this symbolic transaction.

As a Cohen, Élie agrees to perform the ritual for the Hoznys. But when M. Hozny provides him with the ransom, he refuses to return the child. His former lover fears that he will take their child away from her or else reveal the secret of their forbidden love. She pleads with Élie, but her husband silences her, forbidding Élie from addressing her. Tension mounts as Élie refuses to follow the conventional script for the ceremony. He finally relents, releasing his son to the care of Hozny after extracting from him the promise that he will teach the boy to be "honest, upright, virtuous" and "to consider the goods of this world as perishable, to use them nobly if God bestows them upon him" (113). Mme. Hozny recovers her child with relief just as the butler announces that luncheon is served.

This story foregrounds many of the same themes that would preoccupy Foa in her other Jewish fictional works. At the center of the narrative we have a Jewish woman forced into a loveless marriage for financial reasons by a tyrannical father, as well as a verbally abusive husband who flaunts his paternal authority. The rights of the individual once again clash with communal expectations, Jewish law, and the weight of tradition. And an arcane Jewish custom once again becomes the pretext for bringing these issues to crisis. Ultimately Foa resolves the story by upholding the authority of the putative father figure, Hozny, but not without first denaturalizing his claim on his son, showing him to be illegitimate. Hozny recovers his son but only through the magnanimity of the biological father, his wife's lover—whose romantic claims on the boy are sanctioned by his religious status as a Cohen, a representative of God. Social convention may win out over romantic freedom in the story, but its foundations receive a thorough shaking.

Both the stories "Tirtza, ou le divorce" [Tirtza, or the Divorce] and "La kalissa" [The Kalissa] likewise center on aspects of Jewish family law. "Tirtza" takes place in ancient Jerusalem and tells the tragic story of the eponymous heroine who was forced to abandon her lover, Nephtali, and marry a man she did not love. When her husband learns that Nephtali has visited her in the night while he was away, he brings her to a divorce court. She begs the judge's pity but does not deny her fault or affirm that she loves her husband. The judge sentences her to stoning and she dies as a rock hits her head. The narrative ends here, as if the narrator too has been silenced by this blow. An epilogue describes how mothers tell the story of Tirtza to their daughters before their weddings and how husbands recount it to their wives before setting out on a journey.

"La kalissa" casts the plight of women within the Jewish tradition in even bleaker terms. Set in Algeria after the French invasion in 1830, it tells of the rape of Miriam, a Jewish widow, by a French soldier billetted at her home. We learn that according to Jewish law, a widow has the right to marry her dead husband's brother in a ceremony called *la kalissa*. But when Miriam reveals to her brother-in-law, whom she loves, that she is pregnant because of the rape, he repudiates her at the *kalissa* ceremony. Affirming herself "guilty and innocent at the same time" (314), she begs the mercy of all those gathered for the ceremony, but to no avail. In the epilogue, we hear two "Turks" describe how, in Algeria, women "suspected of an intrigue" are put into a sack and thrown into the sea alive. Sometimes cats are placed in the woman's pants. Just then the sack containing a still struggling Miriam is hurled off a cliff. In both these stories, Jewish tradition—whether in the form of paternal authority, religious courts, or ancient customs—serves to oppress the female heroines, not only thwarting their romantic longings but causing their physical abuse and death.

"Rachel, ou l'héritage," the story that lends its title to the volume, describes yet another badly married Jewish woman, but this tale takes place in present-day France, at the spa town of Enghien. The narrator (named "E——e," like the author), becomes fascinated with a mel-

ancholy woman named Rachel who lives in an isolated pavilion and
spends all her time writing. Rachel's black hair and oval face lead the
narrator to suspect her Jewish origin, which the heroine confirms by
telling her life story.[71] An orphan, she was raised by her uncle, a rabbi
from Jerusalem, who prevented her from marrying the man she loved
because he wasn't Jewish: "His religion differed from my own. My
good uncle claimed that such unions were never happy. . . . Alas!"
(xxi). Instead, the uncle forces her to marry a wealthy older man (yet
another!), who abandons her to abject poverty. And because divorce
was illegal in France between 1816 and 1884 and because job opportunities for women were scarce, abandoned women had few prospects.
This "poor victim of marriage" (xv) tells the female narrator how she
has now devoted herself to writing in order to make enough money to
live, braving the insults of those who would denounce her scornfully
as a "woman writer." But she dies of consumption before publishing
her work.[72]

Like the other stories in this volume, "Rachel" views Jewish women
as the innocent victims of a double form of oppression. In Foa's fictional world, Jewish law and tradition compound a despotic paternal
authority. Like the other stories, this one offers the heroine little opportunity to resist her fate. Romantic self-determination succumbs to
the forces arrayed against it. In "Rachel," however, Foa does suggest
the possibility of one form of recourse: fiction itself. The lonely Jewish heroine looks to writing as a solution to her suffering, even while
refusing a more carnal form of compensation in the form of her Christian lover, who visits her in Enghien but whom she refuses to see out
of fidelity to her marriage vows. Suffering the insults of a patriarchal
society that denies women the right to write, just as it denies them
the right to love, Rachel fails to reap the rewards for her labors. But
someone else does. In the epilogue to the story, we learn that she be-
queathed her unpublished manuscript to the peasant who served her,
Madeleine, who turns down offers of both marriage and a dairy farm
to see the manuscript through to publication. We are left to imagine
that the volume we are reading justifies her faith in the talent of her
former mistress.

"Rachel" thus ends on a note of hope, implying that some escape

from authority and tradition may eventually be possible for courageous women. It also departs from both *Le kidouschim* and the other
stories in *Rachel* by placing its Jewish characters in the midst of Christian society. Here the threat to traditional Judaism comes not, or not
only, from the decline of religious belief or from a revolt against traditional laws but also from the temptation of intermarriage. For the
first time, Foa represents a world outside the insular Jewish community. Although her heroine still resists the temptation to violate Jewish
tradition and authority, she thus moves a step closer to asking how
actual nineteenth-century French Jews might confront the dilemmas
of modernity.

La Juive

Foa's later novel *La juive* (1835) follows *Le kidouschim* and *Rachel* in exploring the conflict between Jewish tradition and individual freedom.
But just as Foa would use a proper French title for her later work,
cloaking the Jewish signifier in Gallic form, the Jews in her later novel
find themselves completely engulfed in a Christian world. Whereas
Foa's earlier novel and most of her short stories had conducted a sort
of thought experiment, in which individual freedom and Jewish tradition clash in a hermetically sealed Jewish space, *La juive* introduces a
non-Jewish variable into the equation. As in "Rachel," the catalyst for
conflict comes in the form of a seductive Christian gentleman who
tempts the Jewish heroine not only to disobey her father and break
with Jewish custom but also to leave the Jewish fold entirely.

La juive projects these dangers onto the past. In so doing, the novel
bears a striking similarity to many other Romantic historical works
about Jews from the period, including not only Scott's *Ivanhoe* but
also the popular opera *La juive*, composed the same year as Foa's novel
by her future brother-in-law.[73] Although set in the past, these works
all reflect on dilemmas of ethnicity and identity specific to the period
in which they were written. Indeed, Foa's novels are even guiltier than
Scott's of transposing modern dilemmas onto earlier historical periods. Whereas *Ivanhoe* at least attempts to depict the particular forms

of persecution experienced by Jews in medieval England, in *La juive*, which takes place in Paris in 1720, Foa neglects to mention that Jews were not legally allowed to reside in the capital during this period.[74] The openness with which Foa's Jews proclaim their Jewishness and the close friendship that develops between her Christian and Jewish characters reflect the liberal society of the postemancipation period rather than the repressive Old Regime.

Both Scott and Foa use their historical fiction as a means of reflecting on the place of the Jew in nineteenth-century society, but they imagine different answers to what was coming to be known as the Jewish question, which asked whether Jews belonged in the modern European nation-state and, if so, on what terms. In Scott's novel, the Jew must leave England. At the end of *Ivanhoe*, a heavily veiled Rebecca comes to bid farewell to the Saxon princess Rowena, whose husband, the knight of Ivanhoe, saved her from the predations of the ferocious Templar Brian de Bois-Guilbert. Despite Rowena's offer to protect Rebecca if she remains in England and despite—or perhaps on account of—the Jewess's love for the Christian knight, Rebecca chooses to follow her father to Moorish Spain, where in the twelfth century Jews enjoyed greater freedom. Given Rebecca's narrow escape from being burned at the stake as a heretic and a witch in England, the reader can only approve of her plan for exile. The fact that Rowena implies she will try to convert Rebecca if she stays in England makes her decision to leave an affirmation of her Jewish identity and a rejection of the promise of assimilation.

Before explaining how Foa's Jewish heroine faces similar dilemmas but opts for a different outcome, let me first summarize the plot of *La juive*. The novel takes place during the decadent period of the Regency and plays out against the backdrop of John Law's disastrous attempt to introduce paper money into France. At the start of the story, André de Prezel, a handsome but impecunious nobleman, gets run over in the streets of Paris. Carried back to the home of Schaoul, a wealthy Jewish banker of Syrian origin, André falls in love with the beautiful young woman who tends him. This woman, Midiane, the "juive" of the title, is the daughter of Schaoul, who keeps her hidden in a secret apartment, surrounded by a profusion of oriental carpets and silk pil-

lows. The exotically beautiful Midiane in turn falls in love with André after he saves her from a kidnapping plot hatched by the corrupt
regent, but her father will not consent to her marrying a Christian.
Complicating matters further, Schaoul has promised Midiane to the
son of a man who saved his life years before in the Arabian desert.
This young man, Daniel Samla, a struggling Jewish doctor with a kind
heart and a hunched back, happens to be the best friend of André.
Daniel willingly surrenders his claim on Midiane out of friendship, but
Schaoul will not yield.

On the morning of the wedding between Daniel and Midiane, a
fire breaks out in Schaoul's house. André rescues Midiane once again.
Freed from her parental prison, Midiane gives way to her heart. She
bears André's child and the two live together, although they do not
wed because the law forbids marriages between Christians and Jews
unless one partner converts. Some time later, regretful and homesick,
Midiane sneaks out on a winter night with her baby to beg forgiveness
of her father, who has meanwhile lost his fortune after the failure of
Law's financial scheme. Her mother, who went insane after the fire,
takes the child, but leaves Midiane outside to die in the cold. When
André also dies of grief after hearing of Midiane's death, Schaoul gives
his grandchild to his spinster sisters to raise. In a brief epilogue to the
tragic tale, Midiane's orphaned daughter asks her aunts whether she
will be allowed to marry whom she pleases. "Jew or Christian?"
the child asks. "Jew or Christian," the old women agree with a sigh.

Scott's influence on Foa makes itself felt perhaps most obviously
in the way she exoticizes her Jewish characters. In *La juive*, Foa provides the kind of extended descriptions both of people and objects
that were missing in her earlier work but that Scott had made into
the sine qua non of the historical novel. Foa's new effort to provide
local color leads her to indulge in a host of Semitic stereotypes. Like
Scott, Foa surrounds her Jewish characters with a profusion of oriental luxury: "I thought I had been transported to Damascus, to Con-
stantinople, to Eden or I don't know where, but I certainly was no
longer in France,"[75] André declares, when attempting to describe the
inner sanctum of the Jewish moneylender's house, which is filled with
richly covered divans and Persian rugs. Foa also follows Scott's lead in

endowing her Jewish characters—particularly Midiane—with physical characteristics that increasingly were being seen as marking the Jewish "race." She has the dark hair, aquiline profile, and black eyes typical of the Middle East or North Africa, as the root of her fanciful name, Midi, which means "south" in French, implies. Indeed, so close are the descriptions of the Jewish heroines in the two novels that one suspects that Foa must have had her copy of *Ivanhoe* close at hand while composing *La juive*.[76]

As Leff has shown, early-nineteenth-century Jewish writers found in racial theorizing a way of explaining their own sense of difference. "The Jews, like the Gauls or Franks, could be understood as a once wandering tribe, settled in France, with distinctive and admirable moral and physical characteristics, living alongside other races in peace under a single set of institutions and laws."[77] Before the pseudo-scientific racism that marked the second half of the nineteenth century and found its horrific culmination in the Nazi attempt to exterminate European Jews, racial theory provided Romantic writers, both Jewish and gentile, with a way of explaining the historical origins of current events.[78]

By exoticizing her Jewish characters à la Scott, Foa was no doubt trying to cash in on the success of *Ivanhoe*. But the orientalizing of the Jew serves more than just commercial ends; it offers Foa a means of reflecting on the place of Jews within the French nation. If *La juive* follows *Ivanhoe* in presenting the Jews as physically different, it is because Foa had begun to concern herself, like Scott, with the problem of Jewish foreignness, with the barriers preventing the Jews from integrating into Christian society. As in *Ivanhoe*, the physical distinctiveness of the Jews makes manifest the problem of their social otherness. And the plots of both novels hinge on this problem. But whereas in the oppressive world of *Ivanhoe*, Jews merely react to Christian aggression, in the amazingly tolerant world of *La juive*, where antisemitism almost never rears its ugly head, the fault for the Jews' failure to integrate fully lies with the Jewish characters rather than with the Christian ones.

Despite a certain degree of openness and generosity to people of other faiths, the Jewish banker Schaoul ultimately gives voice to a self-righteous chauvinism that elevates Jewish identity and fidelity to Jewish law over the rights of the individual. When André confesses his love for Midiane, Schaoul refuses to sanction their marriage in the name of religion: "I respect all religions, all beliefs," Schaoul says, "but between you and my daughter, a barrier is erected: he who looks beyond it is crazy, he who attempts to surmount it is a fool" (1: 292). Although Schaoul at first espouses a tolerance of other faiths, this liberalism proves to be but a veneer. When André protests that religion—"that holy and fearsome word" (1: 292)—should not be used to serve retrograde notions, the innate oriental despot in Schaoul emerges from behind the mask of the enlightened cosmopolitan: "My daughter is my property, my life, my blood. She is mine and won't free herself from my authority except to take on that of a husband of my choosing" (1: 293). Despite the rhetoric of blood, Schaoul's stubbornness derives from religious rather than racial scruples; he seeks to prevent the marriage out of fidelity to Jewish law and tradition rather than from a desire to keep his bloodline pure. André begs the banker to elevate his daughter's happiness above considerations of law—"Be a father before being a Jew," he pleads—but Schaoul does not share the Frenchman's notion of paternal rights and responsibilities.

In a later scene, Midiane begs her father to allow her marriage to the Christian: "My father, look here, is not their God ours as well? Does not the sun that shines on us shine on them also?" (1: 335). Midiane's plea calls to mind Shylock's famous speech ("Hath not a Jew eyes?") in Shakespeare's *Merchant of Venice*, yet another model for both this novel and *Ivanhoe*, but reverses its terms. Whereas in Shakespeare's play the Jewish moneylender argues that a common humanity links Christian and Jew, in Foa's novel it is the Jewish moneylender who refuses to recognize this bond. Ultimately, the tragedy of the novel derives from Schaoul's obstinacy, his stubborn—and for Foa, specifically Jewish and specifically male—obedience to the letter of the law rather than to his daughter's desires. "But the fanaticism of their religion cries louder than the heart of their daughter," André tells Midiane when she confesses her desire to visit her suffering parents at the novel's end. "They deserve their unhappiness," he insists, in what the reader interprets as the novel's verdict on the justice of their punishment (2: 180). The destruction of Schaoul's family that follows from his unyielding attitude underscores the degree to which the novel shows Jewish "fanaticism" to undermine the very familial structures it seeks to uphold.

La juive thus asks what keeps the Jews from full participation in French national life and answers, the Jews themselves. The fidelity to patriarchal tradition affirmed in *Le kidouschim*, in Kesil's inability to defy an outmoded Jewish law, comes under fire (quite literally, because Schaoul's house is burned to the ground) as the force holding Jews back from both personal fulfillment and social integration. In the five years separating her two novels, Foa thus reverses her views on this central problem of Jewish modernity, advocating in her later *La juive* a position even more extreme than the one she denounced in her earlier *Le kidouschim*, going so far as to sanction not only violation of Jewish marital customs but also actual marriage with a non-Jew. Scott, it should be noted, does not represent intermarriage in his novel. And whereas the non-Jewish Scott frames the problem of Jewish assimilation in such a way as to indict Christian readers for their intolerant practices, forcing them to sympathize with Jewish suffering even while tacitly recognizing the permanence of Jewish difference, the Jewish Foa calls on Jews, not Christians, to conform to liberal ideology.

To be sure, *La juive* does offer examples of more positive Jewish values to counteract Schaoul's obstinacy. As Leff points out, Foa takes pains to connect Judaism to liberalism by showing that Schaoul offers succor to the Christian André after his injury and provides charity to Christians as well as Jews—the banker even employs a Christian orphan in his house.[79] Moreover, other Jewish characters in the novel prove more flexible than Schaoul, more willing to open themselves to participation in Christian society even at the expense of violating Jewish laws and traditions.

In contrast to the fanatical Schaoul, who fights to keep his daughter from contact with Christians, Daniel's father chooses not to inform his son of his Jewish identity until his thirteenth birthday. Hoping to make his son a man "useful to society" and not just a banker or merchant, he gives him an education that is "the same as that of Christians." Daniel's father himself embodies the ideal of the postemancipation *Israélite*, for whom Jewish identity constitutes a matter of private confession only: "My father hid a religion that he professed in his interior, but which nothing, on the outside, betrayed the appearance," Daniel reflects (1: 199). In a letter to his son, Daniel's father instructs him to follow the commandments of Moses but allows him "to modify their usage, in accordance with the customs of the places where you will live and the peoples among whom you find yourself in relation" (1: 207), in what constitutes an anachronistic anticipation of the program of Reform Judaism as it would be elaborated in the early nineteenth century in Germany and then imported into France in the very years Foa was writing.

Although willing to dispense with customs or laws he considers outdated as well as with all external marks of Judaism, Daniel's father does retain a distinct sense of his Jewishness. Like a nineteenth-century Reform Jew, he has freed himself from Talmudic regulations: "Only, my child, to be happy, do not worship foreign gods; don't deny your God, or your religion." And yet, if conversion remains strictly forbidden for this advocate of Jewish integration in Christian society, so too does mixed marriage: "Above all, be sure not to ally yourself . . . with a woman who belongs to the enemies of our nation" (1: 207), he warns. Daniel's father thus advocates acculturation but specifically denounces assimilation. Whereas the novel seems generally to valorize his principles—the son's happy disposition attests to the sagacity of his father's theories—his reference to "enemy" nations and his opposition to intermarriage seem to contradict the novel's main narrative thrust.

The novel's penultimate tableau, in which Midiane lies dying in the cold outside her father's house, a victim of paternal intolerance and Jewish legal rigidity, implicitly condemns not only the Jewish "fanaticism" that regards Christian society as hostile but also the milder form of traditional authority that inhibits the fulfillment of the individual's desires in the name of perpetuating particular or communal identity. In these terms the most enlightened characters in the novel are Schaoul's maiden sisters, pious Jewish ladies, whose fidelity to tradition bends before their niece's right to choose her own destiny: "Poor child, you will marry whomever you like" (2: 251), they tell her in the story's final scene, showing that they have taken Midiane's tragic story to heart. As Leff remarks, the example of the aunts indicates the extent to which Foa ultimately points to a strain of flexibility within Judaism. Schaoul's tyranny is only one face of the faith that in other instances—particularly in the hands of its female practitioners—proves tolerant and able to adapt to modernity by bending the law.[80]

Leff also sees in Midiane an indication of Foa's desire to valorize Jewish values and tradition. In a letter to André, Midiane cites the example of biblical heroines to vaunt her own courage: "As a Jewess, I derive from my origin the energy that made a young and weak girl, Judith, the liberator of an entire people; the ingenious love that rendered the beautiful Esther a wise and courageous queen" (1: 309). Midiane ascribes her elevation of passion over intellect, of heart over head, to an inherent Jewish cultural—or perhaps racial—trait: "The sun that burns our lands, and the fire of which formed my heart, endowed my soul with an instinct that makes me prefer my own conscience to the cold calculations of a world whose compass only measures the world by shrinking it, and to oppose the lying conventions of a society guided by self-interest with a single sentiment, that of pity!" (1: 309). Here, Midiane denies the conventional stereotype of the Jew as calculating. She claims instead that "pity," often considered a monopoly of Christianity, represents the true expression of her Jewish nature. She thus makes the case for Judaism as a universal religion, equally as capable as Christianity of instilling the values necessary for the virtuous functioning of society.

And yet it is Midiane's courage that allows her to rebel against her father and her passion and pity that drive her into the arms of the lovelorn André. The very values that Foa shows to represent the virtue of Judaism are those that motivate the heroine to turn her back on her family and on Jewish tradition. Midiane might incarnate a more liberal version of Judaism than her father, but it is this liberalism that pushes her away from the faith and from the community. Similarly, the resignation of the aunts, their "enlightened" elevation of personal happiness over tradition, will ultimately sanction the act that most threatens the integrity of Judaism in modern society—intermarriage. Judaism may represent a universal religion for Foa, but the values within it that she shows to be worth defending are the very ones that would—and according to Foa, should—lead to its dissolution.

How can we explain Foa's transition from *Le kidouschim* to *La juive*? How can we account for her shift from Orthodoxy to something bordering on apostasy? Certainly it is tempting to see the change as a reflection of her biography—not only of her own eventual conversion but also of her earlier move from the relatively protected Jewish milieu of Bordeaux in which she was raised into the Parisian literary world, a move that coincided with the publication of her first novel in 1830. Of course, her growing willingness to advocate rebellion against the authority of Jewish fathers also might have sprung from her own life-long struggle against the constraints of Jewish patriarchy and perhaps against her own father, who died in 1834, the year before *La juive* was published.[81] A victim of a bad marriage contracted within the Jewish tradition, Foa would grow increasingly vociferous in advocating the right to romantic self-determination in her fiction, just as she would increasingly ally herself with the feminist movement, which was gaining force in the two decades during which Foa wrote. It is not a coincidence that Foa's willingness to imagine more radical forms of Jewish social or religious integration parallels the shift from male to female protagonists in her fiction.

But I want to suggest that the transition is facilitated as much by genre as by gender. The shift from *Le kidouschim* to *La juive* was also a shift from sentimental to historical fiction, which accompanied a recasting of the way Foa imagined the problem of Jewish modernity. Whereas the primary conflict remains the same in all her fictional works about Jews (the struggle between individual desires and Jewish tradition), in her later historical works, this conflict is not confined to a restricted Jewish milieu but rather plays out against world-historical events and in a larger national context. And in opening her novels to the historical forces shaping modern France, Foa also comes to validate the notions of individualism and rebellion against tradition that defined French modernity. Foa's historical heroines seem to free themselves anachronistically from the yoke of Judaism in order to await the universality that the Revolution would make possible.

"Billette"

In another work of Scott-inspired historical fiction published a decade
later, shortly before Foa's own conversion, Foa once again uses a romantic dilemma to frame both immediate problems facing the French
Jewish community during the July Monarchy (intermarriage, conversion) and larger debates over the authority of Jewish tradition and the
past itself. In *La juive* blame for Jewish exclusion from Christian society lies squarely on the shoulders of the Jews themselves and specifically on the Jewish men who refuse to accept the overtures of a gentile
world that welcomes them with open arms. The novella "Billette ou
la fille du juif Jonathas" (1845) holds out even less hope for Jewish-
Christian harmony than *La juive*, but it assigns the blame for this failure more evenly.

Set in 1290, this novella seeks ostensibly to explain the origin of a
Parisian toponym—the rue des Billettes (later the rue des Archives)—
where a Jewish moneylender named Jonathas, who was burned at the
stake for blasphemy, supposedly lived.[82] Foa adapts the legend by inventing a daughter for Jonathas who bears the name Billette. Far more
resolute and strong-willed than Midiane, Billette is ashamed of her
Jewishness and specifically of the weakness and materialism of the Jewish men surrounding her. She repeatedly complains of the cowardice
of her fiancé, who is beaten in church on Good Friday, and of the
grasping ways of her father. Early in the story, when the handsome
Christian student Ramier Fleming leaves a valuable ring with Jonathas as a guarantee for a loan, Billette secretly returns it to him, thus
earning a declaration of love. Echoing the scene in *Ivanhoe*, in which
Rebecca secretly returns the money Ivanhoe has paid her father for his
suit of armor, the Jewish woman proves herself free of the semitic sin
of greed and, perhaps for that reason, more inherently amenable to
the prospect of redemption through conversion.

When her father is sentenced to death for defiling the host, Billette
agrees to convert to Catholicism to save him. Jonathas is in fact guilty
of profanation, although we learn that he threw the wafer representing the body of Christ into boiling water merely out of curiosity to
see what would happen and without blasphemous intent. It is Ramier

Fleming's influential father, also named Ramier Fleming, who brokers the conversion bargain to save Billette's father and who promises to allow the converted Jewess to marry his son. Yet while Billette fulfills her side of the contract, the Christians do not. Even after Billette's conversion, Jonathas dies at the stake, refusing, in a heroic departure from his earlier cowardice, to abjure his faith. A distraught and newly Christian Billette then discovers that Ramier pretended to love her only to get her father's money. She later retires into a convent to leave him free to marry his cousin. At the close of "Billette," the formerly Jewish heroine comes to understand the true meaning of Christianity and magnanimously forgives Ramier for betraying her.

"Billette" once again thematizes the failure of understanding between Christians and Jews but places blame for this failure not, or not only, on the Jewish characters. Although this highly ambivalent narrative represents Jews in what can at best be described as an equivocal manner—as greedy, cowardly, and sacrilegious in their everyday dealings, although generous, resolute, and devout when put to the test—it also depicts Christians in a highly unfavorable light. In Foa's later tale, Christian hypocrisy, bigotry, and greed rather than Jewish obstinacy and fanaticism doom the Jewish woman and her family. I should note once again that in "Billette" it is only Jewish men who display negative qualities. Both Billette and her mother demonstrate far more noble characteristics, reflecting a gender dichotomy typical of Romanticism's Semitic stereotyping.

Both *La juive* and "Billette" end tragically for their Jewish heroines, but both tales offer the promise of a future redemption. In "Billette" the intermarriage solution offered by *La juive* fails, but conversion represents an alternative and even more extreme means of integrating Jews into the body of the nation. Even if Billette does not manage to join the family of her father's persecutors, she does find acceptance in the Christian religious community of the convent. The act of apostasy that at first had self-interested motives—to save her father and allow her marriage—proves in the end to offer the heroine a genuine consolation as well as an antidote to her social isolation.

Conversions provoked a great deal of acrimony in the Jewish press of the period. One of the most infamous cases in the nineteenth century involved the prominent exponent of Jewish religious reform Olry Terquem (pseud. Tsarphati), who disputed his brother's supposed deathbed conversion to Catholicism, alleging unfair manipulation on the part of the priests. This case occurred in February 1845, shortly before the publication of Foa's novella, and provides a vital context for it.[83] As in the Terquem case, Foa shows her heroine's conversion to be the result of evil machinations and trickery. But, unlike Terquem, she also shows it to be the right solution to her heroine's crisis of family and faith.

A Jewish Writer

Foa's fictional works index topical concerns for French Jews in the 1830s and 1840s, but they also stage issues of larger import. Foa, I want to suggest, reverses Scott's answer to the Jewish question. Whereas Scott's Rebecca survives with her life, honor, and faith intact but pays for her survival with exile, Foa's heroines—in *La juive*, "Rachel," and "Billette"—suffer greatly but remain in France. Foa thus imagines a place for Jews in French society, even if she simultaneously sees the renunciation of Jewish specificity as the desired outcome of this social integration. Despite certain surface similarities, then, Foa is thus quite different from the first Jewish writers in England, her female contemporaries who, according to Michael Galchinsky, responded to Scott's example by writing historical fiction in which Jewish women affirm their Englishness without compromising their Jewishness.[84]

In contrast to her English counterparts, Foa's historical fiction appears to be assimilationist in the strongest sense of the word. It advocates the fusion of its heroines into the body of the nation, even at the price of losing a distinct Jewish identity. As we have seen, however, Foa does allow some of her minor or secondary Jewish characters to remain both Jewish and French. In *La juive*, Daniel Samla, the hunchbacked doctor, achieves a kind of social integration that does not require conversion or intermarriage. Daniel circulates freely among Christians and maintains his link to Judaism as a matter of private confession only. Despite his bodily deformity, Daniel represents a kind

of French Jewish ideal—similar to the Sephardic Jews of Foa's community of origin who would serve as a model for the German Reform
movement[85]—and reminds Foa's readers that Jewish identity could in
fact persist in modern France. In "Billette," the mother refuses to convert and, even in abject suffering, displays a moral rectitude and ethnic
pride that her daughter comes to envy.

In her later fictional works, then, Foa asserts the rights of the individual—including, especially, the female individual—over the collective and in opposition to the claims of Jewish tradition and history.
She valorizes the universal at the expense of the particular, aligning
herself with a new notion of Jewish identity that was taking shape in
legal discourse at the time. However, she also defends the Jewish religious tradition against would-be detractors by showing how it gives
rise to universal values, including tolerance, charity, and a love of freedom. This tension between defending Judaism and seeking to overcome it, between renouncing Judaism as a particularism and finding
in it the seeds of the universal, is not the least of the paradoxes marking Foa's work.

Foa sought to leave Judaism even while remaining a Jewish writer.
To be sure, her relation to the religion and the tradition evolved over
the decades as she moved away from her Jewish upbringing and toward
conversion, but even in a later story such as "Billette," she displays a
concern with the problems of modern Jewish identity that signifies
her continued affiliation with the community. Foa's wrestling with the
problem of the social isolation of Jews in Christian society and with
the claims of the individual within the Jewish tradition aligns her with
the other writers I discuss in this book. Her radical assimilationism
may be an extreme position, but I would argue that it makes her no
less of a Jewish writer.

Indeed, even while advocating the dissolution of Jewish identity
through intermarriage and conversion, Foa simultaneously invented,
more or less single-handedly, the category of Jewish fiction in French.
That the historical novel would offer the vehicle for this invention
comes as no surprise, because the first half of the nineteenth century
saw an outpouring of regionalist imitators of Scott who hoped to do
for their native province what the Scotsman had done for Scotland.

Like her fellow Scott followers, Eugénie Foa wrote historical novels about a particular group. But in place of region she substituted religion. By writing novels about the history of Jews in France, Foa implicitly argued for their place as a constitutive part of the nation, on a par with those groups whose particular identity was more rooted in the French soil. Through her novels, Jews found their place in the national epic alongside the Burgundians, the Corsicans, and other "minority" groups. If Foa ultimately calls for the assimilation of the Jews into the national body, she simultaneously endows French Jews with a historical and literary distinctiveness. And it was on this distinctiveness that Foa staked her own claim to uniqueness as a struggling woman writer in nineteenth-century France.

Two Between Realism and Idealism:
Ben-Lévi and the Reformist Impulse

Thanks to Eugène Sue's serialized bestseller *Le juif errant* [The Wandering Jew] (1844), which features a title character condemned to walk the earth in lonely perpetuity for having mocked Christ, Jews had become something of a literary fashion in 1840s France.[1] Most of these fictional Jews were decidedly more modern than Sue's mythological hero; Balzac's novels of the period feature multiple Jews who manipulate the capitalist system to their own advantage as well as beautiful Jewish prostitutes who seduce men with their oriental charms.[2] These fictional stereotypes mirrored the representations of the Jew in contemporaneous political and sociological tracts, which likewise combined an ancient religious form of Jew hatred with a new modern form of economic antisemitism.[3]

What interests me in this chapter, however, is less these representations themselves than the reaction to them by a writer for *Les Archives Israélites*, the Reform Jewish newspaper. Writing under the pseudonym Ben-Lévi, the Jewish critic praises Sue's portrayal of the Jew, despite the fact that *Le juif errant* resurrects a stock character of popular anti-Jewish mythology. Although he labors under a curse, the wandering Jew becomes, in Sue's telling, a symbol of the oppressed and downtrodden, a sympathetic victim of fanaticism.[4] And yet, even while rejoicing that Sue's text was not as bad as it could have been, Ben-Lévi laments a missed opportunity, imagining "what an Israelite writer would relate, if he attempted to paint the true Wandering Jew." What, he wonders, would a realistic depiction of Jews, by a Jew, be like?

Ben-Lévi had already published an article in 1842 in which he denounced the representation of Jews in French literature. Popular writers, especially writers of fiction, he argued, are guilty of sacrificing truth to convention: "In the theater, from Shakespeare to Scribe; in the novel, from *Ivanhoe* to Paul de Kock; in newspapers, ever since there were serial novels and a public that devours them on a daily basis; everywhere in this world of printed paper and cardboard scenery, they give us conventional Jews with their grimaces, their usury, their mincing ways, their jargon, all more or less mass produced."[5] Ben-Lévi argues that the time has come to bury such stereotypes. Conventional Jews, whose hearts lie in Jerusalem while their bodies reside in France, have given way to the modern French Israelites, French citizens like any other, completely loyal to France while also proud of their Jewish heritage and beliefs. And this new social entity demands a new, realistic portrayal in fiction written by modern French Israelites themselves.

Ben-Lévi set himself the task of becoming just such a writer. In the remainder of the piece on Sue, he experiments with a new fictional mode by imagining a trip with the author of *Le juif errant* to the mythic principality of Gerolstein, where the ending of Sue's earlier best seller, *Les mystères de Paris* [The Mysteries of Paris] had taken place. There the Jewish author discovers a land where the indigenous Jews have attained high-ranking positions in the government as well as in all aspects of civil life. "But there is nothing curious about them, I assure you," his host tells him. "They are men similar in every respect to the other inhabitants of the country" (713). Even more stunning to Ben-Lévi's narrator is that the Israelites of Gerolstein have remained Jews even while integrating so completely with their neighbors. They have maintained a host of thriving Jewish institutions, from synagogues to schools. The comparison to France, where assimilation seemed to threaten the survival of Judaism, could not have been more clear.

Ben-Lévi would write more than a dozen short stories for *Les Archives Israélites* during the 1840s. These fictional works borrow the new literary codes that critics in the period were beginning to label realist to criticize France's assimilating Jewish bourgeoisie and to analyze the paradoxes of their integration into French society. But what makes Ben-Lévi's writing so interesting is the way he fuses realism with its literary and philosophical opposite, with the utopian and sentimental poetics of idealism. Not content to warn of the dangers of modernity for his fellow French Jews, Ben-Lévi uses his fiction to imagine how Judaism itself might offer a counterweight to it. The Judaism envisioned by Ben-Lévi, however, represents a radical departure from Jewish tradition; like the journal in which they appeared, Ben-Lévi's stories advocate a new, Reform vision as a solution to the dilemmas of modernity.

Most historians of Jewish literature have seen not Ben-Lévi but Marcel Proust as the first French Jewish author to have offered a realistic portrayal of nineteenth-century French Jewish life. And yet, although Proust would trace the opposite itineraries of two assimilating Jews, Swann and Bloch, in his modernist masterpiece *À la recherche du temps perdu* [In Search of Lost Time] (1913–1927), Ben-Lévi had provided a similar vision of the process of assimilation some seventy years before. Like Proust, Ben-Lévi's fiction views Jewish social integration with a gaze that is alternately satirical and poignant. Like Proust, who described Swann's Jewish reawakening during the Dreyfus affair, Ben-Lévi views Jewish identity as a political statement and an ethical position in a world that makes such forms of identification morally significant. Indeed, Proust may well be considered the literary descendant of this forgotten nineteenth-century French Jewish writer. Perhaps not coincidentally, he was also his *literal* descendant: The man behind the Ben-Lévi pseudonym was Godchaux Baruch Weil, Proust's great-uncle.

A Parisian Jew

Godchaux (also spelled Godechaux or Godecheaux) Baruch Weil was born in Paris in 1806, but his family, on both sides, had deep roots in Alsace. The Weils, along with other branches of the family—the Blochs and the Mochs—came from small towns with significant Jewish populations near Strasbourg in the Lower Rhine, including Obernai and Niedernai. Godchaux's great-great-grandfather, Joseph Bloch, who died in 1761, was a prominent salt merchant, a banker to Samson

Ferdinand of Landsberg, and a leader of the Jewish community in the region.[6]

The family left Alsace around 1800 to settle first in Fontainebleau and then in Paris, when the capital had fewer than 3,000 Jews.[7] Godchaux's father, Baruch Weil (the great-grandfather of Proust), born in 1780, opened a porcelain factory in Paris in 1805, and by the Restoration he had become a prominent figure in the Parisian business world. He received recognition from Louis XVIII and counted the Duchesse de Berry among his clients. In 1827, he was awarded the Legion of Honor for his contributions to industry, one of the first Jews to receive this prestigious decoration.[8] According to his probate records, which I consulted at the Archives Nationales, Baruch Weil left a substantial estate upon his death in 1828, divided between his three surviving children by his first wife, Hélène Schoubach (1781–1811), and the five surviving children of his widow, Marguerite (Sara) Nathan (1785–1854), which included Proust's grandfather, Nathé Weil (1814–1896). Godchaux, his profession listed as that of rentier (one who lives off the income of investments), administered the estate.[9]

The Weils did not move in the glittering artistic and intellectual circles of Foa and her family, the largely Sephardic Parisian Jewish aristocracy. Grounded in industry rather than banking, the Ashkenazic Weils lived close to the synagogue on the rue Saint-Avoye, later absorbed into the Boulevard du Temple, in what was from the time of the First Empire a Jewish neighborhood. The Weils also remained more firmly committed to a traditional form of Judaism than Foa's friends and neighbors on the rue Montholon, many of whom gravitated to the Saint-Simonian movement. Baruch served as a mohel in his spare time, performing ritual circumcisions on young Parisian Jewish babies, including his own eight sons.[10]

As a member of the business elite and a devoutly Orthodox Jew, Baruch Weil naturally became a leader in the capital's Jewish community. Although he did not participate in Napoleon's Grand Sanhedrin in 1807, in 1820 he was elected to the Paris Consistory, the central governing body of the capital's Jewish community, eventually becoming its vice-president. He served on numerous Jewish charitable bodies, including the Comité du Bienfaisance (Charitable Committee), which he joined in 1813, and the Comité de l'École des Garçons (Boys' School Committee), which he joined in 1819. He also served as the director of the consistorial synagogue on the rue Saint-Avoye.[11]

Whereas many families in Foa's circle sent their male children to the secular lycées established by Napoleon during the first decade of the nineteenth century, Baruch Weil refused this assimilating gesture. Instead, he hired a private tutor to provide his children with an education that, although open to Enlightenment ideas, would also remain firmly Jewish in emphasis. He could not have predicted, however, that the young rabbi he selected to teach his children, David Drach, would later become famous—or rather infamous—in the Parisian Jewish community by marrying the daughter of the chief rabbi of the Central Consistory and then scandalously converting to Catholicism in 1824.[12] The author of a series of evangelical "Letters of a Converted Rabbi" in the late 1820s and of numerous pamphlets attacking his former coreligionists,[13] Drach became a favorite of the Parisian ecclesiastical authorities and a source of shame to the capital's Jews. Before his very public apostasy, however, he evidently excelled as a tutor to the Weils.

Godchaux proved to be a prodigy. At the age of 15, in 1821, he published his first work, an impassioned and scholarly response to Tsarphati (the pseudonym of Olry Terquem), France's leading proponent of religious reform. Tsarphati's first reformist pamphlet, which aroused the ire of the young Godchaux Weil, advocated moving the Sabbath to Sunday (to accommodate poor Jewish workers who had to work on Saturday) and ending the practice of circumcision.[14] Godchaux's response to Tsarphati reveals both a modern sense of patriotic devotion to France for allowing the freedom of Jewish religious practice and a traditional sense of what that practice entails. He bases his argument in favor of maintaining Saturday Sabbath and circumcision on the immutability of God's commandments, citing liberally from the Torah to make his case.[15] The young Godchaux's conservatism seems to have been inspired by loyalty to his traditionalist father, for after his father's death in 1828, he would devote himself to promoting some of the very reforms he had denounced as a teenager.

Godchaux married Frédérique Zunz (d. 1897) and had two children.[16] After his father's death, Godchaux went into the porcelain business, joined the prestigious Cercle de Commerce in the 1830s, and later became a bailiff (*huissier de justice*) for the Tribunal de la Seine. From an early age, he also played a leadership role in the Paris Jewish community, serving on a number of important charitable committees for the Paris Consistory.[17] In her history of the Jews of Paris, Christine Piette views Godchaux as part of a new generation of Jews born as French citizens and steeped in French culture who would modernize the capital's Jewish institutions.[18]

With the founding of *Les Archives Israélites*, in 1840, Godchaux became a writer, appearing in the monthly journal's pages from the first issue. Unlike Foa, however, he never lived by his pen. Rather than attempt to reach a mainstream public, he preferred to write for a specifically Jewish audience and published only in Jewish venues. In addition to writing more than a dozen short stories and forty witty social commentaries for *Les Archives Israélites* during the 1840s, Weil also penned an enormously popular moralistic text for Jewish schoolchildren, *Les matinées du samedi* [Saturday Mornings] (1842), which was widely used in Jewish schools in the francophone world and was translated into English (see Figure 2).[19] His retirement from literary life in 1850[20] coincides with his failure to be elected to the Paris Consistory, no doubt a blow to this pillar of the Jewish community and son of a Consistory member.[21] He died on June 9, 1878, seven years after the birth of his great-nephew Proust.[22]

Les matinées du samedi helped make Ben-Lévi one of the most famous members of the Parisian Jewish community in the mid-nineteenth century. An attempt to explain Judaism and to inculcate Jewish values in children, *Les matinées du samedi* contained a preface by the editor of *Les Archives Israélites*, Samuel Cahen, and an endorsement from members of the Central Consistory, including the renowned jurist Adolphe Crémieux, a relative of the Weils. As an officially sanctioned text, *Les matinées du samedi* offers particularly telling insights not only into Ben-Lévi's vision of what constitutes Judaism, a vision that we will find echoed in more sophisticated fashion in his writing for adults, but also into the ideology of the community's leaders in the 1840s, which he so clearly expressed.

Whereas Ben-Lévi's pamphlet in response to Tsarphati had looked

LES MATINÉES DU SAMEDI,

LIVRE D'ÉDUCATION MORALE ET RELIGIEUSE,

À L'USAGE DE LA JEUNESSE ISRAÉLITE,

PAR G. **BEN LÉVI**,

Ancien Membre du Comité communal des Écoles Israélites de Paris.

AVEC UNE PRÉFACE, PAR **S. CAHEN**,

Rédacteur des ARCHIVES ISRAÉLITES DE FRANCE.

« Continuez à instruire la jeunesse et à combattre, par vos efforts
incessants, les préjugés qui peuvent exister encore contre les Israélites; rappelez-vous que l'eau qui tombe goutte à goutte, finit par
user la pierre la plus dure. »

(*Réponse de S. M. LOUIS-PHILIPPE, 1er, Roi des Français,
à M. Crémieux, Vice-Président du Consistoire central.*)

———

TOME I.

PARIS,

AU BUREAU DES *ARCHIVES ISRAÉLITES DE FRANCE*,
Rue Pavée, No 1, au Marais.

1842.

Figure 2. Title page from Ben-Lévi, *Les matinées du samedi* (Paris: Archives Israélites, 1842). Courtesy of the Library at the Herbert D. Katz Center for Advanced
Judaic Studies, University of Pennsylvania.

to the Hebrew Bible and to a strict sense of religious law for his definition of Jewish practice, *Les matinées du samedi* offers a more cultural vision of Judaism, one grounded in modern Jewish history and
expressed in the form of fictional narrative. Following a brief list of
declarations, modeled on the Catholic catechism, that set forth the
tenets of the Jewish faith,[23] Ben-Lévi provides a series of stories about
Jews—some taken from the Torah or Mishnah and others featuring
more modern subject matter, including a great deal of material drawn
from the Napoleonic wars. One such story, "Le cosaque et le Parisien"
[The Cossack and the Parisian], describes a French soldier about to
be massacred by a Russian during Napoleon's retreat from Russia.
When he recites the Shema before dying, the Cossack, who also turns
out to be a Jew, saves him (see Figure 3). Ben-Lévi emphasizes not
the act of praying but rather the gesture of solidarity between Jews
across national borders as the essence of what it means to be a Jew.
Judaism is less a relation with God or a series of rituals or laws than
an ethical posture, a constellation of attitudes and values governing
actions. These include, first and foremost, a fierce loyalty and gratitude to France for emancipating the Jews; Ben-Levi devotes an entire
chapter to the Abbé Grégoire, the advocate of Jewish emancipation
during the Revolution. Although *Les matinées* draws material from
Jewish history around the world, it focuses on the history of Jews in
France in an effort to solidify a sense of communal identity conceived
in national terms. It contains numerous biographies of famous French
Jews, emphasizing not scholars and rabbis but rather cultural figures,
such as the great actress Rachel Félix, highlighting both the glory she
brought to her country and her loyalty to her Jewish origins.

Les Archives Israélites, the monthly journal that published the bulk
of Ben-Lévi's writing, displayed similar goals and a similar notion of
what modern French Jewish identity should be. We know from its
lists of subscribers that its readership in the 1840s consisted mostly
of elite Parisian Jews.[24] Like similar publications begun at around the
same time in Germany, Austria, England, Italy, and the United States,
Les Archives Israélites dedicated itself to Jewish modernization. For
the writers and editors of *Les Archives Israélites*, this meant replacing
the tradition-bound "Jew," an object of scorn for non-Jews, with the

Figure 3. "Schema Israël," from Ben-Lévi, *Les matinées du samedi* (Paris: Archives Israélites, 1842). Courtesy of the Library at the Herbert D. Katz Center for Advanced Judaic Studies, University of Pennsylvania.

"Israelite," a modern French citizen, free of the complexes resulting from centuries of persecution. Ben-Lévi offered a philosophical and philological justification for this transformation. In his "Fifth Letter from a Humorist," subtitled "The Complicities of an Adjective," he describes how the dictionary of the Académie Française defines *le juif* or "Jew" as "a man who practices usury" (*Les Archives Israélites* [1842], 147). (I verified that this is in fact the case.)[25] The writers for *Les Archives Israélites* would thus treat most uses of the adjective *juif* as an insult because it carried negative connotations.[26]

For Ben-Lévi and his colleagues, inventing the Israelite also meant promoting religious reform. The Reform movement had first taken root in Germany and grew out of the Haskalah, the Jewish Enlightenment of the late eighteenth century. Although Moses Mendelssohn (1729–1786), the founder of the Haskalah, remained a strictly observant Jew, during the first decades of the nineteenth century, as French armies brought civil rights temporarily to the Jews of Germany, certain radical German rabbis began to argue that Judaism need not remain eternal and fixed but rather could evolve to reflect changing historical circumstances. They called for editing the liturgy to shorten the prayers and to remove references to Jewish nationalism, preaching in the vernacular, replacing the bar mitzvah with a confirmation ceremony, and making the synagogue service more decorous. They also advocated abolishing or reducing many of the legal commandments and prohibitions—including kosher dietary restrictions—that kept Jews from freely mixing with their gentile neighbors. They intended these changes to facilitate Jewish social integration, to prove that the Jews deserved emancipation because they had renounced their supposedly backward ways, and to reduce conversion and disaffection by making Jewish practice less onerous. By 1820, Reform temples had been founded in Berlin, Hamburg, and Leipzig, beginning a process that would splinter Germany's Jewish communities.[27]

Tsarphati attempted to import these changes into France as early as the 1820s, but the movement for reform did not really take hold there until the founding of Les Archives Israélites in 1840. Editorials in the early issues of the journal called for following in the footsteps of the German reformers and printed sermons by leading German Reform rabbis.[28] Writers for Les Archives Israélites, including Ben-Lévi, pushed for a series of changes in the synagogue service, including excising references to a return to Jerusalem in the liturgy in order to affirm devotion to France, but avoided most of Tsarphati's more extreme positions, such as moving the Sabbath to Sunday. As Michael Meyer describes it, the centralization of French Judaism, under the control of the Consistory, prevented a schism from taking place in France. Beginning in the 1840s, the Consistory allowed for moderate reforms but refused to sanction separate, more liberal synagogues.[29] The reformist tendencies of *Les Archives Israélites*, however, aroused the ire of a vocal group of Orthodox Jews, who founded a rival publication, *L'Univers Israélite*, in 1844.[30] In the next chapter, I discuss this counter-Reform movement and its leading fictional ideologue, Ben Baruch, who saw himself as the Orthodox Ben-Lévi.

The reformers of *Les Archives Israélites* sought to modernize—or, according to their critics, dilute—Judaism in order to keep a new generation of emancipated Jews from abandoning their links to the community. Yet, even while promoting acculturation by criticizing the outdated manners and customs that had marked Jews as a people apart under the Old Regime, *Les Archives Israélites* resisted the assimilation of France's Jews by promoting autonomous Jewish institutions, such as separate Jewish hospitals, schools, and charities. *Les Archives Israélites* would be written entirely in French; occasional Hebrew and Yiddish words were always translated. With articles devoted to Jewish history and culture modeled on the new German Wissenschaft des Judentums, *Les Archives Israélites* cultivated an intellectualized, scholarly approach to the religion. At once eager to demonstrate the loyalty of Jews to France and keen to promote French Jewish communal identity, *Les Archives Israélites* would constantly vaunt the successes of Jews in French national life.[31] At the same time, monthly articles called attention to the plight of less fortunate Jews still struggling for civil rights in other parts of the world, including England and Germany.

In many ways Ben-Lévi's writing—both his short stories and his nonfiction pieces—mirrors the articles surrounding it in *Les Archives Israélites*. Like his colleagues, he advocated modest reforms to the religion and pushed for Jewish social integration. But his pieces also stand out from the rest of the writing in *Les Archives Israélites* in both form and content. Not only do Ben-Lévi's writings display a worldly, witty, playfully sarcastic tone that seems out of place in a journal that took itself quite seriously, but they also contain a uniquely satirical edge, seeking to hold up a critical mirror to the assimilating French Jewish bourgeoisie. Whereas most articles in *Les Archives Israélites* flatter the ethnic and national pride of its elite readership, Ben-Lévi's stories challenge readers to consider what they left behind in their social ascent. In the remainder of this chapter, I analyze these narratives for the insights they provide into Ben-Lévi's unique vision for Jewish modernity.

Jewish Realism

The tension between tradition and progress in the French Jewish community is one of the principal motors driving Ben-Lévi's fiction. In one story from 1841 called, in a nod to Balzac, "Grandeur et décadence d'un taleth polonais" [Rise and Fall of a Polish Tallith], he traces the history of a prayer shawl (tallith) as it gets passed down through three generations of a Parisian Jewish family.[32] The story opens in the 1780s as the very Orthodox Père Jacob, proprietor of a used clothes and old ironwork shop, imports a prayer shawl from Poland for his wedding. Upon his death, Jacob leaves the tallith to his son Jacobi, who italianizes his name "as much to give it a Corsican air as to erase its overly biblical connotations."[33] A veteran of Napoleon's army—hence the desire to appear Corsican—Jacobi makes a fortune as a military supplier during the Empire. "Much less religious than his father" (753), he nevertheless retains a distinct sense of Jewish obligation; he attends services on the high holidays and gives generously to Jewish charities. He also venerates the old prayer shawl, which he carries with him even into battle.

His son continues the process the father began: "Today Jacobi is dead, and his son, a handsome young twenty-year-old, has inherited his fortune and his tallith. This son goes by Jacoubé so as to hide entirely his Israelite origin." Jacoubé works as a stockbroker and, like many of Balzac's nouveau riche characters, lives in the fashionable Chaussée-d'Antin. "He . . . wears varnished boots, his hair long, a collar shaped like the paths of the Trianon, and a glass that holds itself in place between the eyebrow and the eye" (754). Jacoubé is of an entirely new species from his father and grandfather. Indeed, he is not a Jew at all but a *lion*, as fashionable young men from the time were known: "Needless to say, Jacoubé is only a Jew by birth; he knows nothing of the Israelite religion, and he would blush to be seen at the synagogue. If he is asked about *le père* Jacob, he responds dismissively,

'What is that?'" (754). And what has become of the old prayer shawl in the hands of this fashion plate? The narrator reports having seen just yesterday, at a costume ball at the Opera, a loose woman (*une grisette*) disguised as a stevedore, wearing an exotic piece of old wool adorned with blue stripes.

Like many of Ben-Lévi's fictions, the tallith story functions as a kind of modern parable. Short fictitious narratives carrying a moral message, parables occur occasionally in the Old Testament but with much more frequency both in the New Testament and in postbiblical Hebrew literature. Parables function through allegory; earthly situations, often reflecting contemporary historical conditions, usually signify religious precepts. In the famous New Testament parable of the prodigal son, a magnanimous father welcomes home his spendthrift heir who has spent his portion on high living, just as God accepts all repentant sinners. In Ben-Lévi's story, the tallith does not have a supernatural significance but rather stands for the fate of the Jewish religious tradition in modern France. Jewish identity is able to survive acculturation—the stage represented by the generation of Jacobi—but not assimilation—the stage of Jacoubé.[34] Ben-Lévi's parable also has a more pessimistic thrust than its biblical antecedents; his prodigal son does not repent and serves to warn of the danger of assimilation through a negative example.

Along with its roots in the tradition of religious narrative, the story of the tallith displays many of the characteristics that link Ben-Lévi's writing with the new kind of fiction that his contemporary Balzac had begun writing in the 1830s. This fiction situated its plots in relation to historical processes and placed emphasis on visual observation as the key to unlocking truths about the modern character. According to historians of literature, hostile critics in the 1840s would apply the pejorative label of realism to this fiction to denounce the way it showed too much—including dangerous truths about sex and class.[35] Ben-Lévi clearly associates himself with this new approach. Like Balzac, he calls himself a physiologist, in reference to the new observational fashion, and offers minute visual description of the physical world.[36] He views his characters, their dress and their language, with an eye for the telling detail, like the lorgnon fixed nonchalantly in Jacoubé's jaded brow or the dismissive manner with which he disavows his ancestor. Moreover, Ben-Lévi's narrators, like Balzac's, are omniscient, able to see everything and to read the minds of characters, exposing the ugly secrets many critics would prefer to leave hidden.

And these narrators are not necessarily Jewish. Or rather, they wear their Jewishness lightly. Straight out of Balzac's fictional universe, they are worldly habitués of the opera ball, or *flâneurs* who know the Parisian streets like the palms of their hand, or hermits, bored with pleasure, who have withdrawn from social life after draining it to the dregs. Deeply imbued with French rather than specifically Jewish culture, Ben-Lévi's narrators more often quote Pascal and Racine than the Talmud. Moreover, Ben-Lévi follows Balzac in his heavy use of irony as a tool for social criticism, both in his short stories and in his nonfiction articles satirizing the dreams and desires of the French Jewish bourgeoisie.

Ben-Lévi not only borrowed Balzac's techniques for describing modern life but also shared with Balzac a sense of what modern life entailed. Ben-Lévi's characters are all urban, and many are implicated in modern forms of capitalist economic activity. Although some are doctors or soldiers, others, like Jacoubé, a stockbroker, resemble Balzac's financiers—many of whom, including the master banker Nucingen, are also described as Jews—in their predilection for the more abstract realms of monetary manipulation. Like Balzac and unlike more traditional Jewish tales, Ben-Lévi describes a "disenchanted" world, a postsacred era in which faith and superstition have been evacuated—or rather, like the Polish prayer shawl that winds up on the shoulders of the grisette, recuperated for distinctly nonsacred ends.[37] Uprooted from their villages, cut adrift from religious tradition and from an organic connection with the past, Ben-Lévi's Jewish characters often exemplify, along with a cynical materialism, a selfish individualism. Imitating those eminent Balzacian protagonists, Eugène de Rastignac and Lucien de Rubempré, fashionable gentlemen who extort money from poor relatives to finance their social trajectories, Jacoubé is willing to sacrifice familial bonds for worldly success in the modern metropolis.

Caught in a capitalist nexus of greed and self-interest, deprived of the traditional supports of God and family, Balzac's characters face a set of dilemmas that would come to define the modern experience for generations of readers. It is not a coincidence that Balzac features so many Jewish characters in his fiction because France's Jews faced these dilemmas in a particularly acute fashion. Thrust by the French Revolution's radical gesture of emancipation into the center of a debate about the power of equality and education to transform a backward population into productive citizens, the Jews of France, who had lived for centuries in isolated rural villages, suddenly found themselves confronted with an unprecedented range of opportunities. Many embraced these opportunities by abandoning traditional Jewish ways of life to move to large cities and by taking up new forms of economic opportunity during this age of capitalist expansion. These characters become the subjects of both Balzac and Ben-Lévi. But Ben-Lévi did not merely copy Balzac by describing a modern metropolis filled with Jews. He appropriated Balzacian thematics and Balzacian technique to offer a view of modern Jewish life from within. His stories view Jews not as symbols of the new era but as full-fledged subjects confronting dilemmas in ways that are particular but also universal.

In "Le décret du 17 mars" [The Decree of March 17], also from 1841, Ben-Lévi once again explicitly appropriates Balzacian thematics, but this time in a tragic rather than comic vein. In "Le décret" Ben-Lévi rewrites Balzac's haunting 1832 novella *Le Colonel Chabert* [Colonel Chabert], which describes how a hero of the Napoleonic wars, left for dead on the battlefield of Eylau, returns to Paris only to discover that he has lost his identity. Believing him to be dead, Chabert's wife has used his fortune to marry a minister in the new Restoration government. Defeated by the forces of power and money arrayed against him, as well as by the new bureaucracy itself, the Napoleonic ghost eventually renounces his claim on his fortune and name and lives out the rest of his days in a poorhouse. A commentary on the amnesia of modernity, on the desire to forget the past in the quest for the new, Balzac's story also serves as an indictment of the new capitalist values that leave no place for heroism.

Ben-Lévi borrows this framework to examine a specific event in French Jewish history and its ramifications for the present. His focus is Napoleon's decree of 1808—dubbed by Jews the "infamous decree"—

and its effect on the family of an honest Jewish moneylender in Alsace. Responding to complaints from the Alsatian peasantry over the enormous debts contracted to Jewish moneylenders in the region, Napoleon's decree retroactively nullified loans made by Jews to non-Jews if the lender could not prove that he had given full value for the contracted sum. Because almost no lenders could produce the witnesses and documentation required, many were driven to bankruptcy. The decree, which violated revolutionary principles of equality by applying only to Jews, also required Jews to obtain a special permit before they could engage in trade and forbade Jews from procuring a replacement for military service. It represents perhaps the darkest moment in modern French Jewish history between the Revolution and the Dreyfus affair, because it effectively revoked the legal equality that France, first among European countries, had granted the Jews during the Revolution. In response to Jewish protests, Napoleon exempted the Jews of Paris and Bordeaux—mostly acculturated Sephardim—from the 1808 law, which stayed in effect for a ten-year period, until the Restoration government declined to renew it in 1818.

In Ben-Lévi's story, the infamous decree forces a young Alsatian Jew, David Blum, "a tall and handsome young man of twenty," to abandon both his fiancée and his studies, which include both the Talmud and, in a nod to modernization, more secular subjects, to enter the army.[38] Upon joining his regiment in Spain, David learns that the decree has driven his money-lending father to bankruptcy and his mother to madness. Both parents subsequently die from grief and shame. Consumed with hatred for Napoleon, David fulfills his military duties with such a lack of ardor that his superior officers and fellow soldiers disdain him. When the tide turns against the French army during the retreat from Moscow, however, David's leaden indifference to life enables him to defend his comrades with remarkable bravery. In a scene straight out of another Balzac novella, *Adieu* (1830), Ben-Lévi describes the disastrous crossing of the Beresina, during which Napoleon himself offers David Blum the Cross of the Legion of Honor for his selfless devotion to his fellow soldiers.[39] But David refuses the cross in the name of the Alsatian Jews, ruined and dishonored by the odious March 17 decree. Disconcerted by the rebuke of the Jewish soldier,

Napoleon declares that his advisers misled him and promises to review his Jewish policies, leaving David clutching the cross taken from the emperor's own uniform. Captured subsequently by the Cossacks, David spends the next twenty-eight years in a Siberian mining camp.

David returns to France in 1840, stopping first in his native village. Disoriented by the incipient industrialization that has altered the face of his former home, he recognizes nobody and nobody recognizes him. Cold, hungry, and alone, he then makes his way to the capital. Like Chabert, who must hire a lawyer to prove that he is still alive, David experiences not only material but also both bureaucratic and existential privation in Paris: "He arrived in the capital on December 14, worn down with fatigue, suffering from cold and hunger, without papers, without money and not knowing what would become of him." Ben-Lévi's fictional veteran, like Balzac's, has no place in the modern metropolis: "He wandered for a long while in the streets of the big city, often rubbing elbows with people who were talking about the glories of the Empire but who didn't care that one of the old instruments of that national glory was suffering beside them." Unlike Chabert, however, who returns to Paris during the Restoration, when Napoleonic worship was still suspect, David Blum returns in December 1840—just in time to witness the public celebration of the return of Napoleon's remains from Saint-Helena, organized with great fanfare by the citizen-king Louis-Philippe, intent on appropriating the emperor's prestige to bolster his more banal bourgeois monarchy.[40]

Surrounded by the crowd that has come to pay its respects to the fallen hero, David experiences an epiphany. Remembering Napoleon's apology on the battlefield and identifying with the great man's later suffering, David forgives the emperor for the infamous decree. In the story's final tableau, the broken Jewish veteran, surrounded by the crowd, sinks to his knees to pray as Napoleon's funeral convoy passes. His spirit calmed, the great weight of resentment lifted from his mind, his body then gives way to fatigue. When the crowd parts, David is discovered leaning, lifeless, against the Arc-de-Triomphe. "It is not known whether he collapsed due to starvation or cold, or whether he was crushed by the crowd," reports a newspaper article that concludes the story. This impersonal *fait divers* recounts how the unidentified

man, later exposed at the morgue, was found clutching two items—
the Cross of the Legion of Honor and an old scrap of paper bearing
the words "Imperial Decree Concerning the Jews.—March 17, 1808."

Balzac uses his Napoleonic hero to reflect on the ways the past continues to haunt the present. Ben-Lévi performs a similar gesture, only
from a specifically Jewish perspective. His story analyzes the historical legacies of the Revolution and the Napoleonic eras, which inaugurated modernity for France's Jews. On one level the story functions
didactically to condemn Napoleon's legacy by documenting the tragic
effect of his infamous decree on a representative Alsatian Jewish family. Blameless victims of Napoleon's retrograde policies, David Blum
and his parents illustrate the suffering that resulted from the emperor's
ill-considered effort at social engineering. If Napoleon intended his
decree to encourage the Jews' assimilation by normalizing their economic practices, the story shows how it in fact contributed to their
increased alienation and marginalization in French society; the decree results in the isolation of David's parents (his father in a debtor's
prison and his mother in an insane asylum) and finally in their deaths.
If Napoleon intended the decree to encourage integration by forcing Jews into the army, the decree instead turns David into a pariah,
whose grief and grudge against the emperor keep him apart from his
fellow soldiers. Napoleon's decree, in other words, backfired by exacerbating the very social ills it was meant to counter.

The story thus functions as a kind of critical or revisionist history of
Napoleon's reign. It also figures into a more specifically Jewish historical tradition by placing Napoleon in that long line of oppressive rulers
who have conspired against the Jews since Pharaoh and by fulfilling
the Jewish religious commandment to remember (*zakhor*) the martyrs
of Israel. The repetition of the name of the decree in the story's title
and in its last words figures as a memorial incantation, calling to mind
a painful history for French Jews. Indeed, "Le décret du 17 mars"
resurrects a historical event that the acculturated, elite readership of
Les Archives Israélites might have preferred to leave buried. Ben-Lévi
complicates the triumphant narrative of progress leading from Jewish
emancipation in 1790 to 1831, when France put the Jewish clergy on
the state payroll.[41] By showing Napoleon to have reneged on the revo-

lutionary tradition's liberal promise of inclusion, the story reveals that what is offered can also be taken away. It shows Jewish equality and citizenship in the modern nation-state to be precarious, less a right than a privilege.

Oddly, even though the story denounces the effects of Napoleon's infamous decree, it seeks to absolve Napoleon himself from blame. The emperor's battlefield admission that his advisers misled him and his pledge to revise his prejudicial policy conveniently serve to liberate David—and by extension the reader—from the burden of resenting the emperor.[42] Given Napoleon's notorious antipathy toward the Jews, the apology imagined by Ben-Lévi to the Jewish soldier seems not only unlikely but counterfactual. Fiction serves here as parahistory and as wish fulfillment.

By contriving to excuse Napoleon, the story resolves a dilemma for Jews in the July Monarchy who found themselves trapped between the painful memory of Napoleon's anti-Jewish policies and the desire to participate in the cult of affection for the emperor. As Sudhir Hazareesingh has argued, Napoleonic worship served as a means of promoting national identity in nineteenth-century France.[43] The Jews thus found themselves caught between religion and nation, between *culte* and cult: Could one still be a Jew and worship at the altar of the Saint-Napoleon? Was to idolize Napoleon un-Jewish?[44] Was not to do so un-French?[45] For an intensely patriotic writer like Ben-Lévi, who the next year would publish his moralistic manual for Jewish schoolchildren exhorting love of both religion and country, such a dilemma demanded careful negotiation. Through the fiction of Napoleon's apology to the Jewish soldier, Ben-Lévi's story allows French Jews to have it both ways; the infamous decree lives on in memory along with the plight of its martyrs, and its perpetrator receives absolution.

By absolving Napoleon, the story shifts religious registers from the Jewish commandment to remember to the Christian one to forgive. This symbolic conversion allows David—and by extension the reader—to join the crowd of worshippers lining the Champs-Elysées as Napoleon's funeral convoy passes. But Ben-Lévi's story does not sacrifice Jewish values entirely in its rush to forgive Napoleon. If the Jewish soldier becomes Christian through the act of forgiveness, the

Christian emperor becomes Jewish through the act of suffering. David identifies with the emperor because the great man's martyrdom mirrors his own: "Like me, they robbed you of those who were dear to you" ("Comme moi, l'on t'a ravi les êtres qui t'étaient chers"), David tells the passing coffin, using the familiar form of address (*tu* or *t'*), much as one would speak to a parent or to God. "Like me, they enchained you in a distant land. Like me, your name was covered with the slime of passion. Like me, you return with a frozen heart and a stiffened arm." Napoleon experienced the characteristic Jewish torment of exile, which redeems him in the eyes of the displaced Jewish soldier. "How did you die in exile, you who gave orders to kings and sent men into bondage!" (87), David asks the emperor, less as a question (there is no question mark) than as an affirmation of Napoleon's Jewish bona fides.

If Ben-Lévi resolves the dilemma over Napoleon worship by symbolically converting the emperor to Judaism, he also takes pains to specify that Jewish forgiveness can take place only once France has rectified its wrongs against the Jews. By letting the infamous decree lapse and by restoring the Jews to full equality, the regimes of the Restoration and the July Monarchy made possible the kind of reconciliation envisioned by Ben-Lévi between the Jewish victim and the nation that persecuted him: "And the great Emperor and the humble Jew met for the last time on a soil consecrated once again by liberty, tolerance and justice, for bad laws last but for a day, while liberty, tolerance, and justice are eternal." Here the narrator reassures readers that remembering the infamous decree need not compromise their faith in France as the homeland of liberty. Just as later some Jews would see the Dreyfus affair not as evidence of persistent French antisemitism but as proof that French justice eventually triumphs over prejudice, the story recuperates the infamous decree for a narrative of French-Jewish fusion.

However, Ben-Lévi's story can be read not only as an exploration of the politics of Napoleon worship during the July Monarchy but also as a more general allegory for the paradoxes of Jewish assimilation in nineteenth-century France. Indeed, the process of assimilation for the Jews of France's eastern provinces began during the Imperial period, the result of the increased opportunities opened by the Revolution (freedom of movement, the right to live in cities, etc.) and of Napoleon's perhaps misguided efforts to enforce integration through military conscription. In the story, Napoleon's decree cuts David off from his Jewish roots and from his links to fellow Jews. Forced into the army, he loses at once religious, familial, and local ties. When he returns to his native village following his Siberian captivity, he finds nothing and nobody there, no trace of his former life. This deracination mirrors that of the generation of Jews who, like Ben-Lévi's own family, began the exodus away from traditional Judaism during the Empire. Although at first excluded from the non-Jewish collectivity, David eventually merges with the crowd of spectators watching Napoleon's funeral convoy pass, the "hundred thousand voices" crying "Here he is!" The story thus concludes with the Jew's absorption into the body of the nation through participation in the cult of Napoleonic worship during the July Monarchy. This absorption figures as a liberation for David, as freedom or release from a Jewish identity conceived as suffering: "His soul was calmed by prayer, the hallucination of his mind subsided," the narrator tells us. But what makes this story so interesting, and so important for understanding the stakes of Jewish modernity in France, is the way it reveals not only the pleasures of assimilation but its perils as well.

Even though David is liberated from his past, his assimilation proves fatal. David dies just as he joins the crowd—depicted here as a threatening and faceless mass that perhaps crushes the protagonist and that remains heedless of his misery. The implication is that Jews pay a price for their modernization. By forgiving Napoleon for the infamous decree, by relinquishing his past and his specificity, the Jew may experience the ecstasy of uniting with his fellow Frenchmen, but he dies as a result—if not physically, like David, then spiritually, as a Jew. And to die in the crowd is to die alone. David's fate is ultimately that of the *fait divers*. He ends in the morgue, unidentified, his story told in the impersonal voice of the newspaper, which substitutes for a more specifically Jewish narrative voice once David makes the decision to cut himself off from his past. Having renounced his last link to Judaism, David's body will not be claimed, we assume, for Jewish burial, despite the fact that during his final struggle, his hand violently clutches both the Cross of the Legion of Honor and the text of the March 17 decree. We might read this last desperate grasping as David's turning back from the delirium of complete assimilation, as his dying wish to hold on to not only a modern national identity, which although ostensibly secular, retains Christian overtones (the Cross), but also the Jewish past and Jewish identity (the decree).

Ben-Lévi's story frames the dilemma of modernity for French Jews. Should the Jews renounce their traditional religious identity for a new, modern national one, symbolized here by the cult of Napoleon worship? For Jews, joining this cult offered freedom—from the past and its painful memories. The lure must have been enormous, and Ben-Lévi does his best to justify making the leap. Ultimately, however, he holds back. Although his protagonist joins the crowd and experiences a thrilling—if lethal—freedom, the story itself remains tied to the past, anchored to memory. Ultimately, David's body is claimed by the story itself, which redeems his assimilation as a warning to its readers but also as a sign that complete homogenization was not the only option for French Jews.

Idealism and Reform

If Ben-Lévi borrowed the style and even the plots of Balzac to describe the dilemmas of Jewish assimilation, he did not, however, limit himself to the realist mode. In Ben-Lévi's fiction, we also find elements of idealism, which, as Naomi Schor and Margaret Cohen have shown, vied with realism for the allegiance of the reading public in the 1840s. In France, idealism did not contain the same philosophical overtones it had in Germany; rather, it came to signify a way of imagining positive resolutions to the social conflicts engendered by modernity. It did this by appealing to the best in human nature rather than by dwelling on man's faults and foibles, as realist authors had made it their task to do. Whereas realism exposed capitalism's encroachment on all aspects of modern life and revealed the financial and moral dilemmas of subjects caught in the vise of new economic realities, idealist writers tended to abstract or elide economic concerns. Idealism likewise refused to get bogged down in details, preferring a light touch to the fetishistic obsessions of realism. It found its fullest expression in the novels of Balzac's female contemporary, George Sand.

Ben-Lévi, as we have seen, uses realist literary codes to describe a nineteenth-century world in which spirituality has waned and communal ties have been replaced by capitalist greed. But in many of his stories, the Jewish writer also uses idealist codes to show how these processes can be reversed. In a work from 1846, "Les poissons et les miettes de pain" [The Fish and the Breadcrumbs], a worldly narrator recounts a fishing trip down the Seine with his friend Gustave. Gustave is a modern Parisian gentleman, a typical realist protagonist: "He shops at Renard's, he dines at the Café Anglais . . . and he has studied law, which gives him the right to do nothing at all."[46] A graduate lawyer, Gustave has achieved what so many European Jews, barred from entering the liberal professions by their religion, could not. Yet he takes his opportunities for granted, opting for a life of idleness rather than achievement. Indeed, he resembles Jacoubé, the heartless fop in the tallith story, who represents the sad end point of his family's journey of assimilation.

A godless skeptic, Gustave has freed himself not only from all religious scruples but also from all signs of Jewish particularity: "He was born of Jewish parents, don't ask for anything more; as for our religion and our history, don't question him about them" (631). It is not the implied Jewish reader ("*our* religion" and "*our* history") who does the questioning, however, but rather Gustave. As their boat passes in front of the Hôtel de Ville, he asks the narrator why a crowd of people on the shore are throwing bits of bread from their pockets into the water. The narrator explains to Gustave that these people are fellow Jews practicing the traditional custom of *tashlich*, symbolically emptying their hearts of sin before Yom Kippur, the day of atonement. Gustave, the "avowed enemy of the ridiculous" (632), rails against the custom as an absurd superstition. The narrator—who is hardly a traditionalist himself or he would also be emptying his pockets on shore rather than cruising down the river on a Jewish holiday—does not disagree with

Gustave about the need to modernize the religion by purging it of outdated practices but argues that certain traditions might nevertheless be worth keeping.

After some quiet reflection, Gustave then tells a strange story. He recounts that he has just been privy to a conversation among the fish in the bottom of their boat. He describes witnessing a sole make lewd propositions to a pike while a crayfish complained that the boat wasn't moving fast enough and an eel chastised the other fish for being loud and vulgar. Apparently, by eating the pieces of bread thrown to them by the Jews, these mostly nonkosher fish have ingested their sins and become coquettish, peevish, and snobbish. Although Gustave recounts his vision with a straight face, we suspect that he means to mock the custom of *tashlich* by literalizing it. The narrator responds with a nod to classical French literature (typical for Ben-Lévi), signaling his own ironic distance from the fantastic episode: "Well then, here we are back in the time of La Fontaine, when animals used to speak" (635).

Once Gustave finishes his fantastic narrative, the fishermen witness a touching scene on the far bank, as a beautiful woman, dressed in widow's weeds, helps her young son toss a handful of bread into the water. There follows another silence in the boat, after which a chastened Gustave shakes the narrator's hand and declares with a new note of sincerity, "Yes, there is at the base of every religious custom something sacred that only touches the heart once one has been able to understand it" (638). Moved by his vision of the woman's naïve faith and of religion's power to comfort human misery, Gustave recognizes the value in ancient rites. He understands the metaphorical power of *tashlich* and hence its continued relevance in the modern world.

In this story a disenchanted world is reenchanted by a reformed cynic, who comes to recognize ritual's capacity to express human desire for a realm of perfectibility beyond the material world. Gustave's transformation contains elements of the classic realist bildungsroman, as the protagonist gains knowledge through experience. But whereas for Lucien de Rubempré, the foppish protagonist of Balzac's *Lost Illusions*, the path to insight is characteristically accompanied by a loss of faith in the ideal, Ben-Lévi's character moves in the opposite direc-

tion, from worldliness to something resembling religion: "Les poissons et les miettes de pain," like many of Ben-Lévi's stories, could be
titled *Illusions Found.*

Ben-Lévi is not, however, advocating a return to Orthodox Judaism in this story. He does not mandate that his characters or his readers perform *tashlich* or any other religious rite. He suggests that the
ritual has a certain power and meaning, but he does not specify what
this might be. The little boy may throw the bread into the water because he believes that the fish will ingest his sins. He may accept the
literal meaning of the custom that Gustave and the narrator reject as
superstition. For them, on the other hand, the ritual has a symbolic
significance, one that motivates them to self-scrutiny. We do not really
know what the young mother believes. Perhaps she throws the bread
into the water because her ancestors have always done so; perhaps it
is a way of reconnecting with her dead husband, or perhaps it is just
to please her son. The point is that in Ben-Lévi's fictional universe,
Judaism emerges as a flexible religion, one that evolves and adapts to
new historical circumstances and one in which rituals can signify differently for different practitioners. Here lies what makes these stories
embodiments of the new spirit of religious reform. What counts in
this story is not upholding the law or following tradition but the individual journey that makes for meaning in the present.

This reform ideology comes across in other stories as well, which
also incorporate elements of both realism and idealism. Like the bread-
crumb story, "L'ami du préfet" [The Prefect's Friend] from 1847, begins with the elements of a Balzacian narrative but ends by leaving
realism—and with it, materialism and cynicism—behind. In Balzacian
fashion, the tale starts with a frame narrative, set in the present, as a
Jewish narrator, at a house party in the country, tells a story to distract
his companions from a religious debate over the nature of the messiah,
led by a local priest, that was threatening to get overly heated. The
recounted story begins in Paris during the Reign of Terror, as two
women, one an aristocrat, the other a poor Jew, give birth to sons.
Because the Jewish woman dies in childbirth before circumcising her
son and the marquise goes into exile because of the terror campaign,

both boys are sent to wet nurses in the country. In a twist typical of melodrama and the serial novel, the drunk driver gets into an accident on the way to deliver the children, and although the babies are not harmed, they lose their identifying tags. Unable to tell which child is which, the driver randomly decides one will be an aristocrat and the other a Jew.

Eighteen years later, Paul de Vieuxmenil is a handsome soldier, living a life of debauchery, while the other child, Jacob Samuel, has become a poor peddler. Paul happens to be stationed in the town where the old driver lies dying. Racked with guilt, the driver tells the young marquis the truth about the accident. Paul is then driven by uncertainty over his identity to give up the soldier's life and to go on a fruitless search to find Jacob, who may in fact be the real marquis. Unable to locate the peddler, however, Paul eventually becomes a diligent government bureaucrat, a *préfet*. Twenty years later, Jacob Samuel comes before him with a petition. In an effort at reparation but without revealing the reason for his generosity, Paul sets about using his influence to make Jacob's fortune and provide a dowry for his beautiful daughter. The recounted narrative ends with the daughter's marriage to a young Jewish man. Back in the present of the outer frame story, the narrator resolves the debate over the messiah by showing that, in the face of eschatological uncertainty, Jews and Christians should act as brothers, just as Paul acts toward Jacob.

This stated moral, however, does not exhaust the story's significance. The setting of this story is the same modern world—a provincial prefect's office—that houses Balzac's bureaucrats, but the Jewish writer replaces the cynicism that surrounds these realist characters with a religious ethics.[47] Motivated by guilt over his possibly usurped aristocratic privileges, Paul acts according to the Hebrew Bible's basic moral injunction to treat his brother as he would treat himself. This precept is also, of course, the moral basis of Christianity, and it is significant that the distinctions between religions that serve to separate Paul and Jacob in the social world of nineteenth-century France evaporate in the sentimental realm of the story's conclusion, which points to the universal moral ground underpinning both religions. In becoming a Jew in action if not in name, Paul ironically also becomes a good Christian and truly noble.

But if this story emphasizes a general Judeo-Christian ethics as the basis of social interaction between people of different faiths, it also offers a more specific reflection on the problem of modern French Jewish identity. In all his stories, Ben-Lévi depicts a world that undermines traditional forms of Jewish affiliation. In the story of the prayer shawl, Jacoubé is only Jewish "by birth," just as Gustave in the fish story is merely "born of Israelite parents." Such distinctions were new in nineteenth-century France; before the Revolution, Jews had no choice but to accept the identity that accidents of birth foisted on them. With emancipation came the freedom to abandon the distinctive signs of dress and language that had marked Jews under the Old Regime. The prefect tale allegorizes the Jewish identity crisis that resulted from this liberation. It is literally the founding event of modernity, the French Revolution, that causes the confusion over which child is a Jew in the story. Although traditional Jewish law would resolve this question by determining which child had a Jewish mother, Ben-Lévi rather pointedly does not. Rather, he offers the basis for a new kind of Jewish identity based not on birth but on action. Jacob Samuel is a Jew because he acts like one. But Paul de Vieuxmenil might also be said to be a Jew in this story, not because he possesses any outward marks of Jewish identity or adheres to Jewish law but because he acts morally and seeks to help a fellow Jew in need.

In the prefect story, modernity threatens traditional Judaism, but a modernized Judaism—purged of tradition and reduced to primary ethical impulses and a sense of solidarity with other Jews—forms the basis of a new kind of community. This vision exemplifies the Reform ideology of *Les Archives Israélites*, which finds its ideal representative in Paul de Vieuxmenil, the aristocratic government bureaucrat, rather than Jacob Samuel, the poor peddler, who remains too traditional—too much a ghetto Jew—to serve as a model for Jewish modernity. Hope for the future in this story, however, ultimately rests on the shoulders of Jacob's daughter, who, although perhaps the descendant of Christian aristocrats, will raise a family of modern Jews thanks to the dowry provided by Paul.

Idealism and Social Justice

The aesthetics of idealism had political implications in nineteenth-century France. They expressed the utopian longings of social progressives before the disillusionment of the Revolution of 1848. But according to Schor, idealism also had an identity politics. She argues that Sand's opposition of idealism to Balzacian realism, her refusal of mimesis, serves as "a strategy for bodying forth her difference" and signifies her opposition to a political and representational order that objectifies the disenfranchised, especially women.[48] "Idealism for Sand is finally the only alternative representational mode available to those who do not enjoy the privileges of subjecthood in the real."[49] Idealism, according to Schor, served as a way to protest the politics of a world that refused women equality and to imagine a better one in which more just policies might reign.

The Jewish writer, I would like to suggest, uses idealist literary codes for similar ends. Although male Jews in France could lay claim to citizenship, they did not necessarily enjoy the "privileges of subjecthood in the real" or, more to the point, in *realism*. Balzac, as we have seen, used the Jew to figure both the attractions and repulsions of modernity; he populates his fiction with Jewish moneylenders and Jewish prostitutes. But he never makes a Jew his main protagonist and only rarely attempts to view the world through a Jewish subject's eyes.[50] Ben-Lévi's turn to idealism may thus represent a protest against the way his culture represented Jews—which he criticized in specific terms in his nonfiction pieces for *Les Archives Israélites*—and against the society in which Jews still labored against prejudice and other forms of injustice.

In a story from 1841, "Le médecin des aliénés" [The Alienist], a Jewish doctor in a German town renders a service to an aristocratic woman who then invites him to a ball only to humiliate him in front of her friends. The doctor responds with a dignity that teaches the aristocrat the true meaning of nobility. She apologizes by making a large donation to the doctor's clinic. In this story, Ben-Lévi's highly idealized representation of the Jewish doctor—who exemplifies a saintly humility, intelligence, and compassion—makes for a protest against a society that would exclude Jews or seek to degrade them. Like Sand, then, Ben-Lévi uses idealism as a strategy both to protest against injustice in this world and to sketch the contours of a better one. Unlike Sand, however, Ben-Lévi rarely voices criticism against contemporary France or French society. In the doctor story, the land of injustice lies across the Rhine, in a Germany that in the 1840s still denied Jews basic civil rights, or else in the prerevolutionary French past.

Ben-Lévi's relation to the past is a complicated one, but it offers insights into his vision of Jewish modernity. On the one hand, he seems to reject the reactionary impulses of Balzac, who declared himself a monarchist and a Catholic and constantly criticized such features of modernity as the decline of paternal authority. In contrast, Ben-Lévi refuses to romanticize the Old Regime. In the 1841 story "Mémoires d'un colporteur juif, écrits par lui-même" [Memoirs of a Jewish Peddler, Written by Himself], the narrator is a 100-year-old man who describes his life before the Revolution. He recounts how he was forced to roam the Lorraine countryside selling his goods to peasants, eking out a meager living while facing numerous humiliations: "The Jewish peddler was subject to incessant vexations, to perpetual persecutions."[51] In contrast to Alexandre Weill's village tales, which I examine in Chapter 4, and to Daniel Stauben's *Scènes de la vie juive en Alsace* [Scenes of Jewish Life in Alsace], which I analyze in Chapter 5, Ben-Lévi's stories do not long nostalgically for the "simple" rustic world of the prerevolutionary past.[52] Ben-Lévi is too conscious of history and too pragmatic to gloss over what was genuinely bad about the good old days.

On the other hand, in the peddler's memoirs, Ben-Lévi does point to certain pleasures that the traditional mode of Jewish life allowed, pleasures that have been lost in modernity.

> Forced to be continually on the road and to go on foot from one village to the other, I had only one consolation, which was to spend Saturdays beside my excellent wife and dear children. Today, modern Israelites, who call themselves enlightened, speak of the Sabbath rest with utter disdain, and one could perhaps say that Saturdays were killed off by the July Revolution. But for the man who lives without truce or rest and who has only one day to recover from the travails of

the week, for the man especially who is always on the road and who returns home to spend Saturday with his family, what delight does he not find in that religious observance! (688–689)

For the Jewish peddler of Old Regime France, who made his way on foot from one village to another throughout the week, observance of the Saturday Sabbath represented both rest and reward. To be sure, Ben-Lévi describes the Sabbath ritual as a "consolation" for suffering rather than as a positive boon, but it nevertheless offered the kind of genuine pleasure ("delight") that today's Jews ("modern Israelites"), who no longer know suffering, cannot appreciate.

For Ben-Lévi, the progress of modernity was double-edged: It brought great benefits but also entailed losses. The Jewish peddler serves as a metaphor for this paradox. Social reformers, who sought to cleanse French Jews of the complexes that were the product of centuries of suffering and persecution, saw in the peddler all that was most negative and in need of "regeneration."[53] As Ben-Lévi's peddler puts it, "Today, when one says of a man, 'He's a peddler,' one has heaped upon him all possible scorn and disdain." Ben-Lévi's peddler-narrator goes on to point out, however, that the peddler served an important economic function in prerevolutionary France by linking isolated villages together: "He was the pivot around which turned all important transactions" (687). Outdated by modern innovations such as the railroad—which Jews such as the Rothschilds and the Péreires had recently introduced first in France and then elsewhere in Europe—the peddler was destined to obsolescence in the nineteenth century. Martyr and victim, object of scorn both for "ignorant" peasants and for "enlightened" Jews, the peddler represented all that modernity would attempt to repress in the name of progress. But as Ben-Lévi realizes, along with him vanish the rituals and observances that he alone could appreciate fully.

In the second installment of the peddler's memoirs, published in 1842, the old man recounts his exploits during the Revolution of 1789. Anticipating modernizing trends by renouncing his itinerant ways and setting up shop in Paris, the former peddler receives the patronage of Marie-Antoinette and later contrives to comfort the queen when she is imprisoned at the Conciergerie during the Revolution. Arrested for his counterrevolutionary action, he is saved from the scaffold by his jailer, a member of the Committee of Public Safety named Pereyra, who turns out to be an "Israelite from the South." A Sephardic Jew, Pereyra's sense of solidarity with a coreligionist, even a poor peddler from Lorraine, trumps his revolutionary zeal: "In that fervent soul and in that spirit consumed by revolutionary fire, the first sentiments of religion were never extinguished."[54] Echoing the story about the Cossack helping the French soldier in *Les matinées du samedi*, the memoir's dénouement hinges on the unlikely chance of the old peddler falling into the hands of a fellow Jew in the midst of the Reign of Terror but also on the idealist notion that a sense of Jewish solidarity and human compassion would awaken even in the heart of a revolutionary extremist.

Ben-Lévi ends the peddler's memoirs in the midst of the Revolution, the very event that would free Jews to become citizens of France and set them on the path to modernity. As in his other stories, he expresses the hope that "the first sentiments of religion" will survive the turmoil of modernity and persist, improbably, into the new century—like the 100-year-old peddler himself. But what are these religious sentiments? They are not the virtues of obeying laws and strictures. They are not even the pleasures of enjoying the Sabbath. Ben-Lévi seems to view these elements of traditional Judaism as a lost cause—regrettable, perhaps, but not suitable to the modern world. What Ben-Lévi shows to be capable of persisting, both in this story and in others, is a reformed Judaism, based on universal ethical principles and communal solidarity: Paul helping Jacob, Pereyra helping the peddler. These sentiments are no less threatened by modernity—they would have no meaning for a Jacoubé or a Gustave before his boat trip down the Seine. But these sentiments at least have a chance for survival: They remain, in a dormant state, after a Jew becomes a *lion*, a cynic, a soldier, an aristocrat, or a revolutionary. It is the task set by Ben-Lévi's fiction, and the journal in which they appeared, to revive these sentiments and to actualize them in the modern world. Ben-Lévi is a realist in his analysis of the way modernity threatens traditional structures of Jewish identity. He is an idealist in his belief that a reformed Judaism can also reform modernity.

Revolution and Disillusion

The Revolution of 1848 marked a turning point in French fiction, after which idealism ceased to resonate as a literary or political strategy and realism became more cynical and more ironic. During the initial February uprising, in the Revolution's early phase, hopes for social change had seemed to find fulfillment in the spectacle of cross-class cooperation putting an end to the Orleanist monarchy. However, after the June Days, in which the forces of order brutally repressed the lower-class revolutionaries clamoring for the right to work, many bourgeois writers seemed to lose faith in the transparency of language and in their ability to speak in universal terms. Theorists from Roland Barthes to Ross Chambers have seen in this moment of disillusionment the birth of literary modernism, as such writers as Baudelaire and Flaubert either took refuge in aesthetic autonomy or turned to irony to register their distrust of all forms of political discourse.[55]

The Jewish community also found itself divided by the events of 1848. Despite the fact that two Jews served as ministers in the provisional government of the newly installed Second Republic—Adolphe Crémieux at Justice and Michel Godchaux at Finance—reports of violent attacks against the Jews in Alsace and of the burning of the Rothschild property at Surêne caused many to fear that the Republic had unleashed the people's dormant antisemitic passions. In the next chapter, I describe how Ben Baruch, the Orthodox writer who sought to speak for the Jewish lower classes, welcomed the universal suffrage that the Revolution brought not only to France itself but also to the election of the Jewish Consistory. He rightly predicted the election of more religious traditionalists, who represented the poor Orthodox majority.

Ben-Lévi, on the other hand, increasingly found in the Revolution of 1848 cause for alarm. Immediately after the revolutionary events, his nonfiction pieces register a profound sense of disquiet at the many dangers his fellow Jews faced.[56] Not only did Jews encounter real violence, but the Jewish Consistory also feared that a republic would bring a reduction in state funding to religious institutions. The July

Monarchy, for all its faults, had been good to the Jews. Ben-Lévi also saw danger from within the Jewish community, correctly surmising that giving the Orthodox masses a greater voice in Consistory affairs would place his own moderate, reformist vision in jeopardy.[57] And indeed, he would lose his bid to join the Consistory in 1850, when his rival Ben Baruch's constituents finally made their voices heard.

Ben-Lévi registered these fears for the future in his final story, "L'armoire d'ébène" [The Ebony Armoire], published in October 1848. Once again, he offers a Balzacian beginning to the tale, describing the cold silence of the Kelm abode, "one of those big and silent houses of the Marais,"[58] which resembles a Dutch still life in its spare and sober dignity. The narrator lingers over Moïse Kelm's office, over its oak desk, "blackened by time" (528), strewn with old folios, and lit by a large antique window of the type one finds only in old houses. Moïse himself might have stepped out of a Rembrandt painting of a Jewish patriarch or be one of Balzac's studies of an old miser. We learn that he ventures out only to go to the synagogue, reads the Talmud all day, and laments the ruin of Jerusalem before retiring for the night. His wife, Rébecca, spends her days reading the Bible or the canticles "translated into bad German [*mauvais allemand*], written with Hebrew characters" (528), which is to say Yiddish.

But if their attachment to traditional religious laws, languages, and texts marks the parents as old-fashioned, their son, Nathan, explicitly incarnates modernity. "Moïse Kelm lived in the past, his son dreamed only of the future. . . . The father was an old-time Israelite, the son had transformed himself into an up-to-date Frenchman; the father thought only of Jerusalem, the son lived in the middle of Paris" (529). A low-level employee in a commercial house, Nathan resents that his father won't use his fortune to help him get ahead and comes to despise everything to do with the traditional Judaism his father embodies. Ben-Lévi's narrator blames not Nathan but rather Moïse for this lack of filial and religious piety: "It is wrong for the old-fashioned Israelite to maintain at all costs that his children model themselves on him . . . without taking into account different periods, circumstances, and the enormous abyss dug by time between yesterday and today"

(529). It is the father's fault that the son lacks religious morals, for Moïse has failed to recognize that Judaism needs to change with the times or risk alienating its youth.

When the February Days break out, Nathan throws himself into revolutionary activity, driven by a desire to bring an end to the old world that has stifled his youthful drives. Just as naturally, he begins to gamble and loses at cards a sum he cannot repay. Remembering having seen his father carefully place something in the old ebony armoire, he resolves to steal the fortune he surmises must be hidden there. One night, he enters his father's office, but just as he is about to pry open the armoire, he sees his father's shadow emerge from the dark. To his shock, his father does not thwart his attempted theft but instead opens the armoire to reveal two suits of old clothes—a caftan belonging to a Polish Jewish peddler and a carmagnole, as the revolutionary costume in 1793 was called, complete with a red belt and a "liberty bonnet" (533).

Then Moïse narrates the story of his life. He recounts how he came from Poland, where the persecution of the Jews had made him an inveterate enemy of the aristocracy and the church. Hearing of the revolutionary events in France, he set out for Paris in 1792 and quickly became a participant in the Reign of Terror: "I wallowed in blood, I danced around the scaffold, I set fire to castles" (533). Soon, however, he grew tired of the revolutionary excesses and returned to Poland, where the sight of the paternal home and synagogue restored him to reason. Eventually he made his way back to France, where he retained his two sets of old clothes: the traditional caftan to remind him how far the Jews of France have come as a result of the Revolution and the "hideous red bonnet" as a sign of revolutionary excess, the dangers of too much liberty. "I pray to the God of Israel to pardon me, and I beg him, trembling, to spare France a return to the reign of these horrible images of blood and these emblems of desolation" (534), he tells his son. Chastened by his father's story and perhaps more by his father's clemency, Nathan joins the National Guard to fight against the Revolution. During the June Days, he dies on a barricade, defending "order, property, and family" (535). Moïse returns to his religious routine at the story's close, adding his son's green epaulets to the collection of pious relics in his ebony armoire. His wife, Rébecca, spends the rest of her days reading the Book of Job.

Although the prodigal son returns, this story lacks the hopeful conclusion of "Les poissons et les miettes de pain" and "L'ami du préfet." Those stories had celebrated the consolations of religion and had ended on notes of harmony. Even if modernity threatened the structures of Jewish identity, a reformed Judaism could win out in the end by affirming fundamental ethical principles and solidarity with other Jews. "L'armoire d'ébène" offers no such consolations. The son's death on the barricades, fighting for order, property, and family, hardly causes the heart to exult, even if it signifies a redemption from a life of dissipation and crime.

But is Ben-Lévi really exhorting his readers to join the National Guard and to die repressing workers? Does he really see the future in such negative terms? On closer inspection, it seems to me that the story does not actually sympathize with the son's decision. Rather, it seeks to explain it. What pushes Nathan to join the revolutionaries in the first place and to descend into gambling and theft is his father's excessive piety, which squelches the son's normal and necessary youthful spirit: "There was only life in the house when their son, Nathan, still an adolescent, filled it with noise. . . . But the rigid habits and puritanism of old Kelm eventually froze the joyous gaiety of Nathan and repressed to the bottom of his young heart those clamorous aspirations toward movement and agitation" (529). It is Moïse's reactionary approach to the religion, described not as pure but as "puritanical," that sets the story's tragedy in motion by stifling the youth's energy and driving him away from the paternal home. Indeed, the narrative voice interrupts the story explicitly to condemn such religious rigidity: "Woe! woe! to parents who cause the pure joys of their son's heart to burst forth under a stranger's roof" (530).

If Moïse deserves the blame for his son's actions, then Nathan's ultimate conversion to his father's rigid and joyless worldview cannot be a welcome one. It is this path that leads to his death and his parents' unending sorrow. The story thus does not sanction Moïse's political conservatism and religious Orthodoxy. It actually shows these to be perilously close to their opposite, to revolutionary terrorism and wasteful dissipation. The lesson that Nathan fails to learn from the ebony armoire lies precisely here, in recognizing the dangers of both sets of extremes. The old caftan and the carmagnole represent these two dangerous options for Jewish modernity—religious Orthodoxy and revolutionary fervor—which they show to be linked. Moïse keeps these symbols as a reminder of this message, but he does not seem to take their lesson to heart, for he is unable to achieve the kind of moderation in his own life that would make him a benevolent father and positive role model to his son.

Ben-Lévi's final story, as dark as the ebony armoire itself, is thus in many ways in concert with his lighter, happier tales. Like them, it preaches the virtue of religious reform as a compromise between extremes. Although reform is not named in this story, it is the option that would have saved the Kelms, by tempering the rigidities of Orthodoxy, by accepting the realities of modernity. In Ben-Lévi's view, reform does not repress youthful energy but rather harnesses it toward productive ends. Had Moïse found a third path between the caftan and the carmagnole, he might have saved his son, or so we surmise. This story locates reform as a religious option but also as a political one. Indeed, it shows how the religious and the political are inextricably linked in modern France. Associated with the *juste milieu* politics of Louis-Philippe, reform embodied the interests of the modernizing elite. The Revolution of 1848 would mark the end of the early struggle on its behalf as well as the end of the literary career of its most persuasive proponent, Ben-Lévi.

Ben-Lévi's stories emerge from the archive of the nineteenth century to provide a new perspective on the history of both French and Jewish culture—and on their intersection—in this period. Long seen as paragons of assimilation, French Jews in the period leading up to the Dreyfus affair are frequently depicted as having gladly surrendered their traditional or particular identity for an entrance ticket to France's universal culture. Whereas Foa's fiction might seem to confirm this view, Ben-Lévi's stories indicate that even as early as the 1840s, certain French Jews were able to temper their enthusiasm for emancipation, recognizing the perils of their new situation while welcoming its possibilities. Ben-Lévi's fiction reveals that other fates besides homogenization and assimilation were imagined for French Jews, just as it signals the existence of Jewish agency and creativity in the face of momentous social change.

Ben-Lévi's fiction also sheds light on some more specific conundrums in modern Jewish history. It has long surprised scholars that the first international Jewish aid society, the Alliance Israélite Universelle, was formed in 1860 by those Jews who had the least to gain from it—the French.[59] But the ideology of the Alliance sprang from the commitment of such French Jews as Ben-Lévi to establish new forms of Jewish identity in the modern world. In fact, Ben-Lévi would be one of the first to call for such international Jewish solidarity.[60] The Alliance is the natural outgrowth of the ideology of Jewish solidarity expressed in such stories as "L'ami du préfet" and "Mémoires d'un colporteur juif."[61] Like the Alliance, Ben-Lévi's fiction struggles to navigate between modernity and tradition, universality and particularity, nationalism and religion. It attempts to carve out a third path in which the Jew remains loyal to France while retaining a link to Judaism, articulated less through traditional religious observance than through fidelity to Jewish ethics and solidarity with fellow Jews.[62]

Ben-Lévi's fiction also sheds new light on the history of Jewish religious reform in France. Seen by scholars such as Meyer as derivative of the German movement, French reform emerges in the hands of Ben-Lévi as a homegrown phenomenon, attentive to the specific desires of the French Jews and their unique historical situation. In such stories as "L'armoire d'ébène," Ben-Lévi shows religious reform to be intimately bound up with the volatile French political situation in the 1840s and with the interests of a class of enlightened elite Jews who sought moderate solutions to both political and religious problems.

Ben-Lévi's stories reflect, finally, how modern French literary codes could be used to confront specifically Jewish dilemmas. They fuse the new literary forms of realism and idealism with the aim of transforming Judaism and of reconfiguring modernity itself. The result is unique in both the French and the Jewish literary traditions—but not inevitable. In the next chapter, I show how Ben-Lévi's Orthodox rival approached the same historical situation from a different perspective and how his fiction reflects a nearly opposite set of religious and political, as well as aesthetic, choices.

Three A Conservative Renegade:
Ben Baruch and Neo-Orthodoxy

In 1845, *L'Univers Israélite*, the Orthodox French Jewish newspaper formed in opposition to *Les Archives Israélites*, published a humorous letter addressed to the editor of its reformist rival. Presented by Ben Baruch, a frequent contributor to *L'Univers Israélite*, the letter purports to be from "General Tom Pouff, American citizen." After inquiring about their mutual friend Ben-Lévi, General Pouff refuses the *Archives'* offer to work as a correspondent but agrees to furnish details about his compatriots, "the Redskin Israelites who live among the Hurons," whose customs he knows well since he too is a Jew.[1] So begins a description of the manners and morals of the Jewish Indians, who offer a mirror reflecting contemporary French Jewish society in reverse. Through the lens of this Swiftian satire, Ben Baruch invites his readers to mock the pretensions, as well as the more dangerous errors, of his fellow French Jews, particularly the partisans of the Reform movement.

"The Redskin Israelites are quite uncivilized," General Pouff declares. "They rigorously observe the laws of Moses and traditions . . . the poor folks!" To make matters worse, along with still following Jewish law, the Indians do not even have consistories, "the unlucky ones!" (v. 2, 78). The American general, relying on information supplied by his "aide de camp Lilli-put," goes on to list all the barbaric ways of the Jewish Indians, which include offering extensive religious instruction to their children, encouraging patriotism and piety, and banishing all forms of corruption among their leaders. "And you, Mr. Editor," he concludes, still addressing the editor of *Les Archives Israélites*, "who for the past six years have been pursuing in vain the movement of Reform that manifests itself among the Israelites of France, what might you do among the Hurons!" If the reformers still see room for improvement in France, where the Israelites have made such strides in the direction of immorality and hypocrisy, think how much they could accomplish on the shores of the Mississippi!

The Reform movement, as we saw in the last chapter, developed in France during the July Monarchy as a response to the crisis of modernity. By modifying the religion, reformers sought to free Jews from religious laws and strictures perceived as incompatible with modern life. By making it easier and more pleasant to practice Judaism, they hoped to encourage religious affiliation and communal participation. But did their strategy work? Did reform succeed in resisting the forces of individualism, materialism, and secularism threatening France's Jewish community?

By the mid-1840s certain observers began to register their doubts. "What good is freedom for the synagogue if they never visit it. . . . What good is the right to practice ceremonies that they have forgotten or find ridiculous?" asked Simon Bloch, the secretary to the Central Consistory, in *L'Univers Israélite*, which he founded in 1844.[2] Both in serious editorials and in humor pieces, such as the letter from Tom Pouff, *L'Univers Israélite* taxed the reformers with exacerbating the ills they sought to remedy. By diluting the nature of Judaism, by eliminating the features that made it distinct, did not the reformers also compromise the religion's power to combat the dangers of modernity? Inspired by the German neo-Orthodoxy movement, begun in the 1830s by Samson Raphael Hirsch (1808–1888), the French "conservatives" (as they also called themselves) proposed a different strategy to combat religious indifference, one that sought to maintain the forms of traditional Jewish practice even while subtly modernizing their content.

Just as Ben-Lévi offered the Reform movement a fictional space in which to elaborate the possibilities for a religion purged of tradition and reduced to a primary ethical monotheism, so too did the neo-Orthodox movement find an outlet in fictional narrative. In this chapter I focus on the career of Ben Baruch (the pseudonym of Alexandre Créhange, 1791–1872), a literary persona who initially took shape in the pages of *L'Univers Israélite* as an Orthodox counterpart to Ben-Lévi but who subsequently engaged in a wide range of literary activities, including political propaganda, liturgical editing and trans- lating, and the publication, during the last twenty years of his life, of a Jewish almanac. All these endeavors contributed to a concerted—and seemingly quixotic—effort to foster the cause of Jewish Orthodoxy in modern France.

As I will show, Ben Baruch's traditionalism was no less modern than Ben-Lévi's reform. Indeed, Ben Baruch conceived of religious Orthodoxy as a radical force, as a form of resistance to what he saw as the social, economic, and cultural elitism of the reformers. Tightly bound up with the political conflicts of the period preceding and fol- lowing the Revolution of 1848, Ben Baruch's brand of neo-Orthodoxy offered the Jewish tradition as a solution not only to the particular problems facing France's Jewish community but also to the problems facing France as a whole, including economic segregation and social disintegration. In his fiction we not only meet a new kind of mod- ern Jew but also discover a new set of solutions to the dilemmas of modernity.

Rise of a Radical

Alexandre Créhange (Figure 4) was born on February 10, 1791, in Étain, a small town north of Metz in Lorraine (Meuse).[3] Jews first settled in the vicinity of Metz as early as the fifth century, with stable Jewish populations developing by the ninth century, closely linked to nearby Rhineland Jewish communities. Subject to periodic expulsions and persecutions, the Jewish population of Lorraine fluctuated. When the duchy came under French control in 1552, a limited number of Jews were allowed to resettle in the city of Metz itself, despite their official banishment from the Kingdom of France in order to supply the army garrison in the town, but they were restricted to a small Jewish quarter, or ghetto.[4] Metz eventually became one of the most impor- tant urban Jewish communities in Old Regime France.[5]

The Créhange family had deep roots in the region. The family name

Figure 4. Portrait of Ben Baruch (Alexandre Créhange). Courtesy of the Bibliothèque Nationale de France.

comes from a town in the Moselle, to the east of Metz, where Alexandre's great-great-grandfather, Moïse de Créhange, was born around 1635. Moïse moved to another nearby town, Vantoux, where he died in about 1708. Baruch Créhange, Alexandre's father, was born in Vantoux in 1753, but he moved to Étain to become a *ministre officiant* of the local synagogue—which is to say, a cantor or hazan—sometime between the birth of his first son, Mayer, in 1784 and that of Alexandre in 1791.[6] According to the Declaration of Names of 1808, mandated by Napoleon, Baruch had five boys and three girls and married twice, first to Fegelche, daughter of Moïse de Louvigny, and later to Madeleine, daughter of Moïse Alexandre Polac and Sara Worms. By 1801, the family had moved to Dijon, where Baruch continued to officiate in the synagogue.[7]

During the eighteenth century, the Jews in the semirural areas around Metz lived traditional Orthodox lives. Part of the larger world of Ashkenazic Jewry, they maintained close ties with Jewish communities across the Rhine, spoke Western Yiddish, and engaged in small-scale business activities with the local peasantry, especially peddling and horse trading. A few families in Metz, however, who had made fortunes selling supplies to the French army, opened themselves to French and German culture in the last decades of the eighteenth century, forming the nucleus of the tiny French Haskalah, or Jewish Enlightenment. During the 1780s, about a dozen Jews in Lorraine subscribed to the Hebrew periodical *Hameassef*, the main organ of the Berlin Haskalah, and made contact with Moses Mendelssohn and his circle.[8] The small but influential community of Metz Maskilim promoted secular as well as religious education for the region's Jews and advocated their integration into French society and culture.[9]

Born the very year the Jews of the region became French citizens, Créhange sits astride a great divide in French Jewish history. Although his mastery of the French language and familiarity with French literary sources suggest that he must have benefited from the Maskilic reforms, his command of both Hebrew and Yiddish and commitment to Orthodox values betray the mark of the traditional Jewish culture he absorbed growing up in semirural Lorraine in a deeply religious family. Few Jews at the time chose to send their children to French public schools, which were seen as suffused with Christianity. The first modern Jewish primary schools, at which students studied both secular and religious subjects, were established in the region between 1817 and 1821, so Créhange would have been too old to study at them. Whereas wealthier families engaged private tutors, most Jewish children in the immediate postrevolutionary period attended a traditional heder, or Jewish school, where they studied the Torah and the Talmud.[10] Créhange undoubtedly attended one of these schools. Where he picked up his sophisticated knowledge of both French and English literature is harder to determine.

Créhange's family was not rich, but they no doubt had a certain social standing in the community because of Baruch's role in the synagogue.[11] Alexandre did not follow in his footsteps by entering the religious profession, nor did he become a peddler like the poorest of the region's Jews. Rather, he moved at a young age to Leipzig to work for an established commercial house. According to the *Encyclopedia Judaica*, he went bankrupt in Dresden and subsequently returned to France. He became a traveling salesmen in Saint-Etienne and after 1829 a bookkeeper. During this period he served as chief of the Jewish community of nearby Lyon and president of its charitable committee. In the early 1830s, Alexandre moved to Paris and took a bookkeeping position with the firm of Victor and Gustave-Laurent Mayer. Around this time, he published a how-to guide for bookkeepers before falling out with his employers, who blocked his appointment as a commercial agent by charging him with fraud in his prior bankruptcy.[12] In a scathing self-justificatory pamphlet presented to the Société Industrielle et Commerciale in Paris, Alexandre accused the Mayer brothers of calumny and of perpetrating fraud themselves in their own bankruptcy proceedings.

This early pamphlet testifies to Créhange's penchant for public controversy and provides insights into his views on class divisions within the rapidly growing Jewish community of Paris. Accusing his erstwhile employers of having held back funds during their bankruptcy, Créhange contrasts their opulent lifestyle with his own modest circumstances in order to prove his own probity. "You are Jews, and I too am a Jew . . . but it is precisely that resemblance, that equality with you, that it is important to me to reject, both for the sake of my name and the name of the large majority of my coreligionists."[13] Interestingly, Créhange appropriates both for himself and for the Mayers the label *juif* (rather than the more distinguished term, *Israélite*) but immediately seeks to distance himself from its negative connotations. His former employers, on the other hand, are accused of demonstrating precisely the kinds of shady practices that had made *juif* a synonym for swindler in popular French parlance. Having failed to absorb "the happy influence of our glorious regeneration," the Mayers are declared unworthy of French citizenship. "It is not a question of changing an a to an e,[14] it is your heart that you must change, and that you cannot do; people like you will always be the opprobrium of all nations, the shame and scandal of all religions, of all communions." Créhange adopts the moralizing rhetoric typically used by assimilating bourgeois Jews of the period against their poorer and more traditional coreligionists, whom they blamed for arousing antisemitism through sharp business dealings and uncouth manners. But Créhange reverses the roles; in his pamphlet, the poor Jew (himself) has regenerated, while the rich (his bosses) prove incapable of such a transformation. "A Jew myself," he concludes, "I thank God that I have nothing in common with Jews like you."

I could not determine whether Créhange received satisfaction for his grievance with this pamphlet, but he surely raised his profile within the Parisian Jewish community. By 1839, he had become the spokes-man for the poor Orthodox Jews of Paris in a series of fights against the Central Consistory, the state-controlled governing body of French Judaism.[15] Each French city or town with more than 2,000 Jews had its own local consistory under the umbrella of the Central Consistory in Paris, whose members consisted mostly of laymen elected by a body of Jewish notables. This *collège de notables* was chosen by the govern-ment based on wealth and social influence until 1844, when a new *or-donnance* widened the electorate somewhat.[16] As a result, the *grande bourgeoisie* dominated both the local consistories and the Central Consistory throughout the July Monarchy. A Rothschild was always on the Central Consistory, and representatives of the other wealthi-est Parisian Jewish families (Ratisbonne, Rodrigues, Fould, Cerfberr, Halphen, Worms de Romilly) were also frequently present. By tightly controlling religious practice in France, these elite leaders—who were often not observant Jews—resisted the polarizing elements that had splintered Germany's Jewish community and largely steered French Judaism on a course of moderate reform.

For Créhange, this system guaranteed that those whose lives were most intimately linked to the Jewish community—the poor who re-lied on religious charities and the Orthodox who prayed in the syna-gogues—were effectively denied a voice in its operation. His first major opportunity to do battle against the Consistory Goliath came in the 1830s when the Central Consistory outlawed prayer meetings held by the small, largely Orthodox mutual aid societies. The Consistory had taken this measure not only to maintain religious unity but also to safeguard its monopoly on the sale of seats at the Paris consistorial synagogue, its major source of revenue following the 1831 decree forbidding a special consistorial tax on Jews.[17] As secretary of the mutual aid societies, Créhange bitterly attacked the consistorial leaders for their elitism, greed, and hypocrisy in a series of speeches and pamphlets. He also made his views known in a short-lived journal he founded called *La Sentinelle Juive*[18] and later in *L'Univers Israélite*, to which he contributed both fiction and opinion pieces between 1844 and 1847. Créhange railed against what he saw as the Consistory's misguided attempt to water down the religion.[19] The Consistory eventually decided to allow the prayer meetings (provided that the mutual aid societies contribute funds to the Consistory) and to build another consistorial synagogue to accommodate the capital's burgeoning Jewish population.

According to Phyllis Cohen Albert, Créhange held much more radical views than his constituency,[20] but he nevertheless continued to serve as the principal Orthodox mouthpiece in further disputes with the Consistory over such issues as cemetery plots, the creation of a Jewish trade school, and a tax on kosher meat.[21] In 1844, he complained that the efforts to democratize the *collège des notables*, which elected the Consistory, did not go far enough. In an incendiary speech and later pamphlet in favor of expanding the vote, he pointed to the hypocrisy of a Consistory that determined religious policies they did not practice.

> A Consistory that polices the temples and does not visit the temples; that gives out diplomas [to rabbis] and that wants to dictate the law to rabbis; that names the mohel[22] and does not circumcise its children; that names the sohet[23] and that doesn't eat kosher meat; that regulates the ceremonies of our religious practice and doesn't practice the religion . . . such a Consistory would make us the laughingstock of the civilized world.[24]

According to Créhange, the Consistory represented the interests of the Jewish elite, whose main goal was to purge Judaism of anything that might offend their bourgeois sensibilities or risk embarrassing them in front of their gentile neighbors. He maintained that their prejudice in favor of reform, or in some cases their total irreligiosity, did not reflect the views of the vast majority of their constituents.

Unsurprisingly, Créhange welcomed the February Revolution of 1848 that replaced the July Monarchy regime—supported by the business elite—with a democratic republic. Although the Revolution of 1848 would later give many in the Jewish community reason to pause,[25] in its early stages it seemed to promise a vindication for the rights of the poor workers whom Créhange championed. Shortly after the February Revolution, Créhange published "La Marseillaise du travail" [Marseillaise of Labor], in which he provided new words to Rouget de Lisle's military anthem to celebrate the peaceful cause of the proletariat: "Our Republic of 1848 knows no enemies, it sees around it only the flags of liberty," he declared in the preface to the song (which itself is lost).[26] On February 25, 1848, Créhange published the pamphlet *Des droits et des devoirs du citoyen* [Of the Rights and Duties of the Citizen], in which he used the form of a dialogue between a Jewish schoolmaster and his students to show how the Hebrew Bible prescribes a republic as the optimal form of government.[27]

But although deeply attuned to universal rights, Créhange also saw in the Revolution an opportunity to advance the particular cause of Jewish Orthodoxy—as well as his ongoing battle against the Consistory. Reasoning that the declaration of universal male suffrage in France should also mean an end to the elitist manner of electing the Consistory, he called for the dissolution of the Central Consistory and for new elections by all the (male) Jews of France. A democratic election could not fail to return Orthodox members, given the overwhelmingly poor and traditional character of the vast majority of France's Jews. In the immediate aftermath of 1848, Créhange organized the Club Démocratique des Fidèles to advance his ideas, and he founded another short-lived newspaper, *La Vérité*, to serve as its organ, having meanwhile broken with the editors of *L'Univers Israélite*.[28] "Henceforth, every Israelite is a notable and every notable is an elector. . . . Today, our ancient and holy law, which has never been abrogated and never will be, is brought back to life. That law proclaims:

You will be a nation of priests, all equal, you will all be saints."[29] Unable to refuse or refute Créhange's claims, the Consistory managed to postpone elections for a time. They were finally held by universal male suffrage in 1850, and although more Orthodox candidates were indeed elected, little change occurred in the operation of the Consistory.[30] By the 1860s, the reformers managed to reimpose some restrictions over the electorate.[31]

Like so many disillusioned participants in the Revolution of 1848, Créhange withdrew from political agitation after Napoleon III formally put an end to the Second Republic in 1852. In addition to translating and editing a number of liturgical volumes during the Second Empire, he poured his energy into the publication of a Jewish almanac, which appeared from 1850 until 1872. This popular guide to Jewish life in France, which I examine in detail later in this chapter, contained moralizing fiction and practical information, such as the number of Jews in all major French cities, the dates of holidays, the addresses of kosher butcher shops, and the list of the officers of Jewish organizations in Paris and the provinces. I argue that it represents the culmination of Créhange's lifelong project to foster a sense of French Jewish communal identity and to solidify Jewish solidarity across class boundaries.[32]

Ironically, the success of this venture helped reconcile Créhange with the very men and institutions he had once opposed so vociferously. Scanning the informational pages at the start of each *Annuaire*, one notices not only the rising number of Jews in France (especially Paris) and the soaring price of the *Annuaire* itself (it doubles from 50 centimes to 1 franc by 1856–1857) but also Créhange's corresponding social elevation. In 1862, he lists himself as the secretary of the consistorial temple administration and as the secretary to the Paris Comité du Bienfaisance. By the following year, he appears as a member of the Paris Consistory! In addition to leading a half-dozen Jewish charitable and communal organizations, Créhange was the oldest of the founders of the Alliance Israélite Universelle, the international Jewish aid organization, and served as its vice-president in 1863–1864.[33] Slightly before this apotheosis, Créhange seems to have reconciled with many of his former ideological enemies, and he went so far as to publish articles by Olry Terquem, France's leading advocate of reform, in the *Annuaire*.[34] When Créhange's wife, Elisa, died in March 1866, the grand rabbi of France, as well as Albert Cohn, a close associate of the Rothschilds, spoke at her funeral. Before his own death in 1872, Créhange had arrived financially as well as politically, thanks to this profitable publishing venture. The final almanacs record his move from the more proletarian rue des Petites-Écuries to the fashionable Place Royale.

The Birth of Ben Baruch

Créhange invented the authorial persona of Ben Baruch for the articles—both fictional pieces and social commentaries—that he published during the mid-1840s in *L'Univers Israélite*.[35] In the first issue of *L'Univers Israélite*, the editor, Simon Bloch, announced his goal to make "the mass" of his coreligionists understand that French citizenship does not require breaking with or modifying Jewish tradition, that "civil laws can be reconciled with our religious laws." The newspaper furthered its attempt to "naturalize, so to speak, the religion with social life, and to admit social life into the religion," with articles devoted to promoting the causes of both French patriotism and Jewish Orthodoxy. Its pages reported negatively on the efforts by reformers in Germany and France to modify traditional practices. Despite the reference to a "mass" readership, however, it is unlikely that *L'Univers Israélite* reached a larger, or less elite, readership than *Les Archives Israélites* because of its expensive subscription price and elevated tone.[36]

Just as *Les Archives Israélites*, from its founding in 1840, offered fiction as a means of propagating its program of reform by rendering its ideological battles in concrete human terms, so too did *L'Univers Israélite* attempt from its first issue to embody the principles of neo-Orthodoxy in fictional narrative. And just as Ben-Lévi quickly asserted himself as the leading writer of fiction in *Les Archives Israélites*, so too did his Orthodox counterpart Ben Baruch dominate the early years of *L'Univers Israélite*, publishing nearly ten fictional pieces between 1844 and 1847, along with many nonfiction articles on French Jewish life.[37] Many features link the two writers besides their similar noms de plume. Although they occasionally strike notes of pathos, both are essentially humorists who use the tools of irony and satire to drive home their ideological points. And although their aesthetic and political as well as religious allegiances differ, both attempt to adapt French literary models to address specifically Jewish concerns.

Ben-Lévi reacted negatively to what he perceived as the insulting mimicry of his Orthodox doppelgänger and initiated a battle of the Bens that testified to the increasing autonomy of the newly formed French Jewish public sphere. In a series of witty articles in *Les Archives Israélites* in late 1844 and early 1845, signed "G.," Ben-Lévi attacked Ben Baruch for his attempt to usurp his pseudonym and *L'Univers Israélite* for attempting to steal the readership of *Les Archives Israélites*. Ben Baruch responded huffily—and no doubt disingenuously—by denying any attempt to model his authorial persona on the Reform writer: "Ben Baruch is not a pseudonym," he maintained; "Alexandre ben Baruch is the name under which I am known at the consistorial temple of Paris."[38] Revealing that he knew the true identity and genealogy of his pseudonymous opponent (Ben-Lévi was Godchaux Weil, son of Baruch Weil), Ben Baruch declared, "To dispel any suspicion of wanting to adorn myself with the illustrious name of one of the greatest writers of the *Archives*, who is also a ben Baruch, but who signs ben Lévy [*sic*], I put at the bottom of my fable LE PREDICATEUR ET LE SOUFFLET, ben Baruch, author of the letters in *La Sentinelle Juive*."[39] He signed this article with his real last name, "A. Ben Baruch Créhange." After Godchaux Weil responded by presenting his *carte de visite* to Alexandre Créhange at his home, formally declaring his identity as the man behind the pseudonym Ben-Lévi, Ben Baruch professed little desire to "penetrate the mystery of the trinity Weil-G-Ben Lévi," thus associating the reformer with Catholicism, and expressed outrage that the author of *Les matinées du samedi* would have chosen the Jewish Sabbath to deliver his card.[40] The two would continue to spar in the pages of their respective newspapers for several years.[41]

Like all of Ben Baruch's writings, his first story, "Le prédicateur et le soufflet" [The Preacher and the Bellows], from 1844, has a polemical thrust. It attacks the cause of Reform and advances Orthodoxy as a solution to what Ben Baruch saw as the central problem facing the community, namely, the disintegration of social solidarity among Jews. But unlike his contemporaries Ben-Lévi or Eugénie Foa, Ben Baruch does not use contemporary literary codes to make his case. Whereas Foa had turned to the popular sentimental and historical genres to dramatize the conflicts of Jews caught between tradition and modernity and between the universal and the particular, Ben Baruch largely eschewed the aesthetics of melodrama and the intrigues of romance in his stories for *L'Univers Israélite*. And whereas Ben-Lévi had adopted Balzac's penchant for minute visual description in his narratives of an assimilating and increasingly materialistic bourgeoisie, Ben Baruch opted instead for a broader form of satire. As one might expect from an Orthodox writer, he turned in part to the tradition of Talmudic parable for inspiration, but his main influences can be traced to the eighteenth-century French Enlightenment, never known for its religious piety.

Ben Baruch embraces the contradictions in his endeavor right from the start. Subtitled "Tale Imitated from the Polish," in a gesture to the epicenter of Jewish Orthodoxy, "Le prédicateur et le soufflet" begins with an epigraph by Jean-Baptiste Massillon (1663–1742), the French Catholic bishop and member of the Académie Française. This juxtaposition of the Jewish and the Catholic may at first seem a provocation, but on closer inspection Massillon's brand of Christian orthodoxy proves to have much in common with that of the Orthodox Jew attempting to make his case against reform. "When illustrious talents are given to impious men, it is always to the detriment of their nation and their age," writes Massillon in the epigraph cited by Ben Baruch, who like his Catholic model sees knowledge without religion leading only to "schism and error." Unlike his Catholic model, however, the Jewish writer couples his moralizing purpose with a sarcastic wit.

"Le prédicateur et le soufflet" takes place in a "neighboring country," in which a "great city has just given birth to a petty reform, a new religion."[42] This lightly veiled reference to Germany serves to displace the object of Ben Baruch's satire onto the neighboring land known for the hostile schism between Jewish reformers and partisans of Orthodoxy. Whereas the writers for the Reform-minded *Archives Israélites* constantly looked to the German reformers as a beacon of all that was advanced and enlightened in Judaism, in this story Ben Ba-ruch portrays them as precisely the example not to follow. In Germany, the narrator tells us, the partisans of Reform have formed a group "to reorganize the religion of our fathers and harmonize it, as they say, with civilization, with *their* civilization" (198, emphasis in original). Ben Baruch's irony is biting; he mocks the pretentious rhetoric of the reformers, along with their slavish worship of gentile culture. He also undermines their false belief in the universality of this gentile cul-tural model by emphasizing its particular nature ("*their* civilization"). Speaking to an implied Orthodox reader for whom Judaism ("the reli-gion of our fathers") embodies the true universal values of civilization, Ben Baruch argues that any attempt to alter this tradition to fit the particular cultural prejudices of a particular moment and a particular national group cannot fail but corrupt this ideal.

Because all new religions need preachers to spread the word, the reformers hire a certain M. Freyredner, "whose reputation has crossed mountains and seas" (198), to offer them a sermon. But this Freyred-ner ("free speaker" in German) does not deliver the kind of speech they expect. Beginning by citing Ecclesiastes to mock the reformers' claim to novelty ("There is nothing new under the sun"), he proceeds to tell them a "simple" story of two men in the town of N., Godfried and Jedidjah. The rest of the story unfolds as a sermon, with frequent interruptions by the preacher to comment on his narrative. "Godfried was very rich and very ignorant," he begins, "and his stupidity was proverbial in the land; he was, as a result, a notable, a member of the community council, and one of the leaders of the synagogue" (199). We recognize here Créhange's preoccupation with social injustice in the French Jewish community and in particular with the privileging of wealth over piety and intelligence in the selection of Consistory leaders.[43]

Jedidjah, on the other hand, emerges as a portrait of unappreci-ated merit, which is to say as a portrait of Créhange himself. Poor and intelligent (the two always go together in Ben Baruch's fictional universe), Jedidjah possesses both practical knowledge, "good sense," and spiritual wisdom in accordance with the Jewish faith. The two are not mutually exclusive but rather develop in tandem through the study of Jewish religious texts. He also possesses his creator's penchant for public controversy: "He did not curse others in secret like a coward," the narrator informs us, "but when he wanted to stigmatize idiocy or wickedness, he did it in such a way that he would be understood" (199). A thorn in the side of the synagogue leaders, like Créhange, Jedidjah "allowed himself to call attention to abuses, to indicate practical improvements, to unmask hypocrites" (200). As a result of this honesty, he plays no role whatsoever in the running of his community's religious affairs.

The only person to recognize Jedidjah's superior qualities, aside from the narrator, is the ignorant Godfried, who marvels at his ability to read Hebrew without vowels. The rich man thus invites the poor man to accompany him to the trade fair at Leipzig as his valet. Despite the humiliation of this position, Jedidjah jumps at the chance to expand his knowledge through travel and also welcomes the opportunity to protect his rich friend from the dangers into which his stupidity might lead him. "For M. Godfried is poor, very poor," Jedidjah insists. "He lacks wit and good sense; I must assist him" (201). After Godfried makes all sorts of vain preparations for his own comfort, while Jedidjah commends their souls to God, the two set off on their journey.

Freyredner, the preacher, then interrupts his sermon to reflect on the religious precepts that his story has thus far sought to inculcate through Jedidjah's virtuous example, including "frankness, loyalty, courage, and sincerity," as well as patience, charity, benevolence, and piety. But these are old precepts "and *your* civilization doesn't know what to do with such frippery" (202, emphasis in original), he explains to his Reform-minded congregation, reiterating the particular and hence false nature of their claims to the universal. "Let us hope that thanks to your reforms and to the education that will be its necessary complement, we will no longer have to hear about Moses and the prophets" (202–203). Once again, Ben Baruch has recourse to irony to make his case. Despite his scorn of Jews who slavishly worship gentile culture, Ben Baruch himself is influenced not only by the conservative Catholic writing of Massillon but also by the opposing eighteenth-century French tradition, that of Voltaire. Although Voltaire attacked both Christianity and Judaism, his satiric social critique in *Candide* offers Ben Baruch a model for his own ironic commentary on the faults and foibles of contemporary Jewish society. Ben Baruch's plot, meanwhile, comes straight out of the repertoire of yet another Enlightenment writer, Pierre-Augustin Caron de Beaumarchais, whose play *Le mariage de Figaro* (written 1778, performed 1784) had scandalized censors in the waning days of the Old Regime with its revolutionary depiction of an intelligent valet who bests his master.

Godfried wastes his time in Leipzig at gaming houses and theaters, pursuing fleeting pleasures, while Jedidjah frequents libraries, anatomy collections, and houses of worship, acquiring both secular and religious culture. Godfried returns to their hotel each night a little more exhausted, while Jedidjah returns a little wiser. Finally, it comes time to make a series of purchases before they return home. Jedidjah buys good books and scientific instruments, making sure that his money will benefit honest artisans. Godfried, in turn, wastes his funds on foolish baubles and gets swindled in the process. In one store, his eye falls on a beautiful pair of bellows, which Jedidjah tells him are used to light fires. He buys the bellows and returns to the hotel. But try as he might, the rich man cannot kindle the wood in the fireplace. "You told me that with a bellows I could light a fire," he complains to his valet. "For the last half hour I have been blowing, and look, traitor, how little fire there is. You fooled me; it's a dirty trick; one doesn't treat a notable like this" (208). Jedidjah responds that a bellows can indeed revive a flame, "but first there must be a little fire, there must be at least a spark. If that spark is lacking, the bellows becomes perfectly useless" (208). So ends the narrated portion of the story.

Shifting registers from an Enlightenment to a biblical mode of discourse, from satire to allegory, the preacher then explains the not-so-hidden meaning behind his tale and, in particular, its final tableau of an idiot trying to light a fire without a spark. The fireplace represents their temple, he tells the congregants. The wood symbolizes his Reform listeners, "worm-eaten logs, deprived of true light" (*bûches* vermoulues, dépouvues de la vraie lumière) (208, emphasis in original). The idiot is himself, their preacher, attempting in vain to kindle a fire from dry logs—or from stupid listeners, because *bûche* in colloquial

French signifies idiot. "At your invitation, I came here to bellow the sacred fire of religion; but I can blow and blow and the divine flame will not ignite: THE SPARK IS LACKING" (208, emphasis in original). The Reform preacher thus finally comes fully clean as a conservative, attacking his hosts by revealing to them the sterility of their reformist views. Despite their supposed enlightenment, the reformers cannot generate genuine light without the spark of faith, which comes only from belief in God.[44]

This metaphysical ending may surprise readers who had assumed the point of the story lay in social commentary, in criticizing manners and morals in the material world. Indeed, references to faith in God were rare in both the Reform and the Orthodox Jewish newspapers of the nineteenth century; the contributors to the papers debated questions of practice but largely ignored questions of belief. The problem of which laws to follow occupied nineteenth-century French Jews endlessly, but the reasons they would follow these laws, especially references to divine sanction, tended to remain unspoken. Arnold Eisen has argued that the privileging of practice over belief typifies the nineteenth-century recasting of Orthodox Judaism and suggests that modern Jews continued to obey laws for a variety of reasons, including faithfulness to tradition, rather than simply—or only—because they believed God had commanded them to do so.[45] In this story, however, Ben Baruch seems to insist that faith must underlie all moral action, that belief must precede practice.

And yet, the nature of faith in this story remains vague. Ben Baruch speaks of a spark that must exist in order for a "divine flame" to kindle and implies that those who lack such a spark will not understand the injunction to lead a moral life imparted by the preacher's sermon, but he does not insist on divine sanction for individual commandments. He leaves the exact relation of belief to practice a matter of individual conscience. Moreover, he does not specify what faith entails. The metaphor of the spark has the benefit of encompassing a wide spectrum of beliefs, a spectrum that includes not only a personal deity but also the possibility of a God who has receded from Creation or even an eighteenth-century Deist abstraction. Belief may not be optional for Ben Baruch, but it is flexible. And his focus remains on the practice of morality in the material world, on the values of social equality and solidarity—what the French revolutionary tradition called *fraternité*—that derive naturally from such belief.

If for his debut as a fiction writer, Ben Baruch combined the religious conservatism of Massillon, the satiric irony of Voltaire, and the revolutionary social agenda of Beaumarchais, his next work would look to yet another eighteenth-century French author for a model. "Lettres d'un Israélite de Mogador à son ami à Fez" [Letters from an Israelite of Mogador to His Friend in Fez] is a series of stories that borrows the epistolary format of Montesquieu's *Les lettres persanes* [The Persian Letters] (1721) along with its device of using a fictional foreign visitor to critique French society.[46] In Montesquieu's version, one of the key texts of the French Enlightenment, a Persian prince named Usbek traveling in France writes home a series of letters that evaluate eighteenth-century French social and cultural institutions, calling into question values and hierarchies that the French take for granted. This format proved highly useful to Enlightenment writers: Françoise de Graffigny, in her *Lettres d'une peruvienne* [Letters from a Peruvian Woman] (1747), rewrote Montesquieu's text to view French society through the eyes of a foreign woman in order to cast a critical glance on French gender hierarchies. In Ben Baruch's version, a Moroccan Jew named Rabbi Iéhauschua Hadass, who has come to Paris following the massacre of his family by Kabyle tribesmen, writes a series of letters home to his friend Rabbi Elieser Peri Etz Hâdar, describing the customs of French Jews.

The first letter begins on a somber note, as Rabbi Iéhauschua describes the brutal deaths of his family at the hands of "the barbarians."[47] "We were too happy, my friend, too rich," he tells Hâdar. "Pride had swollen our heart, the Eternal wanted to humiliate us" (268). Here we find Ben Baruch's class antagonism given deadly form as he reminds his elite readers of the perils of prosperity and also of the Jewish religious obligation to thank God for the justice of his punishments. Iéhauschua then relates how he himself survived only because of the timely intervention of the "warriors of France," who defeated the Kabyles and saved the remaining Jews of Mogador. France thus appears at first in the story in a highly idealized light. "No longer having a family or a country, I decided to travel to France," Iéhauschua explains. "I wanted to see the country that gives birth to heroes, the jewel that the Eternal has enshrined in the terrestrial globe. That other promised land of Israel" (268). Over the course of the letters that follow, the rabbi's admiration for France will tarnish as he comes to make the acquaintance of the "Beni-Israel who live under the gold and silk sceptre of the grand sultan Levi-Philippe" (268). And with this Judaizing of Louis-Philippe's name, the story shifts in tone from tragic to comic.

Upon arriving in Paris, Iéhauschua meets a man who vaunts a hotel as offering "good bed, good board, and not expensive" (bon logis, bonne table et pas cher) (269). But the Moroccan Jew, despite his years of studying French, misunderstands the recommendation as "bon logis, bonne table et *Kascher* [kosher]."[48] So the poor foreigner makes his way to the French hotel thinking he has come upon a Jewish inn. Just to make certain, he asks his guide whether his master is in fact a Jew. The guide, however, does not realize that the Moroccan is himself a Jew, so misunderstands the nature of his question: "Don't worry, Mister Arab, we won't fleece you" (Soyez tranquille, monsieur l'Arabe, on ne vous écorchera pas), the man responds to an increasingly puzzled Iéhauschua, who fails to understand the symbolic meaning of the verb "to fleece" (*écorcher*), just as the hotel servant fails to comprehend the literal meaning of "Jew." Terrified his skin will be torn from his body, the Jew then attempts to rephrase his question, asking whether the master of the house has been circumcised. He is about to be thrown out by a scandalized hotel keeper when one of the customers steps forward and explains to the hotelier that "this man is neither crazy nor insolent. He's an Israelite. It seems that his intention had been to stay in an Israelite inn" (271). He then tells Iéhauschua that in France, to ask whether someone is a Jew is equivalent to asking whether he will try to cheat you ("vous écorcher"). "Ask him if he's an Israelite, it's distinguished," the man recommends, after inviting the rabbi to his own home, which is in fact kosher.

Surprised that the word "Jew" is an insult in enlightened France as it is in his own country, Iéhauschua then asks his host, who introduces himself as Jonathan, how he can drink wine in a nonkosher inn. Doesn't he fear the reproach of his rabbi? Jonathan then explains that in France, the rabbi's authority does not extend "to the private conduct of the citizen" (273). A Jew can avoid the synagogue, eat non-kosher food, marry a Christian, and not have his children circumcised, without the rabbi interfering. But surely the Consistory acts to censure such transgressions of the law, the horrified Iéhauschua responds. Jonathan then informs him that the Consistory members, chosen for their wealth and social position rather than their piety, themselves transgress all the Jewish laws. Iéhauschua's remaining illusions of France as a Jewish promised land crumble: "Alas! I believed you to be just and happy because you are free; but, without justice and religion, is there real happiness on this earth?" (274). To the Moroccan's astonishment, Jewish practice finds greater obstacles in enlightened France than in his oppressive homeland. The first letter ends with Jonathan assuring him that "justice will eventually triumph and religion will never die" (275). The terrain in France is good, Jonathan concludes in terms that recall Voltaire's garden metaphor in *Candide*; we just need to learn to "cultivate" it.

In the second letter, Iéhauschua relates his increasing dismay as he learns more about the state of French Jewry. Although the generous Jonathan, his pious wife, Abigail, and their "active and intelligent" children represent a model of enlightened Orthodoxy, the larger Parisian Jewish community strikes the visiting Moroccan as hypocritical and corrupt. After explaining how he has provided his children with a secular education, in order to prepare them for French citizenship, and with "solid religious instruction" (313) to prepare them for leadership within the Jewish community, thus gesturing both toward the universal and the particular, Jonathan relates how a pervasive ignorance about Judaism reigns among his fellow French Jews. This lack of knowledge leaves the general populace without mooring, unable to judge right from wrong or to resist the force of the "imprudent progressives who push and the ignorant retrogrades who hold back" (313). Through his idealized mouthpiece Jonathan, Ben Baruch positions himself as a moderate, open to modest reforms, provided that they are accompanied by genuine religious knowledge and practice. Jonathan's children will "make things better without destroying; they will maintain while ennobling" (313). This approach to change coincides with the program of *L'Univers Israélite*, which despite its "conservative" stance and general hostility to the Reform movement, sought to do away with certain unappealing traditional practices, such as the selling of synagogue honors.[49]

Jonathan then goes on to recount his conflicts with the leaders of the Parisian Jewish community, which resemble down to the smallest detail those of the author. He describes his disappointment at the construction of a "lilliputian hospital" (314) for the Jewish poor, which contains a mere fourteen beds, despite the enormous fortunes of the community leaders. Even worse, the Consistory caved in to the city's demands to reclaim the graves of the poor.[50] Iéhauschua finds this shocking: "In my country, when persecution breaks out, it is the rich who bear the brunt, and if it is only a question of money, like with your cemeteries, our representatives protect the poor and if need be pay for them" (316). Jonathan responds that before Emancipation, when French Jews depended on each other for survival, they too used to practice fraternal solidarity: "But ever since we became equal before the law, we no longer care about being so before God" (316). For Ben Baruch, the political and material "progress" of the nineteenth century goes hand in hand with a breakdown of communal structures and an erosion of traditional Jewish ethics. Liberty and equality have led to the demise of fraternity for the Jews of France.

The next day Jonathan brings Iéhauschua to the synagogue, which furnishes the Moroccan Jew with further cause for despair. Although the consistorial temple does not contain enough seats to accommodate all the pious faithful who wish to attend services, the seats reserved for the members of the Consistory remain empty. The Moroccan cannot believe the lack of attention paid to prayer and the din of gossip about worldly matters that drowns out the voice of the cantor; it reminds Iéhauschua of the "Tangiers bazaar" on market day. "I heard flying about around me: The funds were off by 50 centimes.—Did you see Bouffé yesterday?—It's clear that Guizot is done for" (322). When Iéhauschua complains to his host that he expected "more religion, more genuine devotion in the temple of the capital of the civilized world" (323–324), Jonathan explains that the French Jews need rabbis willing to deliver harsh sermons instructing them in proper comportment and moral virtue according to Jewish religious law.

As in "Le prédicateur et le soufflet," Ben Baruch offers his story in place of such a sermon. Fictional narrative serves as a pretext for social criticism, for observing the institutions and manners of French Jews in the 1840s with a scornful eye. But fiction does not only serve to criticize existing practices; it also allows Ben Baruch to imagine better ones. In the "Fourth Letter from an Israelite of Mogador to His Friend in Fez," dated "12th of Tisseri 5605," according to the Hebrew calendar, Ben Baruch invents a model Jewish community in the Parisian suburb of Pantin, where Jonathan brings Iéhauschua to witness a circumcision.[51] The father of the child, "an upright grocer, very honest in his business, very religious" (64), entertains his guests lavishly, for he believes that the prophet Elijah accompanies the mohel on his mission and should be treated with respect. Jonathan comments that "modern philosophers" dismiss such "puerile ideas" as mere superstitions, which they hope to cure by invading Jewish homes with "the torch of reason" (64). But thanks to this movement of Enlightenment, "These men succeed in disenchanting the life of simple and good men, who used to find happiness in doing and believing what their fathers did and believed" (64). Anticipating Max Weber's theory of modernity as "the disenchantment of the world," Ben Baruch paints a picture of enlightened modern Jews who "no longer believe in anything, hope for nothing, and only see their misfortune" (64). Although such incredulity may suit rich men "in court dress or in frock coats," those who wear a simple worker's smock often require the consolations that superstition can provide. "What is left to the latter? Despair, dishonor, and suicide!" (65). Ben Baruch forecasts in terms that call to mind another later theorist of modernity (and son of a rabbi), Émile Durkheim.[52]

Every aspect of Jewish life in the fictional Pantin contrasts favorably with that of Paris. After visiting a model Jewish school, Jonathan and Iéhauschua tour the generously endowed hospice with its forty-eight beds. In the evening, they visit the synagogue, built in a "simple and elegant" style, in which the rabbi conducts the service with great dignity. To Iéhauschua's shock, the leaders of the Pantin Consistory—all of whom attend the service—occupy the least desirable seats on the west side of the synagogue. The selling of religious honors having been long abolished, everyone participates in the service and takes turns reading from the sacred books. Iéhauschua listens with interest to the sermon delivered to a packed house, in which even Catholic students and priests have come to hear the celebrated rabbi's disquisition, which combines references to the Talmud and to classical French authors, such as Bossuet and Massillon, delivered in a pure French. After the service, they discuss the upcoming Consistory elections. In Pantin, "We don't know the words 'conservative' and 'progressive.' There are only Israelites loyal to the religion of their ancestors, who love and respect one another" (71). They resolve to elect only the most educated among them and those who have rendered the most honorable service to the community. Class still counts in Pantin, but the poor have their own representative on the Consistory. All who contribute to maintain Jewish institutions can vote in the Consistory elections.

In his utopian vision of Pantin, Ben Baruch imagines a world in which Orthodox Jewish values unite rich and poor. The narrative confirms this message of social solidarity by ending, in the final letter, with the marriage of Iéhauschua to Jonathan's daughter Deborah. In the meantime, the Moroccan has recovered the fortune his mother had hidden in Mogador shortly before the Kabyles murdered her. Iéhauschua writes to his friend in Fez that he rejoices in becoming rich once again not in order to enjoy vain pleasure but rather to be able to express his thanks to Jonathan and his admiration for his distinguished daughter. "Ah, if you only knew . . . what virtues this house contains. If you only knew what good works are accomplished by this family, who are not very rich themselves! So this family will be my own" (181), and the Moroccan appends to this sentiment of solidarity a biblical quotation from the book of Ruth.

The vision of unity offered by Ben Baruch crosses class and culture: It allies the rich Moroccan man with the poorer French woman, the Sephardic and the Ashkenazic branches of Judaism. Significantly, however, it remains relatively neutral on the issue of Jewish-Christian relations. Unlike the fiction of Ben-Lévi, it leaves the gentile world largely out of the picture, or at the margin of the stories. Although Jonathan drinks wine at a French inn and pledges to educate his children to serve their country, Iéhauschua prefers instead to affirm his difference from the non-Jewish segment of the French population by insisting on remaining exclusively among Jews. Jewish solidarity is achieved in Ben Baruch's fictional world through a concerted effort to follow both the letter and the spirit of Jewish law, which inspires the characters in Ben Baruch's tales to put aside selfish concerns in order to serve the common good. Of course, the paradox here lies in the fact that the stories preach Jewish unity in an extremely partisan manner, constantly criticizing the reformers and other wealthy Jewish leaders for their lack of piety.

Ben Baruch's fiction demonstrates his familiarity with the eighteenth-century tradition of social satire. Although his critique of French reformers is easily legible, the comic effect of the stories depends on his readers appreciating the references to Enlightenment literary models of Swift and Montesquieu. For a populist who devoted himself to defending the cause of the traditionalist Orthodox proletariat against the elitist, assimilating, bourgeois leadership of the French Jewish community, this strategy had its contradictions. But Ben Baruch was nothing if not versatile. In another story, "Le transfuge" [The Deserter], published in 1845, he turns to a more typically Orthodox source, the Talmudic tradition of parable.[53]

"When the Eternal created iron," this story begins, "the trees shook with fear and horror."[54] God calms the trees by telling them that so long as they band together and banish all discord among them, no harm can come from the iron. This strategy works well for a long time, to the great frustration of iron, until one day a violent quarrel erupts among the trees and "a corrupt branch detaches itself from an ancient oak and grovels ignominiously at the feet of iron" (312). The trees beg this apostate not to abandon his brothers, but their prayers fall on deaf ears: "The corrupt branch united with iron, made an alliance with him, and from that monstrous union, that mixed marriage, was born the axe, which brought terror and devastation to the forest, to the arbors, and even to the gardens" (312). Despite the reference to "mixed marriages," the object of the Orthodox writer's wrath in this story is not literally those who marry outside the faith. Unlike Foa or

Ben-Lévi, Ben Baruch concerns himself relatively little with the question of exogamy, perhaps because it represented so extreme a rejection of his core beliefs. Rather, his prime concern lies with religious schism and with condemning the Reform movement, which like the "corrupted branch" threatens to undermine the integrity of the community. As in all of Ben Baruch's writing, Judaism requires solidarity for survival. Modernity puts this solidarity, which had allowed the Jews to survive centuries of persecution, into peril. But all is not lost: At the end of the parable, the trees "bow their heads with humility" (313), pray, and hope, vowing to remain united in the future.

The Religion of Modernity

Ben Baruch's significance lies in his creative blending of Jewish and French literary codes in order to translate the ideology of the neo-Orthodox movement into narrative form. Unlike traditional Jewish Orthodoxy, neo-Orthodoxy attempted to respond to the dilemmas of modernity, including the threats of materialism and assimilation faced by emancipated Jews. It also attempted to counter the pull of the reformers, who sought to bring Judaism into line with modernity by eliminating elements of the tradition that might be seen to jeopardize the full participation of Jews as citizens in the modern nation-state. Reform gained the most ground in Germany, where Jews in the mid-nineteenth century were still struggling for emancipation and thus needed to prove their worthiness to become citizens. In France, where emancipation had already been granted, the pressure to "regenerate" still made itself felt, but the pressure was more social rather than political. As a result, moderate reform prevailed in France, where the centralization of the Consistory system largely managed to avoid the religious schism that divided Jews in Germany.[55] The French neo-Orthodox nevertheless saw the reformers as a threat and sought to counter their influence by reinventing the tradition.[56]

Ben Baruch argues for Orthodoxy in modern terms, using the literary forms that the French Enlightenment had summoned to critique the influence of religion during the eighteenth century. But even if his goals differed from those of Voltaire and Montesquieu, his methods did not: Ben Baruch makes his case for religion with exclusively rational arguments. Despite his insistence on the necessity of the divine spark, he does not base his plea for following Jewish law on God's will, nor does he offer the incentive of reward in the afterlife. Indeed, with the exception of the parable of the trees and iron, his stories in *L'Univers Israélite* make almost no reference to the supernatural. When his characters do voice supernatural beliefs—as in the story about the circumcision in Pantin, where the father believes that he must entertain the prophet Elijah—the narrator or the other characters qualify them as superstitions and justify them in rational terms as harmless aids in withstanding a life of material struggle. The main reasons for remaining true to Jewish law and tradition, according to Ben Baruch, are that they offer the blueprint for social harmony and provide the basis for social cohesion. Orthodoxy provides the prescription for happiness, whether on the individual or family level—as exemplified by Jedidjah or Jonathan and his brood—or on a broader social plane—as typified by the Jews of Pantin. Ben Baruch locates happiness in this world, however, and sees human perfection as the result of Jewish practice.

Moreover, according to Ben Baruch, the reformers err by assuming that Orthodox Judaism is incompatible with modern citizenship. The heroes of his fiction see adherence to Jewish law as benefiting both the Jewish community and the French nation. Jonathan encourages his children to become productive citizens of France, just as Jewish injunctions lead Jedidjah to acquire both religious and scientific knowledge that will benefit both his coreligionists and society at large. Jews serve society by being Jews. The particular by no means contradicts the universal in Ben Baruch's fictional universe. Jewish difference, even when it leads to social segregation, as evidenced by a refusal to eat in a nonkosher inn, does not preclude full and productive citizenship.

Ben Baruch manifested this ideological program even in the books of Jewish liturgy that he edited and translated throughout his career. Not only do these works promote national feeling within the French Jewish community by translating the sacred texts into the French vernacular, but they also foster religious cohesion by uniting France's disparate Sephardic and Ashkenazic rites.[57] Even more strikingly, they quite explicitly address the apparent problem of incompatibility between Jewish religious and French national aspirations. For reformers, one of the primary obstacles that kept observant Jews from participating fully as citizens in their respective nation-states lay in the traditional messianic hope for a return to Jerusalem. How could Jews feel truly French or German or English if their religion commanded them to long for their own national homeland? In his translation of the Haggadah, the ritual for the Passover (Pesach) holiday that culminates in the declaration "Next Year in Jerusalem," which many reformers sought to suppress, Ben Baruch maintains the declaration but glosses it in a telling way. In a footnote to his French Haggadah, he writes:

> This wish is reproduced in all our prayers, and it does not run at
> all contrary to the duties imposed by our French homeland, nor to
> the love that we have sworn to this land so dear to all Israelites. But
> the re-establishment of a universal metropole in Jerusalem was fore-
> told. . . . "These I will bring to my holy mountain, and make them
> joyful in my house of prayer; their burnt offerings and their sacri-
> fices will be accepted on my altar; FOR MY HOUSE SHALL BE
> CALLED A HOUSE OF PRAYER FOR ALL PEOPLES" (Isaiah,
> LVI, 7). It is that era of peace and union between all peoples that Is-
> rael calls for with all its heart.[58]

According to Ben Baruch, the prayer for a messianic return to Jerusalem does not contradict the exigencies of French citizenship because it applies not just to Jews but to the French as well, and not just to the French but to all mankind. The neo-Orthodox writer reinterprets the nationalist longing for return to Jerusalem that had animated Jews throughout centuries of exile as a desire for world unity, for the convergence of all peoples in the house of God. Orthodox Judaism, in other words, speaks the language of the universal.

Ben Baruch constantly struggled to claim for Judaism the status of a universal religion. Often this meant disputing Christianity's exclusive rights to certain spiritual or moral values. Ben Baruch's story "La charitable mercière juive" [The Charitable Jewish Notions Lady], published in April 1848 in his short-lived journal *La Vérité*, begins with a letter of protest by the Jewish narrator to a Catholic priest who had argued that charity was exclusively Christian. "In support of my claim, allow me to tell you a little story."[59] The narrative describes a Jewish woman named Deborah, raised "in the sweet luxury of the Orient," from an unspecified foreign land. Forced by unhappy circumstances to immigrate to "the hospitable coast of France" (10), Deborah opens a small store selling ribbons and lace, enabling her to provide her old mother and small daughter with the bare necessities. The narrator leads us to believe that her clients patronize her more out of charity than need: "The Talmud says—I like to cite the Talmud to you, reverend Father—the Talmud says: that he who gives in secret is greater than Moses" (11). One day, after calling in vain on a wealthy woman and being told "Madame needs nothing" (11), Deborah returns home to find "a woman poorer than she" who has not eaten for 48 hours. Immediately, Deborah forgets her own sorrows to go out in search of charity for this poor woman and her family. The narrator concludes by asking the priest, "if after hearing this story, which is of the most exact truth, you would still hold that charity is exclusively a Christian virtue" (12).

Published during the still hopeful phase of the 1848 uprising, before the disillusionment of the June Days, when government forces brutally repressed protesting workers, this story offers Jewish ethics as a substitute for the revolutionary Christianity being preached by those on the left.[60] Drawing rather exceptionally for Ben Baruch on melodramatic literary codes (the saintly sufferer, the heroine's reversal of fortune), the story locates the source of the charitable impulses guiding the characters in the Jewish tradition, and specifically in the Talmud, which even certain Jews—such as Alexandre Weill, as I show in the next chapter—thought corrupted the spiritual core of Mosaic monotheism with hairsplitting debates over legal arcana. In the fiction of Ben Baruch, classical rabbinic Judaism provides the basis for a universal religion of brotherhood.

Poor Baruch's Almanac

After years of attempting various genres and venues, of allying with and divorcing himself from diverse editors and publications, Ben Ba-

ruch finally hit on a formula for success in 1850 with his Jewish almanac, which he continued to publish throughout the Second Empire,
until his death in 1872.[61] The format of the *Annuaire religieux et moral
pour l'an du monde X*[62] *à l'usage des Israélites* [Religious and Moral
Annual for the Year X to Be Used by Israelites] remained remarkably
consistent throughout its twenty-year lifespan. A small book (in-18),
able to be carried in a pocket and referred to throughout the day, each
edition of the *Annuaire* began by providing the dates of all Jewish
holidays and fast days according to both the Hebrew and Gregorian
calendars, along with the times of sunset for calculating the start of
the Jewish Sabbath. It also furnished a table comparing the two calendars, meant to help readers commemorate the anniversary of a loved
one's death on the proper day.

But if the calendar was the *Annuaire*'s primary raison d'être, it offered useful information in other domains as well, while inculcating
both French patriotic and Jewish Orthodox ideologies.[63] Each yearly
issue provided a list of all the dignitaries and officers of Jewish institutions in France, including Consistory members for both Paris and the
provinces, and members of various charity boards, both male and female. Indeed, it reads as a veritable Who's Who or *Bottin mondain* of
the French Jewish elite at midcentury. It also provided estimates of the
Jewish populations of all French cities with a Jewish consistory, including Algeria. More practically, it offered the addresses of French Jewish
societies, schools, and businesses, furnishing such useful information
as where to find a mohel to perform circumcisions or a kosher restau-
rant or where to procure matzo or a Hebrew calligrapher in Paris and
the provinces.[64] Every *Annuaire* also included advertisements for Ben
Baruch's other publications, including his various popular translations
of prayers and psalms and his nonreligious publications, such as his
manual for bookkeepers.

The *Annuaire* thus allowed Ben Baruch to promote himself while
also promoting the interests of French Judaism.[65] His desire to forge
a sense of national cohesion, a specifically French community of Jews,
comes across not only in the lists of French Jewish leaders, statistics,
and institutions, all of which reinforce the bonds of imagined community linking Jews living in metropolitan France and in Algeria, but also

in the historical and literary content that fills out the various volumes. In the fifth year of publication (5615, or 1854–1855), Ben Baruch inaugurated a series of sketches of the great rabbis of France, beginning with the two leaders of the Grand Sanhedrin, David Sintzheim and Abraham de Cologna, written by Eliakim Carmoly, a noted Jewish historian.[66] Ben Baruch later supplemented these written portraits with engravings; the first, in 1856–1857, depicts Grand Rabbi Ulmann of the Central Consistory. "Each family, each French Israelite, will want to possess the image of that man who was so distinguished by his learning and by the nobility of his character," the editorial voice declares, uniting the elusive entity of French Jewry by instilling the desire to identify with a common religious leadership and a common past.[67]

Each *Annuaire* also contained short pieces written by Ben Baruch himself, which took a number of forms. These included short tales imitated from Hebrew sources and works dedicated to children. Ben Baruch included in each *Annuaire* a story attached to a Hebrew letter, intended to encourage children to learn the Hebrew alphabet. But the *Annuaire* also included pieces intended for adults, much of it with a polemical tone. Whereas the overall goal of the almanac was to unite French Jews around a shared set of institutions and history, these pieces allowed Ben Baruch to pursue his individual causes, which as we have seen often proved divisive despite paying lip service to unity. We find in these essays many of the same animosities that motivated his polemics in *L'Univers Israélite* during the 1840s, especially a hostility toward reform.

The penchant for controversy never abandoned Ben Baruch, even when he finally became a member of the Paris Consistory himself in the early 1860s. In one sketch, "Entre la poire et le fromage" [Between the Pear and the Cheese], published in 1866–1867, Ben Baruch imagines a dialogue between two Consistory electors. The first elector says that they should for once nominate a real "Yid," that is, a genuine Jew, to the Consistory. The ignorant second elector replies that he thought all the Consistory members were "Yids," and to illustrate his point, he tells a story about the amazing charitable impulses of the Consistory members: At a recent Consistory dinner he attended, they raised 4,000 francs for the poor between the pear and the cheese courses. The first elector then asks whether the dinner was *maigre* [meatless but also scanty]. Scandalized at the suggestion that a Consistory dinner would be anything but lavish, the ignorant second elector replies that of course they had a kosher turkey. The first elector then indignantly explains to his comrade that kosher dietary law forbids cheese after fowl. "I hold to what I said," the first elector declares. "We need Yids on the Consistory; otherwise, do you know what will happen? One fine day these men, the rabbis leading the way, will come together at the Grand Hotel, and there, after a succulent dinner, they will declare the abolition of the Shulchan Aruch[68] between the pear and the cheese" (121). This irreverent dialogue earned the aging writer a flurry of protest letters as well as an outraged editorial in *Les Archives Israélites*, decrying his poor taste.[69]

Another caustic humor piece in the 1864–1865 *Annuaire* satirically announced the latest Reform innovation from Berlin: Jewish temples installed on train cars—*des wagons-synagogues*. "Henceforth, all Israelites in the country who travel on Saturdays and holidays will be able to have a minyan" (131).[70] With conductors trained in the Talmud, the narrator announces exuberantly, the rolling rabbis can double as brakemen while violating Jewish laws by traveling on the Sabbath! Ben Baruch includes a detailed explanation of the rules and regulations of the railroad synagogues. A few examples that illustrate his virtuosic parody of Reform innovations:

> Article 2: The service will begin at the first whistle. It will proceed at great speed.
> Article 3: There will be no station stop between the three obligatory services. All three will be recited together. The evening prayer will be recited in the morning.
> Article 4: Praying aloud is forbidden. Only in the case of collision between two trains will it be permitted to recite the Shema Israel.
> (131–132)

Here Ben Baruch wittily mocks not only the desire of reformers to have their cake and eat it too, to travel on the Sabbath but still consider themselves Jews, but also the fetishization of the modern in all its forms, whether in locomotion or religion, that motivates his contemporaries to tamper with a tradition that has lasted for thousands of years.

The bulk of the fictional pieces in the *Annuaire* are more serious in tone, but they also contain polemics aimed at the reformers. The 1852–1853 *Annuaire* includes the allegorical story "La religion, la civilisation et le chat" [Religion, Civilization, and the Cat], about a magnificent old palace (signifying religion) that has a few mice, which have driven away some of its residents. Civilization offers to help by supplying a cat (signifying reform), which in the process of capturing the mice destroys the palace. "My dear daughter," Religion tells Civilization, "if to get rid of a few pests that annoy me I am obliged to introduce into my home an animal that kills me, I would rather be patient. Those who have left me will return. The future is mine." Moses Mendelssohn had famously used a similar metaphor of a house collapsing in *Jerusalem* (1793) to defend the Jewish religion in the age of Enlightenment. Ben Baruch reappropriates the metaphor of the founder of the Haskalah and spiritual father of the Reform movement to argue against reform and to express his confidence in the ultimate triumph of traditional Judaism.[71]

Many of the stories, however, thematize social rather than religious conflict. These works testify to Ben Baruch's continued preoccupation with the gulf between rich and poor among France's Jews despite the rising fortunes of the French Jewish community in general. During the Second Empire, an increasing number of French Jews entered the bourgeoisie, especially in Paris, which by 1861 was home to 25,000 Jews, or one-quarter of France's Jewish population.[72] In Paris by 1872, 44 percent of economically active Jews engaged in settled commerce or commercial employment, whereas only 6 percent remained itinerant peddlers.[73]

Ben Baruch responds to this increasing prosperity of French Jews during the Second Empire by underscoring its fragility. A surprising number of his stories in the *Annuaire* describe reversals of fortune. One work of fiction from 1856–1857, labeled a "proverb in action," rewrites "Le prédicateur et le soufflet," dispensing with the frame narrative involving the covert Orthodox sermon to focus on his two representative characters: the poor but intelligent man, once again named Jedidjah, and the rich and stupid man, here named Korah. The two embark on a sea journey. Jedidjah earns the respect of the other passengers with his *sagesse* (wisdom), whereas the prideful Korah alienates the others with his *richesse* (riches), the bulk of which he carries with him in the hold of the ship. When a storm destroys the ship, the two manage to swim to a deserted shore. Korah is devastated by the loss of his fortune, but Jedidjah makes the best of the difficult situation. Thanks to some mathematical instruments that Jedidjah stashed in his belt, they find their way to a city. There Jedidjah's superior talents earn him the honor and respect of the citizens, but Korah is forced to undertake "the most abject and rude labor to provide for his subsistence" (89). The story concludes by reiterating its epigraph from Proverbs 3: "Happy is the man who finds wisdom, for its profit is better than gold."

Ben Baruch's reworking of the rich man/poor man theme reflects his increasing dissatisfaction with the direction in which the Jewish community was headed. Whereas the version from the 1840s had lamented the social success of the idiotic rich man and applauded the noble qualities of the poor man but left their social positions unchanged, the narrative from the 1850s rewards virtue and punishes vice. It is as though Ben Baruch must work harder to swim against the current of prosperity. In the later story, his narrative corrects reality rather than merely comments on its injustice. The later story offers less a critique of the overestimation of wealth in the Jewish community than a reflection on the ethics of prosperity from a Jewish perspective.

In another story in the same issue of the *Annuaire*, set in an identifiably modern present, a rich outfitter named Zebulon also loses his fortune in a shipwreck, forcing his daughter, Deborah, a talented artist, to struggle to support her aging parents. Unlike Korah in the preceding story, however, Zebulon had used his wealth to help his neighbors help themselves, in the Talmudic spirit of charity, and his generosity leads to his salvation. Asser, the son of a poor laborer whom Zebulon had helped years before, returns from the colonies where he has made his fortune. He contrives to return the kindness Zebulon provided to his family without it seeming like charity by buying Deborah's paintings at ten times their value. Coming to appreciate the artist's virtues as well as her talents, he eventually proposes marriage to her. The magnanimous Asser invokes the proverb, quoted at the beginning of the story, "The rich and the poor meet together" (Prov. 22:2), and the two families live happily ever after in a "magnificent dwelling."

These stories strike a rare note of pessimism at this moment of greatest optimism for the Jews of France, warning that the traditional Jewish values they have so quickly dismissed in their rush to success may in fact prove necessary should their luck turn. And Jewish history teaches nothing if not that luck can turn. In a story from 1854–1855, one of the few of Ben Baruch's works to involve the supernatural, a poor Jewish family receives a visit from an angel, who offers them ten years of prosperity as a reward for their piety. They can either choose to have the good years now or save them for their old age. Not knowing how long they will live, they choose to have them now; just then, their children return from the forest where they have found a treasure. The family uses its newfound wealth to help the poor. Deborah, the wife, spends her time at the beds of the sick and in the garrets of the indigent, spreading consolation and encouragement. They think not only of the present but also of the future, endowing hospitals, foundations for young girls without dowries, synagogues, and retirement homes. When the ten years come to an end, the angel returns. But instead of plunging them back into poverty, God's messenger allows them to keep their fortune because they have made such good use of it.

This story can be read not only as a morality lesson about wealth aimed at a newly rich readership but also as a more general allegory for the fate of the Jewish community in modern France. Ben Baruch presents French emancipation as the equivalent of the angel's gift: a sudden period of great fortune that may prove limited. The pious family in the story uses its wealth to provide for the community, seeking both to meet present crises and to endow institutions that will continue to provide service in the future. This is precisely the kind of charitable activity that Ben Baruch constantly criticized the wealthy elite among French Jews for not providing with sufficient generosity. The story thus implies that the key to retaining fortune, to preserving the wealth the angel of France has granted them, lies in remaining true to the code of ethics enshrined in the Talmud and Jewish law. The code of ethics governing wealth is placed within a supernatural scheme, but on closer inspection the story proves less magical than it at first appears. The family does good with its fortune not to influence the angel's decision—the angel never promises that their actions will have any effect on their fate—but because they feel a bond of solidarity with others in the community. Although the story implies that continued prosperity may be the reward for generosity and sets men's actions within a divine cosmic scheme, it also implies that good deeds should be accomplished for their own sake and because God commands it.

Simpler in structure than the stories Ben Baruch published in *L'Univers Israélite* and lacking their complex intertextuality, much of the fiction in the *Annuaire* offers straightforward plots illustrating a single moral lesson. In these works destined for a wider and less educated readership, Ben Baruch substitutes the structure and substance of the Talmudic parable for eighteenth-century satire. Although his humor pieces devoted to criticizing Reform—such as the "wagon-synagogue" vignette—still contain the marks of his wit and work largely through irony, his fictional narratives use the more accessible trope of sentimentality, typical of nineteenth-century social fiction and melodrama, to argue for communal solidarity. As in all his stories, Ben Baruch attempts to show how the code of ethics enshrined in Jewish law provides a solution to the problem of social disintegration affecting Jews—and not just Jews—in modern times.

Memoirs and Modernity

To conclude this chapter, I turn now to a unique series of stories published serially in the *Annuaire* between 1857 and 1861 in which Ben Baruch addresses the problems of modernity by turning back to the past. These fictional works, "Mémoires de rebe Züskind" [Memoirs of Reb Züskind], narrate the life and adventures of an Orthodox Jew born at the close of the eighteenth century—a hero whose biographical details resemble those of Alexandre Créhange in every particular.[74] The "Mé-moires" function less as an autobiography of the semi-anonymous author, however, than as a portrait of the Jewish community during the revolutionary period, when old superstitions were beginning to give way to reason and old customs clashed with modern forms of social organization.[75] In this series of stories, Ben Baruch's own life becomes the stuff of myth, a symbol for the process of modernity itself.

No doubt conceived partly in imitation of Ben-Lévi's "Mémoires d'un colporteur juif, écrits par lui-même" [Memoirs of a Jewish Peddler, Written by Himself] (1841–1842), which I analyzed in Chapter 2, "Mémoires de rebe Züskind" likewise take place in the Lorraine countryside during the latter years of the eighteenth century. Although both works describe the customs of a prior age from the vantage point of the modern present, the tone and style of the two works vary greatly. Ben-Lévi's story uses sentimental codes to arouse sympathy for its idealized peddler-narrator; Ben Baruch adopts an overtly comic tone that gently mocks even as it waxes nostalgic. Once again Ben Baruch looks to an eighteenth-century classic for his literary model; these memoirs read as a pastiche of Laurence Sterne's *Tristram Shandy* (1759–1769), one that brings the ironist's gaze to bear on Jewish characters and customs as eccentric as those described by the English author.

Like Sterne, Ben Baruch begins at the beginning. Indeed, by the end of the four installments of "Mémoires de rebe Züskind," the protagonist is only a week old. "My origin is that of all men," the narrative begins modestly. "King and rag picker, the great architect of the universe has constructed everything from the same mud" (107). But this falsely self-deprecating tone quickly gives way to the grandiose: "However," the narrator says in the next sentence, "I claim to be from what one calls good stock." Born to a father who officiated in the synagogue as a hazan, like Créhange's, the young narrator saw the light of day in a small town "between the mirabelle of Metz and the sugarplum of Verdun," which corresponds to the location of Étain, the author's birthplace. The narrator can only speculate that the "sweetness" of the location inspired his parents to name him Züskind, or "sweet child" in Yiddish, a name that (in the case of Créhange) will hardly prove accurate.

The rest of the first installment describes the circumstances of his birth, the comical complications of which recall once again the opening of *Tristram Shandy*. "I in effect declared my intentions to enter the world" (107), the narrator announces, echoing Sterne's determination to relate the minute details of his protagonist's delivery in defiance of the conventions of both biography and good taste. And just as Sterne takes the opportunity to digress on eighteenth-century English legal and medical practices in his description of Tristram's birth, so too does Züskind's delivery provoke a disquisition on the customs and superstitions surrounding birth in Jewish Lorraine. When his mother goes into labor, his father writes on the door in chalk the words from Psalm 20: "The Lord answer you in the day of trouble!" He then takes up a Hebrew book "and set about *lernen*" (107). The rather exceptional entry of Yiddish into Créhange's fiction necessitates a footnote to his assimilated or non-Jewish readers explaining that *lernen* means "to study, to read a book of the law, usually the Mishnah" (107). The midwife surrounds the delivery room with the "holy letters," the *Shir Hamalot*, which another footnote explains are a talisman meant to scare away "the witches (Lilith and her crew) from the bed of the woman in childbirth" (108).[76] Créhange situates the birth of his fictional alter ego at a time when the traditional languages were still spoken and traditional religious beliefs held sway among the Jews of France's eastern provinces, mingled with a kind of popular superstition.

The late eighteenth century, of course, was also the moment in which modernity erupted onto the scene in the form of the Revolution, helping to make these practices a thing of the past. "Indeed, I was, like everyone else at that time (1791), in full revolt" (109), the narrator announces, referring to his difficult birth but also to the Revolution that made the Jews of Lorraine citizens in the very year of Créhange's entry into the world. In deference to the spirit of progress, the practical midwife decides to supplement her superstitions with science and calls for a doctor from Verdun. Similar events transpire at the opening of *Tristram Shandy*, but in Ben Baruch's version the doctor's arrival leads into a digression on the nature of Jewish Sabbath regulations. The doctor, Raphael, "who had never traveled on a Saturday"

(109), takes pleasure in violating the day of rest with impunity be- cause a life is in danger, the one instance in which such a violation is sanctioned by Jewish law. Despite the doctor's secret desire to escape from tradition, the superstitious villagers recuperate his arrival into a narrative in keeping with their premodern worldview; his name, we are told, invokes the "angel of healing" (109), and those who see him arrive swear that his horse has wings.

The second installment describes the events following the birth of the young Züskind, but its real theme is the hospitality offered by vil- lage Jews in bygone times. On the day of his birth, a strange beggar- woman arrives carrying an infant of her own. Rivequesche, the super- stitious midwife, at first suspects the stranger may be Lilith in disguise and performs various "kabbalistic" rituals to ward off the evil spirit. The stranger then recounts how the Spanish Inquisition kidnapped her husband, forcing her to go in search of a distant relative in far-off Lorraine. This relative turns out to be related to Züskind's family as well as to the mohel who will arrive shortly to perform the circumci- sion. After this revelation, the family welcomes the stranger among them, treating her as a member of the household. She returns their affection and even suckles Züskind with her milk.

The third installment narrates the mock-perilous journey of the mohel through a snowstorm. He stops to eat at an inn he knows along the way, where the non-Jewish mistress offers him kosher food and asks only for his prayer in payment: "That I be happy in this here land" (j'soyons heureuse dans c'pays-ci), she says. "That's all I be askin' you." "Yes, Catiche, I shall pray for you," the mohel responds (98). The standard French of the Jew contrasts with the rustic speech of the innkeeper in this idealized vision of interfaith harmony during the revolutionary period, suggesting that the Jew was already closer to becoming an educated citizen of a newly unified France than the Lorraine peasant. But the local dialect of the Jews makes an appear- ance shortly after in the form of the *yitzschkartz*, the party held by neighbor women for the newly delivered baby, "where the steaming *moka* rivaled the chocolate of Prévost, where Federmann's cakes gave the tarts of Caen a run for their money" (103). This nostalgic yearning for the sweets of yesteryear summons the flavors of an idealized but vanished world, one that contrasts—favorably—with the prestige of a modern French present.

The circumcision then follows, bringing together the entire village. "In the little Jewish communities it was like that once upon a time. The celebration of one was the celebration of another, and the mourning of one was the mourning of all" (104). Ben Baruch's vision of the interdependency of the Jews of the small semirural communities in prerevolutionary times anticipates Tönnies' theory of modernity as the move from *Gemeinschaft* to *Gesellschaft*, from a form of society based on mutual association to one based on self-interest: "That happy and holy fraternity still exists here and there," Ben Baruch writes, but "it is in the process of disappearing. One could say that the union of men recedes as civilization advances" (104). For Ben Baruch, the fault lies mostly with those who have pursued their self-interest at the expense of their fellow men: "The rich no longer frequent the poor," forgetting God's desire for them to do so (104). The Orthodox Ben Baruch describes this shift not only in sociological terms but also in religious ones; the move toward individualism, characteristic of modernity, is a move away from not just community but also God's commandment.

The fourth and final installment of the memoirs describes still more celebration following Züskind's birth. "The following Saturday was the date we fixed for my mother to leave her bed and the Haoula-Kraasch" (108).[77] This bizarrely named ritual provokes the astonishment of Ben Baruch's imagined readers, assimilated ladies scandalized by the uncouth Yiddish name: "Surely . . . you jest. Such a language was never spoken," they declare in shocked tones ventriloquized by the narrator. "You made us swallow your Istzchkartz [*sic*], but we won't accept the la Ha-ha-ha-oul-oula, Haoula-Kraasch. Do you take us for Iroquois?" (108). "Calm down, dear ladies," the narrator commands, informing these incredulous imaginary readers that the period he describes goes back seventy years. "At that time we spoke such a language" (108). With this reassurance that the days of speaking such a savage tongue—and here he compares, as in the Tom Pouff story, the traditional Orthodox Jews to American Indians—lie safely in the past, he carries on with his explanation of the customs of this vanished

world. The word *Haoula*, he relates, most likely comes from "hola!"
or the English "hello" and refers to the giving of names, both sacred
and profane, to the child.[78] He then describes the introduction of his
own profane name—Alexandre, or "Suskind" [*sic*]—among Jews, explaining that it goes back to the time of Alexander the Great.

Although he promises a *suite à prochain*, a next installment to follow, Ben Baruch ends his pseudo-autobiographical memoirs here, not
returning to them in the decade he continued to publish his *Annuaire*.
It makes sense, I think, to see this moment of profane naming, in
which the author who had hidden behind the pseudonym Ben Baruch
for so long finally enters the literary field under his own first name, as
an appropriate ending point for his fictional autobiography. What he
leaves unsaid is how he got from Züskind (or Suskind) to Alexandre,
how he effectuated the shift from the Yiddish to the French version of
his secular identity. But perhaps this history would have been all too
well known to the assimilating French readers who feigned ignorance
of the language and customs of traditional Jewish life, for they would
have made a similar transition themselves—or their parents would
have done so. Ben Baruch's point in this story is not to describe the
process of assimilation but rather to criticize its results and to point to
the value inherent in customs that may now seem "barbaric."

In the next two chapters, I return to this theme of the Jewish past,
the lost world of tradition located in the villages of eastern France. This
world was felt to be on the verge of extinction in the mid-nineteenth
century and offered to the Parisian Jewish writer both a touchstone
and a foil for the modern Jew he was attempting to invent. Before
moving on to these village tales and to their modern form of nostalgia, it is worth pausing one last time to consider the innovations of
their precursors. Ben Baruch and his Reform rival Ben-Lévi provided
two different templates for looking backward, contrasting models that
exemplify in their difference precisely what marked the distinction between the Reform and Orthodox visions of modernity.

Like Ben Baruch's "Mémoires de rebe Züskind," Ben-Lévi's peddler story turns a nostalgic eye toward the past, revalorizing the lost
traditions of traditional Jewish life in the Lorraine countryside during
the eighteenth century as an antidote to the problems of modernity.

But several key features distinguish Ben-Lévi's Reform vision from Ben Baruch's Orthodox reworking of this same material. First, Ben-Lévi underscores the injustices of prerevolutionary times—the humiliations faced by his Jewish peddler as well as the legal injustices he encountered. The Reform writer thus inscribes his nostalgia into a narrative of progress that values the material and legal superiority of the present even while bemoaning certain spiritual losses that this great leap forward entailed. Ben-Lévi's peddler narrator recalls the sweetness of the Sabbath ritual as a time of family togetherness and as a recompense for the vexations of his troubled life, but he does not advocate readopting these rituals in the present. Modern Jews, for Ben-Lévi, no longer live in a world governed by traditional Jewish practice and should not seek to do so. The elements of the past that Ben-Lévi hopes to recover for the present are largely ethical: moral uprightness and a form of solidarity among Jews. Ben-Lévi, in other words, extracts the content of traditional Judaism while leaving behind its forms.

And Ben-Lévi's description of the forms of the past is heavily idealized. The scene of his peddler returning from a week of wandering to find a beautifully laid table and a happy family celebrating the joys of the Sabbath represents a kind of whitewashing of memory. This is pointedly not the case for Ben Baruch. In the Orthodox vision of the past, traditional Jews practice not just a heavily edited Sabbath ritual but all kinds of ceremonies, many of which draw not only on the purity of the biblical tradition but also on local custom and popular superstition. Ben Baruch's narrator even calls these ceremonies by their Yiddish names—*Yitzschkartz* or *Haoula-Kraasch*—names that sound "barbaric" to modern French ears. Ben Baruch makes more difficult demands of his modern readers. He asks them to confront the past in all its unenlightened diversity, to lay aside the shame they have internalized of the harsh sounds of their past. For Ben Baruch, the universal truth of Judaism does not need to be extracted from the core of the tradition, like some precious metal surrounded by worthless rock. Rather, it inheres in the very forms of that tradition.

Ben Baruch's nostalgia, then, is very much a *nostalgie de la boue*, but this mud turns out to be precious in and of itself. According to

Ben Baruch, traditional Jewish village life fostered the kind of cross-class solidarity that he found lacking in the modern metropolis. In this world ruled by ritual and governed by Jewish law, a world that seems firmly lodged in the past, the Orthodox writer locates the source of values toward which the revolutionaries of his own day were striving. The problem, of course, was that this world had in fact passed; the Jewish village could not be re-created in modern Paris. Not only had the material conditions of life changed, but also the materialist mind-set of the present along with the gains of Enlightenment precluded the kind of naïve acceptance of tradition and ritual that corresponded in an organic way with the lives of premodern Jews. But this did not mean that the forms of the past had lost their value.

For Ben Baruch, the key to recovering the eternal values of the Jew-ish tradition and to actualizing them in the present lay in reappro-priating ritual and reinterpreting it for modern times. His characters choose to adhere to Jewish laws, to follow rituals and traditions, even to retain certain superstitions, not because they cannot conceive of a world without them but precisely because they can conceive of such a world and have rejected it as lacking. Ben Baruch's fictional world may in fact be disenchanted, but the moral value of following tradition provides its own source of spiritual fulfillment.

Four Village Tales: Alexandre Weill and Mosaic Monotheism

In 1867, Alexandre Weill could state with confidence that among his contemporaries, "Jews can be found, naturally, at the highest levels."[1] Captains of finance, titans of commerce, powerful publishers, popular dramatists and composers—individual Jews had achieved unparalleled success in Second Empire France. To be sure, most of Weill's wealthy coreligionists, willfully ignorant of Jewish culture, "having learned nothing and having forgotten everything . . . don't like to be singled out as Jews. They are French citizens professing the Israelite religion" (291). Not so many years before, he too had been one of these "Israelites," retaining only the thinnest trace of identification with the Jewish religion or tradition, despite his early rabbinical training. But he had seen the error of his ways. At this moment of supreme confidence for the Jews of France, when the path of emancipation seemed the most secure, the self-styled "prophet of the Faubourg Saint-Honoré" sounded the alarm bell of antisemitism and sought to teach his fellow Israelites what it meant to be a Jew.

With the exception of a dozen "philosophers" and "some educated freemasons," Weill laments in 1867, there is not a single French person who does not harbor prejudice toward the Jews. Contrary to expectations for the spread of enlightened tolerance, hatred of the Jews in France "has augmented from one day to the next and is always increasing" (291). True, Napoleon III might protect the Jews, but so too did Caesar and Augustus: "That didn't stop their successors from waging a war of extinction against them." In terms that eerily justify his claim to prophecy, Weill warns of a rising tide of racial hatred in France and foresees not only "a law of exclusion and expulsion" (297) but actual physical violence against the Jews. "Hear and see," the prophet intones. "Somber faces give us threatening looks, blood libels still arise, like in the Middle Ages" (299). In the late 1860s, Weill's contemporaries could still dismiss his pronouncements as paranoid fantasies. Twenty years later, after Édouard Drumont's antisemitic screed *La France juive* [Jewish France] (1886) had become a national best seller, Weill's dire warnings no doubt seemed less far-fetched. In an 1889 pamphlet titled "Cris d'alarme, épîtres aux juifs de France, d'Angleterre, d'Allemagne et d'Amérique" [Alarm Cries, Epistles to the Jews of France, England, Germany, and America], Weill speaks of a day when France would renounce the principles of 1789: "She will set upon the emancipated Jews . . . no hand will be raised, no foot will stir to save the world's Jews."[2]

Like the prophets of the Bible, Weill blames the victim. France's Jews bear responsibility for the coming calamity because of their cupidity, their selfish pursuit of worldly success. "What have they done . . . since their emancipation?" Weill asks. "They have hurled themselves like rabid dogs, competing with Christians not to live ideal and intellectual lives or to win hearts and minds . . . but to earn as much money as possible."[3] Worse than the single-minded accumulation of wealth, however, is their failure to counter the envy aroused by their prosperity through good works. More specifically, France's Jews have failed to support the revolutionary ideals that had motivated their emancipation and that could have served as bulwarks against the very hatreds they now faced. "What have you done in the last sixty years to better the lives of the people who freed you, who were the first to lift you out of the ghetto and elevate you to the role of citizens?" Weill asks his fellow French Jews. "Have you supported those principles of reason and liberty by virtue of which you were transformed from serfs into men?" (295). Weill answers his own question in the negative: The Jews of France have failed in the universal mission they were called on to enact.

Weill's attacks on his wealthy coreligionists grow out of a tradition of Jewish anticapitalism, one that found its leading exponent in Karl Marx, whom Weill describes having met in Paris in the 1840s.[4] But what surprises us about Weill is less his diagnosis of the sickness of antisemitism or his analysis of its causes than his suggestions for a cure. Unlike the convert Marx, whose solution to the so-called Jewish question was communist revolution, Weill sees the answer in a Jewish religious reawakening. French Israelites must once again become French Jews. As I have shown, other contemporaries of Weill called for something similar. Ben-Lévi argued for the distillation of Judaism to a fundamental ethics and a sense of communal solidarity that might remedy the ills of assimilation. His rival Ben Baruch called for a return to Orthodoxy and saw in the strict observance of Jewish law the key to communal salvation. Weill's plan for the modernization of Judaism was at once far more traditional and far more radical than either of these two other options.

Pursuing his own idiosyncratic brand of biblical criticism, Weill advocates a rejection of the Talmud and a return to the Pentateuch. But even the Hebrew Bible itself contains deviations from what Weill identifies as the fundamental Mosaic core of Judaism. In this bedrock Weill discovers nothing less than the principles that had animated the French Revolution of 1789. In Mosaic monotheism, he argues, lies the foundation of a modern political and social organization based on democratic values. For Weill, the mission of the French Jews is to become the agents or apostles of this creed. It is thus paradoxically by returning to the origins of their particular tradition that Jews become the heralds of the universal. Weill would go on to elaborate this theory in numerous theological and political tracts. But as I show in this chapter, it is in his fiction that he attempts to put his theories into practice.

The Prophet's Path

Of all the writers I focus on in this book, Weill achieved the greatest prominence in the nineteenth century. Known, if not admired, by both Jews and non-Jews in his time, he was called the "enfant terrible of literature" in the mainstream *Le Temps* (March 28, 1866) and a "paradox in the form of man" in *Les Archives Israélites* (June 10, 1866).[5] When Weill died in 1899, the *New York Times* printed a detailed obituary.[6] The author of over 130 published works and more than 150 newspaper articles, Weill tried his hand at a dizzying array of genres, including fiction, poetry, theater, philosophy, theology, political propaganda, history, memoir, and journalism. Joë Friedmann attributes the near total eclipse of his fame following his death to the variety—and lack of coherence—of his literary output.[7] Indeed, with the exception of Friedmann's intellectual biography, Weill has received almost no scholarly treatment whatsoever. The few works to discuss him invariably gloss over his voluminous corpus to focus on his friendships with more illustrious figures of his day, including Nerval, Hugo, Baudelaire, Balzac, and Heine.[8] And yet Weill's writings, which span a period of fifty years, constitute perhaps the most original manifestation of Jewish intellectual engagement in nineteenth-century France. Weill also deserves to be remembered as one of the purest examples of a nineteenth-century French type: an autodidact polymath, a political dreamer, a relentless polemicist, and a firm exponent of the power of literature to change the world.

Abraham "Alexandre" Weill (Figure 5) was born in the small Alsatian village of Schirhof (Bas-Rhin), near Strasbourg, in 1811. He was the son of Léopold Yehuda Weill, a modestly prosperous livestock merchant. His mother, Guidel, was the daughter of a secretary to the wealthy Hertz family, Abraham Kellermeister, who took an active role in revolutionary politics ("for which his grandson sincerely thanks him," Weill would write in his memoirs).[9] Alexandre began to learn Hebrew from a local rabbi at the age of 3, but the invasion of the allied armies interrupted his studies. His next teacher, Raphaël Lévy, instructed him in German and French as well as Hebrew. Destined for the rabbinate, the young Weill pursued his Talmudic studies in the larger French centers of Jewish learning (Marmoutier, Metz, and Nancy) before leaving for Frankfurt in 1826 to study with the Orthodox Rabbi Trier.[10] Around this time, Alexandre received recognition for his beautiful tenor voice and considered becoming an opera singer. While in Germany, he subscribed to French newspapers of various political strands, and after 1830 he began a serious study of secular literature and philosophy. This caused him to abandon his religious studies and to opt for a career as a writer and journalist. Although he ceased

Figure 5. Portrait of Alexandre Weill by Nadar. Courtesy of the Bibliothèque Nationale de France.

to practice Judaism at this time, he nevertheless promised his disappointed rabbinic teacher that he would never convert.[11]

In the 1830s, Weill began to write for a number of German newspapers and published the first of his village tales in German. He abandoned a doctorate in philosophy at the University of Heidelberg and edited a short-lived journal in Frankfurt called *L'Iris.* After meeting

Nerval, he moved to Paris in the late 1830s, where despite a heavy Alsatian accent, he managed to penetrate the ranks of the capital's artistic and political avant-garde. He continued to write for German and French publications, including the satiric organ of literary bohemia, *Le Corsaire-Satan*, and Émile de Girardin's *La Presse*. Weill collaborated in the 1840s on the Fourierist newspapers *La Phalange* and *La Démocratie Pacifique*, the latter of which, founded by the antisemite Alphonse Toussenel, repeatedly denounced the Rothschilds and other Jewish capitalists. Weill clearly excelled in making important connections. Aside from Heinrich Heine, whom Weill would count as a close friend, he received support from both the composer Giacomo Meyerbeer and the popular novelist Eugène Sue.[12] In 1847, Weill celebrated his marriage to Agathina Marx in the synagogue, despite his professed atheism. Her successful women's clothing shop on the Faubourg Saint-Honoré financed his subsequent literary career.[13]

The spectacle of mass uprising during the 1848 Revolution shifted Weill's political orientation from far left to far right. "In my writing . . . I have always been a republican. . . . I am less of one since March 17," he wrote in *Le Corsaire-Satan*, denouncing the "political terrorism" of the revolutionaries and their suppression of all opposing political points of view.[14] After a failed attempt to run for the National Assembly on a conservative platform,[15] he began to write for *La Gazette de France*, the prime organ of right-wing Catholic legitimism. Weill would later regret this stage in his career,[16] but in addition to his articles for the *Gazette*, he penned a series of widely read pamphlets in the late 1840s setting forth his increasingly reactionary views.[17] Going so far as to advocate a hereditary monarchy in the aftermath of 1848, Weill came close to converting to Catholicism during this period, despite his youthful promise to his rabbinic teacher never to do so. According to Friedmann, Weill began to believe that Christianity offered the basis for a spiritualization of power, a way to subjugate politics to divine law.[18] By the time of Louis-Napoleon's coup d'état, however, he had broken with the Catholic legitimists and had begun to rethink his spiritual and political orientation.

Weill returned to his republican beliefs in the 1850s, but like many of his disillusioned contemporaries, he largely abstained from direct political engagement during the Second Empire. Instead, he turned his attention to Judaism, subjecting the religious tradition of his youth to intense scrutiny. "I reread the five books of Moses not as a book of faith, imposed by a self-styled revelation, but rather as a work of human philosophy and of religious legislation."[19] In a series of theological tracts, Weill expounded his theory concerning the Mosaic core of Judaism, the kernel of a universal moral code embodied in the first five books of the Old Testament. As Friedmann points out, Weill's approach has much in common with that of two other major nineteenth-century French Jewish religious thinkers: Joseph Salvador and Hippolyte Rodrigues, the brother of Eugénie Foa.[20]

At the center of Weill's theory was a belief that the philosophical contradictions in the Pentateuch were the product not of logical inconsistency on the part of Moses but of subsequent additions and emendations to the sacred books. Biblical scholars since Spinoza had explored the idea that Moses was not the author of the entire Pentateuch, but Weill's originality lay in attributing the contradictions to the additions, or what Weill would consider the falsifications, of the prophets Ezra and Nehemiah. These prophets were responsible, according to Weill, for introducing the foreign notion of pardon into Judaism. Drawing on the Persian (pagan) custom of releasing a scapegoat into the wilderness to free people of their sins, these prophets tainted the strict Mosaic emphasis on the primacy of the law with the addition of a doctrine of forgiveness.[21] According to Weill, this was a terrible error: The law must be absolute or it must not be.[22] Subsequent prophets also corrupted the rationality of original Mosaic Judaism by turning Moses into a supernatural being and attributing the great events of Jewish history to divine miracles. Following them, Talmudic Judaism and Christianity, which according to Weill both grew out of this corruption of the Hebrew Bible, would place emphasis on faith rather than works, on belief rather than reason, and would thus dilute the moral superiority of Judaism.

Weill argued that changing the Jewish religion was necessary, but not along the lines proposed by the Reform movement, which he believed sought merely to copy the outward forms of Christianity.

Rather, Judaism must return to its authentic sources, which involved, first and foremost, freeing itself from the "yoke of the Talmud." The Talmud had long been a *bête noire* for Weill. Already in the 1840s, he had denounced it for fostering obscurantism and for prescribing rules and obligations to separate the Jews from their fellow Frenchmen, thus preventing them from fulfilling their duties to the nation. He had even gone so far as to call on the government to ban its study in France. After his return to Judaism in the 1850s, Weill accorded the Talmudic tradition a grudging respect, crediting it with giving the Jews the strength to withstand centuries of persecution.[23] Nevertheless he continued to accuse it of the crime of "reasonicide" (*raisonocide*) for having distorted the Mosaic basis of Judaism; a modernized Judaism must not look to this "book of errors if ever there was one" for its renewal.[24] For Weill, the key to reinventing Judaism lay in casting off this later corrupted form of Judaism and returning to the original Mosaic core of the Pentateuch itself.

It is in the foundational monotheism of Moses that Weill finds the essence of the universal message of the Jewish people, their gift to world civilization. In Moses, Weill sees not only the founder of a specific religion but the founder of all true religions: "the creator of humanity over and above the different barbarous nations, the initiator of universal civilization, the first legislator who proclaimed the liberty of all peoples."[25] Indeed, Weill makes of Moses not only a religious figure but the world's first great social thinker, the initiator of democracy, the defender of the poor, and the enemy of social hierarchies. "Consciously or unconsciously these principles were borrowed by the men of [1789] from the fundamental principles of Moses."[26] Judaism is thus the religion of revolution, the true republican and universal religion, according to Weill, not only because it is based on reason but also because it admits no class distinctions.[27] As prophet of this true Mosaism, Weill sees his mission as inspiring his Jewish brethren to serve as a light to the nations. "Salvation comes from the Jews," Weill quotes the Christian Gospel as saying, and the mission of the Jews is to inspire the world to embrace the reign of reason, liberty, and solidarity.[28]

Weill found few supporters among the Hebraicists of his day. In

1864, the Jewish author Georges Stenne (the pseudonym of David Schornstein, whom I discuss in Chapter 5) attacked Weill in both the mainstream *Nouvelle Revue de Paris* and *L'Univers Israélite* for reducing the Jewish religion to a cold mathematical formula, for deriving the Hebrew Bible from Spinoza.[29] In a withering review, the great Jewish academic Adolphe Franck, professor at the Collège de France and author of a respected study of the Kabbalah, likewise faulted Weill for basing his argument about the heterogeneity of the Pentateuch not on philological grounds, on the type of Hebrew used in different parts, but on his own subjective passions. "He confines himself simply to making Moses his thing, his creature, his spiritual son, because it's from him, more so even than from Spinoza, that this poor Moses has been obliged to learn the little that he knows. Mr. Weill imposes upon him his small philosophical and social catechism, and everything in the holy book that manifestly contradicts the terms of this formula is repudiated, dishonored, deplored like a work of pious fraud."[30] Weill was undeterred by this criticism and continued to believe he had succeeded in isolating the essential truth of Judaism.[31]

Indeed, Weill's vision of his own achievement reached grandiose proportions: "Not since Moses, Joshua, Samuel, Isaiah, Amos, and Jesus (who was a Mosaic prophet)," he wrote at the end of his life, "has there been, could there be, a Jew like me."[32] Weill took seriously his role as prophet, speaking out not only on issues of scriptural or doctrinal reform but on worldly matters as well. Following his Mosaic revelation, Weill made himself into a kind of moral conscience of French Jewry, rarely missing an opportunity to attack or criticize, especially when it came to the wealthy elite of French Jews.[33] Combining his old Fourierist anticapitalism with a new prophetic sense of the revolutionary mission of the Jewish people, he indicted his rich coreligionists not only in prose but also in polemical poetry.

> The Jew's millions, for whom do you exist?
> Does slavery persist?
> Are your poor brothers still in chains?
> To the oppressor you bow,
> Yesterday's slaves.—Does not still flow
> The martyr's blood in your veins?!!

[Million du Juif, qui sers-tu?
L'esclavage est-il abattu?
Tes pauvres frères sont-ils libres?
A l'oppresseur tu tends les bras,
Esclave d'hier.—Ne bout-il pas,
Le sang du martyr dans tes fibres?!!][34]

Weill directed his wrath both at converts from Judaism to Christianity[35] and at the lay members of the Consistory, who, although superficially remaining loyal to Judaism, actually betray its mission of progress by stubbornly resisting his ideas for reform.[36] Never hesitating to air Jewish dirty laundry in public, Weill nevertheless rallied in defense of Jewish causes. When he was in his 80s, he was one of the few French Jews to attack the antisemitism of Drumont in print.[37]

Throughout his life, Weill supplemented his various polemical and philosophical writings with fiction. According to his own account, he wrote his first works of fiction as a child, and he would continue to write stories for the next fifty years, publishing dozens of works in both newspapers and books. His novel *Couronne* (1857), which I examine later in this chapter, went through four editions and was one of his most widely read works.[38] Yet if Weill has been neglected as a Jewish thinker, he has been even more neglected as a Jewish writer; Friedmann's otherwise comprehensive intellectual biography pays almost no attention to his fiction. Although Weill's nonfiction writing contains little stylistic unity, his fiction bears the trace of a surprisingly coherent artistic vision. The vast majority of his fictional works fall into the category of the village tale, self-consciously simple narratives, usually told in a third-person narrative voice, that feature humble characters in a rustic setting and that document traditional occupations, manners, and religious practices in a lightly idealized manner. In characteristically immodest fashion, Weill claimed to have invented the village tale genre, before Berthold Auerbach in Germany and George Sand in France made it famous.[39] "I was the first to write village tales," Weill maintains in one of his prefaces. "Yes, it's true! I created a separate form."[40] This form, I want to argue in what follows, serves Weill as a remarkably supple instrument for the elaboration of his philosophical, theological, historical, and social theories about French Jews.

Gumper

Weill's description of his first encounter with French literature marks him as a man of his time. The first novel Weill read, like so many young people of his generation, both fictional and real, was Jacques-Henri Bernadin de Saint-Pierre's *Paul et Virginie* (1787), and the book aroused in him a new set of desires and longings. But whereas this sentimental novel, set largely on the island of Mauritius, inspires Flaubert's heroine Emma Bovary to dream of ill-fated love in exotic locales from her convent school in Normandy, it motivates the 15-year-old Talmudic student in Alsace to attempt to become an author. "I know a village tale that always made people cry when I told it," he informed his surprisingly liberal teacher, who lent him Bernadin's novel and encouraged him to imitate it.[41] The result—an early version of the novella later known as "Stasie" and then "Gumper" when Weill translated it into French—determined his subsequent literary development.

Set in the small Alsatian village of Sesenheim, the novella tells the story of a young Christian peasant woman (Stasie Kron) who relies on the help of her family's Jewish confidant (Gumper) to cope with a love affair gone awry. Although on the surface this early text is a cautionary narrative about the pitfalls of misplaced affection among Christians, it contains a reflection on the nature of Jewish identity that resonates in interesting ways with Weill's later, more explicitly Jewish fiction. At the start of the story, a dashing but caddish Christian named Marzolf has just returned to the village after having spent time in Nancy and Paris, where he took on airs and changed his name to Marceau. "He has become proud as a peacock,"[42] Gumper tells Stasie and her mother, also relating how the young man insulted him for being a Jew, despite the fact that Gumper arranged to have money sent to him during his travels. "He threatened to harm me, but he forgot that Old Gumper, Jewish though he may be, was a soldier in the army of Mayence [Mainz], and was at [the Battle of] Marengo" (12). Right from the start of the story, Weill makes it clear that Gumper's heroic past as a soldier in Napoleon's army distinguishes him as superior to the fatuous Marzolf, as does his enlightened, ecumenical friendship with the Christian Kron family, which contrasts with Marzolf's bigotry.

But even as he counters stereotypes of Jewish effeminacy and narrowness, Weill indulges in more conventional ways of portraying Jews. "I well know that you have a little sack filled with hundred *sous* pieces" (10), Stasie's mother playfully chides Gumper, who complains of the dowry he will have to provide for his daughter. Rather than expose the peasant woman's assumption about the Jew's hidden wealth as a misconception, the narrator bears it out. Indeed, Gumper embodies many of the negative characteristics of the typical Jewish moneylender, which Weill exploits for comic effect. A good bit of the humor of Gumper's character derives from his stinginess, which the text clearly associates with his Jewishness, albeit in a self-conscious and comic way. When Gumper advises Stasie not to buy a new dress to impress Marzolf, he jokes, "Take your example from my coat, which dates from '89 [1789]. . . . My motto is: One coat and one God!" (9). By appropriating the terms of antisemitic calumny to laugh at his own expense, Gumper disarms the prejudice of his Christian interlocutors. Weill treads a fine line, seemingly confirming stereotypes about Jews but subtly defusing their danger through humor.

A wily trickster figure who negotiates the amorous as well as business affairs of the Christian characters, Gumper enjoys a powerful role in the village. On one occasion, he manages to rescue Stasie from seduction at the hands of Marzolf, and when she later becomes pregnant with the cad's child, he intercedes on her behalf with Barbe, the mother of Marzolf's fiancée, another one of his Christian friends. "Barbe, we don't share the same religion," he tells her. "This isn't my fault, since I would have made a good Catholic. But there are some Catholics who would make very bad Jews" (44), he says in reference to Marzolf's unkosher behavior. Unfortunately his plea to allow Marzolf to marry the pregnant Stasie fails because Barbe's daughter, Catherine, is also pregnant with Marzolf's child. Having failed in his effort to get her married, Gumper takes Stasie to stay with him during her pregnancy to spare her mother the shame, and he lavishes on her advice as well as affection. "Learn, my child, that on this earth happiness never comes by avoiding duty" (51), he instructs.

Gumper demonstrates the moral importance of duty in his selfless devotion to the Kron family. We learn in the second part of the story that his loyalty to Stasie and her widowed mother dates back to the revolutionary wars. Reluctant to join the army because the revolutionary authorities had prevented Jews from practicing their religion, the young Gumper found himself in the army of the Republic without speaking a word of French and was at first taken for a German spy. Fortunately for him, his commanding officer was a kind Alsatian, Stasie's father, who instructs him how to be a soldier and a citizen: "So you don't even know that you have a homeland?—A homeland, I said to him, what is that?—You'll find that out later. In the meantime, take this gun, get in formation, and prove to me that you aren't a spy. You love your mother, you will love your homeland" (62). Although wounded in his first battle, Gumper quickly takes to army life and devotes himself completely to his commander, whom he serves for seven years. Disappointed by Napoleon's coup d'état, which put an end to his beloved Republic, Stasie's father dies shortly after his military discharge, but not before giving Gumper one more lesson in duty, this time instructing him in devotion to Judaism as well as to France: "He enjoined me to observe my religion strictly; often he even regretted not having any faith" (66), Gumper recounts to his daughter. The Jew's lessons about fidelity and obligation to Stasie thus represent the repetition of the lessons given to him by her father and typify Weill's vision of a shared fundamental moral code, which revolves around obligation to God and country, that unites France's Jews and Christians.

In the story's dénouement, Stasie's brother returns to the village and shoots Marzolf for having disgraced his sister. Before dying, however, Marzolf redeems himself by giving half his fortune to Stasie's child, proving that he has learned the lesson of "devoir." The story's final lines reproduce the words on the tombstone of Gumper, who we learn lived to the ripe age of 90: "Here lies Gumper, the first Jew to shed his blood for the homeland. He feared God, observed His laws, and was the faithful friend of his benefactor Adalbert Kron, one of the brave officers of the Army of Mayence" (83). Weill's return to Gumper at the end of his tale confirms the centrality of the Jew and his moral message to this story about Christian village life.[43] In the end, Gumper's values—fidelity and open-minded tolerance of others—triumph over selfishness, pettiness, and bigotry.

The words on Gumper's tombstone also inscribe Weill's story into a larger narrative of French Jewish emancipation. Although the tomb makes clear that Gumper observed Jewish law, it subordinates this religious fidelity to patriotic devotion to France. Aside from a few references to Gumper's kosher dietary habits, the narrative makes no reference to his actual religious practice or beliefs.[44] If the Jewish character plays a central role in the narrative, Judaism itself remains discreetly hidden from view. The vision of Jewish identity portrayed in this story thus exemplifies the Jacobin model forged during the emancipation period; the Jews retain their specific religious practices so long as they confirm that these do not conflict with the duties of citizenship, including military service. Their primary identification must be to France. Weill's first story exemplifies the values of emancipation, preaching an enlightened form of acculturation but not total assimilation. It shows how even a Jewish moneylender from a backward village can come to embody the values of the modern French citizen. Weill's later fictional works will depart from this model by exploring in greater detail the virtues of a specifically Jewish tradition. They will show how universal values can emerge from a particular form of Jewish religious engagement.

Village People

After Weill quit his rabbinical studies in Frankfurt and began to dream of moving to Paris, he cast about for a means of entering the literary marketplace.[45] Remembering the village tale he had written in French as a student, he reproduced it in German and managed to place it in a journal in 1838. Following the critical and popular success of this first work, other demands for village tales arrived from various German newspapers. The prospect of future earnings from his writing provided Weill with the incentive he needed to move to Paris, where he would later claim to have lived off the proceeds from his village tales for five years.[46] After publishing several more stories in German, he began to publish village tales in French in the mid-1840s in *Le Corsaire-Satan*, the small satirical newspaper that also published Henri Murger's *Scènes de la vie de Bohème*, about struggling artists in the Latin Quarter, in these same years. Weill would write about a dozen stories, many but not all of which centered on Jewish characters, as well as the novel *Couronne*, which also describes Alsatian Jewish village life.

"If I wrote village tales, it's because I made a virtue out of a necessity," Weill writes in the preface to an edition of his collected village tales in 1853, claiming that his lack of familiarity with Parisian salon society compelled him to portray the simpler rustic life he knew as a child.[47] But for as creative an author as Weill, whose ignorance of topics rarely prevented him from writing about them, one wonders whether familiarity alone impelled him to choose the village as a setting. Indeed, given that he continued to write village tales into his 50s, long after he came to know the salons of Paris, this explanation seems all the more lacking. Besides necessity, I want to ask, What other virtues did the village contain for Weill? What did rusticity allow him to say? And what, specifically, did it allow him to say about Jews?

I would like to begin to answer these questions by considering what readers of the time had to say about Weill's fiction. In their comments and reviews we see how the village became a site of intense ideological debate in mid-nineteenth-century France. One such contemporary reader was none other than George Sand, who congratulated Weill in an 1844 letter for having discovered "an inextinguishable vein for the popular and democratic novel."[48] Sand herself began to experiment with rustic fiction shortly after writing this letter, publishing *La mare au diable* [The Devil's Pool] in 1846, *François le champi* [François the Waif] in 1847, *La petite Fadette* [Little Fadette] in 1848, and *Les maîtres sonneurs* [The Bagpipers] in 1853. These works, which earned Sand her reputation as the master of the pastoral novel, represent Sand's own attempt to create a "popular and democratic" form of fiction, one that would draw its inspiration from the peasantry of her native Berry province. For Sand, fiction about peasants set in the villages of France gave voice to people who could not write for themselves and thus opened the novel not only to new subject matter but also to a new revolutionary political point of view.

Sand's first such novel, *La mare au diable*, published the same year that the word *folklore* entered the French language, also offered Sand the opportunity to document the local customs of her native province that she saw as in danger of disappearing.[49] The appendix to the novel describes the wedding between the two characters whose courtship constitutes the plot of the novel itself. "Certain customs are so strange, so curious," she writes, "that I hope to amuse you still for another second, dear reader" (154). Sand laments the rapid disappearance of the distinctiveness that she so admires: "Because, alas! Everything passes. In my lifetime alone there has been more movement in the ideas and in the customs of my village than was seen for centuries before the Revolution" (154). At the same time that Sand hopes to revolutionize the novel by opening it to the voices that the Revolution had empowered, she seeks to use it as a tool for preserving the very customs that the Revolution had endangered.

Jewish critics understood Weill's fiction to perform a similar function. "We congratulate Mr. Alex. Weill on this publication," writes Samuel Cahen, the editor of *Les Archives Israélites*, about Weill's novel *Couronne* upon its publication in 1857. "To present, in a dramatic form, these scenes of family life, so simple and so touching, is to fix that which is in the process of being lost thanks to the progress of civilization." Cahen singles out Weill's depiction of the Jewish matchmaker, who traveled between isolated villages in eastern France and western Germany to bring dispersed Jewish brides and grooms together but who played a much less important role in urban centers with large concentrations of Jews. By documenting the existence of this disappearing social type, Cahen argues, Weill's novel performs an important function for non-Jewish readers curious to learn about the distinctiveness of Jewish culture, for posterity, as well as for those Jewish readers in the present day, many of whom had themselves been born in small Alsatian villages and wished to reminisce. "*Couronne* will be read with pleasure and we recommend it to our readers," Cahen concludes.

Weill's fiction, however, is not merely documentary. He does indeed describe Jewish customs, beliefs, and character types that were in the process of disappearing in the 1840s and 1850s in France, as Jews continued their exodus from rural villages toward urban centers. But he also theorizes the nature of this transition. Far more than Sand's Berrichon peasants, Weill's Alsatian Jews face head-on the very processes of modernity that were rendering them extinct. Like Gumper, who served in Napoleon's army and became the first Jew to shed his blood for France, Weill's village people find themselves swept up in historical currents. His characters confront new ideas, new books, new values. His fictional works are about this confrontation. And significantly, his stories do not long nostalgically for the past. They may serve to document disappearing features of Jewish culture, but they also turn resolutely toward modernity.

Representing village life in mid-nineteenth-century France was a political act, linked to a certain kind of democratic or republican politics, but it was also an aesthetic act, one that forced the writer (or painter) to choose between realism and idealism. In contrast to the pastoral fantasies of eighteenth-century painters such as Watteau, in which well-fed shepherdesses in pretty pink dresses tend fluffy white sheep, artists and writers of the realist school of the mid-nineteenth century strove to depict the poverty and despair of country life. If religion offers Millet's peasants a respite from their backbreaking labor in such paintings as *The Angelus* (1857–1859), Courbet's vision of village life offers no such consolations. His monumental canvas, *Burial at Ornans* (1849–1850), shows ugly peasants and small town bourgeois in all their brute, unvarnished materiality. Even the drink-reddened priest displays little interest in the religious service he conducts.

A Jewish critic, writing in the scholarly journal *La Vérité Israélite*, to which Weill also contributed, praises Weill for steering a course between these two extremes: "Alexandre Weill is not an idealist of the school of the Watteaus and the Florians, nor a realist of the school of Courbet and Champfleury. . . . His peasants are not decked out in ribbons, nor dressed in tender pink and sky blue silk; but they are also not louts wallowing in mud and speaking an uncouth dialect."[50] Although, as we will see, Weill does allow some of the characters in *Couronne* to get muddied, he largely refrains from showing the material aspects of small town life. His characters do not wear silk dresses to draw water from the well, but neither do we see "their callused hands and their faces browned from the sun or frost."[51] Like Sand, Weill strives for a light touch, in which visual description of the physical world plays a small role. And whereas Balzac, a realist, comically renders the Germanic accent of his Alsatian Jewish banker Nucingen, Weill, like Sand, translates the thoughts and words of his provincial characters into standard French.

Ultimately, Weill and Sand share a similar political and aesthetic vision of village life. Following critics of the time, Naomi Schor calls this vision idealist. This is not, however, the decorative, pastoral idealism of Watteau. As we saw in the chapter on Ben-Lévi (Chapter 2), Sand's idealism consisted in an avoidance of realist description, a rejection of the aesthetics of Balzac and Courbet, but also in an ethical posture that foregrounded aspirations for a better, or ideal, world. As Schor points out, the lovesickness of Sand's heroines always contains democratic political longings. Weill's characters also express utopian impulses, but they do so from a specifically Jewish perspective. And whereas Sand's peasant characters exemplify a value system in opposition to modernity, Weill shows how village values can transform modernity.

For Weill, even more explicitly than for Sand, hope for solving the social and political problems of modern life springs from the least modern of places and from the least modern of people. "There is a whole world of difference between the village and the city," Weill writes in a preface to a collection of his village tales in 1853. "The city dweller is polite and cold. . . . In the village, by contrast, any peasant with a bit of natural wit is an original type, a character." This rawness of character derives in part from a lack of self-consciousness, a more unguarded experience of emotion among village dwellers. "Passion breaks out there in a flash and strikes like lightning."[52] But it also derives from proximity to traditional Jewish beliefs and practices.

Weill's characters may feel the winds of change blowing, but they remain firmly entrenched in an ancient culture. Their world is bounded by the routines of country life but most especially by Jewish laws and rituals. This tradition offers a kind of harmony and structure, based around the Jewish calendar and its multiple holidays. It also imposes a set of limitations, proscriptions, and superstitions that inhibit progress and impede development—all of which Weill would ascribe to the Talmud. For Weill's Jews, the village offers both the promise of organic meaning and the obstacle to Enlightenment. And yet it is precisely here, in the most primitive Jewish setting, that Weill discovers the path toward the future.

It is this paradox that animates Weill's fiction and that explains the fascination the village held for him. Along with their "Talmudic superstitions," Weill's village Jews have a seemingly direct access to the original core of Judaism, the ethical code of Mosaic monotheism. Weill finds in this code the solution to the ills of modernity, to the problem of social inequality, as well as the blueprint for a future of democratic egalitarianism. Sand would find something similar in the simple manners and customs of the Berrichon peasants, but for Weill, the Jewish tradition offers a genuinely universal moral code—albeit one obscured by Talmudic obfuscation. The question he poses to his characters is whether they will be able to free themselves from the mud of the village to find the ideal their culture contains.

Couronne

Weill's most widely read work, *Couronne*, subtitled *histoire juive* (meaning "Jewish story" but also "Jewish history"), offers a blueprint for this modernizing process. The novel takes place in the same kind of Alsatian village described in "Stasie"/"Gumper," only here the Jewish characters take center stage. At the start of the story, the unhappily married Mme. Riche, a pious Jewish woman whose husband speaks only of business and knows nothing of love, consults a sorcerer to help cure a pain in her breast. She feels an immediate connection with the hermit who fixes her with his penetrating gaze and "caresses" her breast. Her pain disappears immediately, leaving her swooning and mystified. "Fanatically religious and excessively prude, she was not able to make sense of the extraordinary feeling, the loss of consciousness, that overcame her in spite of herself."[53] A year later, she gives birth to a daughter she names Couronne, who strangely resembles the sorcerer.

In *Couronne*, Weill provides an example of the kind of passion that his unsophisticated village characters feel so spontaneously. Mme.

Riche has deep longings but lacks the ability to express them or even to understand the nature of her dissatisfactions. Her mysterious child, Couronne, emerges as a product of these unspoken desires. The narrator gives no indication that the sorcerer touched more than Mme. Riche's breast. Rather, he hints at a kind of communion of souls between Mme. Riche and the sorcerer, one that implies a longing on her part less for the supernatural as such than for an ideal realm that would transcend the crass materialism of her husband and the village itself. This aspiration toward the ideal will conflict with her practical impulses but will eventually triumph at the story's close.

The name of the family at the center of the story indicates both their social status and the materialist mind-set that governs all their actions and impulses: "Whether by nature or habit, M. Riche only spoke of commerce and business affairs" (2). A one-dimensional character who remains in the background of the story, M. Riche exists only as a foil to the more passionate natures of his wife and daughter. His materialism marks him as a certain kind of Jew, one not far removed from antisemitic caricature, despite his good looks and general probity. He is not scheming or grasping, simply focused on this world and its affairs. With the exception of Couronne, his children resemble him. Héva, Couronne's younger sister, "bursting with freshness and stupidity" (9), cares nothing about books or music and cannot speak a word of French—a sign of her backwardness. She feels frustrated that she must postpone her marriage to the fatuous Léon until Couronne has found a husband. True to her family name, "Héva was a woman perfectly suited for a rich man lacking ideals" (11). Wearing dresses that are "always dirty with the mud of the village" (71), in what is a departure from Weill's idealized exclusion of filth, Héva incarnates the earthbound materialism that sullies small-town Jewish life.

Couronne differs from her siblings both physically and spiritually. Made to do housework and compared at one point to Cinderella (71), she receives only discouragement from her family and consoles herself for their misunderstanding by offering charity to their Christian neighbor (Mme. Sommer). Mme. Riche herself is caught between these extremes, between the secret yearnings of her passionate nature, which produced Couronne, and the conventional demands of village life.

Stifled by her husband's materialism—"Her wedding day was for her like a violent stifling of her heart" (3)—she longs especially for love. She nevertheless remains strictly observant of all religious regulations and adopts the prejudices of her family and neighbors: "Mme. Riche could not help herself . . . from believing, in certain moments, that Couronne was, if not exactly ugly, at least much less beautiful than Héva" (10). Although it is Couronne who lends her name to the story, in many ways Mme. Riche is its real heroine; it is her transformation, her gradual acceptance of the ideal world she has longed for, that will constitute the novel's climax.

Conflict enters the novel in the form of Elias Seibel, a new schoolmaster, who has come to the village for health reasons and who asks to lodge in the home of the Riches, the largest and best-situated house in the village. Mme. Riche at first refuses on the grounds that with two unmarried daughters at home it "would be like letting a fox guard the henhouse" (41). One of her sons, however, manages to convince her that the young teacher "is so small, so frail, so ugly" (44) that he poses no danger and that Héva in particular needs instruction. "You don't know a word of French, and yet you are a Frenchwoman" (42), he tells his sister, implying that contact with French culture will improve her chances of marrying Léon. Mme. Riche eventually consents to give Elias a room but remains on her guard against him, both because she distrusts secular education and because she disapproves of his family background. The son of a "Jewish used clothes seller from Haguenau" (46) who lived for years as a virtual beggar, Elias studied both the Talmud and secular subjects before abandoning his dreams of the rabbinate on account of his weak lungs.

The narrator discourses at length on Elias's physical defects, which seem at first to belie the homonymic resonance of his name (Seibel = c'est bel = "it's beautiful"). "He was as thin as he was small, with arms like spindles and legs no bigger than those of a stork" (50). But although lacking the manly attributes of strength and force prized by the villagers, Elias possesses eyes that provide an indication of his noble spiritual qualities: "He would have been monstrously ugly if it hadn't been for his eyes, which were very expressive, with their blue gaze revealing a strong will tempered by great kindness" (50). The narrator makes it clear that Elias's particular kind of beauty does not appear to anyone but only to those whose own elevated spirituality allows them to recognize a kindred spirit. Still bound by convention, Mme. Riche sees only "the size, the nose, the arms, and the legs of her future boarder" (50), whereas Couronne immediately recognizes in Elias exactly the qualities she longs for in a husband.

Mistaking Couronne for the maid, Elias admires her as well: "What a nobility in the traits of that divine creature! Thus must have Rebecca seemed to Moses about whom he said: 'She is beautiful of face and gracious to behold!'" (65). This Old Testament citation foreshadows the extent to which the teacher will become the mouthpiece for Weill's theory of Mosaic monotheism, for the supposedly pure form of Judaism that Weill believed contained the seeds for societal renewal. But just as Weill would complain that the materialistic modern French Jews obstructed the realization of his Mosaic mission, so too does the Riche family—and in particular Mme. Riche—oppose the union of Couronne with the beggar's son. "In Alsace," the narrator explains, "for the peasants as much as for the village Jews, the lines of social demarcation were more clear and more rarely crossed than in the interior of France and in the cities" (74). Although Weill's narrator makes it clear that such social snobbery is not exclusively Jewish, he also remarks how Mme. Riche clings more tightly to her social position "than a duchess of the Faubourg Saint-Germain" (74) and would be far less likely than such a duchess to give her daughter to a lowly schoolmaster.

And yet one exception contradicts the rigidity of this hierarchy: Among traditional Jews, religious learning trumps wealth and entitles its bearer to his choice of marriage partner. "Among the Orthodox Jews . . . one noble trait was equal to all the others, that of Talmudic science allied with great piety" (74–75). This valorization of learning over money might seem to redeem the Orthodox Jews from the taint of materialism. In theory, it signals the kind of elevation of the ideal over the material that the narrator continually valorizes. In practice, however, it falls short. The type of learning that the Orthodox Jews of the village value is "Talmudic science," the kind of hairsplitting casuistry that Weill continually denounced. The "great piety" that must accompany Talmudic learning also smacks in this formulation of a concern for the letter of the law over its substance and differs from the kind of unconventional religious devotion that inspires Elias. Despite his irreproachable morals, Elias's familiarity with secular culture arouses suspicion in the village: "Even though he never violated a single rabbinic law, like all scholars of profane subjects, he passed for a freemason, harboring heretical desires for reform, and not believing in anything deep down in his heart" (75). As one who teaches "profane subjects" rather than becoming a rabbi, Elias cannot look for a wife beyond his station.

Elias gives lessons to both Couronne and Héva. But whereas Héva cares only for romances and music, Couronne pores over the serious books Elias gives her to read, such as Mendelssohn's translation of the Old Testament and the tomes of the ancient Jewish historian Josephus. Although careful to lock away "any book that resembled a novel" (78), Elias one day accidentally leaves *Paul et Virginie* on his nightstand. Couronne devours it in a single sitting, crying over the fate of the doomed heroine who finds a soul mate in her childhood friend but dies before consummating their love. Her mother, whose sole "poetic" reading consists of Josephus's account of the destruction of the Temple in Jerusalem, chastises her daughter for her profane sensitivity: "Is it possible that a daughter of honest Jews weeps over a story written by a pagan?" (98), she asks in a hysterical rage, misunderstanding the sublime (and sublimated) nature of the love at the center of the novel. Accusing Elias of having cast a spell, she rips the book to shreds over Couronne's head.

Unwilling to be the cause of strife between mother and daughter, Elias accepts a teaching position in Algeria. All the villagers—both Catholic and Jewish—come to say good-bye and even Mme. Riche feels a pang of regret: "She only detested the young man so much because at the bottom of her heart she approved of her daughter's actions" (105), the omniscient narrator reveals. Mme. Riche admits to herself that she prefers Elias to Léon, but still a slave to the material, she cannot condone such a poor match for her daughter. For Couronne, as for Elias, love has nothing to do with such crass worldly calculations. Nor does it involve the kind of physical desire that more modern readers would call sex and that the philosophically inclined narrator refers to as "egotism of the body" (112). Rather, it leads to an overcoming of the body and its material surroundings: "Indeed, love is a desire to transcend the self and to be reflected in a superior soul" (112), the narrator explains. Like Sand's lovelorn heroines, Couronne imbues her carnal passions with utopian ideals.

For Couronne, "in the soul of whom there had never entered a material thought" (113), the loss of her love object leads to a profound ennui that saps her physical strength precisely because it denies her hope for a transcendence of the physical. A rebuke to her family and to the entire culture of materialism surrounding her, Couronne prefers to die rather than surrender her ideal love. Elias shares her disregard for the constraints of mere physicality: "What does it matter if our bodies marry or not," he writes her from his Algerian exile, "since, from what you tell me, our souls are indissolubly married, even though three hundred leagues apart" (140). In this portrait of sublime abnegation, Weill implicitly criticizes the materialism of traditional Jewish life but also reveals that a hidden idealism lurks within the Jewish tradition.

Desperate to save her daughter from wasting away, Mme. Riche contracts with a matchmaker to find a suitable husband. In a comic interlude, Couronne rejects all these suitors, even an Orthodox horse trader who is "neither brutal nor a fool" and who knows how to speak and write French "better than any lawyer" (126). To punish her for her refusal, Mme. Riche dictates a letter to Elias in which she casts scorn on his impoverished origins: "Your father, Sir, was called Jacob the Fool, Jacob the Used Clothes Man, Jacob the Cheat" (161), she insults. Couronne submits to the dictation, reminding herself that her mother, "like all uneducated village women, only understands marriage as a way of becoming rich" (11) and musing that her own family's prosperity, like that of nearly all Jews, does not go back more than a single generation. After mailing the insulting letter at her mother's bidding, Couronne rereads a note from Elias in which he criticizes Jewish pretensions to worldly grandeur: "Who would believe, Elias had written, that a Jew, whose sole and unique nobility lies in his abstract religion, whose ancestors had been slaves and were treated for eighteen hundred years like outlaws that one could pillage and kill with impunity, who would believe that a Jew would swell with pride because of his fortune, or worse, because of his birth?" (166). For Elias, as for his creator, Weill, Jews err by overestimating worldly wealth when their true treasure lies in the Mosaic core of their monotheism. True Judaism is inherently democratic and egalitarian.

The climax of the family conflict occurs during the celebration of Passover. Weill describes the Jewish festivity in great detail, weaving the clash over Elias into the seder ritual commemorating the deliverance of the Jews from slavery in Egypt. After the traditional prayer announcing the desire for a return to Israel ("This year we are here; next year we shall be in the land of Israel"), Couronne's brother suggests a patriotic substitution: "That prayer, said the son of the house, should be rewritten. I don't want to return to Jerusalem at all. I vote that we substitute Paris in its place" (171). Echoing what had become a common liberal argument for reform of the liturgy to reflect the new postemancipation situation of Jews in France, the son finds himself contradicted by Couronne, who argues for a different interpretation of the Passover narrative: "You already made that observation last year," she tells him, "and Elias who was here proved to you that as long as all people do not recognize the abstract and unique God of the Bible, the Jews, whether in Europe, Asia, or Africa, will always be martyrs to the ideal of Moses" (171). Couronne here voices the view that deliverance from slavery in Egypt can only mean a return to the true home of the Jews, not the physical land of Israel but the abstract spiritual home of Mosaic monotheism. The emancipation solution advocated by the brother that would substitute Paris for Jerusalem also misses the mark by remaining too fixated on the material rather than the ideal form of communal salvation.

Couronne's intervention arouses her mother's ire: "Enough already, cried the mother, who was afraid that they were talking too much about Elias" (171). But just like his namesake, the prophet Elijah, who haunts all Jewish homes on Passover, Elias enters in spirit through the door left open by Couronne's ventriloquizing of his views. When it comes time to eat the bitter herb symbolizing the suffering of the Jews in Egypt, Couronne declares that it will kill her if she ever betrays her love. "So I raised a shiksa (pagan woman),[54] a libertine straight out of a novel" (174), declares a scandalized Mme. Riche, who misunderstands once again the nature of her daughter's passion, mistaking it for a physical desire. The simplistic Héva then joins the protest against their mother: "Like a good Frenchwoman, I hope to love my husband" (176). Héva's embrace of French values, like her brother's, becomes a sign not of progress but of crass materialism and sensuality. Her assertion of romantic self-determination, while certainly modern, only underscores the degree to which Couronne's rebellion has a far less selfish motivation.

Eventually Mme. Riche relents, preferring to let Couronne marry Elias than to watch her die of heartbreak. "Ah, I have a mother, cried Couronne" (189), who immediately writes to Elias to tell him to return to France. When Mme. Riche learns from a neighbor that the former schoolmaster has become successful in Algeria, she fears that Elias will misinterpret her change of heart as a form of self-interest. Recognizing that her transformation came from love not greed, however, Elias has the good grace to pretend not to have received her injurious letter. He also recognizes the true morality at the core of Mme. Riche's being: "You, Couronne . . . along with the lessons that I gave you, you perfected your soul by reading serious books . . . but your mother, who has never read a book, and who was raised with all sorts of religious superstitions, never saw anything but examples of egotism and brutality; your mother, who has never spoken to a distinguished man, had to find and create everything within her own soul" (219). Accomplished without the aid of education or outside intervention of any kind, Mme. Riche's feat of moral regeneration testifies to the inherent perfectibility of even the most backward of village Jews. Beneath her superstition, prejudice, snobbery, misguided piety, and overwhelming materialism, we learn, lies a moral center capable of appreciating the call of the ideal.

The surprise ending of the story, however, describes the nature of this ideal in terms that call its specifically Jewish nature into question. As Elias and Couronne prepare to return to Algeria, Mme. Riche declares her desire to accompany them. The couple react with trepidation because they fear offending her religious sensibilities. "It is time to say it all, because you have as much intelligence as you have heart," Couronne says to her mother.

> You are pious and religious, I am as well; but you insist on observing all the Orthodox prescriptions of the Talmud and the rabbis. You have your kitchen, your separate dishes; you don't light a fire on Saturday; you would die rather than pray in a Christian church. Well, Elias and I, even while being proud of our religion, believe in the progress of Christian life, and want to live according to the law of this progress. You are free to live as you please, but you may not want to tolerate our manner of living! (225)

At first glance, Couronne's speech to her mother seems to announce her intention to convert to Christianity. But on closer inspection, the resolution to accept "the progress of Christian life" and to live "according to the law of this progress" indicates less outright apostasy than a willingness to depart from the "Orthodox prescriptions" that govern traditional village life, such as keeping kosher dishes and refusing to light a fire on the Sabbath. Couronne's implied willingness to pray in a Christian church bespeaks an open-minded tolerance of other faiths rather than a desire to join them, for she and Elias remain "proud" of their Judaism. Although nothing indicates an actual acceptance of Christian beliefs or doctrine (no mention is made of Christ), progress in this novel becomes synonymous with the liberation from the "yoke of the Talmud" and from the host of rules that keep Jews from participating fully in a culture still dominated by Christians.

In the novel's closing lines, Mme. Riche agrees to abandon her old ways and to live in Algeria according to the laws of "progress," even if it means violating the religious rules and regulations she had formerly obeyed out of fear for her future salvation. "I want to share with you the same paradise and the same hell" (225), she tells them, in terms that reverse the biblical story in which the widowed Ruth becomes Jewish in order to accompany her mother-in-law, Naomi. Here it is the mother-in-law who adopts the religion of her son-in-law and daughter: "The faith of my children is my faith, the religion of my children is my religion, and the God of my children will be my God!" (225), she declares. The young husband and wife appreciate the difficulty of her sacrifice: "Next to your mother," Elias tells Couronne, "we are only inferior beings. She alone knows love, she alone is great!" (225). At the novel's end, the pious, superstitious, ignorant, materialistic Jewish mother-in-law becomes the very paragon of progress, the model for a new kind of Jew who will help spread the ideals of Mosaic monotheism to the still unregenerated Jews of Algeria.

Written during a period of transition for Weill, just after he broke with the Catholic legitimists to devote his energies to a reconsideration of Jewish texts, *Couronne* reflects an ambivalence if not toward Judaism in its essence, then toward the Jewish religion in its postbiblical incarnation and toward the Jews who practice it in France's eastern provinces. Although the novel reveals that progress can come from within the Jewish tradition—and that regeneration is possible even for the most backward of village Jews—it nevertheless views traditional Talmudic Judaism as an obstacle to future development. Hope lies in transcending Jewish tradition in order to return to the original Mosaic core of the religion, in which Weill (through his mouthpiece Elias) finds the basis for a postemancipation ethics based on social equality and rationality.

Late Stories

Weill's later village tales no longer espouse a rejection of Judaism's outward forms in order to access its inner truths. Published for the first time in an 1860 edition of his collected village tales, both "Braendel" and "Kella" imagine itineraries for their central characters that negotiate the perils of modernity while remaining firmly anchored in Orthodoxy. In these late works, Weill advocates more explicitly Jewish solutions to the problems of materialism and spiritual impoverishment that afflict Jews in modernity. He still advocates a return to an essential Mosaic monotheism, but he no longer sees rabbinic or Talmudic Judaism as such a formidable obstacle on the path to this realization.

"Braendel" begins with a Jewish genealogy that links its central characters to a religious tradition of suffering and piety deeply rooted in the history of the region. "Braendel was a young Jewish woman born in an Alsatian village near Strasbourg. Her grandmother was the great-granddaughter of a rabbi from Mayence who, during a popular riot, was crushed to death in a wine press when he refused to worship an image of the Virgin. Her father was a religious scribe."[55] Whereas in Weill's earlier stories, such a rabbinic filiation might signal backwardness—the stubborn adherence to the arcana of the Talmud—in this later work, it marks the nobility of the central character. The ancestor's martyrdom for refusing to worship the Christian image does not signal his obstinacy but rather his superior fortitude in remaining true to the more abstract (and hence, for Weill, higher) practice of Judaism. The father's profession as a sacred writer, or scribe of religious texts, reinforces the affiliation of this family with the culture of the word. We later learn that Braendel's father worked for Robespierre during the Revolution—like Weill's own much admired grandfather, mitigating religious Orthodoxy with revolutionary politics—another clear sign of the family's moral superiority.

An orphan, Braendel lives with her grandmother, who earns a pittance making tzitzit, which the narrator explains are the fringes of wool that Orthodox Jews attach to their clothing and prayer shawls. Braendel supplements the tiny income from this trade by collecting wood in the forest. As in *Couronne*, Weill's narrator pays special attention to the social divisions within the rural Jewish community, pointing out that although they are the poorest of the poor, Braendel and her grandmother enjoy a privileged status: "Because among religious Jews, from the days of Moses to our own time, there is only one form of nobility, that of the sacred science and of virtue" (213). Once again, the Mosaic value system at the heart of Judaism is shown to contradict modernity's emphasis on material success and to contain the seeds of a more democratic social organization.

The worthy inheritors of their pious ancestors, Braendel and her grandmother know all the prayers and religious traditions and officiate at all religious celebrations. (They are also great Jewish cooks, a virtue Weill also emphasizes in many of his works.) This knowledge gives them the right to feel superior to their rich but ignorant neighbors: "The grandmother of Braendel, despite her poverty, looked down with a haughty scorn upon all the horse traders, dry goods merchants, and prosperous industrialists. They were for her so many *am haarazim*, which is to say ignorant commoners" (213). The use of the Hebrew term for the uneducated, *am haarazim*, which the narrator translates, signals the grandmother's own intellectual elevation, her deep familiarity with biblical Jewish sources.[56] The story's central conflict will turn on this rivalry between the aristocracy of learning, associated with an older Jewish tradition, and the new domination of wealth, which the narrator describes as a corruption brought by modernity.

As in all Weill's stories, a romantic dilemma brings this conflict to the fore. Although the grandmother declares she would rather see Braendel dead than married to an "*am haarez*, even a millionaire" (216), she bridles when the young woman declares she has fallen in love with Joël, a Talmudic student from the village. As Braendel recounts, Joël saved her from an attack by a "goy soldier"—*goy* being another Hebrew term the narrator takes the trouble to define as "anything that isn't Jewish" (217)—and now she sees it as her duty to save him from the even worse fate of having to abandon his studies. The recent scandal of a series of conversions at the rabbinical academy in Metz has terrified all the pious families of budding scholars, including Joël's parents, who want him to return home to take over the family horse-trading business and remain a pious, if uneducated, Jew. "From tomorrow on, I have heard, Joël will cease to be a student and will don the smock of the horse trader. What a sacrilege!" (217), Braendel declares. When her grandmother objects that a brazen declaration of love does not become an Orthodox Jewish woman, Braendel cites the biblical precedent of Rachel's love for Jacob. Jewish women, she maintains, display virtue through their fidelity to a worthy man.

But is Joël worthy? What does worthiness entail? The story attempts to respond to these questions through an inquiry into the nature of Jewish ethics. The narrator provides the basis for an answer by means of a long description of Joël's family background, which would seem exemplary—to conventional observers at least. His father, we learn, made a fortune during the Empire selling horses to the army and passes for one of the wealthiest men in the village. Completely devoted to "the Talmudic religion," he observes all the Jewish rules and regulations with a scrupulous exactitude. "He was even fanatical in his devotion. Now, a fanatical Jew only poses a threat to his coreligionists; he would give his last penny to a Catholic friend but not a crust of bread to a Jew who violated one of the 613 affirmative commandments, not to mention the innumerable prohibitions" (218–219) of the Talmud. Clearly, a piety bordering on fanaticism does not equate with morality for Weill's narrator. Although careful to contradict the popular antisemitic belief that the Talmud encourages Jews to cheat Christians, the narrator mocks the self-righteousness of the supposedly religious Jew who denies charity to his less observant brethren. Here, once again, the Talmud receives blame for emphasizing rules at the expense of a more humane ethics.

And yet the learning that Braendel and her grandmother prize so highly is Talmudic in nature. This apparent contradiction can be explained by the implicit distinction drawn in the story between devotion to the Talmud and study of it. Weill directs his wrath at Talmudic "fanatics," the unenlightened mass of Jews concerned only with observing the letter of the law, and contrasts them with the select few who devote themselves to understanding its deeper meaning. Significantly, however, Braendel has not studied the Talmud. Denied access to the sacred book because of her gender, she has delved instead into the Bible and Josephus's Jewish history. Unlike most Jewish women who read these works "in a German translation, printed in little Hebrew characters" (214), which is to say in Yiddish, Braendel knows Hebrew. Grounded in the Pentateuch, Braendel preaches a higher or purer form of Judaism, becoming a priestess of Weill's Mosaic monotheism.

Joël himself remains caught between his family's desire that he remain an uneducated but observant Jew and his own aspirations to a higher life of the mind. Although he obeys his father's commandment to return home and enter the family business, and even takes to drinking with Christian boys from the village, he regrets having given up his studies. One night, after falling asleep in the forest, he dreams that an angelic figure commands him to return to his books. He wakes up to see Braendel, who has come to gather wood and who resembles the figure in his dream. She continues the antimaterialist discourse of the angel: "What is an animal trader? An *am haarez*, a coarse soul who feels nothing, who is nothing. How can you whom God destined to become a hasid, a zaddik (just, holy man), one of the first sons of Israel, how can you debase yourself in this manner and murder your spirit and your soul?" (226). Bemoaning the fact that Jewish law prevents women from studying, she commands him to do what she cannot. He agrees and begs to marry her. "Be a rabbi and I will be yours," she declares. "Stay a horse dealer and I will snuff out my love along with my life" (228). Braendel's ultimatum makes her an even more strong-willed figure than Couronne, who defers to her lover's religious vision. In the later story, it is the female character who points the way toward the ideal.

Unfortunately, Joël lacks Elias's strength of will, his ability to sublimate and suffer. Whereas Braendel conceives of their love as a way to encourage Joël to study, he has more carnal interests. How, he asks, can he embrace "big books in the place of these fresh pink lips?" (231). Horrified at his sensual materialism, she fears that she has misplaced her affection and fasts in order to destroy the beauty that has served only to distract Joël from higher pursuits. But the disappointment she feels in his weakness for the flesh does not prevent her from rising to an even greater sacrifice. In the story's climax, Joël has an accident while returning from a market in a neighboring village, where he has gone to sell horses and buy a new dress for Braendel as a peace offering. When he does not return for the celebration of the Jewish festival of Purim, Braendel anxiously demands that the men of the village go in search of him. Finally she sets off herself, borrowing a horse from the Catholic mayor of the village, but she has a terrible accident. The guilty villagers find her dying in the forest, victim to her generosity and nobility of spirit. At her funeral, all come to pay their final respects, Jews and Christians alike.

The story ends with Braendel's burial in a simple coffin. "The Jews always bury their dead in this manner, without distinction of fortune or birth" (251). Before the great leveler of death, Weill isolates the true democratic ideals at the heart of Judaism, ideals that the growing culture of materialism obscures. Through her death, Braendel thus unites the village divided by religion and class. From beyond the grave, she also achieves the even more difficult goal of encouraging Joël once and for all to devote himself to study. In the epilogue we learn that profane subjects at times shook his "Talmudic faith" and that he even found himself tempted by conversion, but "always the image of Braendel inserted itself between his heart and his head" (252). Although he leaves the village, one presumes for Strasbourg or Paris, and comes to occupy a "high social position" (252), he never fails to visit Braendel's tomb every time he returns to rural Alsace, placing on it a small stone in accordance with Jewish custom.

In "Braendel" the answer to the problem of modernity for Jews lies in the Jewish religion itself and specifically in the study of its sacred texts, including the Talmud. A bulwark against the temptations of materialism, religious study, when aimed not at fanatic observance but at higher spiritual truths, points the way toward the ideal. This ideal, as in all of Weill's stories, is not only a Jewish one, however. Grounded in social justice, in a democratic form of equality and solidarity, the values that Braendel devotes herself to promoting are the universal values of the French revolutionary tradition. Weill's story shows how universal values emerge from the Jewish tradition at its most basic level—not from the blind following of Jewish law, which leads to a narrow self-righteousness, but rather from study of the most sacred of books, the Jews' greatest gift to Western culture, the five books of Moses.

Clearly, however, not everyone can become a rabbi like Joël or a martyred seer like Braendel. In "Kella," also published in 1860, Weill explores how modest everyday Jews can also achieve redemption through a reengagement with the roots of Jewish tradition. Like all of Weill's village tales, the story takes place in a rural setting near Strasbourg. The narrative begins with a peddler named Kalman taking a shortcut through the woods in order to reach home by the start of the Sabbath at sundown. "He was a Jew, and observed his religion with fervor and exactitude,"[57] the narrator informs, while also pointing out that the peddler does not understand the meaning of the prayers he repeats faithfully and does not know how to read Hebrew. But whereas Weill frequently associates unschooled piety with moral backwardness, particularly when it is linked with material wealth, the figure of Kalman takes on the contours of the ideal, probably because of his poverty. "Poor and having no other education aside from his deceased mother's biblical maxims, for the past six years he had been supporting his old father and his young sister" (456). More concerned with building a fortune than with the complexities of theology, Kalman represents a new kind of hero for Weill: a man whose morality—indicated here by his selfless devotion to family—develops out of his banal form of village Judaism, not in spite of it.

In the forest, Kalman comes upon Tony, a robust Catholic laborer who he assumes will rob him. Although he needs money after having been fired by his evil boss, Jokel, for falling in love with Jokel's daughter, Mariegrète, Tony is offended by Kalman's distrust. The peddler and the laborer quickly become friends, a bond reinforced by the fact that Kalman's Jewish fiancée, Kella, shares a close bond with the Catholic Mariegrète and may be able to speak in Tony's favor. As in "Stasie"/"Gumper" the Christian and Jewish village dwellers enjoy excellent relations in this story. The bond between the two women, we learn, developed when Kella came to cook for Mariegrète's ailing mother, which allows the narrator to indulge in a long discourse on the glories of Jewish food—a clear interest of Weill's. But this association between Jews and Christians can work for evil as well as for good: Jokel employs a Jew named Zodek to deal with his unsavory business affairs, including usury.

The other Jews in the village detest Zodek for his lowly dealings, which give Jews a bad name: "Through his scandals and his lawsuits, he provoked what they called, in their language, a *hilel hashem*. In other words, instead of glorifying the Jewish religion through his virtues, he blasphemed and exposed it to the scorn of Christians" (474). In synagogue, where Zodek goes faithfully to pray on Saturdays, he finds himself shunned. Only the saintly Kella sees the redeeming features of the sinner's nature, the fact that he loved his mother and wept for her after her death. Zodek, however, justifies his neighbors' dislike; jealous of Kella's love for Kalman, he falsely accuses the peddler and Tony of having set a fire in Jokel's barn. The two friends are arrested to the horror of their fellow villagers, who believe in their innocence.

As in many of his stories, Weill weaves the climax into the celebration of one of the major festivities marking the Jewish yearly calendar.

Whereas the crisis leading to Couronne's marriage took place during Passover and Braendel undertook her ill-fated journey to save Joël on Purim, in "Kella" the high holidays of Rosh Hashanah and Yom Kippur furnish the background to dramatic events that bring the narrative to its conclusion. As the narrator explains, on these holidays Jews face the reckoning of God for their sins; those whom God finds deserving or those who repent sincerely for their sins get inscribed in the Book of Life for the upcoming year. Zodek harbors a belief in what the narrator refers to as the Talmudic "superstition" of pardon: "He often broke the law on Sabbath observance and on abstinence. But he would never have not appeared in synagogue on the day of Rosh Hashanah, believing deep down, like all hypocritical pious men, that it suffices to weep and to beat your breast while mumbling Hebrew prayers in order to get yourself inscribed in the great book, and that you are free to sin again the day after Yom Kippur" (488). For Weill, who believed that the notion of pardon represented a foreign or pagan import and a corruption of the Mosaic purity of the Jewish religion, Zodek's criminal actions and superstitious belief in Yom Kippur are of a piece. By allowing for the notion of repentance, the Talmud lets Jews off the hook.

At Kella's urging, the rabbi agrees to set a trap for Zodek, using his sermon to preach against those who bear false witness. As expected, Zodek starts to sweat when he hears the rabbi's words and ends by giving a full confession. The criminal Jew's superstitious beliefs work against him. In the story's happy conclusion, the police arrest Jokel and release Kalman and Tony, who go on to marry Kella and Mariegrète, respectively. The two couples then move to Paris, where they take up occupations in keeping with their abilities and stations: Kalman owns a stationery store and Tony becomes a locksmith. Nodding toward the modernizing trends that drove Jews from their Alsatian villages to the Parisian metropolis throughout the nineteenth century, the story reveals how even simple Jews can achieve happiness and success. Unlike Couronne and Elias or Braendel and Joël, who find solutions to the evils of modernity through an intellectual engagement with the sources of the Jewish tradition, the couple at the center of "Kella" follows a more mundane path. Excelling at the humbler arts of cooking and trade, Kalman and Kella demonstrate their ethics through actions, not words, through practice, not theory.

The story itself, however, provides yet another demonstration of Weill's own rather more abstract theories on Judaism. Zodek is undone by his "pagan" beliefs; encouraged in his criminal actions by the supernatural doctrine of pardon, which Weill thought represented an alien import into Judaism, he allows himself to be trapped by the same false notion. Kella, however, offers the basis for a more rational Jewish ethics. Visiting Zodek in prison after his confession, she advises him to live his life according to moral precepts: "Conduct yourself well during your solitary confinement, and especially don't forget God, the judge of judges" (494). Promising to help him if he redeems himself through proper conduct, she demands a sign of his good will. Zodek obliges by making a clean confession of all his evil actions, not, significantly, in order to free himself from otherworldly punishment but in order to begin a new life of ethical conduct. As the story seeks to demonstrate, the law is absolute. But even if there is no cosmic pardon, there is earthly forgiveness once one has accepted responsibility for one's actions. In the epilogue, we learn that after his prison term, Zodek went to America, where he earned a fortune through honest work. The final lines show Kella and Kalman inviting him to join them in Paris and promising to let him marry Kalman's sister—worldly rewards for a life lived within the bounds of Jewish law.

Returning Home

Alexandre Weill was a restless writer, a true Wandering Jew. He shifted between languages, political positions, and genres of writing throughout his long career. Like him, his characters are on the move in literal as well as figurative ways. In *Couronne*, the protagonists opt at the end for colonial Algeria as the best place to remake their lives according to the laws of progress. The conclusion of "Kella" has the central characters choose Paris to begin their life anew, although America also represents a place in which fortunes can be made by honest and enterprising Jews. Weill's fiction continually asks the same question: Where do Jews belong? The answers he provides reflect his unique approach to the vexed problems of Jewish modernity.

In *Couronne*, when the characters debate the meaning of the Passover ritual, the heroine criticizes her brother for suggesting that Paris replace Jerusalem as the destination of choice for the Jews. Rejecting both traditional Jewish national hopes as well as the modern French faith in emancipation, she suggests that a true homeland exists only in the mind and in an ethical posture derived from a strict Mosaic monotheism. The material opportunities afforded by Paris, and by extension the privileges of citizenship for which Paris stands as a metonym, mean nothing in the absence of moral perfection. The irony of Couronne's choice of Algeria as a place in which such perfection can best be realized cannot help but strike the reader aware of the injustice of the colonial situation. Weill, for all his political progressiveness, was not attuned to colonialist injustice, and Algeria represented for him merely a place in the throes of change, where it was possible for Jews to remake themselves.

At the end of his life, the outpouring of a new, much more violent antisemitism in France caused Weill to view the question of a Jewish homeland in new ways. Weill had always been acutely—I'm tempted to say, uniquely—aware of the dangers that Jews in France faced and of the precariousness of their situation. As early as the 1860s, he warned of a rising tide of antisemitism visible to few at the time. By the 1880s, when Édouard Drumont's *La France juive* (1886) confirmed his worst fears by denouncing the Jews as rootless invaders who had appropriated the nation's wealth for their own profit, Weill was thus able to respond in a way that other French Jews were not. In *Épîtres cinglantes à M. Drumont* (1888), he defends his religion—even the Talmud he spent his life attacking—against the false accusations of Drumont, arguing that the Mosaic faith gave to humanity the basis for a truly universal morality. He defends his coreligionists in similar terms, drawing a line between the bad bankers who deserve the reprobation Drumont heaps on them and the Jewish masses who struggle to live according to ethical precepts and who have as much moral and spiritual, as well as political, right to live in France as any Catholic.

At the close of this document, however, he addresses a startling confession to his antisemitic adversary: "I want to make a confession to you. If there were a Jewish Republic in Palestine, one that proclaimed not the stupid religion of the rabbis whose religious foolishness borders on senile idiocy and from which emerged nonsensical dogmatic Christianity, which borders on dementia, but the pure universal religion of Moses . . . I would gladly leave you to go die in Jerusalem."[58] Formulated before the beginning of the political Zionist movement, Weill's suggestion that he would leave France for Jerusalem represents a dangerous admission to a man who accused the Jews of not belonging in France.[59] Justifying his moniker as the prophet of the Faubourg Saint-Honoré, he seems to call for a Jewish nationalist solution to the problem of modernity, one that the other writers I discuss in this book did not consider. Once again, of course, Weill qualifies his admission by describing the "Jewish republic" in ideal terms, less as a place on earth than as a utopian hope for the future. Weill would have little interest in a Jewish state that did not live up to his moral ideals.

In the meantime, he makes clear, the Jews have only one real home. "But, from here on in, there is only one homeland for which the Jew must sacrifice his fortune and even his life, the one that assures him the rights of man and citizen" (24). Weill does not need to pronounce the word *France* to make it clear which country he means. Weill may have dreamt of creating a Jewish homeland in which the values of pure Mosaic monotheism would reign, but in the short term he saw France as the closest thing to this heaven on earth. And France, or his vision of it, was worth defending as a homeland for the Jews. I would note that Weill says "Jews" rather than "Israelites," signifying an interpretation of the terms by which his coreligionists might lay their claim to Frenchness that is different from that of most nineteenth-century advocates of emancipation. Clearly, Weill no longer saw the need for the more "distinguished" term with its acculturated resonance. For Weill, the glory of France is that it lets Jews be Jews.

But home, for Weill, also had a more specific meaning. In his fiction, as we have seen, he returned again and again to the small Alsatian villages of his youth. There he locates everything that retards Jewish progress as well as the wellspring, the source of that progress. His village characters are ignorant and superstitious but also contain within them the possibility for true enlightenment. Jewish tradition, for Weill, acts in double ways upon its adherents, promoting fanaticism and superstition but also implanting within them the knowledge of and hope for something better. Weill's characters must leave the village to achieve their goals, but he himself returns there to find inspiration.

Weill's Alsatian villages are themselves dynamic places. History has arrived, whether in the form of characters who join Napoleon's army (as in "Stasie"/"Gumper") or daughters who read novels (as in *Couronne*) or rabbinical students who convert (as in "Braendel") or scoundrels who go to America to seek their fortunes (as in "Kella"). Weill may find in his villages remnants of old folkways, but the clash of these traditions with the new realities of modernity provides his plots with their principal motor. Weill may have idealized Jewish village life, he may have washed the dirt off his peasants, but he did not deny them a place in the modern world. He saw his village characters as capable of change and as interesting for that reason. It is important to bear this in mind as we turn in the next chapter to a very different vision of the Jewish village, one that saw it as the antidote to modernity and as the source of a new nostalgic form of Jewish identity predicated on the past.

Five Ghetto Fiction: Daniel Stauben,
David Schornstein, and the
Uses of the Jewish Past

In the difficult aftermath of the Revolution of 1848, a young Jewish scholar used to seek escape from the Parisian "whirlwind" by summoning memories of his childhood in Alsace.[1] Normally his recollections of the "antique simplicity" of semirural Jewish life offered him "a refuge" from the anxiety of contemporary events. One night, however, he found himself in a state of "weariness and depression" after a day spent "both in reading and in the agitation of political questions," and he realized that his powers of recollection had let him down. No longer able to muster in proto-Proustian fashion the lost world of his youth and stricken with terror at the failure of his memory, he decided to go physically in search of his past: "I threw my traveling coat over my shoulder and set out on the road to Alsace." Fortunately, the lost world of his childhood still existed a short journey away. In a few hours, a train would reconnect him with the people, traditions, and stories that seemed to exist frozen in time and that offered him the only reliable antidote to the stresses of modern life.

So begins the first in a series of nine "Lettres sur les moeurs alsaciennes" [Letters on Alsatian Manners], published by Auguste Widal in *Les Archives Israélites* between 1849 and 1853. At once a description of a vanishing way of life and an account of the narrator's feelings as he reconnects with the people and customs of his childhood, the letters unfold in hybrid form, containing both a first-person travelogue and intercalated fiction, told as stories by the various characters or the narrator himself. Documentary in its effort to describe traditional social types, customs, and folktales but also explicitly a kind of therapy for the modern subject, the series struck a chord with readers in the

Reform Jewish newspaper, the majority of whom had, like the author, come to Paris from small villages in France's eastern provinces. The series struck a chord with non-Jews as well; after publishing a serial adaptation in the prestigious *Revue des Deux Mondes*, Widal would publish yet another version as a book under the pseudonym Daniel Stauben. Titled *Scènes de la vie juive en Alsace* [Scenes of Jewish Life in Alsace], the book was enthusiastically reviewed in the mainstream French press.

Several recent studies have shown that Stauben's *Scènes de la vie juive en Alsace* was the initiator of a new form of "ghetto nostalgia" that took hold in French and German literature and art after the Revolution of 1848, just as large numbers of Jews in these countries had successfully distanced themselves from their own Jewish past.[2] This obsession with the ghetto and with the Jewish past more generally has proven extremely durable; it continued to be a central motif in Jewish literature through the twentieth century. Indeed, ghetto nostalgia is arguably one of the defining forms of modern Jewish belles-lettres. Scholars have suggested that the desire to read about and see images of a world that was felt to be on the verge of disappearing served a complex set of psychic functions for the acculturating Jewish bourgeoisie, simultaneously reassuring them about how far they had come and compensating them for what they had left behind.

In this chapter I argue that these texts did more than just assuage the guilt of assimilating Jews in the mid-nineteenth century. Jews returned to the ghetto or village for many reasons. Some of these reasons were no doubt psychological, but others were political, social, religious, and historical. I touch on all these meanings in this chapter but ultimately emphasize the ways in which nineteenth-century ghetto fiction offers up the past as the ground for new forms of Jewish identity in the present. This turning backward represents a departure from the other solutions to the problem of Jewish modernity I describe in this book. It defines what it means to be Jewish in essentially secular terms, holding up traditional religious beliefs and customs as a source of nostalgia but not as a model for action. Stauben's text in many ways initiates this process but also laments it, providing both a model for a new historical form of Jewish affiliation and a profound meditation on the losses that this new relation to the past entailed.

The Jew as Historian

Auguste Widal (Figure 6) was born on June 4, 1822, into a relatively affluent family and was raised in the Alsatian village of Wintzenheim (Haut-Rhin), near Colmar, on the easternmost edge of France.[3] After attending the local primary school in Wintzenheim (most likely one

Figure 6. Portrait of Auguste Widal (Daniel Stauben). Courtesy of the Bibliothèque Nationale de France.

of the new Jewish primary schools established in the region around 1820),[4] he continued his studies at the Collège de Colmar, which was not a Jewish school. His father intended for him to become a rabbi, but just like his slightly older compatriot Alexandre Weill, he rejected sacred texts for secular learning. An exceptional student, Widal left home to attend the prestigious Lycée Charlemagne in Paris, then as now one of the leading secondary schools in France. Accepted at the highly competitive École Normale Supérieure, the summit of the French educational establishment, he began his preparation for a career in academia, studying ancient and modern languages.

Although by midcentury a handful of Jews had scaled the heights of the French university system, their way was by no means assured.[5] Several Jews taught mathematics at the secondary or postsecondary levels at this time, but the humanities remained more difficult to penetrate.[6] The major exception was Adolphe Franck (1809–1893), author of a book on Kabbalah and by far the most famous Jewish academic of the mid-nineteenth century. Franck taught at the Sorbonne in the 1840s and was appointed to the chair in philosophy of law at the Collège de France in 1856.[7] However, several Jews in Widal's generation, including other *normaliens*, faced obstacles to a teaching career because of antisemitism. These included the philosopher Isidore Cahen (1826–1902), the son of Samuel Cahen, founder of *Les Archives Israélites*.[8] Cahen eventually renounced academia for journalism, taking over the helm of *Les Archives Israélites* when his father retired.[9]

The difficulties encountered by other Jews reveal the exceptional nature of Widal's success. In 1847, at the age of 25, Widal accepted a coveted position teaching rhetoric at his alma mater, the Lycée Charlemagne, while he prepared for a career at the university. For the next several years, he continued to pursue his research in both classical and modern literature. In 1851, he published two doctoral dissertations: *Les divers caractères du misanthrope chez les écrivains anciens et modernes* [The Diverse Characters of the Misanthrope in Ancient and Modern Writers] and a treatise on Tacitus in Latin, *In Taciti dialogum De Oratoribus disputatio* [The Debate on Tacitus's Dialogue "De Oratoribus"]. After receiving his *docteur ès-lettres* degree, he took his first university position in the Faculty of Letters in Poitiers, teaching classical languages. Widal would go on to publish several more studies of classical literature, both Latin and Greek: a book on Seneca (1854), a book on Homer (1860), and a magnum opus on Juvenalian satire (1870) that went through multiple editions. He held the chair in ancient literature at the University of Douai before leaving in 1864 for the University of Besançon. In 1873, Jules Simon named Widal inspector general for French primary and secondary schools. He received the Legion of Honor before his sudden death on May 6, 1875, at the age of 52.[10]

Of all the writers I present in this book, Widal is the only one to have achieved a successful career in one of the liberal professions, which would represent the main road to social advancement for French Jews in the decades to come. I draw attention to Widal's scholarly career not only because it typifies a new stage in the process of Jewish acculturation in France but also because it helps explain why he would become the initiator of a new historical form of Judaism. Widal's training as a scholar, and particularly as a modern literary historian, enabled him to conceive of Judaism in a new way. It provided him with the intellectual tools, but also the cast of mind, to discover in the Jewish past possibilities for the Jewish future.

Widal signed his "Lettres sur les moeurs alsaciennes" in *Les Archives Israélites* "Aug. W—— from the Haut-Rhin" or simply "A.W.," and he published them while teaching at the Lycée Charlemagne. By 1857, when he began to publish this material in the *Revue des Deux Mondes* under the pseudonym Daniel Stauben, he was already a university professor. All the earlier vignettes then appear, in slightly altered form, as part one—or roughly the first half—of the volume published by Michel Lévy Frères in 1860 under the name Daniel Stauben. Widal also used this pen name for his translations of three of Leopold Kompert's volumes of ghetto tales from German into French, all of which include prefaces by the translator.

Widal thus pursued his interest in traditional Jewish culture in tandem with his work on ancient Greece and Rome. The fact that he used a pen name for his Jewish writings when he published them in mainstream venues suggests that he saw these texts as distinct from his academic studies—and perhaps also as potentially harmful to his career in the French university system. Indeed, Widal describes turning to the traditional world of Alsatian country Judaism as an antidote to his academic work in the first installment of the *Archives Israélites* version. But it might also be seen as a complement to it: Widal was essentially a literary historian and was accustomed to reviving lost cultures by investigating the stories they told. And although the civilization he sought to evoke in the Alsatian vignettes was less remote in both time and space than that of ancient Greece or Rome, it offered a similar opportunity for immersion in a traditional way of life. The Jews of his native village offered the modern Parisian literary historian the sense of what it meant to live in an ancient civilization.

Stauben's text describes, in first-person narrative, a trip back to Alsace in 1849 (in the 1860 book version, he postdates the trip to 1856). Attempting to reconnect with the people and places of his childhood, the narrator stays as a guest of old friends, the Salomon family, in the village of Bolwiller. Arriving in time for the Sabbath, he describes the celebration in detail in the opening vignette and then devotes an installment (in the book version, a chapter) to the magical tales recounted by their neighbor Samuel, an excellent storyteller, after the Sabbath dinner. The narrator then accompanies the Salomon family to nearby Wintzenheim, where he grew up, to attend a wedding. He revels in the pious customs surrounding this joyous event, dwelling on the unique or colorful details, the "curious ensemble of ideas, rites, ceremonies, superstitions, traits, types of country folk, seasonal festivals, forming, altogether, something like a civilization [*comme une sorte de civilisation*]."[11] The opportunity presents itself for him to describe a funeral as well, for the brother of the bride dies of consumption shortly after the festivities.

The version in *Les Archives Israélites* ends with the narration of the wedding and funeral, the two major events in the traditional Jewish life cycle, but in the second and third parts of the book version, the narrator returns to Alsace to celebrate a year's worth of Jewish holidays. Along with recounting how the local Jews feast and pray, Stauben includes fictionalized narratives of courtship, ambition, success, and failure. He organizes the book according to the seasonal Jewish holidays—one chapter for Purim, one for Passover, and so on—underscoring the extent to which the Jewish sacred tradition is tied to the earth and its cycles. On these trips, his local informants provide the opportunity for the Parisian professor to describe the whole range of Jewish traditions, most of which are common to all Orthodox Jewish communities, although some are local to Alsace. As Arnold Eisen comments in his perceptive pages devoted to the text, Stauben concerns himself much more with practice than with belief in his descriptions of Jewish ritual observance.[12] For the most part, Stauben portrays his subjects as unreflective participants in an ancient cult, and he specifically underscores the oriental nature of many of their rituals. He rarely enters a synagogue, preferring to focus on the way that holidays are celebrated in the family setting.

Stauben's text thus displays a documentary character that aligns it with his other historical work. His *Scènes de la vie juive en Alsace* provides a kind of history of the Alsatian Jews in the sense that it describes the customs and beliefs of an ancient culture, one seen as already in the process of disappearing. But it does far more than this. In the following sections, I explore the meanings that Stauben's text and other contemporaneous forms of ghetto or village nostalgia generated in different contexts and for different types of readers. What, I want to know, did nineteenth-century Jews seek in the ghetto or village? And what did they find there?

Ghetto Nostalgia

First, however, I want to establish the importance of the phenomenon of ghetto nostalgia in the nineteenth century and beyond. Stauben was not, of course, the first Jewish writer to describe the past. In one way or another, all the writers I discuss in this book—Eugénie Foa, Ben-Lévi, Ben Baruch, and Alexandre Weill—looked to the traditional ways of life in prerevolutionary villages or ghettos as a way of developing their programs for the Jewish future—albeit in ways that are different from Stauben and his fellow "nostalgic" writers, as I discuss later in this chapter. But although Stauben did not inaugurate the trend, he was its best-known practitioner in France. In addition to the various versions of his *Scènes de la vie juive en Alsace*, he published historical fiction about Jews in the medieval ghettos of central Europe and nonfiction works about Jewish life in rural France in both *Les Archives Israélites* and in more scholarly publications, such as *La Vérité Israélite*.

The other major midcentury practitioner of the genre in France was David Schornstein (1826–1879), who published a series of serialized novels about life in the Jewish ghettos of medieval and early modern Europe as well as novels about traditional Jewish life in Alsace set in the more recent past, which he published under the pseudonym Georges Stenne (a gallicization of Stein).[13] Later in the century, David-Léon Cahun's *La vie juive* [Jewish Life] (1886), a collection of sketches about traditional Jewish life in Alsace, recast the subjects of Stauben's work in a more explicitly fictional, more sentimentalized, and more patriotic manner.[14]

Germany and Austria also saw an outpouring of ghetto texts. Heinrich Heine might be seen as the initiator of the trend in German, with *The Rabbi of Bacherach*, a historical novel set in a German ghetto in the fifteenth century, written partly in 1824–1825 and completed in 1840.[15] As in France, however, the genre really developed in German only after 1848; in that year Salomon Kohn, Hermann Schiff (the pseudonym of Isaac Bernays), and Leopold Kompert all published fiction set in medieval or modern ghettos.[16] The Viennese writer Kompert became the acknowledged master of the genre, publishing a series of collections of stories about Jews set in the ghettos of *mitteleuropa*, which Stauben translated into French: *Scènes du ghetto* [Scenes of the Ghetto] (1859), *Les juifs de la Bohème* [The Jews of Bohemia] (1860), and *Nouvelles juives* [Jewish Stories] (1873).[17]

Mid-nineteenth-century Jewish fascination with the Jewish past also took the form of visual representation. In 1878, the wealthy composer Isaac Strauss held an exhibition of Jewish religious artifacts, for which Schornstein (Stenne) wrote a detailed guide. This exhibition was the first attempt to collect and present traditional Jewish art. According to Richard I. Cohen, it translated the sacred into a secular context and allowed assimilated Jews to "renew contact with a Jewish world otherwise so distant."[18] At the same time, artists such as Moritz Op-

Figure 7. Alphonse Lévy, "Les boulettes de Pacque" [Passover Matzo Balls], in David-Léon Cahun, *La vie juive* (Paris: Monnier, de Brunhoff, 1886). Courtesy of the Library at the Herbert D. Katz Center for Advanced Judaic Studies, University of Pennsylvania.

penheim and Simeon Solomon in Germany and Alphonse Lévy and Edouard Moyse in France sought to capture the image of a traditional Jewish world.[19] Beginning in the 1850s, Oppenheim's drawings depicting Orthodox Jews in rural settings were avidly consumed by non-observant urban Jews. Sold as illustrated books and as prints, these images were also reproduced on porcelain plates and other collectible items.[20] Lévy's sentimentalized lithographs of hefty Jewish matrons making matzo balls and lighting candles on Friday night and of old men praying were sold in collector's editions and used to illustrate Léon Cahun's *La vie juive* in 1886 (see Figures 7 and 8).

Figure 8. Alphonse Lévy, "Le rabbin" [The Rabbi], in David-Léon Cahun, *La vie juive* (Paris: Monnier, de Brunhoff, 1886). Courtesy of the Library at the Herbert D. Katz Center for Advanced Judaic Studies, University of Pennsylvania.

It is important to note the links between the rise of ghetto fiction and the crisis of 1848, when the revolutionary events in Paris sparked a series of pogromlike attacks against Jews in Alsace.[21] Although the new revolutionary government featured two Jews in top ministerial posts, Parisian Jews worried for the safety of their coreligionists and family members back east.[22] In the preface to the first installment of his Alsatian letters in *Les Archives Israélites*, Widal explicitly alludes to the "agitation of political questions" as one of the motivations for the depression driving him to reconnect with the world of his childhood. First published in 1849, immediately after the revolutionary crisis, Widal's descriptions of life in Alsace offer insight into a community perceived as being under threat. The loss of Alsace to Germany in 1870 further increased the stakes of this form of nostalgia. The cloying sentimentality of some of the later nostalgic texts, such as Cahun's, no doubt responds to the fact that the traditional Jewish past had literally become a foreign country for Parisian readers.[23]

Despite its origins in the specific historical context of the nineteenth century, the fascination for the ghetto or village would have a surprisingly lasting appeal. Today we are perhaps most familiar with a later American incarnation of the nostalgic phenomenon: *Fiddler on the Roof*, the 1964 stage musical and 1971 film, about the eastern European Jewish village, or shtetl, based on the Yiddish stories of Sholem Aleichem (the pseudonym of Sholem Rabinowitz, 1859–1916). Like Stauben's text, *Fiddler* proved popular with Jewish and non-Jewish audiences alike.[24] The appeal of the show to non-Jewish audiences can probably be attributed to a fascination with an exotic culture—and also to stirring music by Jerry Bock and clever lyrics by Sheldon Harnick. For midcentury Jewish American audiences, however, the show had other resonances. It was not a coincidence that *Fiddler on the Roof* appeared on the American cultural horizon just as the eastern European Jewish immigrants and their children had definitively left behind the shtetl culture in which they or their parents were born. Parisian Jewish readers of Stauben's text were at a similar point in the transition to modernity exactly a century before.[25]

Scholars have tended to explain the "return to the ghetto" phenomenon in psychological terms. According to Cohen, these texts and images showing traditional Jewish life allowed assimilating Jews to reconnect with the past that they or their parents had left behind. "The rapid move from the relatively slow-moving Jewish community to the pulsating life of Europe's capitals and cities tended to produce feelings of disorientation and emptiness, which certain Jews tried to counteract by re-establishing an attachment to that 'ghetto' world which they or their parents had abandoned."[26] Cohen's description of the emotional pain caused by assimilation squares with the plaintive tone of Widal's introduction to the *Archives Israélites* version of his text, quoted at the beginning of this chapter, in which he describes his journey back to Alsace as an antidote to the "doubt" and "discouragement" caused by the "whirlwind" of his hectic life in Paris.[27]

According to Cohen, the tales of life in traditional Jewish society fill a void left by modernity both for their authors and for assimilating Jewish readers seeking to reconnect with a world they had explicitly rejected. The descriptions of the solidarity and communal cohesion of the Jewish village found in so much of the ghetto literature compensate for the selfishness and anomie of the modern metropolis. As Cohen puts it, "To retrieve aspects of a community that could no longer be reconstituted, to touch that world in any way was to help overcome the emptiness of a relentless modernization and to integrate the forgotten (or receding) past into contemporary existence."[28] Stauben's text contains numerous examples of joys and sorrows experienced collectively by the entire Jewish community of a village. Perhaps the best example of such communal solidarity, however, comes in a little-known gem of a novel by Schornstein, "La dîme" [The Tithe], published serially in *Les Archives Israélites* in 1864.

In "La dîme," two poor friends in a small Alsatian village, one a Hebrew scribe and the other a cantor in the synagogue, have a falling out after an evil merchant spreads lies about one to the other in order to foil the romance between their children and to marry the scribe's daughter. Resolution comes after the cantor wins the lottery. Although he is not speaking to the scribe, the cantor anonymously sends his former friend a tenth of his winnings (*la dîme*), because the Talmud commands the giving of charity to the less fortunate. The scribe, in turn, anonymously sends 10 percent of his mysterious windfall to his ex-friend, the cantor, who of course knows where the money has come from and reconciles with the scribe. Their children marry and live happily ever after. Schornstein's story celebrates the kinds of bonds that develop between neighbors in small villages as well as the Jewish religious values that govern life in such traditional settings.

According to Cohen, Parisian readers of texts like these sought a simulacrum of a lost world—a sanitized, selective version of their traditional identity to go along with their new modern one. The lithographs of traditional village life by Alphonse Lévy almost exclusively show women preparing food and men studying, while glossing over the dirty, difficult aspects of village life. Like the Jewish comfort foods they celebrate, the tales of traditional ghetto life thus seem to have provided a kind of succor to the assimilating body and soul.

Cohen's explanation for the popularity of these texts is compelling but on closer inspection not quite satisfactory. It seems equally possible that scenes of ghetto life might have produced a disquieting rather than comforting effect for readers who had left this life behind. Wouldn't these texts also have served to remind assimilating Jews of the identity they were trying so hard to forget? An illustrious reader from the time—Bernard Lazare (the pseudonym of Lazare Marcus Manassé Bernard, 1865–1903), the anarchist-socialist and heroic early Dreyfusard—calls attention to precisely this disturbing aspect of ghetto nostalgia in a preface to a 1902 edition of Lévy's drawings of Alsatian village life. From a highly assimilated family of textile mill owners, Lazare became convinced of the need for Jewish collective action during the Dreyfus affair and represented one of the key exceptions in Hannah Arendt's political condemnation of nineteenth-century French Jews. He figures for her as one of the few French Jews in the period who renounced his life as a parvenu to embrace his status as a pariah.[29] Lazare was thus particularly well placed to comment on the phenomenon of Jewish nostalgia.

In his preface, Lazare skewers the assimilating transformations of his fellow French Jews who emerged from villages like the ones represented by Lévy: "Jacob the trafficker now calls himself Jacques and Moses the speculator calls himself Maurice. They have catholicized their religion and only their brain is circumcised." He goes on to evoke the power of Lévy's images of traditional Jewish village life to dredge up old memories—and identities—that nineteenth-century French Jews hoped would remain buried: "How therefore might they receive he who delights in bringing back to life or fixing on the lithographer's stone the types of the old Ghetto, those who have disappeared and those who are on their way out?" Lazare, whose family came from Nîmes and thus did not have links to the rural Alsatian Jews represented in Lévy's images, nevertheless understood that the artist caused a particular kind of pain to his Parisian public: "He shows these parvenus the past that they no longer want to remember. . . . He presents them with a gallery of ancestors they can't leave behind like chaff, a lamentable litany of poor relations that they can't stick at the far end of the table."[30] For modern Parisian Jews to collect these images of their ancestors or country cousins meant painfully acknowledging what their work of assimilation continually sought to suppress.

So why then did these representations become so popular? Were nineteenth-century Jews masochists? Arnold Eisen offers an interpretation along these lines, proposing that the pain caused by these forms of ghetto nostalgia allowed modernizing Jews to relieve the guilt associated with the process of assimilation. Eisen invokes Freud, who struggled with the ghosts of his own Jewish past, to argue that this process of moving from traditional Jewish culture to modern Western culture was tantamount to a symbolic murder of the father: "To abandon Judaism is, in that psychological sense, to kill the parents/ ancestors, by losing touch with that they had stood for and done."[31] Reading ghetto tales or looking at pictures of traditional Jewish life, according to Eisen, thus offered assimilating Jews a way to make peace with the ancestors they had rejected by reconnecting with their way of life on a symbolic level. The pain of looking at these images, in other words, served an important psychological function: It provided a kind of symbolic punishment and thus allowed assimilating Jews to feel absolved of their guilt.[32]

Eisen also reminds us, however, that the remembrance of ancestors has deep roots in the Jewish tradition. All Jewish holiday celebrations, from the recounting of the Exodus from Egypt in the Passover seder to the lighting of candles at Hanukkah to commemorate the miracle of the Maccabean revolt, incorporate memory as part of the ritual of observance. Ghetto nostalgia, then, allowed modern Jews not only to relieve their guilt through painful recollection but also to feel like they were engaging in a traditional form of Jewish ritual practice. It not only reconnected Jews with the forms and figures of their past but also redeemed their present for a larger narrative of Jewish history.

"Nostalgic observances," Eisen concludes, "made the larger transgression of acculturation or assimilation permissible, did penance for it, ennobled it with the ancestors' blessing."[33]

This alternative psychological explanation for the appeal of ghetto nostalgia is just as compelling as Cohen's—and just as difficult to prove. Of course, we cannot read the minds of nineteenth-century Jews to know how they experienced their condition or what they might have felt while consuming texts and images depicting ghetto life. Rather than attempt to guess at the emotions produced in readers by these representations, in what follows I would like to focus on the way the texts themselves go about theorizing the social, political, and existential dynamics of acculturation and assimilation. The meanings that these texts generate can best be appreciated, I argue, by comparing different types of ghetto fiction—some of which seem not very nostalgic at all—and by comparing the framing of the texts for different audiences. My goal is to bring into better focus the new uses of the past in nineteenth-century Jewish culture.

Nostalgia and Regeneration

I would like to begin by returning Stauben's Alsatian letters to their mid-nineteenth-century context in order to understand better the cultural work they performed for readers at the time. That Stauben saw his text as serving different functions for different readerships can be gleaned from the fact that he presented the text differently when he reworked the material from *Les Archives Israélites* for the mainstream *Revue des Deux Mondes* and for the book version in 1860. In these later versions, destined for a not specifically Jewish readership, Stauben dispenses with the angst of the introduction in *Les Archives Israélites*, which I cited at the beginning of this chapter. The introduction to the book makes no reference to the narrator's suffering in Paris, to the tortured existence of the scholar caught up in the midst of literary and political battles in the aftermath of the Revolution of 1848. Indeed, throughout the book version, Stauben carefully edits out all the references to his own emotional need to return to the scene of his childhood to bolster an identity rendered fragile in the modern metropolis.

In place of this personal motivation for his journey, Stauben describes how the idea for his return to Alsace came from reading certain novels of George Sand. "Among the many novels we owe to the pen of our illustrious contemporary, we had just read a few marked by a particular stamp."[34] It is not Sand's early feminist novels depicting the struggles of feisty heroines for romantic and social freedom that inspire him but "those in which, leaving aside all political and social theory along with the painting of heated passions, the author of *La Mare-au-Diable* [The Devil's Pool] and *François le Champi* [François the Waif] takes on calmer, less irritating subjects" (ii). Like subsequent literary historians who excluded Sand's political novels from the French literary canon in favor of her seemingly innocuous pastoral fictions, Stauben admires his illustrious contemporary's ability to depict "rustic life and . . . the poetry of the fields" (ii) and decides to imitate it. Impressed by "these simple tales, these fresh pictures" describing "naïve" country manners and popular traditions, he relates how he found himself overcome with "a pack of reminiscences" (ii) of his own country childhood in Alsace. The irony, of course, is that Sand drew her own inspiration, as we saw in the last chapter, from reading the Jewish village tales of Alexandre Weill, whom Stauben does not cite as a model.

Stauben points out that his account of village life is at once similar to and different from the tales told by Sand of peasant life in the Berry. They are "analogous by the simplicity of the customs, the venerability of the practices, and the originality of certain characters," but they differ in the religion that serves as a "frame to all of that" (iii). And yet, Stauben asks, aren't the Jews of Alsace as unique and interesting as Sand's Berrichon peasants? Don't the Alsatian country Jews offer "customs" just as "venerable" and an "idiom" just as "picturesque" as the farm laborers whose lives and loves Sand chronicles in such touching detail? It is this life that Stauben decides to capture: "Doesn't Jewish life in Alsatian villages, I told myself again, present just as curious an ensemble of ideas, rites, ceremonies, superstitions, traits, types of country folk, seasonal festivals, forming, altogether, something like a civilization?" (iii–iv). Moreover, as one who, like Sand, possesses a unique relation to these country people, as one who can understand their language and participate in their rituals, isn't he the perfect guide to their "something like a civilization"?

As a reviewer for the *Journal des Débats* would point out, the works of Sand and Stauben differ not just in content but also in form. Stauben, for one thing, does not write a novel. His book contains fictional interludes, and he may in fact have fabricated his series of voyages to Alsace, but it does not present itself as fiction or contain a conventional plot.[35] So if Stauben's text bears little structural similarity to Sand's novels, if the actual content of the works is so different, why then does Stauben insist on the link between them? The answer has to do with what I take to be one of the primary political or ideological functions of Stauben's text: to naturalize the Jews in France. What inspires Stauben in the work of Sand is her ability to make the local customs of her home region appear at once quaintly exotic and fundamentally French.

Stauben attempts to depict his Alsatian Jews as the equivalent of Sand's Berrichon peasants. "To the peasants of the Indre, one can contrast in more than one way, in a different sphere of existence and of ideas, the Jews of our Alsatian hamlets" (iii). Like Sand, Stauben calls attention to the rootedness of his subjects in the land: "Established in this region for centuries before the French conquest, haven't they kept a distinct language and a distinct way of life as well?" (iii). Stauben's historical gesture here is not gratuitous; even as he celebrates the picturesque difference of the Jews, their unique language and religious customs, he underscores the fact that their presence in Alsace predates the French annexation of the province in the seventeenth century. The Jews are thus just as French as the Christian Alsatians, as both groups have lived in France for the same amount of time. Stauben thus offers a counterargument to the growing chorus of antisemites who denounced the Jews as opportunistic invaders and as somehow less French than their fellow citizens.

According to Stauben, it is the Jewish particularity of his Alsatian subjects, moreover, that makes them worthy of citizenship, that gives them access to the French universal. Sand had helped to perpetuate this kind of paradox. At a time when peasants were undergoing the arduous transformation into Frenchmen that the Revolution had begun but by no means accomplished, the regional novel attempted a twofold ideological maneuver.[36] On the one hand, Sand and her followers argue for the value of regional distinctiveness—the local identity that the Revolution had begun to eradicate in favor of a cohesive, homogeneous national identity—as a component of Frenchness, but at the same time their novels contribute to its eradication by helping to fortify the national canon of literary works in standard French. Sand and the regional writers help to create a vision of France as an assemblage of individual parts, each unique but each also subordinate to a higher national identity.

Stauben follows this pattern by including examples of the local dialect, Western Yiddish, as well as occasional Hebrew words, to emphasize the uniqueness of his subjects. When the narrator arrives shortly before the Sabbath in the first installment of the *Archives* version, his host Salomon tells him: "Rest assured, my dear *orech* . . . you aren't late. Knowing you were on your way, and fearing that you might involuntarily make *a hole in the Shabbos*, I asked the חזן not to intone the *Boï Becholem* before you arrived."[37] Of all the examples of Jewish literature I discuss in this book, Stauben's text displays by far the most linguistic hybridity. Whereas the other writers might include a Hebrew or Yiddish word here and there, Stauben offers a sampling of entire phrases, only some of which are translated or even transliterated. In this Jewish publication, Stauben includes a footnote to explain that *orech* means *hôte*, or guest, but he does not translate the other, more common terms pertaining to ritual, such as the word in Hebrew (*hazan*, meaning "cantor") and the transliterated *Boï Becholem*, which he assumes his readers in the *Archives* would know or could figure out from context. He also includes an example of a partial French translation of a Yiddish idiomatic expression—"a hole in the Shabbos" (*un trou dans le Schabes*)—designating an interruption of the Sabbath service.

In the book version, intended for a general audience, this passage becomes: "Rest assured, my dear Parisian, he said to me, you aren't late. Knowing you were on your way, I asked the cantor to wait a few

moments and not to intone the Boï Besolem [*sic*] before you arrived"
(12). Although Stauben leaves enough foreignness to provide a taste
of local color, he changes certain terms (*orech* becomes "Parisian"),
deletes a whole phrase ("a hole in the Shabbos"), translates words (the
Hebrew word becomes *chantre*, or cantor), and offers explanations for
the remainder (a footnote tells readers that "Boï Besolem" designates
the first two words of a prayer recited during Friday night services).[38]
Thus, even between the two versions of the text, Stauben enacts the
process whereby French displaces Hebrew and Yiddish, the very process he laments as leading to the loss of the culture he describes. And
on a more general level, Stauben reduces the foreignness of his subjects by rendering their language as a series of words or phrases pep-
pering their discourse in standard—even formal or literary—French
(notice the elaborate construction involving a subjective, "fearing that
you might make" [*de peur que vous ne fissiez*]).

Thanks to Sand, who had pioneered this practice in order to do-
mesticate the Berry, Stauben is able to show how the foreignness of
the Alsatian Jews—including their use of Yiddish and Hebrew, here
reduced to a French "idiom" along the lines of the Berrichon patois—
marks their belonging to a nation formed by the sum of its regions,
each containing its own distinctive language and customs (even when
these seem more Germanic or oriental than French). Stauben thereby
claims for his Jews equal rights to the *terroir* as Christian peasants.
This claim had a strong political and cultural resonance during the period in which the Romantic movement in both France and Germany
had begun to reconceive nations as the expression less of an abstract
political will than of an organic, determined folk spirit rooted in the
land and in traditional culture. Inspired by Johann Gottfried Herder
(1744–1803), the folklorist movement was attempting, at precisely this
moment, to collect oral traditions as a means of documenting the folk
spirit of the nation.

Stauben's rooting of the Jews in the soil of Alsace also implicitly
responds to the portrayals by antisemites of the Jews as rootless invaders who appropriate the resources of their adopted country without
actually belonging to it. The period just preceding Stauben's journey
back to Alsace saw the first spurt of socialist antisemitism in France,

which made political use of these notions. In *Les juifs, rois de l'époque* [Jews, Kings of the Age] (1845), Alphonse Toussenel describes Jews as cosmopolitans without any connection to a particular region or territory: "The Jew is only encamped on the ground he lives on" (*Le juif n'est jamais que campé sur le sol qu'il habite*), Toussenel maintains, repeatedly returning to the image of the Jew as a nomad in order to render illegitimate the Jewish acquisition of wealth or position within French territory.[39] Stauben's text responds to this kind of rhetoric by underscoring Jewish rootedness in the Alsatian region.

Along with addressing accusations of Jewish cosmopolitanism, Stauben's text works to localize Jews in the countryside rather than in the city. Countering notions (and actual demographic trends) that associated Jews with urban centers, Stauben provides a portrait of a rural or semirural Judaism. Unlike their author, who journeyed to nearby Colmar and eventually to Paris for his education, Stauben's characters never leave their country hamlets. Tied to the land, they venture as far as the neighboring village for a wedding, but this constitutes a major journey requiring elaborate preparations. Indeed, the horizon of even the merchant characters is completely local—or, for the peddlers, regional—and Stauben never mentions the kind of commerce with Jews in neighboring regions, or even Germany, that we know was common at the time.

The only exceptions are the characters who leave home to join the army. In the second chapter of the second part of the book version, Stauben's narrator tells the story of Rachel, who waits patiently for her fiancé, Maïerlé, to finish seven years of army service. After returning from the Crimea a hero, the young Jewish soldier settles down to farm near his native village: "He tends with success to a few acres of land near Beisheim. He is the model of the soldier-farmer" (147). This country identity constitutes the ideal toward which social reformers had long pointed. Stauben thus aligns his text with the ideology of regeneration that had motivated the Abbé Grégoire and other eighteenth-century liberals to grant the Jews citizenship during the Revolution as a means of normalizing their occupations and rendering them more "productive."[40] These reformers hoped that after becoming citizens, the Jews—especially the supposedly backward Alsatian

Jews—would cease to practice peddling or money lending and would opt en masse to become farmers and artisans. That relatively few Jews followed their advice when accelerating industrialization was rendering such occupations less viable economically should have come as little surprise, but it did not stop the inheritors of the regeneration rhetoric in the nineteenth century from continuing to advocate this program.[41]

Ghetto fiction served as one of the prime vehicles for the propagation of the ideology of regeneration in the nineteenth century both in French and in German. Kompert, the Viennese Jewish writer whose collections of short stories Stauben translated into French, endows his tales of traditional ghetto life with a strong regenerative message. In "Trenderl," a typical story, a young Jewish man in a Bohemian ghetto becomes a locksmith, marries his sweetheart, and lives happily ever after. In "The Princess," a spoiled Jewish girl from a wealthy urban family gets sent to the country to recover her health by living with a family of Jewish farmers. At first she disdains country ways, but eventually she falls in love with the son of the farming family. Casting her novels into the river in a sign of renunciation of the decadent city mentality, she agrees to become a farmwife and recovers her health in the rustic setting.

These lessons were not lost on Kompert's translator. In his introduction to the 1859 French translation of one of Kompert's works, Stauben remarks on the Austrian writer's ability to "slip a lesson into a dialogue."[42] Calling Kompert a "moralist," Stauben notes, "One can detect, without it seeming so, [Kompert's] own thoughts, aspirations, goal: the time of the ghetto is past; soon it must only be a poetic memory; it is necessary to renounce old prejudices; the Israelites must become secular, leave off peddling and petty commerce in order to work outdoors, trade in their scale and sack of goods for a scythe and plow. That is what the author wants."[43] Note the temporizing gesture Stauben reads into Kompert's works; the point of journeying back to the ghetto, of describing traditional Jewish life, is to declare it passé. Stauben understands these tales of ghetto life as an attempt to "inspire his coreligionists with a love of the fields" as well as a fondness for low-paying artisanal trades.[44] And without a doubt he seems to approve of Kompert's desire to describe the Jewish past in order to cast Jewish modernity in a new form.

The Alsatian Jews did not live in ghettos like their coreligionists in central Europe. For certain writers, however, they nevertheless embodied the degenerate characteristics associated with ghetto life, such as cowardice and laziness. And French writers, like their German counterparts, did not hesitate to seek their regeneration through literature. Isaac Lévy, a rabbi in Verdun, specialized in the production of moralizing tales addressed to the poor Jewish youth in France's eastern provinces. In 1862, he published a novel with the programmatic title *Isaïe ou le travail* [Isaiah or Work], in which he recounts the adventures of a model Jewish country waif who rejects the temptation of becoming a merchant in Paris to return to his Alsatian village and become a locksmith (yet another!). By dedicating himself to labor and thrift, he achieves happiness and respectability. In the serialized novel *Joseph Rosenkolb* (1864), published in the short-lived journal Lévy edited for Jewish youth, *Le Foyer Israélite*, the rabbi of Verdun recounts the obverse of Isaïe's story; in this chilling tale, a young Jew's laziness results in the loss of his family's modest fortune and his confinement to a hospice. Despite their heavy-handedness and inelegant style, Lévy's works earned the praise of Jewish critics. One reviewer describes with a seemingly genuine appreciation how reading Lévy's novel to a group of rowdy schoolchildren reduced them to stunned silence.[45]

It helps to situate *Scènes de la vie juive en Alsace* in the context of these contemporaneous works to understand the politics of Stauben's enterprise. In contrast to Kompert and Lévy and despite his praise of Kompert's moralizing message, Stauben does not show Jews in need of regeneration. His Jews are not cowardly, lazy, or backward in any way. The one exception in *Scènes de la vie juive en Alsace* is the character of Lazare, who appears at the Passover seder of the Salomon family, when it is customary to share the ritual meal with the poor. Lazare combines the occupation of schnorrer (a deprecatory Yiddish word, which the narrator translates as mendicant or beggar) with that of peddler of Hebrew books.[46] He denounces all forms of modernity, including the innovation of translating the Hebrew liturgy into French, which has threatened his business. Placed next to the servant at the far end of the table, dressed in a shabby old coat, Lazare typifies the kind of unregenerated Jew whom writers such as Kompert and Lévy hoped to render obsolete through their fiction. Stauben's narrator refers to him as a "little old man, a personification of nomadic Judea" (111), asking us to read him as the embodiment of the negative stereotype of the Wandering Jew and urging us to share his belittling scorn.

In his chapter on Stauben, Arnold Eisen devotes several pages to the figure of Lazare, asking why this "wandering Jew," this "*ostjude* at the door," would surface in a text that otherwise offers such carefully edited nostalgia. Pointing out that the mythical figure of the Wandering Jew had acquired positive connotations in certain "leftist circles" in France by midcentury, thanks in part to Eugène Sue's popular serial novel *Le juif errant* [The Wandering Jew] (1844), Eisen suggests that "Lazare served as a mouthpiece for truths and anxieties that the readers of *Scènes* would not have been willing to hear" (168).[47] Lazare's tirade against modernizing the religion represents for Eisen one of the few moments in the text when Stauben deals with debates over observance, even if Stauben "acts immediately" to dismiss the beggar's view: "It comes via a silly beggar, and Stauben's audience, unlike Lazare's, does read French. And Parisians were no longer wandering Jews! They were at home."[48]

Although correct to call attention to the strangeness of Lazare's presence in this text, Eisen attributes to him a more positive role than he really plays. Stauben does more than dismiss Lazare's tirade; he mocks it from the start. The beggar's tirade against translating Hebrew texts into French constitutes exactly the kind of retrograde mentality that Stauben's colleagues in *Les Archives Israélites* continually attacked. As I showed in Chapter 3, even such a stalwart of Orthodoxy as Ben Baruch, who constantly lambasted Reform in the pages of *L'Univers Israélite*, devoted himself to providing patriotic French translations of the liturgy. To attack French translations of Hebrew texts was a position so extreme—and in the case of Lazare, so obviously self-interested—as to be ridiculous. Far from voicing truths that Stauben wanted his assimilated readers to hear, Lazare represents the lone example in the text of the Jew who must be transformed, or perhaps merely condescended to, as an amusing reminder of what not to wear and what not to do or say. Lazare offers the necessary foil for the other characters, whose pure manners and enlightened ideas emerge in contrast to the peddler's retrograde persona.

Stauben's journey back to Alsace, which figures as a journey back in time as well as space, reveals that the vast majority of the supposedly "unregenerated" village Jews are not so degenerate after all. Whereas liberal reformers at the time held that, in order to become a worthy citizen, the village or ghetto Jew needed to reform his manners and mentality to purge himself of the taint that years of oppression had instilled, Stauben represents the village dweller as embodying the most noble of characteristics. Whereas sympathetic reformers traced the Jews' supposed love of money to the fact of their persecution, to the need to realize their capital at a moment's notice in order to flee ahead of some death warrant, Stauben does not seek to excuse such materialism; he denies its very existence. Seemingly uninterested in money or business, Stauben's village Jews display an open-hearted generosity and elevate the spiritual over the material in every aspect of their lives.[49]

Stauben may have shared the ideological program of Kompert and Lévy in his advocacy of manual labor in a country setting as the goal for the newly enfranchised Jews of France, but he portrays the Alsatian Jew as always already embodying this ideal. This is not to say that the Alsatian Jews betray no signs of backwardness. Throughout the text, Stauben describes their many superstitious beliefs. The story told by the père Samuel in the second chapter features witches who transform themselves into cats and the *Schamess* (or beadle) of the synagogue has strange visions.[50] Harmless folkways, these superstitions pointedly have little to do with the actual religious practices of the Alsatian Jews, which exemplify an austere monotheistic purity. The Alsatian Jews may not have benefited from the Enlightenment, but the small signs of backwardness in their behavior and belief only serve to underscore the purity of their manners and morals in their primitive state. If anything, these quaint superstitions link the Jews more closely to their Christian neighbors—or to the peasants described by Sand in *La mare au diable*—further absolving them of the stigma of degeneration.

One of the main functions of Stauben's *Scènes de la vie juive en*

Alsace was thus to present a positive image of traditional Judaism to counter the negative presumptions inherent in most of the other fictional works of ghetto life. By showing the rural Jews of France's eastern provinces to lack the degenerate characteristics attributed to them by both Jewish and gentile reformers, Stauben challenged assumptions about what the Jews should do to modernize. In his work, the Jewish tradition comes to serve as the origin of positive values and, as such, as a source of nostalgia. Stauben aims these lessons both at non-Jewish readers, curious about—or perhaps suspicious of—Jewish difference, and at would-be Jewish reformers ashamed of their country cousins.

The Rise of Jewish History

At the same time, Stauben's text and other forms of ghetto fiction served a different, more existential function specifically for their Jewish readers. They helped institute a new relation to the Jewish past and a new use for Jewish history. Although Stauben and Kompert largely set their narratives in the present, they show this present to be continuous with an unbroken chain of Jewish tradition for their ghetto dwellers. Indeed, their stories of ghetto or village life could almost be said to take place in a kind of eternal past in which the Jewish characters perform the same occupations and worship in the same ways as their ancestors have for centuries. Stauben takes pains to contrast this traditional setting with the modern Parisian existence of his narrator. When this narrator throws on his coat and sets out on the train to Alsace, his journey takes him back in both space and time to a world that seemed in the 1840s on the verge of disappearing.

The effort that these fictional and quasi-fictional texts make to document the customs of an almost bygone world form part of a much larger revolution in Jewish attitudes toward history that took place in the mid-nineteenth century. As Yosef Hayim Yerushalmi makes clear, Judaism had in some sense always treated the past with veneration. The Hebrew Bible functions as a history of the nation of Israel and enjoins the reader to remember (*zakhor*) the events of the national past. Jews incorporated these events into their religious rituals, many of which involve the narration of important events in the history of the people, such as the Exodus from Egypt recounted in the yearly Passover ritual. Yerushalmi explains how this form of collective memory, expressed in ritual remembrance, served to bind the Jewish people together following the loss of their national homeland. Selective in its contents, collective memory filtered out extraneous detail to better serve religious and nationalist ideologies, such as the faith in messianic redemption and a return to the land of Israel.

Beginning in the early nineteenth century, however, history began to take the place of memory for western European Jews. "The modern effort to reconstruct the past begins at a time that witnesses a sharp break in the continuity of Jewish living and hence an ever-growing decay of Jewish group memory. In this sense," Yerushalmi writes, "history becomes . . . the faith of fallen Jews."[51] All the secular Jewish ideologies that developed in the nineteenth century used the past to justify their goals for the future. Those who believed in emancipation saw the French Revolution as ushering in a new era in Jewish history and viewed the sufferings of the past as leading up to this watershed moment. Zionists likewise invoked history to support their call for a return to the Jewish homeland. The Jews, of course, were not the only group to experience a renewed interest in history in the nineteenth century, as the peoples of Europe increasingly turned to historical narratives, including novels, to come to terms with the radical reorganization of their social structures and to develop a new sense of national belonging.[52] But as Yerushalmi has argued, the historiographic revolution of the Romantic period was particularly wrenching for Jews because it represented such a rupture with prior ways of relating to the past.

Although the break with tradition may not have been as sharp as Yerushalmi suggests—even in France, Jews retained ritualized forms of collective memory long after emancipation—the rise of new historiographic practices did constitute an innovation in the nineteenth century. This new form of history valorized the more recent diasporic period of the Jewish past neglected by traditional collective memory and sought a much greater specificity in its historical reconstructions. It also invested history with new meanings, substituting for the traditional faith in messianic redemption a confidence that emancipation represented the telos of the Jewish past. At the same time, it produced a sense of loss, or mourning for collective memory, that I argue echoes throughout Stauben's text.

The renewed Jewish interest in history began in Germany, where the Wissenschaft des Judentums movement attempted, from the 1820s onward, to place the Jewish people on an equal footing with other European *volk* by recovering their modern history.[53] As Yerushalmi points out, whereas traditional Jewish collective memory was highly selective in its approach to the past, the modern historians sought a more total picture of Jewish life and recovered details and facts that had no place in ritualized remembrance. The new scientific approach to Jewish history culminated in Heinrich Graetz's multivolume history of the Jews, published in German between 1853 and 1870, which documents the diasporic period in great detail.[54] The German Jewish historians associated with the Wissenschaft movement also turned their sights on non-Jewish history, recasting it from a Jewish perspective in what Susannah Heschel has argued constitutes the first example of postcolonial contestation of the West's intellectual hegemony.[55]

The Jewish historical novel formed a vital part of this historical renaissance. Scholars of German Jewish culture have shown that beginning with Berthold Auerbach's *Spinoza: Ein historischer Roman* [Spinoza: A Historical Novel] and Phöbus Philippson's *Die Marannen* [The Marranos], both published in 1837, and continuing with the works of Ludwig Philippson and Markus Lehmann in the 1860s and 1870s, Jewish authors writing in German offered a mostly Jewish readership fictionalized narrative accounts of the Jewish past.[56] According to Jonathan Skolnik, the Institut zur Förderung der Israelitischen Literatur (Institute for the Promotion of Israelite Literature), a book club formed by Ludwig Philippson and a group of Jewish scholars in 1855 to promote the new Jewish literature in German, distributed more than 182,000 copies of 55 different works by 1865. Historical novels composed roughly one-fifth of their titles.[57] I would point out that in the case of the historical novel, the French take primacy: Eugénie Foa's historical fiction about Jews from the early 1830s preceded those of her German coreligionists by several years.

French Jewish historians, however, lagged somewhat behind the Germans. Aron Rodrigue has shown how Léon Halévy's *Résumé de l'histoire des juifs modernes* [Summary of the History of the Modern Jews] (1828), the first postbiblical history of the Jews written by a French Jew, hails the French Revolution as a sacred event in Jewish history and views France as a new promised land.[58] It does not yet bear the traces of the new scientific mode of history writing, but it does represent a significant departure from traditional forms of Jewish memory in its revaluation of the modern period and its elevation of emancipation over messianic redemption as the goal of the Jewish trajectory. In the following decades, French Jewish historians such as Éliakim Carmoly, Moïse Schwab, Élie-Aristide Astruc, James Darmesteter, and Théodore Reinach would import the methods of the Wissenschaft movement into France.[59] From its inception in 1840, *Les Archives Israélites* contained articles devoted to modern Jewish history. Although many of the early articles in the journal were translations from the German, gradually French authors began to produce their own histories, many of which focused on specifically French Jewish people and events.[60]

The short-lived weekly journal *La Vérité Israélite* provided a forum for this new Jewish historical scholarship. Founded in 1860 by Joseph Cohen (1817–1899) and with its collaborators consisting of "a society of rabbis and men of letters," the journal combined a scholarly examination of the Jewish religion with articles of a literary and historical nature.[61] In his opening editorial in the first issue, Cohen announces victory in the struggle for Jewish emancipation and declares that the time has come for French Jews (or in his terms, Israelites) to dedicate themselves to analyzing their own culture and tradition. "Our goal, our single goal, is a mission of teaching and religious instruction,"[62] he declares, signaling the journal's difference from the more worldly focus of *Les Archives Israélites* and *L'Univers Israélite* as well as from their polemics over ritual reform. *La Vérité Israélite*, by contrast, would focus exclusively on "that Jewish law, that Israelite truth, which has survived the ruin of every empire" and on the diverse ways that the religion has been practiced through time. Despite Cohen's efforts to distinguish his journal from the competition, however, many of the collaborators on *La Vérité Israélite* also wrote for *Les Archives Israélites* or *L'Univers Israelite*, including both Alexandre Weill and Alexandre "Ben Baruch" Créhange.[63]

It is not surprising, therefore, that both Widal and Schornstein collaborated on this journal. Along with its programmatic editorial, the first issue of *La Vérité Israélite* contains an article signed by Daniel Stauben titled "Le Hanouka en Alsace: Souvenirs de la vie juive" [Hanukkah in Alsace: Memories of Jewish Life], which reprises his descriptions in *Scènes de la vie juive en Alsace* of the way Alsatian village Jews celebrate the December holiday. This piece recounts the history behind the Hanukkah story in a manner that goes beyond the performance of collective memory: "Who doesn't know the famous story of the Maccabees, those heroes of Jewish independence, from the time of the Second Temple and the domination of the odious Seleucids?" the narrator asks, adding to his description of traditional forms of celebration a wealth of historical facts not contained in ritualized remembrances of the event.[64] In subsequent issues, the journal would print excerpts from his *Scènes de la vie juive en Alsace*, which, it notes, presents "in a dramatic and eminently literary form the manners of our little Alsatian communities."[65] It also featured some original works by Stauben, including the short story "Joker Dai," a work of historical fiction about Jews set in the sixteenth-century Frankfurt ghetto.[66] In its effort to present Jewish history with a new level of detail and specificity and in its refusal to become engaged in doctrinal debates, *La Vérité Israélite* epitomizes the modern approach to Judaism that would take the past as its primary focus.

Schornstein's Ghetto Fictions

As a contributor to *La Vérité Israélite*, David Schornstein would combine a concern with documenting the disappearance of traditional forms of collective memory with a new kind of Jewish history writing. Schornstein was born in the Alsatian village of Brumath (Bas-Rhin) in 1826, the son of Joseph, a cantor in the synagogue, and Madeleine Weil. Despite his traditional religious upbringing, he studied secular subjects. From 1843 to 1846, he trained to be a teacher at the École Normale of Strasbourg, before pursuing a literary career in Paris. Once in the capital, he wrote several plays and volumes of nostalgic ghetto fiction (*La dîme*, 1864; *Perle*, 1877). Mainly, however, he worked as a journalist, collaborating on both Jewish and mainstream publications, including both *Les Archives Israélites* and *L'Univers Israélite*, as well as *Le Charivari*, *L'Artiste*, and *Le Petit Journal* (one of the first truly mass market Parisian dailies, founded in 1863 by Moïse Polydor Millaud, a Jew from Bordeaux), where Schornstein served as an editor until his death in 1879.[67] A specialist in Jewish art and antiquities, Schornstein wrote a yearly review of Jewish artists in the Paris Salon for *Les Archives Israélites* in the 1860s. As mentioned earlier, he also wrote, under his pen name Georges Stenne, an introduction to the catalogue of the Strauss collection of Jewish antiquities, which showed at the Universal Exposition of 1878.[68]

The second issue of *La Vérité Israélite* contains a typical piece of ghetto nostalgia by Schornstein, "Le vendredi soir dans les familles juives de l'Alsace" [Friday Night in the Jewish Families of Alsace], which documents traditional forms of Jewish Sabbath observance in his Alsatian homeland. In later issues, he furnishes a historical piece on the capture of Jerusalem by the Romans as well as one on the Jewish community of Prague and its legends. Schornstein's most notable contribution to *La Vérité Israélite*, however, consists in a series of six novellas about Jews in different historical periods that he published serially between the second issue in 1860 and the journal's final issue in 1863. These lurid, action-packed fictional works stand out from the dry erudite articles that make up the rest of the contents of *La Vérité Israélite* and were no doubt intended to reach a wider readership than the "rabbis and men of letters" who no doubt constituted not only the journal's primary collaborators but also its primary readers.[69] I want to turn now to Schornstein's historical fiction to show how it exemplifies the way history had become the basis of identity for a new generation of secular modern Jews. And not just any history: For Schornstein, as for Stauben, the past that serves to found the new form of Jewish identity can be found only in the ghetto.

According to Yerushalmi, Jews before the modern period viewed their period of national exile, characterized by persecution, as largely unworthy of history, a "shameful" epoch better forgotten.[70] Schornstein, by contrast, draws his fictional subjects exclusively from this history of diasporic oppression. All of Schornstein's novellas in *La Vérité Israélite* describe either the horrible suffering of the Jews at the hands of their Christian neighbors or their narrow escape from such suffering in medieval and early modern Europe. In "Le sauveur ou le nouveau Mardochée" [The Savior or the New Mordechai] (1860), the Jews of sixteenth-century Prague are rescued from expulsion through the influence of a community leader who receives a warning from a government minister he has saved from bankruptcy. "Le Kaddisch avant Col-Nidré" [The Kaddish Before Kol-Nidre] (1860), set in sixteenth-century Worms, focuses on pogroms and forced conversions in Germany during the Wars of Religion.[71] In "La légende du kabbaliste de Mayence" [The Legend of the Kabbalist of Mainz] (1861), the characters run afoul of the Christian authorities who threaten violence if they do not convert.

"Deborah, la juive de Nuremberg" [Deborah, the Jewess of Nuremberg] (1861) presents the most detailed and disturbing representation of Jewish suffering in Schornstein's corpus. Set in fifteenth-century Nuremberg, the story describes how Reb Baruch and his daughter, Deborah, attempt to help their local prince put down a conspiracy but fail to thwart an attack by the local mob against the town's Jewish ghetto. Unwilling to take up arms to defend themselves, all the Nuremberg Jews take refuge in the synagogue, cowering in a gesture of passivity that the narrator ascribes to their tradition of suffering: "As for resisting themselves, the number of their enemies, the passive resignation that an unending and pitiless persecution imprinted upon them, had prevented them even from thinking of self-defense. Assembled altogether in the synagogue, they awaited their harrowing fate with prayers and tears."[72] The only man willing to come to their aid is Dietrich, a poor Christian orphan whom Deborah had cared for as a child and who pines for her love. "Indeed, Dietrich was not a poor Jew who would let himself be slaughtered without resisting" (141), the narrator informs. The Christian Dietrich tries to shame the Jews—including Deborah's bookish fiancé, Emmanuel—into taking up the sword in self-defense: "Must you, your wives, and your children go like lambs to the slaughter?" (237), he asks in terms that reproach Jewish passivity.

Emmanuel eventually does overcome his fear and inertia to take up arms but is immediately killed by the angry rioters, along with Reb Baruch, who likewise sacrifices himself heroically. The Christians then set the synagogue, with all the town's Jews in it, on fire. Dietrich manages to save Deborah from the burning building, which collapses in an image of horrifying destruction. At the end of the story, Dietrich and Deborah seek refuge in nearby Trèves (Trier), where the Christian orphan Dietrich converts to Judaism in order to marry Deborah and takes the name of her father, Baruch. An epilogue informs readers that restrictions forbade Jews from dwelling in Nuremberg until the lifting of residence restrictions in 1848.

This is clearly not the same type of writing about the Jewish past that Stauben and Kompert were producing, nor even that of Schornstein himself in his portrait of Alsatian Jewish village life in "La dîme." We have no hefty Jewish matrons making matzo balls in these stories, no rustic celebrations of the Jewish life cycle, no neighbors sharing their humble rewards together. If all those texts idealize to a greater or lesser degree traditional Jewish life in the ghetto, Schornstein here focuses instead on the horrible suffering that it produced. How to account for this difference?

Schornstein's obsession with historical persecution, his drive to document in excruciating and often gory detail the multiple ways in which Jews suffered in medieval and early modern ghettos, has diverse functions. On a purely narrative level, this fetishization of violence offers the kind of lurid excitement that readers of historical fiction had come to expect of the genre. Schornstein's novellas are page-turners in the way that Dumas père's swashbuckling historical adventures are and in a way that Stauben and Kompert are most definitely not. Schornstein turns the Jewish past into an adventure tale, one that could be consumed alongside, or perhaps in place of, the serialized novels, the *romans feuilletons*, that his Jewish readers would have found in mainstream middlebrow publications and one that offered the same cheap thrills.

But these fictional works do more than just provide a Jewish version of a popular literary genre. We have already seen how Stauben and Kompert used their ghetto fiction to comment on the regeneration debate. Kompert explicitly offered a program for the transformation of lower-class Jews, whereas Stauben argued that they are less degenerate than one might think. And whereas Schornstein's "La dîme" resembles Stauben's idealized portrait of the village dweller in deemphasizing the need for regeneration, his historical fiction stigmatizes negative aspects of the preemancipation Jewish psyche in a manner similar to Kompert's. In "Deborah, la juive de Nuremberg," Emmanuel's weakness and passivity in the face of danger, his cowardice and apathy, figure as a regrettable but understandable response to the overwhelming force directed against the Jews by their oppressors. The story reinforces the idea that these traits can be overcome through historical change, through granting Jews equality. When motivated by Dietrich, both Deborah's fiancé and her father do prove capable of surmounting their apathy to make heroic if doomed stands against their oppressors. In the case of Deborah's future offspring with Dietrich, the influx of vigorous and brave Christian blood cannot but help this process along.

Schornstein displays a special fascination with not only gruesome death scenes but also the multiple restrictions on Jewish life in the ghetto. This is ghetto fiction, then, in the true sense of the term. Nearly all Schornstein's stories dwell in detail on the rules and regulations restricting Jewish movement in medieval times. In "Deborah, la juive de Nuremberg," the characters constantly seek to avoid getting locked out—and eventually locked in—the part of the city that confines them. Like the images of anti-Jewish violence in Schornstein's fiction, this recurring motif of isolation and restriction had deep ideological resonance in nineteenth-century France. It once again helps bring into focus some of the differences separating the practitioners of ghetto fiction.

In *Scènes de la vie juive en Alsace*, Stauben presents the Jewish villages of eastern France as a world unto themselves. His characters do not leave the village—except on rare occasions to attend a celebration nearby—but neither do they feel trapped in a place that contains within it everything necessary for a happy life lived according to Jewish ritual and law. Likewise, in Schornstein's "La dîme," the characters seem only dimly aware of a world beyond the confines of their small Alsatian village and then only look to the nearby Jewish community of Frankfurt. Kompert too would look back longingly to the tight-knit Jewish communities of the Bohemian ghettos even while advocating a moral renewal, achieved through physical labor, that would cleanse the Jews of the lingering negative aspects of the ghetto mentality. In these more classic instances of ghetto nostalgia, the social solidarity of the Jewish ghetto or village offers a contrast to the pressures and anomie of the modern metropolis.

Schornstein's historical fiction in *La Vérité Israélite*, however, bears no trace of nostalgia for the ghettos it describes. In contrast to Kompert and Stauben and to his own nonhistorical fiction, he does not sentimentalize or idealize traditional Jewish life in his historical works. Schornstein makes no attempt to celebrate colorful ghetto characters or to glorify the warmth produced by communal confinement. Moreover, his historical ghetto dwellers display little of the communal solidarity that might compensate for their isolation. In "Deborah, la juive de Nuremberg," the heroine's initial impulse to stay behind with her fellow Jews almost dooms her, and she ultimately abandons her community in the conflagration of the synagogue. In "Le sauveur ou le nouveau Mardochée," the hero does save his fellow Jews of the Prague ghetto from expulsion, but the story celebrates Jewish charity toward Christians beyond the ghetto walls rather than communal affiliations *intermuros*. These historical works function as a kind of counterweight to the romanticization of the ghetto in contemporaneous Jewish fiction, serving to remind readers of the pain and suffering such confinement entailed.

Schornstein seems equally at pains to criticize the ghetto way of life. We have already seen how he censures Jewish passivity in the face of violence, denouncing it as a by-product of persecution. But he also targets more positive values cherished by Jews as compensation for their suffering. These include the premium placed on intellectual achievement, and religious study in particular, within the Jewish tradition. Whereas in Stauben's historical story "Joker Dai," published in

La Vérité Israélite in 1861 and set in the Middle Ages, the hero saves his fellow Jews by winning a religious debate with the Christian authorities (and later by using his medical knowledge to save the prince), few of Schornstein's heroes are scholars and even fewer have devoted themselves to religious study.[73]

The message to the Jews of nineteenth-century France was clear. For Schornstein, the lessons of the past taught that salvation for Jews lay in breaking free of the material as well as psychological confines of the ghetto, the legacy of their difficult history. The path of emancipation provides Schornstein's readers with the only hope for the future. What redeems these tales from despondency is the reader's knowledge that in an egalitarian France they cannot be repeated. The fact that all of Schornstein's violent narratives of persecution take place in neighboring Spain and Germany, where emancipation had not yet been fully achieved in the 1860s, only serves to underscore the implicit assumption of French redemption for the history of Jewish suffering. Indeed, Schornstein completely ignores the issue of *French* oppression of the Jews in the past, preferring to point to France's more magnanimous future role. He offers no stories, for example, of life in the *carrières* of Provence.

This vision of France as the new Jerusalem comes across most clearly in "Les marannos, chronique espagnole" [The Marranos, A Spanish Chronicle], published in 1861. Set in late-sixteenth-century Saragossa, the story begins when Don Diego, a respected Christian nobleman, reveals to his marriageable daughter, Juanita, that they are secret Jews. Threatened both by the Inquisition and by the powerful Count de Ramira, whose son he has rejected as a suitor for Juanita in favor of the obscure orphan Fernando, another crypto-Jew, Don Diego plots his family's escape from Spain. After a series of hair-raising adventures, in which Diego and his daughter barely elude their pursuers, they eventually cross the border into France along with Fernando in the story's happy conclusion.

Their newfound home inspires feelings of intense gratitude in the Marranos, who do not seem aware of the fact that they still cannot practice Judaism openly in France: "Juanita considered for an instant that land, which offered to her and her people asylum and protection against pitiless enemies, and where hope and happiness smiled at her again."[74] Here Schornstein's anachronism echoes that of Foa, who also displaced postemancipation tolerance onto the prerevolutionary past in her novel *La juive*. Schornstein's story implicitly references the narrative of the Exodus of the Jews from Egypt in its depiction of France as the new promised land of the Jews: "Blessed are you, O land of deliverance," the Spanish Jewess intones in her hymn to France. "May heaven always watch over you so that you become one day the leading country in all the world, the asylum of justice and the hope of all oppressed peoples" (791). The prophetic tone places this story of Jewish suffering in the context of a larger narrative of Jewish redemption, modeled on the Bible, but with emancipation as its ultimate goal. Jewish collective memory enshrined in biblical history is thus rewritten for a new generation of emancipated French Jews.

The representation of extreme forms of violence against historical Jews serves another function as well: It helps to cement a new sense of French Jewish identity in the postemancipation context. Schornstein's images of Jewish suffering in the ghettos of Europe promote Jewish ethnic identification in a world in which other ties binding Jews to the community—such as religious practice—were waning. By recounting the horrible persecution that the readers' real or imagined ancestors suffered for being Jews, Schornstein encourages them to value an identity they might otherwise neglect. In this sense, the stories serve a function akin to much Holocaust fiction today. They mark a key stage in the celebration and secularization of suffering that would become a central dynamic in Jewish fiction.

Note that even as these stories celebrate the goals of emancipation, they do not advocate assimilation. This difference from the precedent established by Foa's historical fiction is key to Schornstein's fictional and ideological project. Although he condemns Jewish isolation, he does not condone the kind of complete integration that would lead to the disappearance of Jewish specificity, as does Foa. His characters resist, whenever possible, the acts of intermarriage and conversion that Foa imagines as solutions to the dilemmas of her Jewish characters. The only intermarriage that occurs in his oeuvre is that of Deborah and Dietrich in "Deborah, la juive de Nuremberg," which ends with the Christian orphan converting to Judaism. In "Les marannos," the crypto-Jews convert outwardly but risk life and limb to practice Judaism in secret and eventually sacrifice their high social position in Spain for religious liberty. "It is at once our duty and our greatness to transmit to our descendants, amid perils without number, in the face of the cruelest torments, of death and infamy, the gift of that faith that makes for the hope and support of our people across the centuries,"[75] Don Diego tells his daughter when he reveals the secret of their Jewish identity, and she readily accepts the responsibility and the heroism that her newfound faith entails.

Schornstein represents conversion to Christianity as a spiritual and intellectual annihilation far worse than the physical death that remaining true to Judaism might entail. In "Le Kaddisch avant Col-Nidré," José-Abraham Silva, a Sephardic Jew who has fled the Spanish Inquisition to practice his religion openly, braves a mob in his adopted home of Worms to save his fiancée, Miriam, who has lost her mind after being attacked by hostile Christians, from forced conversion. Subdued by the mob, the forlorn Silva watches as the dazed Miriam is led off to a convent and accepts conversion to save his own life. At the end of the story, however, and after saving the Jews of Prague from destruction, Silva attempts to rescue Miriam from the convent, but she dies after recovering her sanity and her Judaism.[76] He then retires from the army to Worms to practice Judaism in seclusion. The epilogue recounts how the rabbis of Prague continue to this day to recite a special Kaddish for their crypto-Jewish savior on the eve of Yom Kippur.

The hostility to conversion in Schornstein's fiction functions not only as a literal warning to his readers but also as a more general admonishment against the lack of interest in Judaism and Jewishness that was becoming increasingly common among French Jews. By reminding his readers of the sacrifices their ancestors made to stay Jews, he exhorts them to continued fidelity. Schornstein's fiction may reflect the ideology of emancipation by instructing Jews to leave the ghetto, both physically and psychologically, but they resolutely do not advocate leaving Jewish identity behind.

But what does Jewish identity entail for Schornstein? Despite the sacrifices of his characters for their religious freedom, few scenes of actual Jewish religious practice occur in his fiction. The crypto-Jews in "Les marannos" do congregate for a secret Jewish service amid the ruins on the outskirts of Saragossa, but the narrator provides little sense of either the form or the content of their worship. The other stories pay even less attention to Jewish ritual or religious belief. At the end of "Le Kaddisch avant Col Nidré," we learn that Silva has instructed the rabbis of Prague to say the mourner's Kaddish in his honor, but we do not learn the significance this prayer has for him. Neither do we see Silva himself pray.

This lack of religiosity stands out next to the other articles in *La Vérité Israélite*, about three-quarters of which provide erudite analyses of the Jewish religious tradition. The same issue of the journal that contains the second half of "Les marannos," for example, also contains a long article by Joseph Cohen discussing the Talmud from a historical perspective as well as Cohen's "profession of faith," elaborating the tenets of his religious belief.[77] Schornstein's lack of concern for the religion also contrasts with the historical sketches that make up most of the other quarter of the articles in the journal. These include the excerpts from Stauben's *Scènes de la vie juive en Alsace*, which document in enormous detail the religious practices and traditional celebrations of the Jews in France's eastern provinces, and Schornstein's own nonfictional contributions to the journal, such as his description of Sabbath celebrations in Alsace.

If the other articles in *La Vérité Israélite* innovated by viewing the Jewish religion from a historical perspective, Schornstein's fiction pushed one step beyond, dispensing with the religion and retaining the history. What makes these tales important for understanding the function of ghetto fiction in the nineteenth century ultimately lies here, in the suggestion that history itself can serve as the basis of Jewish identity. Indeed, just as Schornstein's characters sacrifice themselves for the "faith of their fathers," so too do his narrators present the stories of Jews in the ghettos of the past as justification for remaining Jewish in the present. As Yerushalmi puts it, history becomes the faith of fallen Jews. The new kind of writing about the past that Schornstein implements, the effort to reconstruct in detail the legacy of oppression faced by Jews in the European Diaspora, substitutes here not only for religious practice itself but also for more traditional, ritualized forms of Jewish communal memory.

This substitution of history for ritualized memory is thematized throughout Schornstein's oeuvre but perhaps most poignantly at the end of "Le Kaddisch avant Col-Nidré," when the narrator instructs an imaginary reader, curious about the unusual addition of the Kaddish during the middle of the Yom Kippur service in Prague, to ask an old member of the Prague community for its meaning. "If by chance you happen to ask one of the old-time inhabitants of Prague, who along with the historical traditions of their community has kept that of Jewish hospitality, he will respond by offering you to break the fast with him the next day in his home and there he will tell you the moving story we have tried to narrate."[78] History, and specifically his own form of historical narrative, the narrator implies, is what will be left to modern Jews after the last guardians of memory have disappeared. Religious ritual here depends on a form of fiction for its meaning.

Schornstein's fiction thus demonstrates the importance of historical fiction for a new secular definition of Jewish identity. Here we begin to understand the stakes of Schornstein's project and to recognize its importance. Despite their melodramatic excesses, the liberties they take with historical fact, and their brutal violence, these works see themselves as a kind of secular scripture. Indeed, one might say that it is precisely these characteristics that approximate Schornstein's works to the religious literature, including the Hebrew Bible, they seek to replace.

Nostalgia for Memory

Despite their differences, all these texts about traditional village or ghetto life that I have discussed in this chapter perform a similar kind of cultural work: They all turn the past into the basis for a new kind of Jewish identity in the present. Just as Schornstein attempts to cement the loyalty of modern French Jewish readers by asking them to identify with the sacrifices made in past times for the sake of Judaism, so too does Stauben offer up traditional Jewish life in France's eastern provinces as the ground for a new kind of Jewish affiliation. Whereas Schornstein uses the past to bind modern Jews to a legacy of suffering, Stauben uses it to remind them of lost pleasures. Like the daring escapes and brutal massacres in Schornstein, remembering the homey idioms, the tasty foods, and the rustic occupations in Stauben offers modern French Israelites a reason to remain Jews. These narratives fill the gap left by the decline of traditional forms of faith and ritual.

This use of the past differs from the historical reflections of the writers I have described in previous chapters. In Ben-Lévi's peddler memoirs, the representation of life in prerevolutionary Lorraine offers the model for a new, reformed Judaism reduced to primary ethical impulses. Ben Baruch presents a more chaotic picture of the past in his fictionalized memoirs, also set in prerevolutionary Lorraine, meant to inspire readers to mourn not only the content but the form of traditional Jewish ritual in all its roughness. Alexandre Weill returns to the Alsatian villages of his youth to search for the essence of Mosaic monotheism lurking beneath traditional rabbinic Judaism. And Eugénie Foa recalls the sufferings of Jews in medieval ghettos to make the case for assimilation, advocating intermarriage and conversion as ways out of Jewish isolation. All these writers use the past as the means to reinvent (or in the case of Foa, to reject) Jewish religious practice for the present.

By contrast, the evocations of traditional Jewish life by Stauben and Schornstein do not contain prescriptions for Jewish religious practice. They do not advocate adapting ritual, following laws, or rejecting them altogether. Rather, they reconceive Judaism along historical lines. Jewish identity for them consists in a recollection of the traditions, and also the suffering, of ancestors. It requires a kind of affirmation of these customs but not their adoption or even their adaptation. True, Judaism always made use of history in its rituals, but it could be said that history *replaces* ritual. It is a secular approach to being a Jew. It offers a way of being Jewish without following laws or attending synagogue. And fiction provides its scripture.

I also think it is possible, however, to identify in Stauben's text, which perhaps more than any other work helped to generate this new historical form of Jewish identity, a resistance to it, or at least a recognition of the losses it entails. His *Scènes de la vie juive en Alsace*, I suggest in conclusion, theorizes the effects of the Jewish "historical turn" for the scholar-narrator and for the French Jewish community as a whole. To see how, let us return to the introduction to the first version of the text with which I began this chapter. Published in *Les Archives Israélites* and thus—unlike the later versions—intended for a specifically Jewish audience, this introduction describes the disorientation produced by Parisian life and the narrator's quest to find a remedy in the memories of his Alsatian childhood. "My dear editor," he begins:

> As you know, I left my native Alsace when still young, and transplanted suddenly into the middle of Parisian life, thrown into study by my vocation, and drawn into the whirlwind of that literary existence, where through wanting to know and explain everything you are consumed like a scorpion in the sun, where very often, after excursions into the fields of history and philosophy, you return pale of forehead and occasionally, alas! doubting in spirit, I for my part, in those difficult times, used to have the singular good fortune of finding the remedy along with the sickness. For that remedy is none other than the faculty I possess, thanks to my early education, of finding a refuge from the discouragement that often overtakes us in my memories of childhood.[79]

Although Cohen and Eisen do not discuss the *Archives* version of Stauben's text, focusing instead on the volume he published for a mainstream audience, this introduction seems in many ways to confirm their psychological reading of the text. It is difficult not to hear in the young professor's complaints about his Parisian existence an echo of the anxiety produced by the assimilation process and by the entry into modernity.

Yet, alongside the difficulties caused by "Parisian life," we find more specific anxieties related to the author's profession as a scholar and, even more specifically, as a scholar of ancient cultures. It is not just the disorientation of the city itself that plagues him, but the "whirlwind" of his *studies*. Indeed, on closer examination, the narrator does not actually mention the difficulties of assimilation or conflicts over following Jewish religious laws but rather complains of the exhaustion caused by his drive to "know and explain everything," which he likens to a scorpion scorched by the sun. This is a peculiarly academic kind of angst, an existential doubt produced by scholarly labors, by "excursions into the fields of history and philosophy."

This introduction, in other words, explicitly positions the first-person narrator as a historian, as a practitioner of the new kind of historical science for whom the labors of reconstructing the past produce a particular kind of ennui. Describing his struggles to "explain and know everything," the narrator laments the exhaustion and discouragement his work produces: "After excursions into the fields of history and philosophy, you return pale of forehead and occasionally, alas! doubting in spirit" (644). This doubt is existential in nature; it derives from a fear that his scholarly labors have yielded the wrong kind of results. As Yerushalmi notes, the modern historian produces a whole range of facts and figures that collective memory has neglected while failing to generate the organic connection with the past that traditional forms of memory have so effortlessly achieved. Like a scorpion in the sun, the historian consumes himself in the quest for information but can never achieve the connection with the past embodied in ritualized forms of remembrance.

The only antidote for the excesses of history, the text suggest, lies in memory. The narrator's "old reminiscences" (644) of his youth spent among traditional Jews in Alsace provide him with the diversion and respite necessary to continue his work of analyzing the traces left by the ancient civilizations of Greece and Rome. But if the narrator's own personal memories at first offer a counterbalance to his historical practice, they ultimately prove "powerless" (*impuissant*), incapable of compensating him for his pains and sustaining him in his labors. The trip back to the scene of his childhood, he hopes, will allow him to refresh his "slightly tarnished memories" but also to connect with a different and more authentic way of life: "I wanted to dip myself once more into the very source of reality" (645), the narrator states.

The Jews still living in Alsace incarnate the past because they still practice old traditions. In the introduction to the 1860 edition, Stauben refers to them as "that sort of *contemporary Judaic antiquity*" (cette sorte d'*antiquité judaïque contemporaine*) (v, emphasis in original), which in its oxymoronic formulation signifies the degree to which he considers them ahistorical holdovers from ancient times, similar to the Greek and Roman antiquities he spends the majority of his time studying. This antiquity emerges as a function of their "patriarchal" social structure and of their closeness to the land and the cycles of the seasons. They live much as their ancestors had for centuries, despite the modern technological innovations, such as the railroad, that bring the Parisian voyager to them in a matter of hours. But their antiquity also proves to be a function of their worldview. Like the Greeks and Romans, the Jews of Alsace live within what Yerushalmi calls "the enchanted circle of tradition."[80] They have yet to lose the faith in the supernatural. They hold firmly to the belief that a divine force governs their destinies.

Most significantly for the historian-narrator, Stauben's Alsatian subjects exemplify the traditional Jewish relation to the past. This emerges most clearly in the second and third parts of the book, the part not printed in *Les Archives Israélites*, in which the narrator describes how the Alsatian Jews celebrate the yearly cycle of holidays and festivals. Each of these holidays involves the performance of the past as ritual. On Purim, for instance, the Alsatian Jews read the story of how Esther saved her people from the destructive fury of the evil Haman, minister of King Ahasuerus in ancient Persia. The narrator summarizes the Purim story in detail and does so not as a modern scientific historian but rather as a traditional reader of Jewish sacred texts. He does not attempt, in the style of the Wissenschaft historians, to explain the actual historical conditions surrounding the Purim story—how, for instance, the Jews found themselves in the Persian empire after Babylonian captivity—or to evaluate the diverse source material composing the book of Esther—how it became the last of the twenty-four books of the Hebrew Bible to be canonized—but contents himself with summarizing the tale, as told by the *Megillat Esther*, which Jews the world over read in its entirety during the celebration of the holiday. This version of the Purim story sacrifices the kind of detail fetishized by the modern historian for the sake of collective memory.

The narrator goes on to describe how the Alsatian Jews reenact the main events of this story in symbolic form. "Is that all?" the narrator asks, "and doesn't this reading offer other incidents? There is one especially that it is my duty as a historian to mention" (204). Here the evocation of his status as a historian contrasts with the role he attributes to the participants in the Purim ritual, who actually seem to relive the events they describe.

> You haven't forgotten our youngsters armed with wooden hammers? They have remained there, following very attentively the voice of the hazan, and each time that he pronounces the name of Haman, son of Amdatha, you would have been able to see them, like one man, bend down and deliver, for at least five minutes, a pitiless series of hammer blows to the floor of the synagogue. All these blows are supposed to fall on the head of Haman. It's a tribute that the Jewish youth of our villages pay him, every year, in the same currency. And if, after more than two thousand two hundred years of inflicting that punishment upon him, the old minister of Ahasuerus doesn't yet have a flat back, we must admit that the fault doesn't lie with his young enemies, but with his solid shoulders. (204)

Unlike the modern historian or reader of historical fiction, the Alsatian Jews experience the past as a contemporary event. They project themselves into the story, banging the synagogue floor as if hitting Haman himself. Moreover, in doing so, they enact a ritual that their ancestors have performed for "two thousand two hundred years," further collapsing the distance that separates the ancient Jewish past from its fallen present. The precision with which the historian-narrator quantifies this time period contrasts with the lack of temporal awareness of the participants in the Purim festivities. Whereas the modern historians concern themselves with measuring the distance of the past from the present, those within the "enchanted circle of tradition" seek to close the gap, to make the past come alive in the present.

The second and third parts of Stauben's book are concerned nearly entirely with the celebrations of the various Jewish holidays. All these celebrations, like that of Purim, repeat this double historical gesture. On the one hand, the writing recalls the events befalling the ancient

nation of Israel and materializes them in the present through the ritualized act of remembrance: "It's mainly during the religious holidays
that the antique Hebraic civilization rises once again and relives, in
a way, its poetic grandeur" (99). On the other hand, the ritual re-
enactment of these memories serves to inscribe present-day Jews in
a continuum of ritual that links them with their ancestors who have
performed the same acts of remembrance for thousands of years. In
regard to Passover, an "antique and curious holiday, instituted to remember the Exodus from Egypt and the miraculous deliverance of
Israel" (101), the narrator thinks of "those thousand invariable customs that date from the most remote time of Jewish history" (101),
the identical forms of observance that collapse the distance between
past and present, such as the baking of unleavened bread to recall the
haste with which the Jews had to flee from Egypt and which current
Alsatian Jews reenact with a "minute exactitude" (101).

The pain experienced by the narrator in Paris, I would argue, derives from the loss of this organic relation to the past. Toiling to reconstruct the civilizations of Greece and Rome, the narrator experiences doubt and discouragement because he will never achieve the
connection with the ancient world experienced effortlessly by the
Jews banging on the floor of the synagogue or baking matzo. Indeed,
the more he labors to understand history, the further he finds himself
from it, because modern historiography seeks to establish the difference of the past, not to collapse it. Returning to Alsace thus offers the
narrator not only the opportunity to see the people and places of his
own personal past but to sense again what it felt like to experience the
past itself in a different way.

Written during the period when modern historical studies were
changing the way Jews thought about the past and about themselves,
Stauben's *Scènes de la vie juive en Alsace* documents and theorizes this
transition from memory to history. Throughout the text, Stauben
peppers his anthropological investigation of traditional forms of Jewish memory with reflections on their obsolescence. The "contemporary Judaic antiquity," he describes in the preface to the 1860 edition,
is "alas! about to disappear" (v), thanks to the progress of such inven-

tions as the railroad, the very mode of transportation that brings him from Paris to Alsace. But the railroad is not alone to blame; the new science of Jewish history, which was supplanting the obsolete forms of collective memory, also helped doom traditional modes of Jewish life to disappearance even while instituting a new, secular form of Jewish identity.

Conclusion: Proust's Progenitors

The writers I have discussed in this book use fiction as a laboratory for the invention of new forms of Jewish identity. They construct plots in which characters confront the central questions concerning Jewish modernity in the French context, including how to reconcile their Jewish particularity with the demands of citizenship. The solutions they suggest run the gamut from total assimilation—including intermarriage and conversion—to a version of neo-Orthodoxy that advocates maintaining fidelity to ancient Jewish laws and traditions. In between these two extremes, writers recommend reforming the religion to accommodate the demands of modern life or returning to its most archaic form to rediscover its true essence. Finally, some writers see the future of Judaism in the past and seek to ground a new kind of secular Jewish identity in historical representation. Taken together, these writers reveal the spectrum of options contemplated by French Jews in the mid-nineteenth century, the first Jews to face modernity as full and equal participants in the life of their nation.

I have emphasized that although some of these solutions resemble those proposed by Jewish writers in other European countries at the time, especially Germany, others were unique to France. I have also stressed the uniqueness of the forms these fictional works took in France. Eugénie Foa used the common generic models of the sentimental and historical novel, but she adapted them in interesting ways to suit the specific problems facing elite, modernizing French Jews. Ben-Lévi's combination of realism and idealism, like Ben Baruch's blend of Enlightenment satire and Talmudic parable, reflect their particular French literary heritage.

If these writers borrowed from the past, they also inaugurated literary trends. Weill's village tales influenced as important a non-Jewish writer as George Sand, and Stauben's brand of ghetto nostalgia continued to inspire Jewish writers into the twentieth century. The pseudonymous writers—Ben-Lévi (Weil), Ben Baruch (Créhange), Stauben (Widal), and Stenne (Schornstein)—all published in relatively widely read and discussed Jewish periodicals. Some of Weill's works, especially his novel *Couronne*, went through several editions, suggesting a readership beyond the French Jewish community. Foa was referred to as "our famous coreligionist" in *L'Univers Israélite*, indicating a large contingent of readers. In general, however, the claim I am making for the importance of these literary figures does not have to do with their influence either on the literary practices of subsequent generations of writers or on the religious practices of readers at the time. Their Jewish contemporaries may in fact have followed their prescriptions, but evidence that they did so would be nearly impossible to discover. If Foa emboldened her Jewish readers to marry their Christian lovers or if Weill inspired acolytes to seek a pure form of Mosaic monotheism in colonial Algeria, we will probably never know. Rather, what strikes me as perhaps most significant about these writers is the mere fact of their having written at all.

By this, I mean the fact that they wrote both as French Jews and, at least in part, for French Jews. To do so meant entering uncharted literary territory. French readers had never before heard the voices of minority writers. French literature had seen some regionalist imitators of Walter Scott beginning in the 1820s—writers who sought to describe the history of a particular province and the customs of its inhabitants with attention to "local color." There had also been literary attempts to imagine the experience of members of a minority group by writers from the majority culture. One thinks here of *Ourika* (1823), by the aristocratic Claire de Duras, about an African girl raised in France. To my knowledge, however, the Jewish writers I have discussed in this book were the first members of an ethnic or religious minority group in France to describe their own experience in fiction. Certainly they were the first to do so in the modern period, after the French Revolution made pluralism a possibility but also a problem.

These writers charted new territory, then, by defining a new role for French literature. In their hands, fiction became not just a form of ethnography but a potent tool for exploring the nature of social adhesion and self-definition in a modern liberal state. It also became a vehicle for countering negative images propagated by the dominant culture. The writing of French Jews in the nineteenth century, as I have shown, is very much a writing back—to Scott and all those who had traded in stereotypes of the predatory Jewish moneylender and the doomed *belle juive*. In the fictional worlds of these Jewish writers, we find bankers and beauties but also a whole range of more ordinary Jews—soldiers, scholars, seamstresses, storekeepers, and stockbrokers. Balzac used the figure of the Jew as a stand-in for the new economic and social processes of the era, but his Jewish contemporaries viewed the effects of modernity on average Jews. These Jewish fictional works reveal the ways in which a minority culture made itself at home in French literature, using it to present a more positive vision of themselves to the culture at large and to confront issues of relevance to the community itself.

I have also argued that these fictional works shed light on a number of important historical questions. Whereas Hannah Arendt and historians writing in her wake faulted nineteenth-century French Jews for their blind faith in emancipation and cast them as paragons of assimilation, the fiction of these French Jewish writers reveals how they imagined other fates for themselves and their descendants besides merely blending in. We find in their novels and short stories a desire to remain Jewish even while becoming French and a desire to confront head-on the difficulties such a novel conjunction of identities might entail. Even a writer like Foa, who advocated a radical form of assimilation, simultaneously created her literary persona around a model of Jewish difference. Her contemporaries and followers still more boldly proclaimed their Jewishness in the public sphere and sought to create new forms of Jewish solidarity to replace the old bonds of corporate identity that the Revolution had sundered. Taken together, their writings reflect the enormous creativity and versatility of a community in the throes of momentous social change.

As a result of the increase in antisemitism after 1870, French Jews became more circumspect about their Jewishness, but at the same time they sought a more active role in French political and cultural life. Several leading literary figures of the fin de siècle were Jewish: the Parnassian poet Catulle Mendès, the symbolist poet Gustave Kahn, and the large number of Jews involved in the extremely influential avant-garde journal *La Revue Blanche*, including Marcel Proust, Bernard Lazare, Léon Blum, and Tristan Bernard.[1] This journal was seen and denounced by antisemites as the agent of a Jewish infiltration of French culture; Edmond de Goncourt called it "a real nest of young Yids" (*un vrai nid de jeunes youtres*).[2] But it remains the case that neither the critics at *La Revue Blanche* nor the prominent Jewish poets thematized Jewish concerns in the way that their predecessors, the writers I have discussed here, so explicitly did. Devotees of art for art's sake, they largely separated the realms of art and politics.

As I discussed in the Introduction, literary historians have conventionally assumed that Jewish fiction in French emerged only in response to the Dreyfus affair, as a new generation of Jews born after 1870 rejected the assimilatory strategies of their parents and grandparents at the start of the twentieth century. This new generation included such writers as André Spire, Édmond Fleg, Jean-Richard Bloch, Bernard Lazare, Henri Hertz, Benjamin Fondane, and Henri Franck. They wrote explicitly as Jews and about Jews. Their fiction reflects a self-conscious attempt to forge a community through their writing, to establish links with their readers and perhaps with each other as well in order to reclaim a sense of Jewish difference. This attempt to build identity led many of this generation to Jewish nationalism and support of the Zionist cause. What strikes me as odd, therefore, is their total ignorance—or is it ignoring?—of the rich tradition of Jewish fiction in French that preceded them in the nineteenth century.

Although it is certainly the case that many of the works I describe were not readily available at the fin de siècle, they had not vanished into thin air. I was able to find them a century later at the Bibliothèque Nationale. These works may not have been for sale in bookstores, but many of them must still have been in circulation. Alexandre Weill did, in fact, continue writing into the 1890s and would have been known to the later generation. Moreover, some of the texts I discuss in this book went through several editions during the nineteenth century and probably could have been found on the bookshelves in the extremely literary homes in which many post-Dreyfus Jewish writers grew up. I think there is an element not just of ignorance but of repression at work, linked perhaps to a desire to reject what they held to be the strategies for negotiating Jewish identity of their parents' generation—or perhaps to a desire to believe that what they were doing was really new, when reading the nineteenth-century texts may have suggested otherwise.

This perhaps deliberate rejection of the legacy of their forebears is most surprising in the case of Marcel Proust—born in 1871, just after the period I have studied came to an end. Proust, as we have seen, was related to one of the most prominent nineteenth-century Jewish writers, Godchaux Weil, the man behind the pseudonym of Ben-Lévi. He was the grandson of Weil's half-brother, Nathé Weil. Godchaux died when his great-nephew was 7, but Proust continued to visit his widow, Frédérique (née Zunz), Tante Friedel, on New Year's Day until her death in 1897. Both Godchaux and his wife are buried in the Weil mausoleum at Père-Lachaise cemetery, alongside Proust's beloved grandparents, whose marriage Godchaux had witnessed.[3] And yet I could find no mention of this literary ancestor in Proust's correspondence or any reference to him in his fiction.

I can imagine all sorts of explanations for this lacuna. But instead of speculating on the reasons for an absence, I would like to turn, by way of conclusion, to the undeniable presence of Jewishness in Proust's fiction. This presence has attracted the attention of a number of prominent historians and literary critics—including Hannah Arendt, Jonathan Freedman, Julia Kristeva, Pericles Lewis, Elaine Marks, Henri Raczymow, and Eve Kosovsky Sedgwick. They have all investigated Proust's complicated and contradictory scrutiny of Jews and Judaism, turning it into one of the central terrains of critical disagreement as well as one of the major spurs to critical brilliance in the vast literature on Proust.

If Jewishness has come to be seen as one of the major keys to the puzzle of Proust, then Proust's representation of Jewishness has, in turn, come to be seen as one of the key sources for understanding the history of Jews in France. Proust's vast novel, *À la recherche du temps perdu* [In Search of Lost Time] (1913–1927), which I refer to here as the *Recherche*, offers a penetrating vision of fin de siècle Parisian high society as filtered through the extremely sensitive eyes of a young man who eventually becomes a writer. In the process, it focuses in detail on such important events to French Jews as the Dreyfus affair and on more quotidian struggles of French Jews for social acceptance and against antisemitism. Proust thus merits our attention here not only because he has long been seen as the greatest French Jewish writer but also because he has been considered one of the keenest historians of French Jews.

But what exactly constitutes Proust's view of the Jews and the Jewishness of his novel has never been easy to define. To a certain extent, Proust has become a kind of mirror in which readers see their own feelings about Jews—both positive and negative—reflected. Proust's younger contemporary, the great French writer and virulent antisemite Louis-Ferdinand Céline, denounced Proust's overwrought style as Jewish, likening his "Arabesque" constructions to the Talmud.[4] Writing in 1931, the American critic Edmund Wilson, who was more favorable both to Proust and to Jews, saw in Proust's moral indignation something of the Jewish prophet and thought his social satire was akin to "Jewish literature" and was hence "un-French."[5]

One of the problems with even such a well-disposed reading as Wilson's is his failure to delineate the Jewish literature to which he compares Proust's novel. Another problem, of course, lies in the way he denies to this Jewish literature the status of Frenchness, as if writing that is Jewish cannot also be French. In what follows, by contrast, I want to compare Proust's novel to a specific corpus that is both Jewish and French—the fiction by and about Jews produced in nineteenth-century France that I have described in the previous chapters. I want to ask what is to be gained by reading Proust as his uncle's nephew—gained both for our understanding of Proust's fiction and for our understanding of the nineteenth-century French Jewish literature that preceded it.

The perils of such a reading should not go unacknowledged, for in almost every way the fictional oeuvres of Proust and Ben-Lévi could not resemble each other less. The uncle wrote modest short stories in a Jewish newspaper and a didactic work aimed at schoolchildren. The nephew's multivolume novel, perceived by many as the greatest single work in all of French literature, is nothing if not monumental and universal. And yet, the two writers share a deep sociological and historical interest in the nineteenth-century French Jewish community, one that I argue emerges from a similar perspective. They also frame the dilemmas that Jewishness poses in modern France in similar ways.

I realize, of course, that to speak of Proust as a Jewish author is highly problematic. He was baptized a Catholic and received Catholic last rites before his death. But his mother, Jeanne Weil (1849–1905), was born a Jew and remained one even after her marriage to Proust's father, a non-Jew.[6] This alone would qualify him as a Jew according to Orthodox Jewish religious law, which traces Jewish identity through matrilineal descent. It would also qualify him as a Jew according to the new racial pseudoscience, which emerged in France in the second half of the nineteenth century and which believed Jewishness to be transmitted through the blood and manifested in physical features. As Jonathan Freedman points out, Proust's dark coloring and prominent nose were perceived as Jewish by those in his circle. "One night, after having let his beard grow, it seemed all of a sudden as if an ancestral rabbi reappeared from behind the charming Marcel we once knew," commented Proust's friend Fernand Gregh, Jewish himself and the possible model for the character of Bloch in Proust's novel.[7] Gregh's antisemitic—or rather, self-hating—opposition of the charming Marcel to the ancestral rabbi reveals the degree to which Jewish physicality had transformed from a mark of distinction, as it appears in Foa's fiction from the 1830s, into a source of shame in Belle Époque France.

Proust's affiliation with the Jewish community, however, went beyond any supposed "racial" connection. Proust remained extremely tied to his actual Jewish relations, who themselves remained both culturally and religiously Jewish. As all his biographers note, although his novel dwells in detail on the narrator's non-Jewish relatives, Proust had a much stronger bond with his Parisian Jewish family than with his father's Catholic family in the provinces. Indeed, many of the supposedly Catholic relatives of the narrator in the novel are modeled after Proust's Jewish family. Biographers have also shown that Proust's literary consciousness was shaped by his mother and maternal grandmother, Adèle Weil (née Berncastel), nieces of Adolphe Crémieux, president of the Jewish Consistory, and products of a cultivated Jewish milieu that emphasized the importance of female education.[8] Moreover, many of Proust's most intimate friends were other well-integrated Parisians of Jewish origin, including Geneviève Straus (Eugénie Foa's niece), Daniel and Élie Halévy (more Foa cousins, who did not consider themselves Jews), and Reynaldo Hahn.

Proust's political affiliations also aligned him with other Jews. As Hannah Arendt notes, the half-Jewish Proust was "in emergencies ready to identify himself as a Jew."[9] She is referring here to the Dreyfus affair, which divided France just as it divided Proust's own family; his Jewish mother supported Dreyfus, whereas his Catholic father believed Dreyfus guilty. Proust sided with his mother, becoming in his own words one of the "first Dreyfusards," and signed a pro-Dreyfus petition as early as January 1898, shortly after Zola's incendiary article "J'accuse" made the case for the Jewish officer's innocence.[10] Proust assiduously attended Zola's trial, which he described in detail in his novel *Jean Santeuil*, a precursor to the *Recherche*. His early and ardent pro-Dreyfus stance represents an especially courageous choice on the part of an assimilating half-Jew such as Proust. Another ardent Dreyfusard, Léon Blum, who was Proust's almost exact contemporary and who would later go on to become France's first Jewish prime minister, describes how the Dreyfus case posed a conundrum for French Jews, who did not want to appear to support the Jewish officer merely out of sectarianism.[11] Added to this was the social opprobrium surrounding the Dreyfusards, which led to their expulsion from certain prominent Catholic nationalist salons. Supporting Dreyfus meant putting hard-won assimilation in jeopardy. And yet Proust made this choice.

Scholars attempting to understand Proust's relation to his Jewishness invariably cite a revealing letter to his friend, the count Robert de Montesquiou, the model for the antisemitic Baron Charlus in the

Recherche. The letter dates from 1896, after the initial conviction of Dreyfus but before the eruption of the affair.

> Yesterday I did not answer the question you put to me about the Jews. For this very simple reason: though I am a Catholic like my father and brother, my mother is Jewish. I am sure you understand that this is reason enough for me to refrain from such discussions. I thought it more respectful to write this to you than to answer you in the presence of a third person. But I very much welcome this occasion to say something to you that I might never have thought of saying. For since our ideas differ, or rather, since I am not free to have the ideas I might otherwise have on the subject, you might, without meaning to, have wounded me in a discussion.[12]

Among the many interesting things in this letter, such as the author's supreme social tact, one notices Proust's affirmation of his Catholicism but also his unwillingness to disavow his Jewishness. Although he presents Catholicism as his religious identity, his Jewishness emerges as a more diffuse sort of affiliation, a bond between the writer and his mother. And yet, he presents this diffuse connection as a force determining his worldview and ideas—"I am not free to have the ideas I might otherwise have on the subject"—and as the source of a potential "wound," a relation of great affective intensity. So great is this intensity that it can be expressed only in writing. And indeed, it is only in his long novel that the meaning of this identity and the powerful sentiments that attach to it come into clear focus.

If one part of my definition of French Jewish fiction in this book has depended on the writer's biographical connection with Jews and Judaism, the other part depends on the fiction itself being about Jews and Judaism. Proust unambiguously fits the bill: That Jewishness is a major theme of the *Recherche* no reader can overlook. But I want to take this argument a step further by maintaining that Proust provides a meditation on Jews not as an outsider looking in but from a specifically Jewish perspective. In arguing this, I realize that I am treading once again on dangerous ground, for the narrator of Proust's novel, through whom the vast majority of the *Recherche* is focalized, is not presented as Jewish. Neither is he presented as homosexual, although the novel might be said to present an "insider" view of homosexuality as well. And indeed, the two *races maudites* are frequently compared in the novel.[13]

It is certainly true that the Christian heterosexual narrator, who is so lacking in particularizing traits, regards both the Jewish and the homosexual characters with a degree of fascination that seems to mirror the gaze of those scientific observers—the anthropologist, sociologist, and sexologist—who all emerged in France at precisely the historical moment described in the novel. This gaze is exoticizing. It even at times resembles something we might call racist and homophobic in its willingness to attribute certain innate tendencies to Jews and homosexuals. In so doing, it gives voice to the doxa of the moment. But it also engages with the problems of Jewish identity or same-sex desire in ways that belie or transcend this doxa and that expose its certainties to irony.

It does this first of all by holding stereotypes up to scrutiny. One of these is the literary cliché of the *belle juive*. As we have seen, Walter Scott's *Ivanhoe* helped inaugurate a tradition of splitting representations of the Jew along gender lines, depicting the male Jew as hideous and grasping and the female as the opposite—as beautiful, generous, and capable of seducing all who see her with her oriental charms. As I have argued elsewhere, fictional Jewish prostitutes fill the bordellos of nineteenth-century French literature, appearing in the works of Balzac, Baudelaire, Hugo, Huysmans, Maupassant, and the Goncourts as well as a host of less prominent writers.[14]

Proust plays with this tradition in self-conscious and often hilarious ways. On a trip to a brothel with his friend Robert de Saint-Loup early on in the novel, the narrator encounters a madam who tries to sell him on a certain prostitute named Rachel by billing her as a Jewess. "'She's Jewish! How about that?" (It was doubtless for this reason that she called her Rachel.) And with an inane affectation of excitement that she hoped would prove contagious and that ended in a hoarse gurgle, almost of sensual satisfaction, the madam continued: "Think of that, my boy, a Jewess! Wouldn't that be thrilling? Rrrr!"[15] Here we find the attribution of the quintessential Jewish name, Rachel, revealed as a marketing scheme aimed at arousing fantasmatic desire for the mythological *belle juive*. But although the aristocratic Saint-Loup falls for Rachel's Jewish masquerade, the narrator does not. By nicknaming her "Rachel when from the Lord," in reference to the famous aria from the Scribe and Halévy opera *La juive*, the narrator mocks the stereotype of the beautiful Jewess. His refusal to become aroused signals an end to the long tradition of viewing the Jewess as modernity's erotic plaything.[16]

Proust also skewers more overt forms of antisemitism. In one telling interchange, the Baron Charlus, upon meeting Albert Bloch, congratulates the narrator on having a foreigner among his acquaintances.[17] The narrator responds that Bloch is French. "'Indeed,' said M. de Charlus, 'I took him to be a Jew.'"[18] Charlus's blithe revocation of Jewish emancipation, his assertion of the incompatibility between Frenchness and Jewishness, is immediately censured by the narrator, who replies that were there to be a war, the Jews would be called up as soldiers like everyone else. Throughout the *Recherche*, the narrator gives voice to similarly liberal views. Although he does not always denounce the intolerance of the other characters as explicitly as he does here, the narrator does act as a touchstone of reason, in comparison to which the prejudices of Charlus and others appear eccentric and repellent.

The baron's antisemitism, however, proves immune to the narrator's reasonable rejoinders. After making the provocative assertion that Dreyfus is actually innocent of treason because he is not really French and therefore cannot betray a country that is not his own, Charlus lays his cards on the table, providing a glimpse into the deep well of hate he possesses for the Jews and the twisted psychosexual fantasies in which this hate is clothed. "Perhaps you could ask your friend to allow me to attend some great festival in the Temple, a circumcision, or some Hebrew chants." He continues:

He might perhaps hire a hall and give me some biblical entertainment. . . . You might perhaps arrange that, and even some comic exhibitions. For instance a contest between your friend and his father, in which he would smite him as David smote Goliath. That would make quite an amusing farce. He might even, while he was about it, give his hag of a mother a good thrashing. That would be an excellent show, and would not be unpleasing to us, eh, my young friend, since we like exotic spectacles, and to thrash that non-European creature would be giving a well-earned punishment to an old cow. (v. 2, 298)

Charlus here carries his antisemitism to its extreme dehumanizing conclusion in what I take as one of the most *anti*-antisemitic passages in the novel. Not only does the narrator denounce "these terrible, almost insane words" (298) in clear, forthright language (albeit only to the reader and not to Charlus's face), but Proust also shows the extent to which Charlus's antisemitism and anti-Dreyfusism are not rational opinions to which moral and sane French people might subscribe but rather spring from a deep perversity. By pointing to the insanity lurking beneath what passed at the time as an acceptable form of political and social discourse, Proust helps rob this discourse of its legitimacy and prestige.

It doesn't take a Jewish writer, of course, to denounce antisemitism. Where I think Proust really reveals his affinity with the Jewish authors I have discussed in this book is in his representation of Jewish characters. At first glance, however, the descriptions of the social awkwardness produced by the partial assimilation of certain Jewish characters—particularly the family of Bloch—are so biting that the text veers perilously close to enacting the antisemitism it elsewhere denounces. In one passage, Bloch's father and his uncle, Nissim Bernard, refer to their servants as *meschorès*, which the narrator informs us is a Hebrew term designating servants of God in the Bible. "In the family circle the Blochs used the word to refer to the servants, and were always delighted by it, because their certainty of not being understood either by Christians or by the servants themselves enhanced in M. Nissim Bernard and M. Bloch their twofold distinction of being 'masters' and at the same time 'Jews.'"[19] The narrator mocks the clannishness of these nouveaux riches Jews as well as the narcissistic delight they take in their difference and their privilege. But he also reveals that he understands the Hebrew term and thus comprehends the Bloch family on a deeper level than at first seems apparent.

Apparently the narrator understands not only Hebrew but Yiddish as well, for he also reports how Nissim Bernard dismisses the writer

Bergotte as a "Schlemihl" and describes Bloch père's embarrassment to hear the term designating someone who is "gauche" used in front of non-Jews: "The epithet 'Schlemihl' formed part of that dialect, half-German, half-Jewish, which delighted M. Bloch in the family circle, but struck him as vulgar and out of place in front of strangers [*des étrangers*]" (830), the multilingual narrator explains. Whereas in the first passage the narrator seems to mock the use of Jewish languages, in the second he satirizes the shame surrounding them. This is the critique of an author less scandalized by the presence of Jewishness than by the ridiculous efforts made by Jews to hide it. Moreover, the narrator's unusual use of the term *étrangers* (meaning both strangers and foreigners) to designate non-Jews, which I take to be a translation of the Hebrew term *goyim*, once again places the supposedly non-Jewish narrator within the world he criticizes.

Like Ben-Lévi, Proust does not hesitate to mock the graceless social contortions of his Jewish characters as they attempt to fit into gentile society. And like Ben-Lévi, his satire of the Jews proves less malicious than didactic. Proust mocks his fellow Jews to correct them. An even more blatant example of Proust's sleight of hand, whereby an observation that may at first seem antisemitic proves to be a Jewish self-critique, occurs on the beach at Balbec. The narrator and Saint-Loup overhear a tirade against the Jews emanating from a changing tent.

> One day when we were sitting on the sands, Saint-Loup and I, we heard issuing from a canvas tent against which we were leaning a torrent of imprecation against the swarm of Jews that infested Balbec. "You can't go a yard without meeting them," said the voice. "I am not in principle irremediably hostile to the Jewish race, but here there is a plethora of them. You hear nothing but, "I thay, Apraham, I've chust seen Chacop." You would think you were in the Rue d'Aboukir. (v. 1, 793)

Here Drumont's complaint about Jewish invaders taking over France, expressed in a biological language ("the swarm of Jews") likening the Jews to insects and containing a cruel parody of a Yiddishized French, appears at first as a kind of disembodied doxa. One at first suspects the author of displacing his hatred of the Jews onto an unseen speaker in order to voice prejudices without owning them. But in the next moment, the narrator reveals the identity of the speaker, completely changing the tenor of the scene: "The man who thus inveighed against Israel emerged at last from the tent, and we raised our eyes to behold this antisemite. It was my old friend Bloch" (793).

In this passage the object of satire turns out to be not the Jewish beachgoers with Yiddish accents but rather the discourse that would denounce them. It is not Jewishness but Jewish antisemitism—here named as such, despite its relatively recent coinage—that comes under fire.[20] To be sure, the passage does not totally escape from antisemitism by mocking it. Part of the humor in the revelation of Bloch as the scourge of the vulgar Jews lies in the fact that he fails to count himself as one of their number. And although the narrator and Saint-Loup are nothing but gracious to Bloch, the elevation of their own manners serves only to underscore the abjection of the Jew. There is certainly something more cruel in Proust's treatment of Bloch and his family than anything one would find in Ben-Lévi's representations of self-hating Jews. Nevertheless, Proust's focus on the complex psychological gyrations produced by Jewish assimilation and on their humorous but ultimately tragic social manifestations signals that something besides Jew baiting is at work in the novel.[21]

One could in fact argue that Proust is never more Jewish than in this passage. By mocking Bloch's vulgarity, by laughing at the vulgar Jew for laughing at the vulgar Jews, Proust repeats the very conduct he ridicules, tars himself with his own brush. In a sense, Proust becomes Bloch in this passage. He is the Jew he mocks. And Jewish readers might then mock Proust for mocking Bloch for mocking the Balbec beachgoers if this didn't lay us too open to the very same mocking (in an endless *mise-en-abyme* of Jewish self-hatred). I prefer instead to believe that the text is conscious of the effects it produces and that what comes out of the tent, or what Freedman calls "the Jewish closet," along with Bloch on the beach at Balbec is Proust's own tortured relation to a community he binds himself to even while ridiculing it.

Like the nineteenth-century Jewish writers but in an admittedly much more complex fashion, Proust satirizes both antisemitic stereotypes and Jewish assimilation. More significantly, I think, he also follows these writers in struggling to define what it might mean to be a Jew in modern France—"to invent the Israelite." We thus begin to see how viewing Proust in the tradition of the nineteenth-century French Jewish writers helps illuminate a vital part of his project. Most critics have viewed Proust's fascination with Jewishness as part of his larger philosophical undertaking; along with homosexuals and aristocrats, Jews serve Proust as heuristic tools for examining the nature of identity formation in modern society.[22] This is true. But it is also true that his inquiry into the possibilities for Jewish identity yields results that are particular as well as universal.

Like Ben-Lévi and his fellow nineteenth-century Jewish writers, Proust uses fiction as a kind of laboratory; the *Recherche* can be read as an experiment in which different types of Jews are put into a given social crucible (Parisian high society) and exposed to an external catalyst (the Dreyfus affair). From this experiment emerge new ways of being a Jew. So telling and apparently truthful are the results that Hannah Arendt would use them as evidence for her historical theories about the nature of Jewish assimilation in France—despite their explicitly fictional nature.[23]

As we have seen, Proust's narrator does not share his creator's Jewish background. Instead, Jewishness is projected onto two of the most prominent secondary characters in the novel—Charles Swann and Albert Bloch. They are the subjects of Proust's experiment, and by their very difference, their nearly opposite backgrounds and personalities, Proust makes the essential point that Jewish identity is never single or unitary but always the product of a unique combination of social determinants. Swann is the extremely cultivated son of the narrator's grandfather's close friend, who was a stockbroker (*agent de change*) like Jacoubé in Ben-Lévi's story about the prayer shawl.[24] At the start of the novel, Swann has achieved a seemingly effortless assimilation into the highest realm of French society, becoming "one of the most distinguished members of the Jockey Club, a particular friend of the Comte de Paris and of the Prince of Wales."[25] An art connoisseur, he hides his erudition behind a veil of good taste and impeccable manners. On the other hand, the narrator's schoolmate, Bloch, is a pretentious know-it-all from a family of uncouth Jewish parvenus. The contrast with Swann is explicit.

In fact, it is as an aside in the narrator's description of Bloch's reception by his family that we first learn of Swann's Jewishness: "It is true that my grandfather made out that, whenever I formed a strong attachment to any one of my friends and brought him home with me, that friend was invariably a Jew; to which he would not have objected on principle—indeed his own friend Swann was of Jewish extraction—had he not found that the Jews whom I chose as close friends were not usually of the best type."[26] We are made to understand that Swann—merely "of Jewish extraction," elsewhere referred to as the son and grandson of converts, with a Protestant grandmother—is the right kind of Jew, according to the narrator's family. And, to a great extent, we are asked to share this view; as Henri Raczymow notes in his study of the character of Swann and his real-life model, Charles Haas, "The less Jewish he is, the more refined he is."[27] Bloch, on the other hand, whose Jewishness is undiluted, furnishes a constant source of mirth and scorn. His absurdity derives not from his religious beliefs, which are never at issue, but from his manners—a curious mixture of overrefinement and vulgarity, which the novel encourages us to see as a product of his Jewishness.

Over the course of the novel, Swann and Bloch transform in ways that mark two approaches to Jewish identity seemingly as opposite as the two walks the narrator takes through the village of Combray. Despite taking a strong stand in favor of Dreyfus in the middle part of the novel, Bloch endeavors at the end to distance himself from his Jewish identity in order to penetrate more completely aristocratic circles that at first only tolerate him out of a "taste for the oriental."[28] Changing his name to Jacques du Rozier, he deploys an "English *chic*"[29] to mask his semitic origins; combing his curly hair straight and affecting a monocle, he manages to transform his physiognomy into a passably gentile configuration. Even his telltale nose assumes less threatening proportions: "And thanks to the way in which he brushed his hair, to the suppression of his moustache, to the elegance of his whole figure— thanks, that is to say, to his determination—his Jewish nose was now scarcely more visible than is the deformity of a hunchbacked woman who skilfully arranges her appearance" (v. 3, 996). But no amount of costuming can alter his fundamental Jewishness. As many Proust scholars have noted, even his ill-chosen pseudo-aristocratic name calls to mind the rue des Rosiers, the center of Paris's most Jewish neighborhood.[30] At the end of the novel he appears in an aristocratic salon, nervous as an "old Shylock" preparing to go on stage.[31]

Swann, in contrast, comes to reidentify as a Jew in response to the Dreyfus affair. Breaking with his former society friends, anti-Dreyfusards whom he accuses of antisemitism, this crypto-Jew (or "marrano" in the terminology of Marks) returns "to the spiritual fold of his forebears."[32] If Bloch represents a later incarnation of Ben-Lévi's Jacoubé, the dandy who gives his grandfather's prayer shawl to a grisette, then Swann is Gustave, the fisherman who rediscovers the meaning of Jewish ritual on Rosh Hashanah. Swann's passionate defense of Dreyfus leads him to a late-in-life conversion, a rediscovery of his Jewishness that signals the possibility that assimilation need not run in a single direction, that its losses can be reversed.

Recent critics, such as Marks and Kristeva, have tended to view Proust's representation of Jewishness as illustrating the performative aspect of identity in modern society. As the reference to Bloch's well-heeled turn as Jacques du Rozier illustrates, Proust presents Jewishness as a costume drama, in which identities can be dressed up or down for effect. The result, these scholars argue, is that Proust destabilizes the very idea of Jewish identity, indeed of all claims to group or national belonging, by showing them to be artificial rather than natural creations.[33] In Marks's reading of the Balbec beach scene, in which Bloch imitates the jargon of the Jewish masses, the tent from which he emerges becomes a sign of the latent homosexuality (in French, *tente* sounds like *tante*, slang for homosexual) hovering over the characters—especially Saint-Loup, the model of manly Frenchness—which undermines not only their heterosexual identities but also any claim to a stable, fixed identity, including Jewish.[34] Likewise, Kristeva analyzes Proust's Jewish thematics to ultimately argue that the novel's goal in representing Jews is to "untangle clannishness" and thus to oppose any sort of group identity.[35]

Although ingenious and often illuminating, these readings seem to me utopian in their attribution to Proust of a postnational, postracial sensibility. Proust does at certain moments in the text present Jewish and other identities as unstable and performative, but he also presents them at other moments as inherent and fixed. Indeed, Proust flirts with a racial notion of Jewishness that even a Gobineau[36] or a Drumont would have approved. "How marvellous the power of the race," he writes of Bloch's mysteriously reappearing Jewishness, "which from the depths of the ages thrusts forward even into modern Paris."[37] Moreover, the narrator presents the rediscovery of Swann's "semitism" not only as a religious or political reawakening but also as a racial reversion.[38] If Bloch's nose becomes less Jewish with age, Swann's olfactory organ comes to resemble that of "an old Hebrew."[39]

Even though it is true that the perception of the Jewishness of Swann's nose, or Bloch's for that matter, is presented as just that—the narrator's perception and for that reason colored by a racist ideology that at times Proust seems to mock—it is also true that the novel repeatedly presents Jewish identity in physical and racial terms.[40] Just as Swann is destined to die young from the same disease that killed his mother, so too does his return to Jewishness prove in part an unavoidable destiny. Describing the sudden appearance of hereditary characteristics in old age, the narrator remarks, "These changes were usually, in fact, atavistic, and the family—often even—especially among Jews—the race—filled up the gaps left by the passing of time."[41] If Jewishness is performative in Proust, it is clear that the Jews must follow a script dictated to them in part by their biology. Jews seem if anything more subject to these racial laws than other groups. In what I find to be one of the most perceptive readings of Jewishness in Proust, Freedman remarks that Proust reveals Jewishness to be more "essential" than other forms of identity and not in the end purely performative.[42]

But if Jews are somehow barred on a fundamental level from escaping their Jewishness, it remains their prerogative to determine the ways in which they assume it. Here, I think, lies the key to understanding what Proust has to say about the affirmation of Jewishness in the absence of religious faith or a legal framework inherited from scripture and tradition. To understand the novel's position, let us return to the passage in which Swann's semitic nose emerges from its dormancy at the end of the novel, after he has broken with his aristocratic friends over the Dreyfus affair and begun to succumb to cancer. Quoted in full, this passage reveals Jewishness to be a racial inevitability but also a moral choice.

> Whether because of the absence of those cheeks no longer there to modify it, or because arteriosclerosis, which is also a form of intoxication, had reddened it as would drunkenness, Swann's punchinello nose, absorbed for long years into an agreeable face, seemed now enormous, tumid, crimson, the nose of an old Hebrew rather than of a dilettante Valois. Perhaps too, in these last days, the physical type that characterises his race was becoming more pronounced in him, at the same time as a sense of moral solidarity with the rest of the Jews, a solidarity which Swann seemed to have forgotten throughout his life, and which, one after another, his mortal illness, the Dreyfus case and the anti-semitic propaganda had reawakened. There are certain Jews, men of great refinement and social delicacy, in whom nevertheless there remain in reserve and in the wings, ready to enter their lives at a given moment, as in a play, a boor and a prophet. Swann had arrived at the age of the prophet.[43]

The transformation of Swann's buffoonish "punchinello nose" serves as a pretext for the narrator's most profound reflection on the vicissitudes of Jewish identity. Interestingly, the racial explanation for the emergence of Swann's Jewishness is presented as merely a possibility ("Perhaps too . . ."), and not the most interesting one at that. Instead, the physical characteristics of Swann's change are juxtaposed with an ethical transformation involving the emergence of a feeling of "moral solidarity with the rest of the Jews," a solidarity that he had repressed or "forgotten" but that now reemerges as a result of antisemitism. It is this sense of solidarity that makes Swann a "prophet."

I have shown throughout this book, but particularly in the chapters on Ben-Lévi and Ben Baruch, how the idea of solidarity with other Jews came to define a modern and specifically French brand of Jewish identity that was not necessarily predicated on religious sentiment or inherited tradition. As I have argued, French Jewish fiction writers invented, or adapted, this modern form of Jewish solidarity, which was later actualized in the Alliance Israélite Universelle, the Jewish international aid organization. Formed in Paris in 1860 and headed for several years by Proust's great-uncle, Adolphe Crémieux, the Alliance took as its motto, "All Israelites are in Solidarity."[44] Even if Proust was not conscious of the legacy of the nineteenth-century Jewish writers I have discussed here, he uses their vocabulary to define Swann's sense of connection and moral responsibility to his fellow Jews. Yes, he presents Swann's incarnation as a prophet as yet another kind of performance—an identity waiting in the wings to go onstage. But he also endows it with a kind of moral intensity, described with an uncharacteristic lack of irony, that stands out among the other descriptions of Jewishness in the *Recherche*. Jewishness may be a performance, but the role is an important one.

I realize that I am beginning to sound rather utopian myself and perhaps as guilty as Marks or Kristeva of projecting my own desires onto the novel. My goal is certainly not to make Proust into a modernist Ben-Lévi. Without a doubt, the nature of Jewish identity proves far more complicated for Proust than for his great-uncle. Although there is something undeniably noble in Swann's solidarity with his fellow Jews, precisely because it requires him to turn his back on the attractive aristocratic world of the Faubourg Saint-Germain he has spent his life cultivating, there is also something limiting about it—and in the end, vaguely pathetic. Might Proust in fact be closer to Eugénie Foa, who advocated rejecting Judaism, than Ben-Lévi—despite their glaring differences in tone and style, not to mention literary quality?

Just after the quoted passage, in which the narrator refers to Swann as a prophet, he appears to the narrator, and to the reader, once again as a buffoon. Approaching the narrator and Saint-Loup, both fellow supporters of Dreyfus, at a society fete, Swann makes a "Jewish joke" of dubious taste: "Heavens!" he says, "All three of us together—people will think it's a meeting of the Syndicate." His mention of the Syndicate, a reference to the anti-Dreyfusard fantasy of a Jewish cabal in league against France, embarrasses the narrator and Saint-Loup, encouraging the latter to distance himself from the Dreyfusard camp. "[Swann's] Jewish gaiety was less subtle than his socialite witticisms," the narrator comments wistfully.[45]

Only able to view the world through the optic of Dreyfus and the Jews at the end of the novel, the once socially adroit Swann not only makes bad jokes but also more serious forms of social miscalculation. "Swann's Dreyfusism had brought out in him an extra-ordinary naïvety," the narrator remarks.[46] Even more troubling, Swann's Dreyfusism leads him to affirm what he knows to be false: "I chatted for a minute or two with Swann about the Dreyfus case," the narrator relates, "and asked him how it was that all the Guermantes were anti-Dreyfusards. 'In the first place because at heart all these people are anti-semites,' replied Swann, who nevertheless knew very well from experience that certain of them were not."[47] Clearly, along with the status of the prophet, Swann's return to Jewishness makes him something of a *mufle*, or boor: "[He] showed himself nevertheless quite comically blind. He subjected all his admirations and all his contempts to the test of a new criterion, Dreyfusism."[48] And Proust punishes this transformation brutally, belaboring Swann's skin and stomach ailments that seem to accompany and in a way provoke his newfound Jewish solidarity. The narrator refers to these symptoms as "ethnic eczema and . . . constipation of the prophets," thus associating the character's return to Jewishness, in both its cultural and political manifestations, with his physical decline.[49]

It must be acknowledged, then, that if Proust uses his novel as a laboratory to invent new possibilities for Jewish identity, his experiment does not yield very positive results. Even in approaching the dignity of the prophet, Swann cannot shake off the cloak of the buffoon. There seems to be no right answer to the Jewish question. Either the Jew attempts to hide his Jewish identity like Bloch, an enterprise doomed to failure, or he affirms it like Swann, which leads to a foolish, hypocritical, and even diseased form of tribalism. It is not difficult to see why Arendt found so much evidence in the novel to support her theories about the debilitating effects of assimilation on French

Jews. The *Recherche* presents Jewish life in fin de siècle France as a series of bad jokes, as a tragedy performed by its unwitting actors in a comic mode.

But for all that, the novel does not advocate the rejection of Jewish affiliation. Proust might complicate the Jewish question, but he is by no means an "anti-Jew."[50] The characters in the novel who reject their Jewishness or seek to deny it receive far worse treatment than Swann. Bloch is one example. Gilberte, Swann's daughter, is another. At the end of the novel, after her adoption by the aristocratic de Forcheville, her attempt to dissimulate her Jewish ancestry makes her look far more foolish than her father's blundering affirmation of it. Swann at least approaches the dignity of the prophet, even with his eczema and constipation. The self-denying Jews are just plain buffoons.

The central unanswered question concerning Jewish identity in the novel amounts to this: Can there be Jewish solidarity without clannishness? Or to put it another way, in a period in which the dangers facing French Jews threatened to transform comedy into tragedy, could the prophet be separated from the buffoon? The examples of Swann and Bloch would seem to provide a negative answer. They are not, however, the novel's only experimental subjects. The example of the narrator might be said to come the closest in the novel to resolving these paradoxes by affirming a principled solidarity with Dreyfus and the Jews without closing himself off from the world or devolving into buffoonery. But the narrator is not supposed to be a Jew—despite his odd familiarity with Yiddish and Hebrew.

Perhaps, then, Proust himself, the narrator's partly Jewish double, provides the kind of positive model for being a Jew that eludes his Jewish characters. Perhaps he is the one positive result of the experiment with Jewish identity he performs in his novel. By writing about Jews, Proust found a path to Jewish identity that otherwise eluded him. To argue thus not only attributes an identity to an author that he explicitly (although incompletely) rejected but also flies in the face of Proust's own injunction against biographical reading, against judging a work by evaluating its author, expressed in his polemical essay *Contre Sainte-Beuve*. But not to argue thus is to miss the novel's most important context, its productive tension with a life that it doubles and completes.

Only in writing, Proust tells us, can the contradictions of Jewish identity be held together without compromising their complexity. As Proust implied in his letter to Montesquiou, only in writing could he profess Catholicism while remaining somehow a Jew. Only writing would allow him to express solidarity with other Jews while criticizing their faults, to describe the reality of a difference that defines him and that he in turn defines. Only in writing could he avoid the pitfalls, the social missteps, of Swann and Bloch that Proust himself feared repeating in person. And it is through writing about Jewish specificity that Proust found his path to the universal, transcending the clannish while at the same time expressing solidarity with his fellow Jews. For Proust, it seems, the only solution for the Jew is to become a writer or artist.[51] Ultimately, however, the effort to find a positive result in Proust's experiments with Jewish identity matters less than the experiments themselves, which provide the most complex and penetrating analysis of Jewish modernity in French literature, perhaps in all literature.

Reading Proust in the context of his nineteenth-century Jewish forebears sheds light on important aspects of his project. Proust, in turn, sheds light on the nineteenth-century Jewish writers. Writing more than a half century later, he reveals where the social and cultural processes observed by Foa, Ben-Lévi, Ben Baruch, Weill, Stauben, and Schornstein would lead and how the dilemmas of the nineteenth-century French Jews would be transformed in the more difficult context of the Belle Époque. In many ways he confirms the results of their experiments; in other ways he contradicts them or exposes their certainties to beneficial scrutiny. Most of all, however, Proust reveals how the meaning of Jewishness remains an open question, one that can best be asked by fiction and one that fiction, perhaps, alone can answer.

Notes

Introduction

1. Alphonse Toussenel, *Les juifs rois de l'époque: Histoire de la féodalité fi-
nancière* (Paris: L'École Sociétaire, 1845). Zeev Sternhell analyzes the politics of
French antisemitism in *Neither Right nor Left: Fascist Ideology in France*, trans.
David Maisel (Berkeley: University of California Press, 1986).

2. Édouard Drumont, *La France juive: Essai d'histoire contemporaine* (Paris:
Marpon and Flammarion, 1886). Drumont's two-volume denunciation of the
Jewish presence in French political and cultural life sold 65,000 copies in the first
year and roughly 100,000 copies by 1914. On Drumont's success, see Élisabeth
Parinet, *La librairie Flammarion, 1875–1914* (Paris: Imec, 1992), 256.

3. By assimilation I mean the abandonment of religious and cultural specificity. Acculturation, on the other hand, refers to the adoption of linguistic, cultural,
and social norms of the host country without relinquishing some basic but dif-
ficult-to-define particular identity.

4. Hannah Arendt, *The Origins of Totalitarianism*, pt. 1, *Antisemitism* (New
York: Harcourt Brace Jovanovich, 1968), 117.

5. Arendt, *Antisemitism*, 118.

6. In *Proust: Questions d'identité* (Oxford: Legenda, 1998), Julia Kristeva provides a perceptive gloss of Arendt's text and its political subtext: "Beyond the
Dreyfus Affair, Hannah Arendt calls attention to the hidden, sociological, religious, and psychological causes that resulted in the extermination camps and the
Holocaust. Desired or imposed assimilation . . . is interpreted as one of the conditions of an unprecedented massacre, and the courageous Zionist return to origins
as the only possible way to resist it" (21–22).

7. My definition of Jewish literature would thus exclude literature by Jews that
does not thematize Jewish concerns. It would also exclude literature about Jews
by non-Jewish writers. (Of course, what makes a writer Jewish is another question, one that I discuss at some length in the Conclusion.) In her introduction
to *What Is Jewish Literature?* (Philadelphia: Jewish Publication Society, 1994),
Hana Wirth-Nesher points to the problems inherent in attempts to define Jew-

ish literature according to the identity of the author or by reference to language or theme. Rather than advancing any single definition of Jewish literature that is valid transnationally and transhistorically, Wirth-Nesher advocates a more strategic and flexible definition that "answers specific needs of time and place" (12). In *Jewish American Literature: A Norton Anthology* (New York: Norton, 2001), the editors Jules Chametzky, John Felstiner, Hilene Flanzbaum, and Kathryn Hellerstein provide a helpful and inclusive definition of Jewish literature as all literature "created by authors who admit, address, embrace, and contest their Jewish identity, whether religious, historical, ethnic, psychological, political, cultural, textual, or linguistic" (3).

8. In *The Structural Transformation of the Public Sphere: An Inquiry into a Category of Bourgeois Society*, trans. Thomas Burger (Cambridge, MA: MIT Press, 1989 [1962]), Jürgen Habermas refers to the "public sphere" as a discursive space in which individuals could debate societal problems in eighteenth-century Europe. Habermas sees the public sphere as already in decline in the nineteenth century because of the rise of consumer culture and the mass press. For my purposes here, I take the public sphere to mean a discursive space outside the home or synagogue in which Jews might confront non-Jews.

9. By emancipation I mean the acquisition of equal rights as well as, more generally, the full participation by Jews as citizens in national life.

10. Jeffrey Mehlman discusses pre–World War II denunciations of the Jewish infiltration of French literature in his "'Jewish Literature' and the Art of André Gide," in his *Legacies of Antisemitism in France* (Minneapolis: University of Minnesota Press, 1983), 64–82.

11. One of the best collections of essays on contemporary French Jewish philosophy and literature is Lawrence D. Kritzman, ed., *Auschwitz and After: Race, Culture, and "the Jewish Question" in France* (New York: Routledge, 1995). Thomas Nolden's *In Lieu of Memory: Contemporary Jewish Writing in France* (Syracuse, NY: Syracuse University Press, 2006) provides a helpful overview of fiction published by French Jews born after World War II.

12. Armand Lunel, "Vers une littérature judéo-française," in his *"Les chemins de mon judaïsme" et divers inédits*, ed. Georges Jessula (Paris: L'Harmattan, 1993), 100–101. Alan Astro refers to this article in "Two Best-Selling French Jewish Women's Novels from 1929," *Symposium* 52 (1999), 241–254. Lunel names Alexandre Weill, my subject in Chapter 4, and the religious philosopher Joseph Salvador as exceptions. Lunel was the author of *Nicolo-Peccavi, ou l'Affaire Dreyfus à Carpentras* (1926), a novel about the Judeo-Provençal community at the fin de siècle. All the translations from the French in this book are my own unless otherwise stated.

13. Michel Trebitsch, "Les écrivains juifs français de l'affaire Dreyfus à la Second Guerre mondiale," in *Les juifs de France: De la Révolution française à nos jours*, eds. Jean-Jacques Becker and Annette Wiviorka (Paris: Liana Levi, 1998), 171.

14. "From this moment, a decade after the beginning of the Affair, we can date the beginning of Jewish writing in the literary field, between 1905, when André Spire publishes in the *Cahiers de la quinzaine*, 'Et vous riez' [And You Laugh], the first collection of 'Jewish Poems,' . . . and 1913, when Edmond Fleg publishes the first volume of *Écoute Israël* [Hear O Israel], his 'Legends of the Jewish Ages'" (Trebitsch, "Les écrivains juifs français," 179).

15. Gozlan's *Balzac en pantoufles* (1856) is still in print. Among d'Ennery's best-known plays are *Gaspard Hauser* (1838) and the French stage adaptation of *Uncle Tom's Cabin* (1853).

16. Lehrmann cites a telling remark by d'Ennery on the subject: "When asked if there were any Jewish characters in his plays, Adolphe d'Ennery, a half-Jew and very popular author at the end of the nineteenth century, replied, 'No, and the reason is very simple. I believe that in the theater you should never fight against public feeling. . . . The first task of the writer is to please the audience, which means respecting its tastes and habits. If I had put a Jew on stage, I would have naturally had to make him a usurer, a crook, a traitor, or some kind of low-life character.'" Cuno Charles Lehrmann, *L'élément juif dans la littérature française* (Paris: Albin Michel, 1961), v. 2, 41.

17. Schor writes, "The abstract rights-bearing individual, the citizen, is a neutral subject who must be divested of all particularities to access those rights; universalism is enjoined upon the would-be citizen of the Republic." Naomi Schor, "Universalism," in *The Columbia History of Twentieth-Century French Thought*, ed. Lawrence Kritzman (New York: Columbia University Press, 2006), 345.

18. Émile Zola described his fiction as a similar kind of laboratory in *Le roman expérimental* (1880) but saw it as capable of producing objective data.

19. Gerald Prince, *Narratology: The Form and Functioning of Narrative* (New York: Mouton, 1982). Jack Goody defines narrative and fiction along similar lines in "From Oral to Written: An Anthropological Breakthrough in Storytelling," in *The Novel*, v. 1, *History, Geography, and Culture*, ed. Franco Moretti (Princeton, NJ: Princeton University Press, 2006), 4–6.

20. Jacob Katz, *Out of the Ghetto: The Social Background of Jewish Emancipation, 1770–1870* (Cambridge, MA: Harvard University Press, 1973). In *Paths of Emancipation: Jews, States, and Citizenship* (Princeton, NJ: Princeton University Press, 1995), Pierre Birnbaum and Ira Katznelson argue that because Jews in France and the United States had achieved citizenship by the beginning of the nineteenth century, these countries should be taken as models for Jewish modernity rather than Germany (21–22). The essays in Jonathan Frankel and Steven J. Zipperstein's *Assimilation and Community: The Jews in Nineteenth-Century Europe* (Cambridge, U.K.: Cambridge University Press, 1992) also provide a corrective to the Germanocentric model.

21. The two best overviews of French Jewish history in English are Paula E. Hyman, *The Jews of Modern France* (Berkeley: University of California Press,

1998), and Esther Benbassa, *The Jews of France: A History from Antiquity to the Present* (Princeton, NJ: Princeton University Press, 1999).

22. Although France had one of the larger communities in western Europe, it was small compared with the communities in eastern Europe. In 1820, there were 50,000 Jews in France, 20,000 in Great Britain, 25,000 in Italy, and 45,000 in the Netherlands. By contrast, there were 223,000 in Germany, 240,000 in Galicia, and 1,600,000 Jews in Russia at that time. I derive my statistics from Victor Karady, *The Jews of Europe in the Modern Era: A Socio-Historical Outline*, trans. Tim Wilkinson (Budapest: CEU, 2004), 44–45.

23. The Sephardim originally pretended to be "New Christians" but gradually shed the trappings of Christianity. By the end of the seventeenth century, they ceased to baptize their children. In 1723, they received official permission to practice Judaism.

24. Christine Piette, *Les juifs de Paris (1808–1840): La marche vers l'assimilation* (Québec: Laval University Press, 1983), 10.

25. Frances Malino, *The Sephardic Jews of Bordeaux: Assimilation and Emancipation in Revolutionary and Napoleonic France* (University: University of Alabama Press, 1978), 12. Francesca Trivellato describes the economic networks linking the Jews of Bordeaux with other Sephardic Jewish communities in *The Familiarity of Strangers: The Sephardic Diaspora, Livorno, and Cross-Cultural Trade in the Early-Modern Period* (New Haven, CT: Yale University Press, 2009).

26. Hyman, *Jews of Modern France*, 8. In *The French Enlightenment and the Jews* (New York: Columbia University Press, 1968), Arthur Hertzberg notes that, although "the linguistic and cultural world" of the Jews of eastern France "remained, even into the Revolutionary era, Yiddish and Hebrew," certain groups of businessmen and intellectuals did know some French (139).

27. In *Rites and Passage: The Beginnings of Modern Jewish Culture in France, 1650–1860* (Philadelphia: University of Pennsylvania Press, 2004), Jay R. Bercovitz points to the increased power of the laity in the Jewish communities of Alsace and Lorraine to argue that these communities were already changing, or modernizing, before the Revolution (14), but he does acknowledge that the "main features of medieval life," such as civil legal restrictions against Jews and the primacy of the Halacha (the body of Jewish law regulating Jewish life), continued into the late eighteenth century.

28. Ronald Schechter, *Obstinate Hebrews: Representations of Jews in France, 1715–1815* (Berkeley: University of California Press, 2003).

29. Arthur Hertzberg argues that Voltaire inaugurated a new, modern anti-semitism by casting the Jews not as Christ killers but as innately backward and corrupt. One of the many examples of Voltaire's antipathy cited by Hertzberg is *Il faut prendre un parti* (1775), in which Voltaire has a "theist" say to the Jews, "You have surpassed all nations in impertinent fables, in bad conduct, and in barbarism.

You deserve to be punished, for this is your destiny" (cited in Hertzberg, *French Enlightenment*, 301). Voltaire's verdict, according to Hertzberg, applied equally to the ancient Hebrews and their modern descendants. Other Enlightenment philosophes, such as Montesquieu, believed that the Jews could be transformed into modern, productive citizens.

30. In 1787, the Metz Academy sponsored an essay contest on the topic, "Are there ways of making the Jews more useful and happier in France?" Grégoire's prizewinning entry maintained that the Jews were degenerate but were capable of being transformed. In *The Abbé Grégoire and the French Revolution: The Making of Modern Universalism* (Berkeley: University of California Press, 2005), Alyssa Goldstein Sepinwall argues that Grégoire's call for the "regeneration" of the Jews became "the dominant paradigm for the treatment of difference in modern France and its empire" (56). On debates over regeneration, also see L. Scott Lerner, "Beyond Grégoire: A Third Discourse on Jews and the French," *Modern Judaism* 21(3) (2001), 199–215.

31. On the emancipation of Jews during the Revolution, see Gary Kates, "Jews into Frenchmen: Nationality and Representation in Revolutionary France," in *The French Revolution and the Birth of Modernity*, ed. Ferenc Feher (Berkeley: University of California Press, 1990), 103–116.

32. Cited in Hyman, *Jews of Modern France*, 27.

33. Hyman, *Jews of Modern France*, 29–30.

34. According to Katznelson, in 1787 all the states except New York had laws barring Jews from holding high political office. These laws were withdrawn gradually throughout the nineteenth century. The last state to do so was New Hampshire in 1877. Ira Katznelson, "Jews on the Margins of American Liberalism," in Birnbaum and Katznelson, *Paths of Emancipation*, 157–205. Jon Butler describes the conflict over religious establishment in the post-Revolutionary United States in *Awash in a Sea of Faith: Christianizing the American People* (Cambridge, MA: Harvard University Press, 1990), 258–268.

35. The Italian and German Jews saw their rights revoked after Napoleon's defeat at Waterloo. The Jews of Holland became emancipated in 1795 and did not lose their rights after the fall of Napoleon.

36. Among the most significant books on Napoleon and the Jews are Robert Anschel, *Napoléon et les juifs* (Paris: PUF, 1928); Simon Schwarzfuchs, *Napoleon, the Jews, and the Sanhedrin* (London: Routledge and Kegan Paul, 1979); and most recently Pierre Birnbaum, *L'aigle et la synagogue: Napoléon, les juifs et l'état* (Paris: Fayard, 2007).

37. England, of course, had the example of Queen Victoria's prime minister Benjamin Disraeli, but he had converted to Christianity.

38. These were Achille Fould (elected in 1834), Adolphe Crémieux, and Lieutenant-Colonel Max Cerfberr.

39. These were Adolphe Crémieux (Minister of Justice) and Michel Goud-chaux (Minister of Finance). Achille Fould went on to become Minister of Finance during the Second Empire.

40. Pierre Birnbaum describes this phenomenon in his *Les fous de la République: Histoire politique des juifs d'état de Gambetta à Vichy* (Paris: Fayard, 1992).

41. These were Léon Blum, René Mayer, Pierre Mendès-France, Michel Debré, and Laurent Fabius.

42. "In France, access to the state for Jews passed by way of the army first, a phenomenon that has been underestimated for a long time because of purely ideological interpretations of the effects of the Dreyfus affair." Pierre Birnbaum, "Between Social and Political Assimilation: Remarks on the History of Jews in France," in Birnbaum and Katznelson, *Paths of Emancipation*, 124.

43. Piette, *Les juifs de Paris*, 59.

44. Hyman, *Jews of Modern France*, 60.

45. Landau provides the statistics on the July Monarchy in "Les débuts de l'émancipation des femmes juives sous la monarchie de juillet, 1830–1848," in his *Rachel, une vie pour le théâtre, 1821–1858* (Paris: Adam Biro, 2004), 109. He provides a wealth of information on conversion in "Se convertir à Paris au XIXe siècle," *Archives Juives* 35(1) (2002), 27–43. According to Landau, church records show that 877 Jews in Paris converted to Catholicism between 1807 and 1914. Many of these—496 cases—converted after 1870. Landau estimates that 5 percent more may have become Protestant. The net loss to the Jewish community because of conversion was very small, however, because 497 Christians became Jewish between 1807 and 1914, most because they married Jews. Most of these conversions to Judaism also took place after 1870 (466 cases).

46. The major exception to this was Marie-Théodore Ratisbonne, a member of one of France's most prominent Jewish families, who converted to Catholicism in 1826 and founded the Order of Notre Dame de Sion, dedicated to converting poor Jewish girls, in 1842. The Jewish press constantly complained of the tactics of this order, which they believed preyed on the poor by offering them charity in exchange for conversion. On Ratisbonne and other high-profile French converts, see Jay R. Bercovitz, *The Shaping of Jewish Identity in Nineteenth-Century France* (Detroit: Wayne State University Press, 1989), 115–119, as well as Landau, "Se convertir," 30. Michael Ragussis describes English conversion societies and the British novel in *Figures of Conversion: The Jewish Question and English National Identity* (Durham, NC: Duke University Press, 1995).

47. According to Benbassa, the intermarriage rate among bourgeois Jews in Paris (the most likely to intermarry) during the Second Empire remained less than 14 percent (Benbassa, *Jews of France*, 194).

48. Phyllis Cohen Albert, *The Modernization of French Jewry: Consistory and Community in the Nineteenth Century* (Hanover, NH: Brandeis University Press, 1977), 24.

49. Albert, *Modernization of French Jewry*, 3.

50. According to Albert, in 1808, 78.87 percent of France's Jews lived in Alsace-Lorraine and only 5.83 percent lived in Paris. By 1861, 56.50 percent lived in Alsace-Lorraine and 26.20 percent lived in Paris (Albert, *Modernization of French Jewry*, 19).

51. By comparison, the general population of Paris nearly doubled in this period, going from 547,756 in 1801 to 1,053,262 in 1851. Piette, *Les juifs de Paris*, 51.

52. Pierre Birnbaum, "Introduction," in *Histoire politique des juifs de France: Entre universalisme et particularisme*, ed. Pierre Birnbaum (Paris: Fondation Nationale des Sciences Politiques, 1990), 11.

53. See Birnbaum, *Les fous de la République*.

54. In *The Politics of Assimilation: A Study of the French-Jewish Community at the Time of the Dreyfus Affair* (Oxford, U.K.: Clarendon Press, 1971), Michael Marrus describes the urge of nineteenth-century French Jews to "avoid the Affair and to take refuge in silence" (212). He explicitly cites Arendt as the prime influence on his study: "[Arendt] is concerned with the 'disintegrating' effects of assimilation, and with the corresponding disintegration of European society. Ultimately, it seems to us, she is concerned with the terrible breakdown of community in our time. Her work, more than that of any other, has influenced the chapters which follow" (6).

55. In "Between Social and Political Assimilation," Birnbaum traces the history of several "state Jews" (high-ranking government officials and army officers) and notes how they "did not abandon their particularism in the public sphere" (121). Even if they did not practice the Jewish religion, they did not convert, change their names, or intermarry, and most had Jewish funerals.

56. Phyllis Cohen Albert, "L'intégration et la persistance de l'ethnicité chez les juifs dans la France moderne," in *Histoire politique des juifs*, ed. Pierre Birnbaum, 221.

57. *Les Archives Israélites*, which began in 1840, was obviously read primarily by Jews, but it also listed such prominent non-Jews as the king Louis-Philippe and the journalist Delphine de Girardin among its subscribers, suggesting that it saw itself as addressing a mainstream public. Béatrice Philippe, Les Archives Israélites de France *de leur création en 1840 à février 1848 ou un journal juif sous Louis-Philippe: Étude de mentalités*, Mémoire de Maîtrise, Université de Paris IV (1974–1975), vii.

58. With the Loi Guizot (1833), which authorized state-sponsored religious primary schools, many Jewish schools became communal schools. When the original formulation of the Loi Falloux (1849), which allowed for state-sponsored religious secondary schools, inadvertently made no mention of the Jews, the Consistory complained. The final version of the law specifically granted Jews equal status, leading to the construction of Jewish schools paid for by both the state and the Consistory. Albert, *Modernization of French Jewry*, 153–156.

59. Dominique Jarrassé discusses the construction and refurbishing of the large Parisian synagogues during the mid-nineteenth century in "La synagogue de la rue Notre-Dame de Nazareth, lieu de construction d'une culture juive parisienne et d'un regard sur les juifs," *Romantisme* 25 (2004), 43–56. Also see Albert, *Modernization of French Jewry*, 221; and L. Scott Lerner, "The Narrating Architecture of Emancipation," *Jewish Social Studies* 6(3) (2000), 1–30. Monumental synagogues were also built in Lyon and Marseilles in 1864 and in Bordeaux in 1882.

60. In *The Jews in Nineteenth-Century France: From the French Revolution to the Alliance Israélite Universelle*, trans. Jane Marie Todd (Stanford, CA: Stanford University Press, 1996), Michael Graetz argues that the Alliance was founded by Jews on the periphery of the community. Also see Aron Rodrigue, *French Jews, Turkish Jews: The Alliance Israélite Universelle and the Politics of Jewish Schooling in Turkey, 1860–1925* (Bloomington: Indiana University Press, 1990); and Lisa Moses Leff, *Sacred Bonds of Solidarity: The Rise of Jewish Internationalism in Nineteenth-Century France* (Stanford, CA: Stanford University Press, 2006).

61. Leff, *Sacred Bonds*, 14.

62. This declaration from a Jewish observer at the time of the Dreyfus affair is typical of the new desire to avoid public manifestations of particularity: "Let there be neither Jews nor Christians, except at the hour of prayer for those who pray! That is what France proclaimed on 26 August 1789, by the Declaration of the Rights of Man. From that day on France recognized only citizens." Ernest Crémieu-Foa, *La campagne antisémite: Les duels, les responsables—mémoire avec pièces justificatives* (Paris: Alcan-Lévy, 1892). Cited in Marrus, *Politics of Assimilation*, 87.

63. Schor reveals how the revolutionaries in 1789 drew on the tradition of Catholic universalism in their formulation of a new republican universalism (Schor, "Universalism," 345). Joan Wallach Scott describes recent feminist challenges to the French universalist model in *Parité! Sexual Equality and the Crisis of French Universalism* (Chicago: University of Chicago Press, 2005).

64. On second-generation immigrant literature, see Michel Laronde, *Autour du roman beur: Immigration et identité* (Paris: L'Harmattan, 1993).

65. Walter Benjamin, "Paris, Capital of the Nineteenth Century," in his *Reflections*, trans. Edmund Jephcott (New York: Schocken, 1986).

66. Walter Benjamin, *Charles Baudelaire: A Lyric Poet in the Era of High Capitalism*, trans. Harry Zohn (London: Verso, 1983).

67. Walter Benjamin, *The Arcades Project*, trans. Howard Eiland and Kevin McLaughlin (Cambridge, MA: Harvard University Press, 1999). Interestingly, Benjamin, who worked on *The Arcades Project* while in exile from Nazi Germany in Paris, is nearly silent on the topic of Jews despite his almost panoramic vision of the nineteenth-century city.

68. On Haussmannization and modernity, see David P. Jordan, *Transforming*

Paris: The Life and Labors of Baron Haussmann (Chicago: University of Chicago Press, 1995), and David Harvey, *Paris, Capital of Modernity* (New York: Routledge, 2003).

69. Harvey describes the activities of the Rothschilds and the Péreires in *Paris*, 117–124. Barrie M. Ratcliffe describes the Jewish identity of the Péreires in "Some Jewish Problems in the Early Careers of Emile and Isaac Péreire," *Jewish Social Studies* 34(3) (July 1972), 189–206.

70. Siegfried Kracauer, *Jacques Offenbach and the Paris of His Time*, trans. Gwenda David and Eric Mosbacher (New York: Zone, 2002). Vanessa Schwartz describes Meyer's role in fostering a new Parisian journalistic and entertainment culture in her *Spectacular Realities: Early Mass Culture in Fin de Siècle Paris* (Berkeley: University of California Press, 1998), 99–118.

71. The main protagonist in these attacks, George Dairnvaell, wrote under the pseudonym Satan and published a series of pamphlets with such titles as *Histoire édifiante et curieuse de Rothschild Ier, roi des juifs* (Paris: J. Labitte, 1847). *La Démocratie Pacifique*, a newspaper founded by the Fourierists Alphonse Toussenel and Victor Considérant in 1843, launched a campaign denouncing the Rothschilds and their railroad "monopoly" from the very first issues. (It should be noted that Alexandre Weill, one of the Jewish writers I examine in this book, collaborated on *La Démocratie Pacifique* during this period.) Toussenel attacks the Rothschild railway monopoly in more specifically antisemitic terms in *Les juifs*, xxxv.

72. Paula Hyman, *The Emancipation of the Jews of Alsace: Acculturation and Tradition in the Nineteenth Century* (New Haven, CT: Yale University Press, 1991), 4.

73. Albert, *Modernization of French Jewry*, 22.

74. In *From Dreyfus to Vichy: The Remaking of French Jewry, 1906–1939* (New York: Columbia University Press, 1979), Paula Hyman notes that, on the eve of World War I, as much as one-third of Paris bankers were Jews (47).

75. On German Jews in Paris in the early nineteenth century, see Michel Espagne, *Les juifs allemands de Paris à l'époque de Heine* (Paris: Presses Universitaires de France, 1996); and Liliane Weissberg, "Metropole der Freiheit: Berliner Juden in Paris, 1789–1812," in *Jüdische Literatur als europäische Literatur*, eds. Caspar Battigay and Barbara Breysach (Munich: Verlag Text und Kritik, 2008), 17–43.

76. Balzac, *Splendeurs et misères des courtisanes* (Paris: Gallimard, 1973), 169. See my reading of the role of Jewishness in this novel in "Metaphors of Modernity: Prostitutes, Bankers, and Other Jews in Balzac's *Splendeurs et misères des courtisanes*," *Romanic Review* 97(2) (March 2006), 169–184.

77. Michael Meyer, *Response to Modernity: A History of the Reform Movement in Judaism* (New York: Oxford University Press, 1988), 170.

78. For the classic account of how *Bildung* became a source of identity for acculturating German Jews, see George L. Mosse, *German Jews Beyond Judaism*

(Bloomington: Indiana University Press, 1985). In *The Transformation of German Jewry, 1780–1840* (Detroit: Wayne State University Press, 1999), David Sorkin describes how "the ideal of Bildung stood at the center of the modern German culture that appeared in the last half of the eighteenth century, epitomizing its secular nature in being entirely self-referential" (15). Liliane Weissberg discusses these issues in "Literary Culture and Jewish Space Around 1800: The Berlin Salon Revisited," in *Modern Jewish Literatures: Intersections and Boundaries,* eds. Sheila Jelen, Michael Kramer, and L. Scott Lerner (Philadelphia: University of Pennsylvania Press, in press).

79. In *Germans, Jews, and the Claims of Modernity* (New Haven, CT: Yale University Press, 2002), Jonathan Hess emphasizes Jewish agency in the creation of a distinct German Jewish subculture (9). Hess's *Middlebrow Literature and the Making of German-Jewish Identity* (Stanford, CA: Stanford University Press, in press) describes how popular Jewish literature similar to that which I discuss here played a key role in the modernization of nineteenth-century German Jews.

80. Jonathan Freedman, *The Temple of Culture: Assimilation and Antisemitism in Literary Anglo-America* (Oxford: Oxford University Press, 1999).

81. De Man's article "Les juifs dans la littérature actuelle" (1941), which resurfaced only after his death in 1983, argued for resistance to the pollution of semitic influence in French culture. This and other of his antisemitic essays can be found in Paul de Man, *Wartime Journalism 1939–1943,* eds. Werner Hamacher, Neil Hertz, and Thomas Keenan (Lincoln: University of Nebraska Press, 1988). Also see Werner Hamacher, Neil Hertz, and Thomas Keenan, eds., *Responses: On Paul de Man's Wartime Journalism* (Lincoln: University of Nebraska Press, 1989), in which de Man's many students and admirers respond to the revelation of his antisemitic past.

82. In *Tragic Muse: Rachel of the Comédie-Française* (New York: Knopf, 1993), Rachel Brownstein writes that Rachel was "praised as an uplifting avatar of the *patrimoine,* or cultural legacy of the nation, as a priestess of Art, as the precious embodiment of a lost ideal" (7). Rachel refused to convert and in fact accentuated her Jewishness as a form of self-promotion, including adopting a Jewish stage name (Leff, *Sacred Bonds,* 103). On Rachel, see also Anne Hélène Hoog, "La marge, l'exemple et l'exception: Le parcours d'Élisa Félix dite Mademoiselle Rachel," *Romantisme* 125 (2004), 91–102.

83. During the Revolution of 1848, Rachel was chosen to declaim "La Marseillaise" at the Comédie Française, proof that an immigrant Jew could incarnate an ideal not only of French culture but also of French patriotism. According to Anne Hélène Hoog, critics commented frequently on Rachel's Jewishness during her lifetime but mostly saw it as "a certificate of aptitude for tragedy" rather than as a liability. After her death, however, antisemitic clichés became much more frequent: Rachel is frequently described in later biographies as having had "an unstable character, overwrought, money hungry, and manipulative." Anne Hélène

Hoog, "'L'enfant du miracle': Ambivalences du discours sur les origines de Rachel et de son génie," in *Rachel, une vie pour le théâtre*, 72–73.

84. For discussions of Jewishness and *La juive*, see Diana R. Hallman, *Opera, Liberalism, and Antisemitism in Nineteenth-Century France: The Politics of Halévy's* La Juive (Cambridge, U.K.: Cambridge University Press, 2003); Olivier Bara, "*La juive* de Scribe et Halévy (1835): Un opéra juif?" *Romantisme* 125 (2004), 75–90; and L. Scott Lerner, "Jewish Identity and French Opera, Stage, and Politics, 1831–1860," *Historical Reflections/Réflexions Historiques* 30(2) (2004), 255–281.

85. See, for instance, Leff, *Sacred Bonds*, 102.

86. *Le Journal des Débats*, May 27, 1830.

87. In *The Location of Culture* (London: Routledge, 1994), Homi Bhabha argues against notions of originary and self-contained national or cultural subjectivity to suggest that selfhood emerges only through the articulation of difference, in the "in-between" spaces produced by the contact of cultures. "Culture only emerges as a problem, or a problematic, at the point at which there is a loss of meaning in the contestation and articulation of everyday life, between classes, genders, races, nations" (34). The hybridity and mimicry of the Jewish writers under consideration here in many ways provide an example of Bhabha's theory in practice. I want to suggest that the French literary tradition serves as a mediating term, a condition of enunciation, that the Jewish writers appropriate, rehistoricize, and read anew (37).

88. See especially, Hess, *Middlebrow Literature*.

89. Gabriella Safran, *Rewriting the Jew: Assimilation Narratives in the Russian Empire* (Stanford, CA: Stanford University Press, 2000), 36–37.

90. Perl wrote an anti-Hasidic satire in 1819. Of the supposed thirty novels and plays Aksenfeld wrote, only one novel survives: *Dos shterntikhl* [The Headband], published in 1861 but most likely written in the 1840s. As proponents of the Haskalah, or Jewish Enlightenment, these two writers resembled their French contemporaries in their use of satire as a tool of social critique. Dan Miron, *A Traveler Disguised: The Rise of Modern Yiddish Fiction in the Nineteenth Century* (Syracuse, NY: Syracuse University Press, 1996 [1973]), 2–3.

91. Y. Y. Linetzki's *Polish Boy* [*Dos poylishe yingl*], about a Hasid, was published in *Kol-Mevasser* in 1867 and became a sensation.

92. Miron, *A Traveler Disguised*, 34.

93. Michael P. Kramer, "The Origins of Jewish American Literature," in *The Cambridge Companion to Jewish American Literature*, eds. Hana Wirth-Nesher and Michael P. Kramer (Cambridge, U.K.: Cambridge University Press, 2003), 23–25.

94. Olga Borovaya, "The Serialized Novel as Rewriting: The Case of the Ladino Belles Lettres," *Jewish Social Studies* 10(1) (2003), 30–68. Also see her entry, "Judeo-Spanish Literature," in *Encyclopedia of Jews in the Islamic World*, ed.

Norman Stillman (Leiden: Brill, 2009), as well as her manuscript "Modern La-dino Literary Culture: Press, Belles Lettres, and Theater in the Late Ottoman Empire (1845–1908)."

95. Although Miron and other Yiddish specialists have long assumed that Yid-dish was originally used by Enlightenment-inspired novelists in order to reach the masses, Alyssa Quint argues that in actuality bourgeois enlighteners were most likely not only the producers but also the consumers of this brand of Yiddish fic-tion until the 1870s. Alyssa Quint "'Yiddish Literature for the Masses'? A Recon-sideration of Who Read What," *AJS Review* 29(1) (2005), 61–89.

96. According to Guy Bedouelle and Jean-Paul Costa in their *Les laïcités à la française* (Paris: PUF, 1998), the term *laïcisme* had come to mean "a doctrine that tends to give institutions a non-religious character" by 1842. The term *laïcité*, considered a neologism in 1871, first appeared in the context of debates over re-ligion in public education (10). Marcel Gauchet draws a distinction between the *laïcisation* of predominantly Catholic countries and the *sécularisation* of Protes-tant ones in *La religion dans la démocratie* (Paris: Gallimard, 1998), 15–16.

97. Caroline Ford, *Divided Houses: Religion and Gender in Modern France* (Ithaca, NY: Cornell University Press, 2005), 66–67.

98. Theodore Zeldin, *France, 1848–1945* (Oxford, U.K.: Oxford University Press, 1977), 994.

99. See, for example, an article by Ben-Lévi in *Les Archives Israélites* (1848), 378. I discuss the Jewish reaction to the Revolution of 1848 in Chapters 2 and 3.

100. The ultras, as the extreme-right monarchists were known, sought to merge throne and altar, which would have led to a loss of Jewish equality. Leff shows that French Jews saw state secularization as the best way to guarantee a place for Judaism in the public sphere. Secularization in the French context thus did not imply a total separation of church and state in the mid-nineteenth century but rather public equality for the three major religions. See Leff, *Sacred Bonds*, esp. 40–41.

101. Arnold Eisen, *Rethinking Judaism: Ritual, Commandment, Community* (Chicago: University of Chicago Press, 1998), 3.

102. In his lecture "Science as a Vocation" (1919), Max Weber describes the "disenchantment of the world" in modern times and the replacement of the sa-cred by technology and calculation. Max Weber, "Science as a Vocation," trans. Michael John, in *Max Weber's "Science as a Vocation,"* eds. Peter Lassman and Irving Velody (London: Unwin Hyman, 1989), 13.

103. Gauchet, *Religion*, 7. Gauchet sees the "return of religion" as essentially a foreign import in France: "The phenomenon mainly comes to us from the out-side, even if it affects us directly because of its representatives living on our soil" (28). The nativist overtones of Gauchet's phrasing strike me as problematic be-cause they seem to imply that Muslim fundamentalists are not fully French.

104. Although both Ben-Lévi and Ben Baruch use the Hebrew *ben* (son of)

in their pseudonyms, Ben-Lévi chose to follow French grammatical convention by hyphenating it, whereas Ben Baruch did not.

105. This "tragic" reading is exemplified by the opening lines of Michael Marrus's *Politics of Assimilation*: "A sense of tragedy hovers about any historical study of European Jewry in the late nineteenth century. Tragedy clings to the subject because the reader knows that the historical path was leading ultimately to the Nazi extermination of European Jews" (1).

106. By minor literature I mean a literature concerned with the interests of a minority group but articulated in a majority language. My use resembles but ultimately differs from that of Gilles Deleuze and Félix Guattari, who argue in *Kafka: Toward a Minor Literature*, trans. Dana Polan (Minneapolis: University of Minnesota Press, 1986), that as a Jew writing in Prague in German, Kafka produced a "minor literature" with inherently subversive tendencies—including the ability to subvert the dominant language from within. In *The World Republic of Letters*, trans. M. B. DeBevoise (Cambridge, MA: Harvard University Press, 2004), Pascale Casanova criticizes this prophetic notion of Kafka's politics as anachronistic (203–204). Like Casanova, I do not see the main goal or effect of the Jewish writers under discussion here to be the subversion of the French language, even if their existence does undermine ethnically deterministic notions of a unified French national subject.

Chapter 1

1. Walter Scott was by far the best-selling contemporary author in France during much of the nineteenth century, and *Ivanhoe* was his most popular work. According to Martyn Lyons, there were twenty-eight editions of *Ivanhoe* published in France by 1851 for a total circulation of at least 60,000 copies. This is in addition to the dozens of editions of Scott's complete works. Martyn Lyons, "The Audience for Romanticism: Walter Scott in France, 1815–1851," *European History Quarterly* 14(1) (January 1984), 27–28. Also see the tables of publishing statistics in Martyn Lyons, "Les best-sellers," in *Histoire de l'édition française: Le temps des éditeurs*, ed. Roger Chartier and Henri-Jean Martin (Paris: Promodis, 1990), 415–423.

2. I describe the fascination with the *belle juive* for Balzac and other nineteenth-century French writers in "Metaphors of Modernity: Prostitutes, Bankers, and Other Jews in Balzac's *Splendeurs et misères des courtisanes*," *Romantic Review* 97(2) (March 2006), 169–184. In *Bodies of Art: French Literary Realism and the Artist's Model* (Lincoln: University of Nebraska Press, 2001), Marie Lathers discusses the representation of beautiful Jewish women in French painting and their role in the modeling trade during the nineteenth century. Luce Klein provides a sustained account of the era's fascination with the beautiful Jewish woman in *Portrait de la juive dans la littérature française* (Paris: Nizet, 1970).

3. Léon Poliakov describes Scott's representation of the Jew in *Histoire de l'anti-sémitisme* (Paris: Calmann-Lévy, 1981), v. 2, 174–175.

4. Augustin Thierry's popular Romantic historiographic work, *Histoire de la conquête de l'Angleterre par les Normands* (1825), followed Scott in ascribing current social conflict to a historical battle between different races.

5. Following Napoleon's defeat, the civil emancipation that conquering French armies had brought to Europe's Jews was revoked in many countries, including most German states. Debates over Jewish emancipation would grow increasingly vociferous throughout the nineteenth century, particularly in Germany, where most Jews did not receive full civil rights again until German unification in 1870.

6. In *The Jewess in Nineteenth-Century Literary Culture* (London: Cambridge University Press, 2007), Nadia Valman discusses representations of Jewish women by Scott and other nineteenth-century British writers, including several Jewish women writers, such as Grace Aguilar and Amy Levy. Michael Galchinsky describes the response to Scott by British Jewish women writers in *The Origin of the Modern Jewish Woman Writer: Romance and Reform in Victorian England* (Detroit: Wayne State University Press, 1996).

7. Arthur Hertzberg, *The French Enlightenment and the Jews* (New York: Columbia University Press, 1968), 89.

8. At the time of his death, Abraham's estate was valued at over 10 million livres. Frances Malino, *The Sephardic Jews of Bordeaux: Assimilation and Emancipation in Revolutionary and Napoleonic France* (University: University of Alabama Press, 1978), 14.

9. Eugénie's brother wrote, "The Gradis family rendered such services to the French navy under Louis XV and Louis XVI that noble titles were offered to them by Louis XVI. And these titles were refused by them—as they were unable, they said, to take an oath on the Gospels, the religion of which they did not consider sufficiently monotheistic." Hippolyte Rodrigues, *Papiers de famille* (Paris: Vve. P. Larousse, 1893), n.p.

10. By the provisions of the Code Noir of 1683, Jews could not own property in the French colonies, but the Gradis family received special permission to do so in 1779. Hertzberg, *French Enlightenment*, 92.

11. Although it is likely that some Gradis ships carried slaves in the mid-eighteenth century, they did not play a major role in the slave trade. Hertzberg explored this question at length in *The French Enlightenment and the Jews* and concluded that, although the Gradis firm dealt mostly in shipping provisions directly to the French colonies, they did on at least one occasion take payment in slaves for supplies delivered to Africa; they then sold the slaves in Saint-Domingue for sugar (Hertzberg, *French Enlightenment*, 92). More recently, Saul S. Friedman has estimated that the role of the Gradis firm in the Atlantic slave trade was small. He maintains that there were no Jewish slave traders and that French Jewish bankers in Bordeaux were "of no consequence" in financing the slave trade. Saul S.

Friedman, *Jews and the American Slave Trade* (New Brunswick, NJ: Transaction, 1988), 86.

12. Malino, *Sephardic Jews of Bordeaux*, 41.

13. Jean Cavignac describes Foa's family in *Dictionnaire du judaïsme Bordelais aux VIIIe et XIXe siècles* (Bordeaux: Archives Départementales de la Gironde, 1987), 111–112. He also provides a tree of the Gradis family (152). I thank Lisa Moses Leff for helping me to piece together the complicated elements of Foa's genealogy.

14. Visits to the building by the future business magnates (Jacob) Émile and Isaac Péreire, also cousins of Eugénie, inspired them to join the Saint-Simonian movement as well. Léon Halévy, *F. Halévy, sa vie et ses oeuvres* (Paris: Ménestrel, 1863), 17.

15. Léonie showed at the salon beginning in 1877 and became famous for sculpting a bust of her husband. Adrian M. Darmon, *Autour de l'art juif: Encyclopédie des peintres, photographes et sculpteurs* (Paris: Carnot, 2003), 316. She also suffered from mental illness and spent stretches at Dr. Blanche's asylum in Passy. Chantal Bischoff, *Geneviève Straus: Trilogie d'une égérie* (Paris: Balland, 1992), 21.

16. Geneviève Halévy married the composer Georges Bizet and, following his death in 1875, Émile Straus, a lawyer to the Rothschilds. She drew many writers, including Marcel Proust, as well as members of the aristocracy, to her salon. "From the mid-1880s to the late 1890s . . . all who counted, or wanted to count, appeared chez Madame Geneviève Straus." Emily D. Bilski and Emily Braun, *Jewish Women and Their Salons: The Power of Conversation* (New Haven, CT: Yale University Press, 2005), 66.

17. The name Hippolyte Rodrigues appears on an 1845 list, published in *Les Archives Israélites*, of Jewish notables eligible to vote in Consistory elections, marking him as one of the wealthiest of the capital's Jews.

18. The catalogue of the Bibliothèque Nationale de France lists 107 works by Busnach.

19. In *Zéidouna* (no date), Gradis presents the same central conflict that obsesses Foa but in a different religious context: A Muslim princess does not want to marry the man her father has chosen for her.

20. Henri Gradis wrote histories of Bordeaux (1888), of the Revolution of 1848 (1872), and of the Jewish people (1881).

21. See Michel Prévost and Jean-Charles Roman d'Amat, *Dictionnaire de biographie française* (Paris: Letouzey, 1979), v. 14, 151–152; and Camille Lebrun, "Foa, Eugénie," in J. C. F. Hoefer, *Nouvelle biographie générale* (Paris: Firmin-Didot, 1856), v. 18, p. 19.

22. Eugénie Foa, "Rachel, ou l'héritage," in Foa, *Rachel* (Paris: Henri Dupuy, 1833), xv. Subsequent references appear in the text.

23. Foa also comments on the career of the "woman writer" in the prefaces to *Le kidouschim* and *La laide*.

24. The particularly mean-spirited Lebrun, whose account contains errors, says Foa received some financial help from her father but spent it carelessly.

25. Annie Prassoloff, *Littérature en procès: La propriété littéraire sous la Monarchie de Juillet*, doctoral thesis (Paris: École des Hautes Études en Sciences Sociales, 1989), 287, cited in Elisabeth-Christine Muelsch, "George Sand and Her Sisters: Women Writers in the Société des Gens de Lettres (1838–1848)," *George Sand Studies* 16(1–2) (1997), 97.

26. Married women, for example, needed their husband's signatures on legal contracts, which posed a problem for women writers, such as Sand, who were separated from their husbands. See Muelsch, "George Sand and Her Sisters," 100.

27. Anne Sauvy argues that the early nineteenth century saw an "explosion" in the number of women writers thanks to new laws on authors' rights and the fact that middle- and upper-class women had few other ways to earn money. Anne Sauvy, "Une littérature pour les femmes," in *Histoire de l'édition française: Le temps des éditeurs*, ed. Roger Chartier and Henri-Jean Martin (Paris: Promodis, 1990), 502–503.

28. Muelsch, "George Sand and Her Sisters," 97.

29. These are *Le kidouschim* (1830), *Philippe* (1831), *La laide* (1832), *Les blancs et les bleus* (1832), *La fiancée de l'exilé* (1833), *Rachel* (1833), and *La juive* (1835). In the preface to *La laide* (Paris: Vimont, 1832), Foa jokes at her own expense: "How is it—I said to my bookseller!—that there is not a single author whose books don't go through at least three editions! I have known some whose books went through eight, nine, ten, etc., etc.! and me . . . me! Sir, I'm lucky if mine go through a second!" (i).

30. Muelsch describes the participation of women in this organization in "George Sand and Her Sisters," 101. She notes that the society advocated on behalf of Foa when she lost her state pension.

31. Founded by Jules de Castellane in the 1840s as a female equivalent to the Académie Française, the Institut des Femmes provided a space for women artists and writers to discuss their works. Members included George Sand and Delphine Gay de Girardin. See Elisabeth-Christine Muelsch, "Eugénie Foa et le Institut des Femmes," in *Women Seeking Expression, France 1789–1914*, eds. Rosemary Lloyd and Brian Nelson (Monash Romance Studies 6) (Melbourne, Australia: School of European Languages and Cultures, Monash University, 2000), 86–100.

32. Foa presented her project in an article in *La Voix des Femmes* on April 3, 1848. Evelyne Lejeune-Resnick, *Femmes et associations (1830–1880)* (Paris: Publisud, 1991), 85.

33. Cited in Lejeune-Resnick, *Femmes et associations*, 86. According to Lejeune-Resnick, Foa's charity, which counted only women of the "financial and political high bourgeoisie" among its directors, typifies the recuperation of the proletarian revolution by the ruling classes in 1848. But it also marks the entry of women into the arena of politics with a force not seen since the march on Versailles. "You

consider me an obscure woman and you scorn me, and yet even though I am a woman, my voice is as strong as the voices of many men," Foa wrote to the same minister in another letter, also in December 1848, when the association was already foundering (Lejeune-Resnick, *Femmes et associations*, 86).

34. Lejeune-Resnick, *Femmes et associations*, 86.

35. Lebrun, "Foa, Eugénie."

36. The entry on Foa in the *Jewish Encyclopedia* notes that she was "famous for her beauty." The encyclopedia cites Édouard Féret, *Statistique de la Gironde* (Bordeaux, 1878), v. 3, 250, and *La grande encyclopédie*.

37. *L'Univers Israélite*, v. 1A, 416 (1844).

38. The "Registre des abjurations, 1807–1878" at the Paris Archdiocese contains the following entry (4.r.E-6): "A Rebecca FOA, née RODRIGUES-GRADIS, from Bordeaux, and aged 46 years, converted in Paris on January 20, 1846, under the care of the Abbé RATISBONNE." Although the register lists her middle name (Rebecca) and the wrong birth date, this entry surely refers to Eugénie. I thank Philippe-E. Landau for this reference.

39. Leyla Ezdinli cites this letter (found in the Bibliothèque Marguerite Durand, Fonds 091, FOA) as proof of Foa's conversion in "Altérité juive, altérité romanesque," *Romantisme* 81 (1993), 39n20.

40. Elisabeth-Christine Muelsch, "Foa, Eugénie (1796–1852)," in *The Feminist Encyclopedia of French Literature*, ed. Eva Martin Sartori (Westport, CT: Greenwood, 1999), 215.

41. According to Philippe-E. Landau, 160 Parisian Jews converted during the Restoration and the July Monarchy, a small number when one considers that the Jewish population of the capital approached 10,000 during this period. Philippe-E. Landau, "Se convertir à Paris au XIXe siècle," *Archives Juives* 35(1) (2002), 29.

42. I discuss the conversion in 1824 of David Drach, the son-in-law of Grand Rabbi Isaac Deutz, in relation to Ben-Lévi in Chapter 2. The rabbi's son, Simon Deutz, caused an international scandal when he converted to Catholicism in 1828, became friends with the Duchesse de Berry, and later betrayed her plan to foment rebellion against Louis-Phillipe during the early years of the July Monarchy.

43. Letter dated October 10, 1886, in Rodrigues, *Papiers de famille*.

44. Bischoff, *Geneviève Straus*, 66. Also cited in Bilski and Braun, *Jewish Women*, 66.

45. On May 27, 1830, a notice in one of the leading Parisian daily newspapers, *Le Journal des Débats*, announced the publication of a new work, "translated from the Hebrew," titled *Le kidouschim*.

46. In 1838, the newspaper publisher Émile de Girardin divided novelists into five categories: those who sold 2,500 copies (Hugo, de Kock); those who sold 1,500 (Balzac, Sue, Janin, Soulié); those who sold 900–1,500; those who sold 600–900; and those who sold fewer than 600. Foa's print runs thus place her in the middle of the pack, even though she may not have sold all the copies printed

(as the decline in her print runs suggests). "De l'invention des ouvrages de lit-térature, de science et d'art," *Études Politiques* (1842). Cited in Odile Martin and Henri-Jean Martin, "Le monde des éditeurs," in *Histoire de l'édition française: Le temps des éditeurs*, eds. Roger Chartier and Henri-Jean Martin (Paris: Fayard, 1990), 194.

47. Christine Piette, *Les juifs de Paris (1808–1840): La marche vers l'assimilation* (Québec: Laval University Press, 1983), 95.

48. In *Sacred Bonds of Solidarity: The Rise of Jewish Internationalism in Nine-teenth-Century France* (Stanford, CA: Stanford University Press, 2006), Lisa Mo-ses Leff writes that by the 1830s Jewishness had become "not only acceptable, but a selling point" in the Parisian artistic world (103).

49. Numerous references place *Le kidouschim* in the present of the Resto-ration. For example, it is noted that one of the characters, a middle-aged man, eluded military service during the Empire. Eugénie Foa, *Le kidouschim, conte de ma tante Rébecca par madame Foy* (Paris: Boulland, 1830), 1: 80. Subsequent ref-erences to the novel appear in the text.

50. *Le kidouschim* does not appear in the catalogue of the Bibliothèque Natio-nale de France in the list of Foa's works (most likely because her name on the title page is listed with the alternate spelling of Foy). The novel can, however, be found at the Bibliothèque Nationale de France under call number Y2.44853.

51. The first preface consists of an imaginary dialogue between the narrator ("Eugénie F.") and her absent friend Sophie, who advised her against writing. The second preface describes how the story that follows was originally told by the narrator's blind aunt Rebecca.

52. An "editor's note" at the bottom of the page informs the reader that the *kidouschim* designates a ring with which a young "Hebrew" betroths a woman. After the ring is given, the young man "respects" his fiancée until a rabbi blesses the union (1: 147). Foa's information is essentially correct. The Mishnah recog-nizes *kiddushin* (betrothal) as the first stage of the marriage process; during this period, the couple is considered legally married, although they cannot have sexual intercourse until the second stage, *nisu'in.*

53. Some of the names in the novel have a biblical origin (Noëmi, Nephtali), but others seem purely fanciful. It was not uncommon for Romantic writers and artists to choose biblical names (Rachel, Esther) to exaggerate the Jewishness of their characters (one thinks also of the great actress of the period, Élisa Félix, who took on the name Rachel). Foa, however, endows her characters with an ad-ditional exoticism.

54. Here is a typical exchange, involving two characters engaged in a lawsuit: "'Monsieur is too gallant for a plaintiff,' said Alaï smiling. 'One can hardly be so with such a pretty adversary, said Nephtali bowing with respect'" (2: 14).

55. Margaret Cohen describes the avoidance of physical and material descrip-tion as a "light touch" and sees it as a hallmark of the female-authored sentimen-

tal novel of the early nineteenth century. Margaret Cohen, *The Sentimental Education of the Novel* (Princeton, NJ: Princeton University Press, 1999), 48–50.

56. Mme. Lemuel employs Esther in her embroidery workshop in Bordeaux. Sent to make a delivery, she falls in love with a handsome solider, who later turns out to be her promised husband, proving that her father had wisely chosen her intended suitor.

57. Ezdinli cites the fact that Foa explains certain Jewish customs in this and other of her novels as evidence that "Foa consciously intended her work for a non Jewish public" (Ezdinli, "Altérité juive," 35).

58. Referred to by Michael Meyer as the "self-appointed *enfant terrible* of French Judaism," Terquem was an eccentric weaponry expert and mathematics professor at the Royal Academy for Artillery. Michael A. Meyer, *Response to Modernity: A History of the Reform Movement in Judaism* (New York: Oxford University Press, 1988), 166.

59. Already in the eighteenth century, members of Foa's prominent family had lapsed in their religious duties. The famous Jewish traveler from the Holy Land, Hayyim Joseph David Azulai, describes two visits to the Gradis home in Bordeaux. On his first trip in 1755, he does not suggest that Benjamin Gradis was anything but a conforming Jew. By 1777–1778, however, he refers to Abraham Gradis as "one of the heretics who do not believe in the oral law and who eat forbidden foods in public." Cited in Hertzberg, *French Enlightenment*, 160–161.

60. Cohen, *Sentimental Education*, 34. In *Foundational Fictions: The National Romances of Latin America* (Berkeley: University of California Press, 1991), Doris Sommer provides a model for reading the romantic intrigues at the heart of nineteenth-century novels as allegorical representations of political or national ideologies.

61. Alyssa Goldstein Sepinwall provides an excellent account of these issues in *The Abbé Grégoire and the French Revolution: The Making of Modern Universalism* (Berkeley: University of California Press, 2005).

62. "Opinion de M. le Comte Stanislas de Clermont-Tonnerre, député de Paris, le 23 décembre, 1789." Cited in Paula Hyman, *The Jews of Modern France* (Berkeley: University of California Press, 1998), 27.

63. According to Paula Hyman, Napoleon's question, "Can a Jewess marry a Christian and a Jew a Christian woman? Or does the law allow the Jews to marry only among themselves?" aroused the most acrimonious debate in the Grand Sanhedrin. Although the delegates acknowledged that, following the Revolution, it was possible for a Jew to have a civil marriage with a Christian and remain a Jew, they underscored that rabbis would not give their blessings to such unions. Hyman, *Jews of Modern France*, 42.

64. Leff, *Sacred Bonds*, 45.

65. Leff, *Sacred Bonds*, 56.

66. Leff, *Sacred Bonds*, 5–6. On the effort to revive local identity in nine-

teenth-century France, see Stéphane Gerson, *The Pride of Place: Local Memories and Political Culture in Nineteenth-Century France* (Ithaca, NY: Cornell University Press, 2003).

67. Leff, *Sacred Bonds*, 86. Olinde Rodrigues attended the Lycée Charlemagne.

68. In her discussion of Foa's "Rachel," Ezdinli notes that "Foa's Jewish heroes and heroines fight within Judaism; they do not convert, even while their narrators complain about the inexorability of religious law that condemns them to death" (Ezdinli, "Altérité juive," 37). Although this applies to *Le kidouschim* (which Ezdinli was unable to locate), it does not hold true for "Billette ou la fille du juif Jonathas" (which I discuss later), in which the heroine converts.

69. Foa's novel *Phillipe* (1831), for example, centers on a non-Jewish student at the École Polytechnique during the Revolution of 1830.

70. I would note that once again the name Hozny is not typical of either the Sephardic or Ashkenazic Jews of France. Foa seems intent on adding an oriental exoticism to her Jewish characters at the expense of sociological accuracy.

71. "Long curls of black hair framed a pale and elongated face, which hinted at a Jewish origin" (Foa, "Rachel," ix).

72. Ezdinli offers an interesting reading of "Rachel," comparing it to Sand's portrayal of a Jewish woman in *Lavinia*, also of 1833. She notes that Foa's heroine is a victim of Jewish patriarchy, "Hebraic law" (Ezdinli, "Altérité juive," 35).

73. It seems possible that Foa wished to capitalize on the success of the opera by borrowing its title, but the setting and plots of the two works are very different.

74. However, a certain number of Jews managed to reside in Paris in the eighteenth century, including some moneylenders resembling the characters in Foa's novel, although they constantly faced the threat of expulsion. Léon Kahn, *Histoire de la communauté israélite de Paris* (Paris: Durlacher, 1894), 61–65.

75. Eugénie Foa, *La juive, histoire du temps de la régence* (Paris: Arthus Bertrand, 1835), 1: 65. Subsequent references appear in the text. André's exclamation mirrors the almost identical reaction of Ivanhoe, who like André had been healed by the beautiful Jewess in her mysterious oriental apartment: "To his great surprise, he found himself in a room magnificently furnished, but having cushions instead of chairs to rest upon, and in other respects partaking so much of Oriental costume that he began to doubt whether he had not, during his sleep, been transported back again to the land of Palestine" (Walter Scott, *Ivanhoe* [New York: Penguin, 1986], 298).

76. Compare the "profusion" of Rebecca's "sable tresses" (Scott, *Ivanhoe*, 82) to the "long tresses of black hair" (Foa, *La juive*, 67) belonging to Midiane; or the "superb arch" of Rebecca's eyebrows to "lightly arched" brows of Midiane; or the "brilliancy" of Rebecca's dark eyes to Midiane's eyes, "the brightness of which

is tempered by her long lashes." The physical descriptions of the two Jewish fathers are also almost identical; both men are tall and thin with high foreheads and sharp eyes.

77. Leff, *Sacred Bonds*, 99.

78. In *The Politics of Assimilation: A Study of the French Jewish Community at the Time of the Dreyfus Affair* (Oxford, U.K.: Clarendon, 1971), Michael Marrus argues that "race, in fact, provided Jews with the means to express their sense of a distinct Jewish identity, a sense which was difficult to define in other terms, and which they themselves were not always prepared to admit" (10).

79. When André asks the boy whether he is Jewish, the orphan responds: "No sir, a note found on me declared that I was baptized with the name of Jehan" (Foa, *La juive*, 1: 97).

80. Leff, *Sacred Bonds*, 114.

81. The *inventaire après décès* of Isaac Rodrigues Henriques preserved in the Fonds Gradis at the Archives Nationales dates from 1834. Muelsch puts the date of Foa's father's death in 1836, but also sees it as a turning point in Foa's literary career: Elisabeth-Christine Muelsch, "Creativity, Childhood, and Children's Literature, or How to Become a Woman Writer: The Case of Eugénie Foa," *Romance Languages Annual* 8 (1997), 69. Chantal Bischoff dates Isaac's death to 1826 (Bischoff, *Geneviève Straus*, 15), but this is clearly wrong.

82. According to legend, a Jewish moneylender named Jonathas accepted a wafer representing the Christian host in exchange for a loan made to a Christian woman. Denounced for blasphemy after plunging the host into boiling water, Jonathas cedes his property to the king, Philippe-le-Bel, and dies at the stake. Philippe gives the Jew's land to a bourgeois named Ramier Fleming, who builds an expiatory chapel on the spot, in which the hospitalier monks of Notre Dame take up residence. Originally called the rue-ou-Dieu-fust-bouilli (Street-where-God-was-boiled), the street eventually became the rue des Billettes after a piece of metal worn by these monks. See Charles Lefeuve, *Les anciennes maisons de Paris* (Paris: C. Reinwald, 1875).

83. Thomas Kselman provides an account of the controversy over this conversion in "Turbulent Souls in Modern France: Jewish Conversion and the Terquem Affair," *Historical Reflections/Réflexions Historiques* 32(1) (2006), 83–104.

84. The existence of Foa's fiction contradicts Galchinsky's claim that "Anglo-Jewish women writing in the 1830s preceded women elsewhere in Europe and the United States into print by fifteen years" (Galchinsky, *Origin*, 19). Indeed, Foa began to publish fiction about Jews in 1830, several years *before* her British counterparts Grace Aguilar and Marion and Celia Moss.

85. Ismar Schorsch, "The Myth of Sephardic Supremacy," *Leo Baeck Institute Yearbook* 34 (1989), 47–66.

Chapter 2

Portions of this chapter were originally published in *Judaism: A Quarterly Journal of Jewish Life and Thought* 213–214(54) (Winter–Spring 2005), 17–25; and in *Nineteenth-Century French Studies* 34(3–4) (Spring–Summer 2006), 287–302. I gratefully acknowledge the permission to republish the material here.

1. Subscriptions to *Le Constitutionnel*, which serialized Sue's novel, rose from 3,600 to more than 40,000 in the space of a few months. Francis Lacassin, "Preface," in *Le juif errant*, by Eugène Sue (Paris: Laffont, 1983), 3. Ahasvérus, the title character, figures only occasionally in the sprawling page-turner, set in the present, about the diabolical attempts by the Jesuits to rob a Protestant family of a secret treasure.

2. I am referring to Balzac's *Splendeurs et misères des courtisanes* [A Harlot High and Low] (1838–1847), in which the Jewish prostitute Esther seduces the rapacious Jewish banker Nucingen, among others. Nucingen figures in many Balzac novels. Other major novels of the period by Balzac that feature Jewish characters include *La cousine Bette* [Cousin Bette] (1846) and *Le cousin Pons* [Cousin Pons] (1847).

3. The Fourierist journalist Alphonse Toussenel produced the most notable such tract, *Les juifs, rois de l'époque* [The Jews, Kings of the Age] (1845).

4. *Le juif errant* contains other Jewish characters as well, including the banker Samuel, who, although possessed of stereotypical physical features, "the pure and oriental racial type" (464), and "endowed with an admirable aptitude for business" (468), protects the secret fortune of the Rennepont family with great probity. Moreover, Sue does not hesitate to use his novel as a platform to speak out against the persecution of the Jews in Poland and Russia. Samuel describes the death of his son: "The Russian government, treating him like they treat our brothers and sisters in that country of cruel tyranny, condemned him to cruel torture" (465).

5. *Les Archives Israélites* (1842), 151. (Throughout this chapter, I give page references to Ben-Lévi's pieces by referring to the year of the *Archives Israélites* issue in which the piece was published, followed by the page number, as pagination for each year of the journal was continuous. If consecutive citations come from the same piece, I provide page numbers in the body of the text.) Also cited in Léon Poliakov, *Histoire de l'anti-sémitisme* (Paris: Calmann-Lévy, 1981), v. 2, 194, and in Leyla Ezdinli, "Altérité juive, altérité romanesque," *Romantisme* 81 (1993), 29. The immediate impetus for Ben-Lévi's diatribe was the nonfictional text "Le juif" [The Jew], by Alphonse Cerfberr de Médelsheim, the son of a convert who, although he came from one of France's most distinguished Jewish families, describes the Jew as a dirty, scheming, rapacious fanatic, an oriental invader who has taken advantage of France's generosity by sucking its peasants dry. Ben-Lévi

mobilizes the full force of his wit to denounce the text and its author, mocking not only his bad writing and vicious lies but also the pretentious addition of the aristocratic "de" to his name. "The Marquis de Médelsheim is certainly happy that the baptismal waters ran over his forehead with sufficient force to cleanse him of the dirt that disfigures the rest of us German Jews" (*Les Archives Israélites* [1842], 154). Cerfberr de Médelsheim's "Le juif" originally appeared in *Les Français peints par eux-mêmes* (1842) and then as a stand-alone text in slightly different versions.

6. Evelyne Bloch-Dano, *Madame Proust*, trans. Alice Kaplan (Chicago: University of Chicago Press, 2007), 256.

7. Berlin's Jewish population during the first two decades of the nineteenth century was only slightly larger. Hamburg, the city with the largest Jewish population in Germany, had 6,000 Jews by the beginning of the nineteenth century. Michael A. Meyer, *Response to Modernity: A History of the Reform Movement in Judaism* (New York: Oxford University Press, 1988), 43, 53.

8. Frédéric Viey, *Fontainebleau-Avon: Journal d'une communauté juive de la Révolution à nos jours* (Avon: Frédéric Viey, 1991), 101–102, 159.

9. The *Inventaire après décès* for Baruch Weil, dated May 7, 1828, listed property valued at more than 95,000 francs. AN Cotconsu et/xxxv/1092 (ref 140529).

10. "My respectable father," Godchaux would write, "has performed circumcision at least six hundred times, and always, thank God, without the least accident. He circumcised his eight sons himself." Godchaux Weil, *Réflexions d'un jeune Israélite français, sur les deux brochures de M. Tsarphati* (Paris: Chez l'Auteur, 1821), 23.

11. Christine Piette, *Les juifs de Paris (1808–1840): La marche vers l'assimilation* (Québec: Laval University Press, 1983), 133–140.

12. Drach provides a fascinating autobiographical sketch, describing his birth and early rabbinical education in Edenhorf, near Strasbourg, his Talmudic studies in various Alsatian cities, his move to Paris, his work as a tutor teaching "theological and profane" subjects "in the family of a very estimable Israelite" (i.e., Baruch Weil), his growing religious doubts, and his very public conversion, along with that of his children, at the hands of the archbishop of Paris. Paul Louis Bernard Drach, *Lettres d'un rabbin converti, aux Israélites ses frères sur les motifs de sa conversion* (Paris: Belin-Mandar, 1825), 27–49.

13. The full title of one of these evangelical works gives a sense of the self-importance of this converted rabbi: "Of the Harmony Between the Church and the Synagogue or the Perpetuity and Catholicity of the Christian Religion by The Chevalier P. L. B. Drach, Doctor of Philosophy and of Letters, Member of the Pontifical Academy of the Catholic Religion, as well as of the Arcadians, the Asian Society of Paris, the Faith and Light Society of Nancy, etc. Member of the Legion of Honor, of Saint-Grégoire le Grand, of Saint-Louis, of the Civil Order of

Lucques, 2e classe, of Saint-Sylvestre, etc., Honored librarian of the Holy Congregation of Propaganda" (Paris: Paul Mellier, 1844).

14. Tsarphati [Olry Terquem], *Première lettre d'un Israélite français à ses coreligionnaires* (Paris: Bachelier, n.d. [1821]).

15. "A few citations of the Bible will suffice to establish, with the utmost evidence, that transferring the celebration of the Sabbath to another day of the week, replacing circumcision by a symbolic ceremony, would be an act diametrically opposed to the expressed will manifested by the Eternal." Weil, *Réflexions*, 8.

16. Although it is possible that Frédérique was distantly related to Léopold Zunz (1794–1886), one of the founders of the Wissenschaft des Judentums movement in Germany, I have not found the link.

17. On Godchaux Weil's charitable activities, see Piette, *Les juifs de Paris*, 40, 64, 166, 186–187. Phyllis Cohen Albert also discusses Weil's participation on various Consistory committees in *The Modernization of French Jewry: Consistory and Community in the Nineteenth Century* (Hanover, NH: Brandeis University Press, 1977), 62, 64, 204, 237–238, 275, 301.

18. Piette, *Les juifs de Paris*, 32.

19. Ben-Lévi, *Moral and Religious Tales for the Young of the Hebrew Faith*, adapted by A. Abraham (London: Whittaker, 1846).

20. In one of his last regular articles for *Les Archives Israélites* (1850), 436–442, "Defunct Ben-Lévi," signed G. Weil, he attributes the death of his pseudonym to the passage of a law on July 16, 1850, "the year III of the French Republic, Second of that Name," mandating that all newspaper articles must be signed by their authors. In a mock funerary oration for his defunct pseudonym, Weil intones: "With what devotion he always defended the holy cause of Israelitism! With what courage he battled tirelessly against our adversaries within and against our enemies without! . . . He perhaps too often saw a comic side to things, he didn't always cite big chunks of Hebrew or of Chinese . . . but he was basically a good man" (437). Over the course of the next decade, Weil wrote occasional pieces, including letters to the editor regarding the plight of Jews in other parts of the world, and the obituary for Samuel Cahen, the journal's founder, in 1862.

21. An article in *Les Archives Israélites*, after the August 11, 1850, Consistory elections, complains that the entire list the journal had put forward passed with one exception: G. Weil.

22. The obituary in *Les Archives Israélites* begins, "The Israelite Community of Paris has just suffered a grievous loss, which will be felt most especially, we dare say, here at the *Archives*." *Les Archives Israélites* (June 15, 1878), 381.

23. One such statement reads: "We understand by Religion, the cult of the Divinity, the principle that makes us recognize the celestial power." Ben-Lévi, *Les matinées du samedi, livre d'éducation morale et religieuse à l'usage de la jeunesse israélite par G. Ben Lévi, ancien membre du comité communal des écoles israélites de Paris* (Paris: Au Bureau des *Archives Israélites de France*, 1842), 1.

24. According to the lists of subscribers published in the journal, at its beginning in 1840, the *Archives* counted 450 subscribers. By 1843, this number had risen to about 1,000. Parisian Jewish subscribers came mostly from the upper bourgeoisie and the liberal professions. Many of the prominent Jews of the time subscribed, including the Rothschilds, the Péreires, the Foulds, the Halévys, Olinde Rodrigues, and Adolphe Crémieux. Subscribers also included some Jews in the provinces (mostly merchants) as well as a small number of foreigners. The small number of non-Jews on the published subscription list includes Delphine de Girardin and, after 1843, King Louis-Philippe and his family. Béatrice Philippe provides an overview of the journal's history in *"Les Archives Israélites de France de leur creation en 1840 à fevrier 1848 ou un journal juif sous Louis-Philippe,"* Mémoire de maîtrise, Université de Paris IV (1974–1975), vi–viii.

25. The entry under *juif* in the sixth edition of the dictionary, from 1835, contains the following: "JEW is also used, figuratively and familiarly, of he who practices usury or sells at exorbitant prices; and in general of anyone who seeks to make money through unjust and sordid means." *Dictionnaire de l'Académie française*, 6th ed. (Paris: Firmin Didot, 1835). The supplement to the sixth edition also adds a verb, *juiver* ("to jew"), which it defines as "to commit usury; to cheat in a deal, in a business affair." *Supplément au dictionnaire de l'Académie française* (Paris: Gustave Barba, 1836).

26. Significantly, Simon Schwarzfuchs titles his study of nineteenth-century French Jewry, *Du juif à l'israélite: Histoire d'une mutation (1770–1870)* (Paris: Fayard, 1989).

27. Meyer, *Response to Modernity*, 10–61.

28. Meyer, *Response to Modernity*, 168.

29. According to Meyer, whereas the German Reform movement followed the path laid down by the Protestant Reformation, in France, Jewish reformers looked to Catholicism as a model. Rabbis began to dress like priests, and the synagogue service came to resemble the Catholic mass. Because Catholicism continued to rely on Latin, Hebrew retained its primacy, except for sermons, which the Consistory required to be in French (Meyer, *Response to Modernity*, 170).

30. The editors of *L'Univers Israélite* did share the belief in the need for certain reforms, however, such as ending the practice of selling synagogue honors. On the Reform movement in France, also see Jay R. Berkovitz, *Rites and Passages: The Beginnings of Modern Jewish Culture in France, 1650–1860* (Philadelphia: University of Pennsylvania Press, 2004), 152–156, 191–212.

31. Famous Jews such as the actress Rachel Félix, the composer Fromental Halévy, and the jurist and politician Adolphe Crémieux received constant mention, but *Les Archives Israélites* also singled out Jews who attained a high grade in the army, won prizes, or graduated from prestigious schools.

32. Balzac published *Grandeur et décadence de César Birotteau, marchand parfumeur* in 1837.

33. *Les Archives Israélites* (1841), 753.

34. In a nonfiction article published a few months before, Ben-Lévi makes a similar sociological observation: "Three generations of French citizens are alive at this moment: the first saw the degrading reprobation that the French before the Constituent Assembly attached to the name of the Jew; the second, contemporaries of the Empire, fought in the army and enriched itself in business; the third has garnered, in the schools of the Restoration, ideas of independence of spirit and character that it has put to use since the Revolution of 1830." And with this generational change comes a loss of religious sentiment: "The grandfather believes, the son doubts, and the child denies." *Les Archives Israélites* (1841), 528, 530.

35. Jann Matlock, "Censoring the Realist Gaze," in *Spectacles of Realism*, eds. Margaret Cohen and Christopher Prendergast (Minneapolis: University of Minnesota Press, 1995), 28–65.

36. In his nonfictional "Deuxième lettre d'un humoriste," *Les Archives Israélites* (1841), 19–27, Ben-Lévi offers a "physiologie" of three types—rabbis, rabbi lovers, and rabbi haters—to be found in the Paris Jewish community. Balzac published his *Physiologie du mariage* in 1829.

37. In his lecture "Science as a Vocation" (1919), Max Weber describes the "disenchantment of the world" in modern times and the replacement of the sacred by technology and calculation. Max Weber, *Max Weber's "Science as a Vocation,"* trans. Michael John, eds. Peter Lassman and Irving Velody (London: Unwin Hyman, 1989), 13.

38. Ben-Lévi, "Le décret du 17 mars," *Les Archives Israélites* (1841), 79–88.

39. Chased by the Russians, the French hurriedly constructed bridges to cross the freezing river but had to abandon a large part of their army on the far bank to face capture and slaughter. One of the great French military disasters, the episode was recounted in the second part of Balzac's *Adieu* as well as in many popular histories and theatrical productions from the time. On the historical resonance of this episode, see Maurice Samuels, *The Spectacular Past: Popular History and the Novel in Nineteenth-Century France* (Ithaca, NY: Cornell University Press, 2004), 208–224.

40. Michael Paul Driskel describes the festivities surrounding the return of Napoleon's body to France and his interment at Les Invalides in *As Befits a Legend: Building a Tomb for Napoleon, 1840–1861* (Kent, OH: Kent State University Press, 1993).

41. Along with the abolition of the More Judaico (the special oath required of Jews in court) in 1846, the decision of the July Monarchy government to pay the salaries of rabbis removed the last official barriers to full equality for French Jews. French rabbis would continue to be paid by the state until the Combes Law of 1905 officially separated church and state.

42. This apology, of course, is pure fiction. Although it is true, according to Anschel, that the anti-Jewish measures of the March 17 decree had in fact been

suggested to Napoleon by Portalis, his Ministre des Cultes (minister of religion), it is also true that Napoleon chose to disregard the advice of Champagny, his minister of the interior, who favored more equitable policies. In other words, not all of Napoleon's ministers "deceived" him regarding the Jews. Anschel further specifies that the decree reflected opinions that Napoleon himself had expressed to the Conseil d'État (Council of State) in April 1806, when he demanded repressive measures against Jewish money lending in Alsace: "I want to take away from them," Napoleon said of the Jews, "at least for a certain time, the right to make loans, because it is too humiliating for the French nation to find itself at the mercy of the most vile nation [i.e., the Jews]." He went on, "The Jews are not in the same category as Protestants and Catholics; they must be judged according to political law and not according to civil law, because they are not citizens." Cited in Robert Anschel, *Napoléon et les juifs* (Paris: PUF, 1928), 91. Schwarzfuchs likewise describes how Napoleon dismissed the concerns of the politicians and lawyers serving on the Council of State who upheld revolutionary principles of equality and argued that it is wrong to ask a lender's religion before deciding whether he should be paid. Napoleon insisted that Jews constituted a "nation within the nation" and clearly demanded special measures against them (Schwarzfuchs, *Du juif à l'israélite*, 46–50). Also see Pierre Birnbaum, *L'aigle et la synagogue: Napoléon, les juifs, et l'état* (Paris: Fayard, 2007).

43. Sudhir Hazareesingh, *The Saint-Napoleon: Celebrations of Sovereignty in Nineteenth-Century France* (Cambridge, MA: Harvard University Press, 2004).

44. The story calls the dead Napoleon the people's "idol," a loaded term for Jews because the Jewish religion explicitly forbids idolatry.

45. Hazareesingh describes how religious Catholics faced a similar dilemma (*Saint-Napoleon*, 73).

46. "Les poissons et les miettes de pain," *Les Archives Israélites* (1846), 631. The French text contains a pun on the word *droit*: "Il s'habille chez Renard, il dîne au café anglais . . . enfin, il a fait son droit, et tout cela lui donne celui de ne rien faire."

47. Balzac published *Les employés* (originally titled *La femme supérieure*) in 1838.

48. Naomi Schor, *George Sand and Idealism* (New York: Columbia University Press, 1993), 47.

49. Schor, *George Sand*, 54.

50. One exception might be *Gobseck* (1840), in which the miserly Jewish moneylender of the title tells the story of his life to the narrator, the lawyer Derville. Gobseck's worldly philosophy and probity make him a more sympathetic character than Balzac's Christian miser, the father in *Eugénie Grandet* (1833), who also learned his wily ways from a Jew.

51. *Les Archives Israélites* (1841), 687.

52. Alexandre Weill began publishing his *Histoires de village* first in German

and later in the French newspaper *Le Corsaire-Satan* in the 1840s. Daniel Stauben published the first part of his text serially in *Les Archives Israélites*, beginning in 1849.

53. In *The Shaping of Jewish Identity in Nineteenth-Century France* (Detroit: Wayne State University Press, 1989), Jay R. Berkovitz describes how the movement for Jewish regeneration paradoxically defined progress as a "return to an idealized past" (140). Also see his discussion of regeneration in *Rites and Passages* (105–107).

54. *Les Archives Israélites* (1842), 466.

55. In *Le degré zéro de l'écriture* (Paris: Seuil, 1953), Roland Barthes argues that the Revolution of 1848 served as a watershed for French bourgeois writers. In *Mélancolie et opposition* (Paris: Corti, 1987), Ross Chambers discusses strategies of literary resistance against the authoritarian regime of the Second Empire.

56. In an article published in April, "The Pillagers of Alsace," Ben-Lévi describes the attacks in the eastern provinces as "a lugubrious spot on the brilliant sun of our beautiful revolution." *Les Archives Israélites* (1848), 215.

57. Ben-Lévi voiced his fears explicitly: "How will universal suffrage be implemented in our consistories? . . . Will the religion continue to be paid for by the State?" *Les Archives Israélites* (1848), 378.

58. *Les Archives Israélites* (1848), 527.

59. Dedicated to the modernization of Jews throughout the world, the Alliance Israélite Universelle, headquartered in Paris, established Jewish schools for boys and girls in the Middle and Near East. On the origins of the Alliance in nineteenth-century France, see Michael Graetz, *The Jews in Nineteenth-Century France: From the French Revolution to the Alliance Israélite Universelle*, trans. Jane Marie Todd (Stanford, CA: Stanford University Press, 1996), esp. 249–288; and Aron Rodrigue, *French Jews, Turkish Jews: The Alliance Israélite Universelle and the Politics of Jewish Schooling in Turkey, 1860–1925* (Bloomington: Indiana University Press, 1990), esp. 1–24.

60. Rodrigue notes that Ben-Lévi called for the foundation of committees to help Jews abroad in *Les Archives Israélites* as early as 1844 (*French Jews*, 20). In 1845, Ben-Lévi helped found such a committee. *Les Archives Israélites* (1845), 552–558. In an article in 1865, Ben-Lévi vaunts his long-standing advocacy on behalf of the Jews of Rome. *Les Archives Israélites* (1865), 292–298.

61. Lisa Moses Leff describes the movement for Jewish solidarity, culminating in the founding of the Alliance Israélite Universelle, in *Sacred Bonds of Solidarity: The Rise of Jewish Internationalism in Nineteenth-Century France* (Stanford, CA: Stanford University Press, 2006).

62. Graetz argues that it was "peripheral" Jews who represented the most dynamic and forward-looking segment of the French Jewish community in the mid-nineteenth century and who took the lead in founding the Alliance. Born into

one of the most "insider" families, and a community leader from an early age, Godchaux Weil would seem to contradict this hypothesis, although he did find himself excluded from the Consistory in 1850.

Chapter 3

1. Ben Baruch, "Correspondance," *L'Univers Israélite* (1845), v. 2, 77. Subsequent references appear in the text. The pagination of *L'Univers Israélite* is complicated. The journal had continuous pagination from its first issue in April 1844 through December 1844. In January 1845, the page numbers started again at zero. Then in April 1845, they started again at zero for what they called "Volume 2." I therefore refer to the issues between April 1844 and December 1844 as "v. 1A," those between January 1845 and March 1845 as "v. 1B," and those between April 1845 and December 1845 as "v. 2."

2. Simon Bloch, "La stabilité et le mouvement," *L'Univers Israélite* (1844), v. 1A, 33–34. Also cited in Arnold Eisen, *Rethinking Judaism: Ritual, Commandment, Community* (Chicago: University of Chicago Press, 1998), 170. Before founding *L'Univers Israélite*, Simon Bloch (1810–1879) published a short-lived bilingual (German-French) Jewish journal in Strasbourg called *La Régéneration/ Die Wiedergeburt* in 1836–1837 that likewise defended Orthodox religious values while advocating acculturation. He also published several books of Jewish theology and liturgy. M. Prevost and Roman d'Amat, eds. *Dictionnaire de biographie française* (Paris: Letouzey, 1959), v. 6, 683.

3. According to Étain's official Web site, the town had one of the largest Jewish populations in the department in 1806, numbering fourteen families (http://www.ville-Étain.fr/01/histoire.html). In this period, there were about 7,000 Jews in the Lorraine province.

4. Restrictions existed on Jewish mobility, including prohibitions against leaving the quarter on Sunday and holidays, until the Revolution. Esther Benbassa, *The Jews of France: A History from Antiquity to the Present* (Princeton, NJ: Princeton University Press, 1999), 60.

5. The number of Jews in Metz grew from 20 households in 1595 to 585 households, or about 2,223 Jews (roughly 2 percent of the total population), on the eve of the Revolution. Benbassa, *Jews of France*, 60.

6. In a story published in *L'Univers Israélite* in 1845, Ben Baruch refers rather gratuitously to the Créhange cloth manufacturers of Sédan, suggesting that members of his family may have engaged in the textile business, like other Jews of the area (including the family of Alfred Dreyfus). Ben Baruch, "Dixième lettre d'un Israélite de Mogador à son ami à Fez," *L'Univers Israélite* (1845), v. 2, 186.

7. My information on the Créhange family comes from Jean-Pierre Bernard and Pascal Faustini, *Vantoux, Vallières, Méy et Grimont: Une communauté juive*

aux portes de Metz du 17e au 20e siècle (Paris: Cercle de Généalogie Juive, 2005). I thank Yves Niquil and Alain Créhange for this reference and for their help in piecing together the Créhange family tree.

8. In the 1780s, Isaïe Berr Bing of Metz published a Hebrew translation of one of the works of Moses Mendelssohn.

9. In 1782 Berr Isaac Berr of Nancy translated into French the Haskalah pamphlet *Divrei Shalom ve-Emet* [Words of Peace and Truth], which advocated the integration of secular subjects into Jewish education. See Paula Hyman, *The Jews of Modern France* (Berkeley: University of California Press, 1998), 13–14.

10. Hyman, *Jews of Modern France*, 66–67.

11. In *Scènes de la vie juive en Alsace* (Paris: Michel Lévy, 1860), Daniel Stauben describes the social position of the hazan in semirural Alsace: "Salaried by the community, the cantor is an important functionary whose position is rather lucrative" (77). I examine Stauben's text in Chapter 5.

12. Créhange, *Vade-mecum du jeune teneur des livres* (n.p., n.d.).

13. Créhange, *A MM. les membres de la Société Industrielle et Commerciale à Paris* (Paris: imp. J. Smith, 1835), 13. Subsequent references in the text are also from this page.

14. I assume this implies changing the spelling of Meyer/Mayer to make it sound less Jewish.

15. The Jewish Consistory regulated issues from school curricula to circumcision methods and took responsibility for such administrative tasks as building and maintaining synagogues, regulating kosher slaughter, and until 1830 determining the amount of the special tax each Jewish family had to pay. The Protestant consistories, established in 1802, were less centralized than the Jewish Consistory and allowed for greater diversity of religious practice. See Lisa Moses Leff, *Sacred Bonds of Solidarity: The Rise of Jewish Internationalism in Nineteenth-Century France* (Stanford, CA: Stanford University Press, 2006), 57–61; and Daniel Robert, *Les églises réformées en France (1800–1830)* (Paris: PUF, 1961).

16. In 1844, a new regulation redefined the criteria for the selection of notables to include not just the wealthy but also those who exercised certain functions, including government administrators, army officers, members of the chambers of commerce, rabbis, professors, and teachers. See Phyllis Cohen Albert, *The Modernization of French Jewry: Consistory and Community in the Nineteenth Century* (Hanover, NH: Brandeis University Press, 1977), 106–107.

17. This despite the fact that the consistorial synagogue on the rue Notre-Dame-de-Nazareth had only 500 seats during a period in which the Jewish population of Paris had swelled to more than 8,000 (in 1840). Albert, *Modernization of French Jewry*, 210–214.

18. Three issues of this journal appeared in 1839–1840. Albert points out the irony that the reformer Olry Terquem (pseud. Tsarphati) supported Créhange's call for independent prayer meetings in the pages of *Les Archives Israélites*.

"Créhange angrily retorted that he had no need for support from such quarters" (Albert, *Modernization of French Jewry*, 214).

19. "There are in Paris a crowd of learned doctors who want to endow us with reform; let these little Luthers abandon their childish discussions. It is by instructing the people that they will uproot the prejudices they abhor. They can judge for themselves since they have become so smart: ever since they know EVERYTHING they believe in NOTHING." Alexandre Créhange, *Discours prononcé le 24 juin 1839, dans la séance du Consistoire israélite du departement de la Seine* (Paris: Chez Tous les Délégués, 1839), 12.

20. Albert, *Modernization of French Jewry*, 210.

21. Zosa Szajkowski (the pseudonym of Szajko Frydman) discusses Créhange's battles against the Consistory in *Internal Conflicts in French Jewry at the Time of the Revolution of 1848* (New York: Yiddish Scientific Institute, 1947–1948), but his account contains inaccuracies, including the date of Créhange's death (105–111).

22. The mohel performs circumcisions.

23. The sohet prepares kosher meat.

24. A. Créhange, *Discours de M. Créhange prononcé dans la réunion préparatoire des Israélites de Paris, le 1er décembre, 1844* (Paris: Dondey-Dupré, 1845). Cited in Albert, *Modernization of French Jewry*, 103.

25. Although the Revolution provoked the destruction of the Rothschild property, which could not have displeased Créhange greatly, it also led to antisemitic riots in Alsace (Hyman, *Jews of Modern France*, 56). Editorials in *L'Univers Israélite* also complained about the loss of financial support to Jewish institutions occasioned by the Revolution as well as the general attack on traditional religious authority that the Revolution seemed to legitimate.

26. A. Créhange, *La Marseillaise du travail* (Paris: Bureau de la Vérité, 1848).

27. In "Religion and Association in French Political Thought," *Journal of the History of Ideas* 69: 2 (April 2008), 219–243, Michael C. Behrent discusses how certain nineteenth-century republican thinkers were not anticlerical but rather saw religion as essential to social cohesion.

28. In the fall of 1846, Créhange founded another newspaper to defend the interests of Orthodoxy, *La Paix*, which I was unable to locate. He published *La Paix* for a year before being sued for libel. As he described it in his first editorial in *La Vérité* the following year, "We told some truths, they brought us to court. We signalled some abuses, they wanted to fine us and imprison us." He then merged *La Paix* with *L'Univers Israélite* in 1847, but this led to a rupture with his former editors: "But alas! Never was there a worse marriage: after a few days, our home was full of discord and three months later we had to file for divorce." He offered *La Vérité* as a new alternative to the established Orthodox journal. *La Vérité* (April 17, 1848), 1.

29. Créhange, *La Vérité* (April 27, 1848), cited in Albert, *Modernization of French Jewry*, 78.

30. Szajkowski argues that the democratic elements were unable to make effective use of the expanded electorate (*Internal Conflicts*, 116).

31. Albert provides a comprehensive discussion of the debates over the electorate in *Modernization of French Jewry*, 78–82.

32. Leff explains that the term *solidarité* originally had a precise legal definition in the Civil Code of 1804, defining a relationship in which people are held accountable for other people's debts and promises. Well into the 1840s, French Jews argued that they should not be held responsible for debts contracted by Jewish communities before the Revolution, thus disavowing a certain form of communal solidarity that they saw as antithetical to the revolutionary principles of individual autonomy enshrined in the code (Leff, *Sacred Bonds*, 45–49). They thus did not use the term "solidarity," which they felt retained corporate connotations, until after 1848, when they borrowed it from Christian socialist discourse. The motto of the Alliance Israélite Universelle, founded in 1860, used the Hebrew term *Arevim*, which they translated as *solidaires*, to express a feeling of responsibility to Jews across the world (Leff, *Sacred Bonds*, 171–177).

33. Michael Graetz, *The Jews in Nineteenth-Century France: From the French Revolution to the Alliance Israélite Universelle*, trans. Jane Marie Todd (Stanford, CA: Stanford University Press, 1996), 282.

34. The 1857–1858 edition of the *Annuaire* contains articles of a scientific nature by Terquem.

35. Whereas *Les Archives Israélites* itself was modeled on the German *Allgemeine Zeitung des Judenthums*, the mouthpiece of the liberal movement in Germany, *L'Univers Israelite* (founded in 1844) actually predated its German neo-Orthodox counterparts, Rabbi Jacob Ettlinger's *Der treue Zionswächter* [The Faithful Guardian of Zion], founded in 1845, and *Jeschurun*, founded by Rabbi Samson Raphael Hirsch in 1854. See Jonathan Hess, "Fictions of Modern Orthodoxy, 1857–1890: Orthodoxy and the Quest for the German-Jewish Novel," *Leo Baeck Institute Year Book* 52 (2007), 49–86. Also see chapter 4 of Hess's *Middlebrow Literature and the Making of German-Jewish Identity* (Stanford, CA: Stanford University Press, in press).

36. In its second year (1845), the subscription price was 10 francs for Paris, 12.50 francs for the provinces, and 15 francs for foreign subscriptions.

37. *L'Univers Israélite* also published fiction by other Jewish writers, including Adolphe Millaud and Alphonse Ennery (not to be confused with Adolphe d'Ennery), as well as poetry.

38. A. Ben Baruch Créhange, "Correspondance," *L'Univers Israélite* (1845), v. 1B, 21.

39. *L'Univers Israélite* (1845), v. 1B, 21. Godchaux Weil (Ben-Lévi) was the son of Baruch Weil, a leading member of the Parisian Jewish community. See my discussion of him in Chapter 2.

40. *L'Univers Israélite* (1845), v. 1B, 88.

41. In a particular telling exchange in the spring of 1845, Ben-Lévi mocked a meeting of Orthodox Jews at which Créhange gave a speech quoting the Bible to the effect that "from dust we were created . . . and to dust we shall return" (*L'Univers Israélite* [1845], v. 1B, 119). In his response to Ben-Lévi's attack, Ben Baruch writes: "In the last issue of the *Archives*, Mr. Weil (G. Ben Lévi) felt he should protest against my idiotic pretension to equality. He admits that we are dust; what is more, he declares that we are *mud* and that he is a *river*! If Reform counts many such partisans in its number, our religious affairs will soon be *liquid* and we will have a *flood* of improvements" (119).

42. *L'Univers Israélite* (1844), v. 1A, 198. Subsequent references appear in the text.

43. Lest the reader have any doubt that this "neighboring land" resembles France in every way, the author includes explicit references to specific features of French religious life, such as the selling of religious honors to raise money for the synagogue, the subject of much criticism in the pages of both *L'Univers Israélite* and *Les Archives Israélites* during the 1840s: "In this country [synagogue] honors are sold to the highest bidder, and he who can pay thinks he has deserved them" (*L'Univers Israélite* [1844], v. 1A, 199). He also informs the reader in a footnote that the type of political maneuvering that Godfried uses to receive a government decoration are not "without example among us" (199n1).

44. The idea of the spark (*nitzotzot* in Hebrew) of divinity comes from the Jewish mystical tradition.

45. Eisen, *Rethinking Judaism*, 2–3.

46. The choice of Montesquieu is itself significant. As Arthur Hertzberg notes, unlike Voltaire, Montesquieu favored tolerance for the Jews. Arthur Hertzberg, *The French Enlightenment and the Jews* (New York: Columbia University Press, 1968), 275.

47. *L'Univers Israélite* (1844), v. 1A, 268. Subsequent references appear in the text.

48. Ben Baruch rather surprisingly finds the need to translate the common word *kascher* parenthetically as "pure, allowed," suggesting that he imagined a non-Jewish, or very assimilated, readership for his tale.

49. In the first issue of *L'Univers Israélite*, the editors opine in favor of adding a piano and a choir to "initiation" services: "Why therefore take away such a powerful tool, the influence of music on the soul and on the senses of the young initiated?" (*L'Univers Israélite* [1844], v. 1A, 16).

50. When the city of Paris insisted on reclaiming all plots after a period of five years, unless the deceased had paid 500 francs for perpetual care, the rich Consistory leaders acquiesced, because they themselves had no problem paying the fee. This was another actual battle that aroused an angry protest from Créhange on behalf of the poor Orthodox Jews of Paris.

51. Jonathan reveals himself to be a *Mohel non-assermenté*, which means that

he performs circumcisions in clandestine fashion, without the official approba-
tion of the Consistory, "because he refuses to grant the Consistory the right to
restrict all or part of the religious ceremony and to demand of those who practice
to renounce it" (*L'Univers Israélite* [1845], v. 1B, 63; subsequent references appear
in the text). Although Ben Baruch does not explain what part of the ceremony
Jonathan refuses to renounce, those familiar with the debates of the time would
surely recognize the *mezizah*, or sucking of blood from the wound, prescribed by
the Talmud as the third and final stage of the circumcision process, which *Les Archives Israélites* denounced as unsanitary and barbaric. Jonathan refuses to abandon a practice explicitly commanded by the law, but perhaps more importantly he
refuses to grant the Consistory the power to dictate to individual Jews how best
to practice their religion. The renegade mohel allies his libertarian principles with
social conscience by offering his services gratis.

52. Durkheim was the author of the pioneering study of anomie in modern
society, *Le suicide* (1897).

53. Ben Baruch reprints this story in the 1863–1864 edition of the *Annuaire*.

54. *L'Univers Israélite* (1845), v. 2, 310. Subsequent references appear in the
text.

55. In *Rites and Passages: The Beginnings of Modern Jewish Culture in France,
1650–1860* (Philadelphia: University of Pennsylvania Press, 2004), Jay R. Berkovitz
argues that "the organization of French Jewry within the consistorial system precluded the emergence of a radical reform ideology. As the official representative of
all regional, ethnic, and religious sectors of the Jewish population, the consistorial
system discouraged measures that might fragment the unity, whether imagined or
real, of French Jewry" (197).

56. Eisen describes the efforts of Samson Raphael Hirsch and his followers to
make the case for Jewish practice to an enlightened audience in Chapter 5 of *Rethinking Judaism*, titled "New Reasons for Old Commandments: The Strategy of
Symbolic Explanation," 135–155.

57. Ben Baruch's French-language Haggadah, for example, includes indica-
tions for both the Ashkenazic and Sephardic rites, offering the French liturgy as
the union of the two disparate branches of Judaism.

58. A. Ben Baruch Créhange, *La haggada ou cérémonies religieuses des Israélites
pendant les deux premières soirées de Paque: Hébreu-Français—traduction nouvelle*,
4th ed. (Paris: Librairie Israélite, 1860), 49.

59. *La Vérité* (April 1848), no. 1, 10. Subsequent references appear in the text.

60. Frank Paul Bowman provides a magisterial study of the nineteenth-century
French Catholic revolutionary tradition in *Le Christ des barricades, 1789–1848*
(Paris: Cerf, 1987).

61. According to the printer's declaration I consulted at the Archives Nationales, the Annuaire had a print run of 1000 in 1856 (AN F18*II19).

62. The date was always provided according to the Hebrew calendar with the

corresponding date in the Gregorian calendar added parenthetically. So the full title of the first edition is *Annuaire religieux et moral pour l'an du monde 5611 (1850–1851) à l'usage des israélites contenant La Constitution de Moïse, etc., etc., par A. Ben Baruch* (Paris: À la Librairie Israélite, 5 rue de Tracy).

63. Ronald Gosselin describes how revolutionaries used almanacs to advance their political program among the uneducated masses during the years preceding and following the Revolution of 1848 in *Les almanachs républicains: Traditions révolutionnaires et culture politique des masses populaires de Paris (1840–1851)* (Paris: L'Harmattan, 1992).

64. Later editions detail such practical information as the cost of holding a wedding in the Consistorial Temple of Paris, which varied according to the number of candles one wanted lit and whether there was to be choir and organ music.

65. In an 1862 article published in *La Vérité Israélite* titled "Une lacune dans la presse Israélite" [A Lacuna in the Israelite Press], Lazare Wogue calls for a different kind of *annuaire*, one that would summarize the events of historical interest relating to Jews that occurred in the prior year. He dismisses attempts by *Les Archives Israélites* and *L'Univers Israélite* to offer something similar in their yearly recapitulations of events of interest, attributing to them a petty partisan bickering: "You find in these reviews, very nearly always, three things: a little history—a lot of personal advertisements—and a great deal of insulting of rivals. . . . One's own works and beliefs are extolled, those of one's neighbor are deplored; judge what becomes of history when it is thus mixed with mercantilism and passion, and what a sorry face it must show!" (7: 86). Although he does not mention Ben Baruch's *Annuaire* by name, he implies that it and its author represent precisely the kind of self-promoting partisanship he loathes. Proclaiming that he does not care whether an *annuaire* provides dates according to the Hebrew or Gregorian calendars, Wogue states in a footnote, "This is a heresy. I signal it to the thunder of Brother B., the grand-inquisitor of French Judaism and the sworn guardian of 'conservative principles'" (7: 87). He can only mean Ben Baruch.

66. A later edition of the *Annuaire* (5616, 1855–1856) contains an advertisement for Carmoly's *La France Israélite, galerie des hommes et des faits dignes de mémoire*, described as "the intellectual history of French Judaism from the earliest days to our own time."

67. The addition of the engraving justifies raising the price from 50 centimes to 1 franc.

68. The *Shulchan Aruch* [The Set Table] was the compilation of the rules and practices of Jewish law prescribed by the rabbis and local custom. It was compiled in the sixteenth century by Joseph Caro and governed Jewish life in all traditional societies. According to Michael Meyer, nineteenth-century reformers held it responsible for causing Judaism to resist change and hence to stagnate. Meyer, *Response to Modernity: A History of the Reform Movement in Judaism* (New York: Oxford University Press, 1988), 1.

69. "What a joke! *Les Archives* judges matters of taste!" Ben Baruch responded in the following year's *Annuaire* (1867–1868). The controversy did not end there, however. The following year, Isidore Cahen, the editor of *Les Archives Israélites*, son of the journal's founder, denounced Ben Baruch's *Annuaire* as "a mountain of figures decorated with some stunted lampoons." In the 1868–1869 *Annuaire*, the 80-year-old Ben Baruch fired back: "L'Annuairophobia has broken out once again at the *Archives*. . . . I used to enjoy breaking a lance with the father; there is no merit in unhorsing the son" (116). In 1869–1870, he penned a sequel to the pear and the cheese dialogue, in which two pickles discuss reforming the liturgy.

70. A minyan is a group of at least ten men, required for Jewish prayer.

71. Mendelssohn had argued that if Enlightenment contradicts Judaism, it makes no sense to convert to Christianity as a solution, because Christianity is built on Judaism. If a house is about to collapse, "do I act wisely if I remove my belongings from the lower to the upper floor for safety?" Moses Mendelssohn, *Jerusalem*, trans. Allan Arkush (Hanover, NH: University Press of New England, 1983), 87. Cited and discussed in Eisen, *Rethinking Judaism*, 26.

72. Already by the 1840s, the percentage of Jews who were bourgeois equaled that of the general population and Jews had secured a firm presence in the liberal professions. Christine Piette, *Les juifs de Paris (1808–1840): La marche vers l'assimilation* (Québec: Laval University Press, 1983), 19.

73. The percentage of artisans among the Jewish population of Paris declined from 30 percent for the 1809–1840 period to 25 percent by 1872. Hyman, *Jews of Modern France*, 60.

74. Signed "Alexandre du Mat-de-Cocagne," the story features a complicated pun on the identity of the author. Here Créhange joins to his actual first name a homonymic allusion to his famous contemporary, Alexandre Dumas, the author of historical dramas and fiction, but also to a French medieval tournament, the Mât-de-Cocagne, in which contestants climbed a pole to reach a prize at the top, which often contained edible delicacies. This reference resonates with Créhange's own view of life as a perpetual struggle to attain a reward that is both earthly and supernatural, for in French popular speech, *cocagne* (or *pays de cocagne*) designates a land of mythical happiness.

75. In *Rites and Passages*, Berkovitz shows that the stirrings of modernity in the French Jewish community began long before the Revolution.

76. In *Juifs en Alsace: Culture, société, histoire* (Paris: Privat, 1977), Freddy Raphaël and Robert Weyl describe the superstitions surrounding birth in Alsatian Jewish culture in terms similar to those evoked by Ben Baruch. According to the modern sociologists, the real dangers that childbirth posed for mother and child were represented in supernatural terms for traditional Alsatian Jews: "The moment of birth was crucial both for the mother and the child because demons allied to snuff out the feeble flame of life hovering between two worlds" (232). They

describe the custom of marking the walls with the words from Psalm 121, which begins *Shir ha-Mallot* (232).

77. According to Raphaël and Weyl, the *Hollekreisch*, or *Holekrash*, was a ceremony unique to Jews in eastern France, southern Germany, and Holland and took place forty days after a child's birth or when the mother left her home for the first time to attend synagogue. Young children would gather around the newborn's crib and chant, "Helles Kreisch, Hollekreisch, wie soll das Kind heissen?" before pronouncing the newborn's profane or non-Hebrew name. Fruits and candy would then be given to the children (*Juifs en Alsace*, 236).

78. Raphaël and Weyl give a slightly different origin for the term: *Kreischen* comes from the German for "to cry out" and *hol* from the Hebrew for "profane" or "common." "That hybrid expression would thus signify that one pronounce out loud the profane name of the child, the name that he uses in daily life" (*Juifs en Alsace*, 237).

Chapter 4

1. Alexandre Weill, *Mes batailles* (Paris: Agence Générale de Librairie, 1867), 291. Subsequent references appear in the text.

2. Alexandre Weill, *Cris d'alarme, épîtres aux juifs de France, d'Angleterre, d'Allemagne et d'Amérique* (Paris: Dentu, 1889), 81.

3. Weill argued that France's ranks of Jewish millionaires acted as a lightning rod for antisemites: "It is they, it has always been they, who, everywhere and always, have caused us to be hated and persecuted" (*Mes batailles*, 295).

4. Alexandre Weill, *Souvenirs intimes de Henri Heine* (Paris: Dentu, 1883), 137. According to Friedmann, Weill no doubt read Marx's *On the Jewish Question* in 1846. Joë Friedmann, *Alexandre Weill, écrivain contestataire et historien engagé (1811–1899)* (Strasbourg, France: Istra, 1980), 40.

5. Cited in Friedmann, *Alexandre Weill*, 15.

6. "M. Alexandre Weill Dead: The Noted French Novelist and Publicist Dies at Paris," *New York Times* (April 20, 1899), 2. The obituary notes that Weill was "of Jewish parentage" but does not discuss his writing on Jewish themes.

7. Friedmann, *Alexandre Weill*, 253.

8. One exception is Richard I. Cohen's "Nostalgia and 'Return to the Ghetto': A Cultural Phenomenon in Western and Central Europe," in *Assimilation and Community: The Jews in Nineteenth-Century Europe*, eds. Jonathan Frankel and Steven J. Zipperstein (Cambridge, U.K.: Cambridge University Press, 1992), which briefly compares Weill to Berthold Auerbach (142–144). Cohen argues that Weill wrote about Alsatian village life as a testament to a vanishing past (144). I discuss Cohen's article in detail in Chapter 5.

9. Alexandre Weill, *Ma jeunesse* (Paris: Dentu, 1870), 1: 23.

10. "Not having found free education in France, neither books to teach myself, nor men to support me, I went to Germany, where I found all that among my Jewish coreligionists from Frankfurt." Alexandre Weill, *Code d'Alexandre Weill* (Paris: Sauvaitre, 1894), vii.

11. Friedmann, *Alexandre Weill*, 33.

12. According to Weill, Meyerbeer subsidized his writing and Sue offered to help him publish his *Guerre des paysans*, a history of a seventeenth-century German peasant uprising that Weill argued served as a rehearsal for the French Revolution. Weill, *Souvenirs intimes*, 72–80.

13. "From the age of fifteen I only had one desire: to live free and independent! . . . To force myself to conform, to submit to slavery, not to have the freedom to go to bed and to wake up when I wanted, never! Not for Rothschild's fortune!" (Weill, *Souvenirs intimes*, 73).

14. Friedmann, *Alexandre Weill*, 49–50.

15. Weill ran as an independent candidate from the Seine and received a respectable 15,000 votes (Friedmann, *Alexandre Weill*, 50). Ben-Lévi wrote, "We thought for a moment we would see M. A. Weil [*sic*] arrive at the National Assembly. He is a writer of great intellect and originality, and what is more, of great courage and good common sense." *Les Archives Israélites* (July 1848), 382.

16. Weill writes that Heine "contributed greatly to detaching me from the *Gazette*, knowing better than I that the Catholic principle did not offer the possibility of liberty and that a Jew who was a Catholic and a legitimist could only do one thing: lock himself in a cell, put a lock on his lips and a helmet on his brain" (Weill, *Souvenirs intimes*, 139).

17. Weill's *Ce que j'aurais dit à l'Assemblé nationale* [What I Would Have Said at the National Assembly] (1848) still contains elements of his earlier socialist concern with the problem of labor. In *Au président* [To the President] (1849) and *De l'hérédité au pouvoir* [Of Heredity in Power] (1849), he turns far more to the right, coming out against the republic and in favor of a hereditary monarchy. His *Questions brulantes, république et monarchie* [Burning Questions, Republic and Monarchy] went through eight editions.

18. Friedmann, *Alexandre Weill*, 57.

19. Alexandre Weill, *Le centenaire de l'émancipation des juifs* (Paris: L'Auteur, 1888), ii. Cited in Friedmann, *Alexandre Weill*, 61.

20. Joseph Salvador's scholarship on the ancient Hebrew legal system makes him an especially important model for Weill. Salvador's widely discussed *Loi de Moïse ou système religieux et politique des hébreux* [The Law of Moses or the Religious and Political System of the Hebrews] (1822) argued for the universality of ancient Jewish legal doctrine. L. Scott Lerner discusses Salvador's unique brand of Jewish historiography in "The Modern Counterhistories of Joseph Salvador," in *Modern Jewish Literatures: Intersections and Boundaries*, eds. Sheila E. Jelen,

Michael P. Kramer, and L. Scott Lerner (Philadelphia: University of Pennsylvania Press, forthcoming).

21. Weill saw Yom Kippur as a late—and un-Mosaic—addition to Judaism.

22. See Friedmann, *Alexandre Weill*, 123–125.

23. In his *Épîtres cinglantes à M. Drumont* (Paris: E. Dentu, 1888), Weill defends the Talmud against Édouard Drumont's calumnies, pointing out that it does not encourage Jews to trick non-Jews or drink their blood. He also points out that the Talmud does not constitute Jewish law but rather individual opinions about that law (7).

24. Weill, *Mes batailles*, 294. He continues: "Nobody exists for himself alone. That is one of the great laws of Moses, who proclaims solidarity even between men, beasts, and plants. The Talmud, it is true, preaches the opposite. At the most it admits solidarity among Jews. The hardness of the Jew comes from the Talmud and the rabbis" (*Mes batailles*, 298). In this passage Weill comes close to echoing antisemitic rhetoric that accuses the Talmud of teaching Jews to cheat Christians.

25. Weill, *Souvenirs intimes*, 21.

26. Weill, *Code*, viii.

27. "Where finally is the tithe rightfully appropriated by Moses from the rich Jew and intended to provide for the material well-being of the poor? Where are your modern martyrs to that eternal and regulatory right of the oppressed against the oppressor?" (Weill, *Mes batailles*, 300).

28. Weill, *Mes batailles*, 301.

29. Friedmann, *Alexandre Weill*, 128.

30. Cited in Friedmann, *Alexandre Weill*, 129.

31. In his *Souvenirs intimes de Henri Heine*, written toward the end of his life, Weill boasts of having convinced the German poet, a convert from Judaism, of the truth of his Mosaic system (*Souvenirs intimes*, 21–22).

32. Weill, *Code*, ix.

33. Weill spares his more humble contemporaries in his attacks on the Jews: "It is not to you, workers, artisans, scholars, Israelite merchants that I address myself" (*Mes batailles*, 294). Among the few Jews he singles out for praise for having lived up to the Mosaic universal mission of spreading freedom and truth is Samuel Cahen, the founder of *Les Archives Israélites* (300).

34. Weill, *Croquants financiers* (Paris: E. Dentu, 1861), 25. This published 400-verse excerpt from an even longer poem denounces financial speculation as a Jewish "scourge" but does so from a specifically Jewish point of view. The effect is less one of Jewish self-hatred than of a prophetic attempt to clean house, to purge (French) Judaism of what Weill sees as its negative elements. He begins the poem, "I am the son of a dealer in horses and glue/I was born a gentleman and am proud to be a Jew!" (Je suis fils d'un courtier de bestiaux et de suif/Je suis né gentilhomme et suis fier d'etre juif!) (12).

35. "Any converted Jew is a dishonest man, and any converted Jewess is a dishonest woman, even if she is loyal to her husband, because their lives are lives of lies and falsehoods" (Weill, *Épîtres cinglantes*, 10). No Jew ever converted out of conviction, Weill maintains.

36. "This consistory is composed of investors, merchants, agents, brokers, dealers, all no doubt honest citizens, but totally lacking as motors or engines of progress" (Weill, *Mes batailles*, 300).

37. See his *Épîtres cinglantes à M. Drumont*. Weill takes pains to distinguish his own brand of attacks on the Jews from those of Drumont, who, like him, was a disciple of the Fourierists.

38. Weill claimed that his first attempts at fiction date to his primary school days. Weill, *Histoires de village* (Paris: L. Hachette, 1860), ii.

39. In an 1847 preface to an edition of Weill's village tales in German, Heine confirms Weill's claim: "Mr. Alexandre Weill, the author of Alsatian Idylls, to which we owe some lines of introduction, pretends to have been the first creator of the genre. This pretension is perfectly justified, according to a large number of my friends, who add that the author in question not only wrote the first Village Stories but the best ones." Weill translated this preface for a later French edition. Weill, *Mes romans* (Paris: Cohen Frères, 1883), iii.

40. Weill, *Histoires de village* (1860), i, iii.

41. Alexandre Weill, *Mes romans* (Paris: Cohen Frères, 1886), 5.

42. Alexandre Weill, *Gumper, histoire de village* (Paris: Chez Tous les Libraires, 1854), 12. Subsequent references to the story appear in the text. The story first appeared in French in the *Revue de Paris* 20 (Février, 1854).

43. Note that Weill changed the title to "Gumper" when he translated the novella into French. This change signals the centrality of the Jewish character.

44. Stasie's mother offers him only cabbage, potatoes, and coffee. "I offer you nothing else because your religion forbids it" (Weill, *Gumper*, 10).

45. "But how to go to Paris without being certain of being able to support my literary life there in an honorable fashion?" he wonders. "And how to support myself without knowing anyone, afflicted as I was and still am by a German accent?" Alexandre Weill, *Histoires de village* (Paris: Dentu, 1853), 6.

46. Weill, *Histoires de village* (1853), 7.

47. Weill, *Histoires de village* (1853), 9.

48. In Sand's *Correspondance*, v. 4, Lubin dates this letter to March 4, 1844. Cited in Friedmann, *Alexandre Weill*, 215. Weill would later accuse Sand of having plundered his "vein" for her own sentimental village tales.

49. On the invention of folklore, see the notice by Léon Cellier in George Sand, *La mare au diable* (Paris: Gallimard Folio, 1999), 221. Subsequent references to the novel appear in the text.

50. Ben Jona, "Variétés: 'Histoires de village,' par Alexandre Weill," *La Vérité Israélite* 1 (January 19, 1860), 239–240.

51. Ben Jona, "Variétés," 240.

52. Weill, *Histoires de village* (1853), 9.

53. Alexandre Weill, *Couronne, histoire juive* (Paris: Poulet-Malassis, 1857), 7. Subsequent references to the novel appear in the text.

54. Weill provides the translation of the common term *shiksa*, suggesting his assumption of a non-Jewish readership for the novel.

55. Weill, *Histoires de village* (1860), 211. Subsequent references appear in the text.

56. Hebrew, of course, had far more prestige in traditional Jewish culture as a sacred language than everyday Yiddish.

57. Alexandre Weill, "Kella," in *Mes romans* (1886), 456. Subsequent references appear in the text.

58. Weill, *Épîtres cinglantes*, 23–24. Subsequent references appear in the text.

59. The first Zionist Congress was held in Basel in 1897, although major Jewish immigration to Palestine—the so-called First Aliyah—had begun in 1882.

Chapter 5

A portion of this chapter originally appeared in *Jewish Social Studies* 14(3) (Spring/Summer 2008), 38–59, and is republished here with permission of Indiana University Press.

1. A. Widal, "Lettres sur les moeurs Alsaciennes," *Les Archives Israélites* (1849), 643–644.

2. In *Rethinking Modern Judaism: Ritual, Commandment, Community* (Chicago: University of Chicago Press, 1998), Arnold M. Eisen refers to Stauben's 1860 version as "one of the first [texts] to offer its readers a pilgrimage back in space and time to the sacred precincts of authentic ancestral Judaism" (159). Richard I. Cohen also discusses Stauben in "Nostalgia and 'Return to the Ghetto': A Cultural Phenomenon in Western and Central Europe," in *Assimilation and Community: The Jews in Nineteenth-Century Europe*, eds. Jonathan Frankel and Steven J. Zipperstein (Cambridge, U.K.: Cambridge University Press, 1992), 147–150.

3. Jews had been expelled from Colmar in 1510 and forbidden to live there until the Revolution. After the lifting of residency restrictions during the Revolution, however, Jews from the country villages of Alsace and Lorraine flocked to nearby towns such as Colmar, as well as Nancy, Strasbourg, and Mulhouse. By midcentury, Colmar had one of the largest Jewish populations in France and was home to a Talmudic academy.

4. According to Paula Hyman, the curriculum at these schools combined general and Jewish studies but privileged the former over the latter. Hyman, *The Jews of Modern France* (Berkeley: University of California Press, 1998), 67.

5. See Jay R. Berkovitz, "Jewish Scholarship and Identity in Nineteenth-Century France," *Modern Judaism* 18(1) (February 1998), 1–33.

6. A notice in *L'Univers Israélite* in February 1850 lists eight Jewish professors in France, along with Adolphe Franck. Of the five whose fields are given, three are mathematics professors (289). This list is not complete, and Widal does not figure on it.

7. A native of Liocourt in Lorraine, Franck at first intended to become a rabbi but chose instead to study philosophy at the University of Toulouse. Number one on the competitive *aggrégation* exam in philosophy in 1832, which he was the first Jew to pass, he held a teaching post at the Lycée Charlemagne in the 1840s, where he may have taught Auguste Widal, and at the Sorbonne, before being elected to the Collège de France. The author of more than twenty books on moral philosophy as well as on the Jewish mystical tradition, Franck also contributed frequently to *Les Archives Israélites* and held leadership positions in French Jewish organizations, including the Central Consistory. Aron Rodrigue discusses Franck's career in "Totems, Taboos, and Jews: Salomon Reinach and the Politics of Scholarship in Fin-de-Siècle France," *Jewish Social Studies* 10(2) (Winter 2004), 131.

8. Isidore Cahen received the third highest score on the competitive *aggrégation* exam in philosophy but was the only *normalien* of his year not to receive a teaching position. When in 1849 he finally landed a job at the Lycée Napoléon in the Vendée, France's most conservative and Catholic province, he was prevented from taking it by church leaders, who objected explicitly to his Jewish faith. An editorial in *Les Archives Israélites* recounts the scandal asking, "Might it therefore be the case that our emancipation in France exists only on the surface, that actions lag behind the law?" *Les Archives Israélites* (1850), 8. Hyman discusses this scandal in *Jews of Modern France*, 64.

9. Isidore Cahen went on to become one of the founding members of the Alliance Israélite Universelle.

10. My biographical information on Widal comes mostly from Antoine Meyer, *Biographies alsaciennes avec portraits en photographie* (Colmar: Ant. Meyer, 1884–1890), v. 4, 40. I have corrected, where possible, the mistakes in this volume.

11. Daniel Stauben, *Scènes de la vie juive en Alsace* (Paris: Michel Lévy Frères, 1860), iii–iv.

12. Eisen, *Rethinking Modern Judaism*, 162–163.

13. See, for example, Cohen's "Nostalgia and 'Return to the Ghetto': A Cultural Phenomenon in Western and Central Europe," which provides one of the first, and most sustained, treatments of the two authors.

14. In his preface to Cahun's *La vie juive*, Zadok Kahn, chief rabbi of France, writes, "What lends still more charm and further interest to the work that I have the honor to present to the reader is the patriotic note that vibrates on each page" (iii). Cahun's *La vie juive* (Paris: Monnier, de Brunhoff, 1886), with illustrations by Alphonse Lévy, sold for 5 francs, although a special signed limited collector's edition on Japanese paper sold for 100 francs.

15. Jost Hermand, "1840, Heinrich Heine's Ghetto Tale 'The Rabbi of Bache-

rach' Is Published," trans. James Steakley, in *Yale Companion to Jewish Writing and Thought in German Culture 1096–1996*, eds. Sander L. Gilman and Jack Zipes (New Haven, CT: Yale University Press, 1997), 152–157.

16. Florian Krobb, "Between Exile and Assimilation: Language and Identity in German-Jewish Texts Around 1848," in *Exiles and Migrants: Crossing Thresholds in European Culture and Society*, ed. Anthony Coulson (Brighton, U.K.: Sussex Academic Press, 1997), 45.

17. The original titles in German were *Geschichten aus dem Ghetto* (1848), *Böhmische Juden* (1851), and *Neue Geschichten aus dem Ghetto* (1860), respectively.

18. Cohen, "Nostalgia," 131.

19. In the 1860s, Schornstein would write a yearly article in *Les Archives Israélites* about Jewish artists showing at the Salon. These included Alexandre Laemlein, Benjamin Ulmann, Edouard Moyse, Émile Lévy, Edouard Brandon, Mayer Léon, Ernest Hirsch, Alexandre Hirsch, Henry Lévy, Auguste Mayer, and Benjamin Netter. Most of them did not paint Jewish subjects, although some did turn to the Bible for inspiration. Benjamin Ulmann, for example, who won the Prix de Rome, showed a picture of Delilah and Samson at the Salon of 1863. Only Edouard Moyse (1827–1908) devoted himself to Jewish genre scenes; for example, he painted Talmudic scholars for the Salons of 1863 and 1864.

20. Cohen, "Nostalgia," 138.

21. Eisen makes the connection with 1848 in his discussion of Stauben (Eisen, *Rethinking Modern Judaism*, 160).

22. See, for example, the editorial expressing alarm in *Les Archives Israélites* (1848), 215. For their part, *L'Univers Israélite* did not publish during the revolutionary crisis.

23. I refer to Leslie Poles Hartley's dictum in the novel *The Go-Between* (1953) that "the past is a foreign country: they do things differently there," as well as to David Lowenthal's more recent scholarly exploration of modern nostalgia in *The Past Is a Foreign Country* (Cambridge, U.K.: Cambridge University Press, 1988).

24. *Fiddler on the Roof* was the first American musical to surpass 3,000 performances. Michael Kantor and Laurence Maslon, *Broadway: The American Musical* (New York: Bulfinch, 2004), 302. The musical was based on Sholem Aleichem's *Tevye and His Daughters*, originally published in the 1890s.

25. On American representations of the eastern European Jewish past, see Steven J. Zipperstein, *Imagining Russian Jewry: Memory, History, Identity* (Seattle: University of Washington Press), esp. 15–40.

26. Cohen, "Nostalgia," 131.

27. Marshall Berman provides a classic account of the social and psychological disruptions of the nineteenth-century metropolis in *All That Is Solid Melts Into Air: The Experience of Modernity* (New York: Penguin, 1982). The description of Parisian life as a *tourbillon*, or whirlwind, might be a reference to Jean-Jacques

Rousseau's description of *le tourbillon social* from *Émile, ou de l'éducation* (Paris: Gallimard, 1959 [1762]), v. 4, 551. See Berman, *All That Is Solid*, 17.

28. Cohen, "Nostalgia," 131–132.

29. Arendt describes Lazare as a "conscious pariah," in *The Origins of Totalitarianism*, pt. 1, *Antisemitism* (New York: Harcourt Brace Jovanovich, 1968), 65n26. Also see Nelly Wilson, *Bernard-Lazare: Anti-Semitism and the Problem of Jewish Identity in Late Nineteenth-Century France* (Cambridge, U.K.: Cambridge University Press, 1978).

30. Bernard Lazare, preface to Alphonse Lévy, *Scènes familiales juives* (Paris: Félix Juven, 1902), i.

31. Eisen, *Rethinking Modern Judaism*, 181. Eisen references Freud's *Totem and Taboo*, trans. James Strachey (New York: W. W. Norton, 1989 [1919]), 21–27, 144–145.

32. Eisen, *Rethinking Modern Judaism*, 182–183.

33. Eisen, *Rethinking Modern Judaism*, 183.

34. Stauben, *Scènes de la vie juive*, ii. Subsequent references appear in the text.

35. "If the *Scènes de la vie juive* are . . . interesting because of their subject matter, we will not astonish anyone, nor Mr. Widal himself, by saying that they do not recall either in their composition or their style the inimitable masterpieces that inspired them." Émile Deschanel, "Revue de quinzaine," *Journal des Débats* (September 6, 1860), 2.

36. As Eugen Weber makes clear, this process was still not completed by the dawn of the Third Republic. See his classic account of the transformation of rural France in *Peasants into Frenchmen: The Modernization of Rural France, 1870–1914* (Stanford, CA: Stanford University Press, 1976).

37. Widal, "Lettres sur les moeurs alsaciennes," 649. All emphasis in the original.

38. "Boi Bishalom," or "Boï Becholem" or "Besolem" in French transliteration, is Hebrew for "Enter in Peace." The phrase begins the last paragraph of the Lecha Dodi prayer, in which worshippers welcome "the bride" of the Sabbath into the synagogue.

39. Alphonse Toussenel, *Les juifs, rois de l'époque: Histoire de la féodalité financière* (Paris: Marpon et Flammarion, 1886 [1845]), xlii.

40. The 1787 Metz essay contest, to which the Abbé Grégoire submitted his essay on the regeneration of the Jews, specifically asked whether Jews could be made "more useful and happier" in France. On Grégoire's response, see Alyssa Goldstein Sepinwall, *The Abbé Grégoire and the French Revolution: The Making of Modern Universalism* (Berkeley: University of California Press, 2005), 56–77.

41. In the first issue of the short-lived journal *La Régénération*, a "monthly review intended to improve the religious and moral condition of the Israelites," founded in 1836 by Simon Bloch (future founder of *L'Univers Israélite*), an article describes the mission of the Society for the Promotion of Work for the Israelites

of the Bas-Rhin: "Give a better education to your children; preserve their young souls from the contagion of the pernicious mercantile spirit; inspire them with a taste for industrial and agricultural professions" (10).

42. Daniel Stauben, preface to Léopold Kompert's *Scènes du ghetto*, trans. Daniel Stauben (Paris: Michel Lévy Frères, 1859), 3.

43. Stauben, preface to *Scènes du ghetto*, 3.

44. Daniel Stauben, preface to Léopold Kompert's *Nouvelles juives*, trans. Daniel Stauben (Paris: Hachette, 1873), ix.

45. In his review of *Isaïe ou le travail*, published in *La Vérité Israélite*, Élie-Aristide Astruc (1831–1905), future grand rabbi of Belgium, laments the lack of an edifying literature for Jewish youth in French. Praising Lévy's foray into this market, Astruc excuses the novel's simple style, "without any affectation of elegance," arguing that it suits the subject matter and audience of the book perfectly. The majority of the readership, poor Jews in Alsace and Lorraine, still did not speak perfect French and would have had trouble understanding more complicated language. Astruc dismisses imputations that Lévy tried to "servilely imitate some Israelite writers who came from Alsace, and who have managed to make a name for themselves in Parisian literature by presenting to the public original studies of the manners of their native land." Obviously referring to Stauben, a fellow contributor to *La Vérité Israélite*, and perhaps Alexandre Weill, Astruc asserts that Lévy's didactic purpose overshadows his ethnographic impulse.

46. Kompert's first published story was "Der Schnorrer" (1846).

47. Sue's novel uses the figure of the Wandering Jew as a symbol for social oppression. As I discuss in the chapter on Ben-Lévi (Chapter 2), Jewish readers did in fact welcome the novel's sympathetic attitude toward Jews (and hostility to the Jesuits). Fromental Halévy composed the opera *Le juif errant* (1852) based on Sue's novel. Earlier, the non-Jewish Edgar Quinet had published *Tablettes du juif errant* (1823), in which the Wandering Jew symbolizes the progress of humanity. He also composed the prose poem *Ahasvérus* (1833), in which the Wandering Jew receives sympathetic treatment.

48. Eisen, *Rethinking Modern Judaism*, 163.

49. Describing the preparations of the Wintzenheim Jews for Yom Kippur, the day of atonement, Stauben emphasizes the degree to which modern Jews follow their ancient forebears in the scrupulous observance of this ritual of repentance by mortifying themselves before God. A footnote then informs readers that "even in Paris," this holiday is celebrated with a "particular devotion" and that a certain family known for their place at the summit of the financial establishment (obviously the Rothschilds) are also known for the zeal of their performance of the Yom Kippur ritual.

50. "The Schamess is also the man of strange visions. The one from Wintzenheim will tell you how, a few hours after the death of the venerable Rabbi Hirsch, he saw, at dusk, a celestial flame move across the hairless forehead of the pious

deceased and, at the same time, kabbalistic letters appear on the walls" (Stauben, *Scènes de la vie juive en Alsace*, 83).

51. Yosef Hayim Yerushalmi, *Zakhor: Jewish History and Jewish Memory* (Seattle: University of Washington Press, 1982), 86.

52. On these new uses of history, see Maurice Samuels, *The Spectacular Past: Popular History and the Novel in Nineteenth-Century France* (Ithaca, NY: Cornell University Press, 2004).

53. Leopold Zunz (1794–1886) published a history of the Jewish sermon (1832), signaling the Wissenschaft movement's interest in the history of the postbiblical period and in the variety of forms of modern Jewish experience.

54. Graetz's work was translated into French by Lazare Wogue and Moïse Bloch between 1882 and 1897.

55. Susannah Heschel writes, "Nineteenth-century German-Jewish historians were the first to call into question accepted 'truths' about the history of the West and the respective roles played in it by Christianity and Judaism." Heschel, *Abraham Geiger and the Jewish Jesus* (Chicago: University of Chicago Press, 1998), 3.

56. As discussed earlier, Heinrich Heine's novel fragment, *Der Rabbi von Bacherach*, preceded these two works. Jonathan Hess discusses the first Jewish historical fiction works in German in *Middlebrow Fiction and the Making of Jewish Identity* (Stanford, CA: Stanford University Press, forthcoming). Also see Nitsa Ben-Ari, "The Jewish Historical Novel Helps to Reshape the Historical Consciousness of German Jews," in Sander L. Gilman and Jack Zipes, eds., *Yale Companion to Jewish Writing and Thought in German Culture, 1096–1996* (New Haven, CT: Yale University Press, 1997), 143.

57. Jonathan Skolnik, "Writing Jewish History in the Margins of the Weimar Classics: Minority Culture and National Identity in Germany, 1837–1873," in *Searching for Common Ground: Diskurse zur deutschen Identität, 1750–1871*, ed. Nicolas Vazsonyi (Köln, Germany: Böhlau Verlag, 2000), 231. Skolnik studies Auerbach's novel in detail in "Writing Jewish History Between Guzkow and Goethe: Auerbach's *Spinoza* and the Birth of Modern Jewish Historical Fiction," *Prooftexts* 19(2) (May 1999), 101–125.

58. Halévy also published *Résumé de l'histoire des juifs anciens* [Summary of the History of the Ancient Jews] (1825), a history of Jews in biblical times, which relied heavily on the work of another (half-)Jewish contemporary, Joseph Salvador's *Loi de Moïse ou système religieux et politique des hébreux* (1822), which argued for the universality of ancient Jewish legal doctrine. Aron Rodrigue, "Léon Halévy and Modern French Jewish Historiography," in *Jewish History and Jewish Memory: Essays in Honor of Yosef Hayim Yerushalmi*, eds. Elisheva Carlebach, John M. Efron, and David N. Myers (Hanover, NH: Brandeis University Press, 1998), 415.

59. Rodrigue mentions Schwab, Astruc, Darmesteter, and Reinach ("Léon Halévy," 413). Carmoly was born Goschel David Behr in Sulz (Haut-Rhin). He

studied in Colmar and worked at the Bibliothèque Nationale in Paris before becoming the chief rabbi of Brussels. His major works include *Histoire des médecins juifs anciens et modernes* (1844), *La famille Almosnino* (1850), *Notice historique sur Benjamin de Tudèle* (1852), *La France israélite* (1855), and *Biographie des israélites de France* (1868).

60. The August 1840 issue of *Les Archives Israélites* contained an article on the history of the Jews of Paris, and the September 1840 issue had an article on the history of the Jews of northern France. A review in the June 1840 issue of Lion Mayer Lambert's *Précis de l'histoire des hébreux depuis le patriarche Abraham jusqu'en 1840* faulted the author, who was the grand rabbi of Metz, for using the term *Hebrews*, implying that the Jews still constitute a distinct national group and thus were not really "French." *Les Archives Israélites* (1840), 385.

61. Originally from Aix, Joseph Cohen was primarily a biblical historian as well as a political and social writer. His *Les déicides*, a defense of the Jews from charges of having murdered Jesus based on biblical sources, originally published in *La Vérité Israélite*, was later published as a book (1872) and translated into English (1873). According to Zosa Szajkowski, Cohen opposed the Saint-Simonians despite working for *La Liberté*, a publication owned by the prominent Jewish Saint-Simonian Isaac Péreire. Szajkowski, *The Jewish Saint-Simonians and Socialist Antisemites in France* (New York: Conference on Jewish Relations, 1947), 45.

62. Joseph Cohen, "A nos lecteurs," *La Vérité Israélite*, v. 1 (1860), 7.

63. Ben Baruch contributed the story "Les amis" to *La Vérité Israélite* in 1861. Other well-known contributors included Adolphe Franck, Lazare Wogue, and Olry Terquem, who also contributed to *Les Archives Israélites*.

64. Daniel Stauben, "Le Hanouka en Alsace: Souvenirs de la vie juive," *La Vérité Israélite*, v. 1 (1860), 186.

65. *La Vérité Israélite*, v. 2 (1860), 64.

66. Publication of "Joker Dai" begins in *La Vérité Israélite*, v. 3 (1861), 43.

67. Nicolas Stoskopf, entry on Schornstein in *Dictionnaire de biographie alsacienne*, ed. Jean-Pierre Kintz (Strasbourg: Fédération des Sociétés d'Histoire et d'Archéologie d'Alsace, 1985–2002), v. 34 (1999), 3531–3532.

68. Dominique Jarrassé credits Schornstein as one of the inventors of Jewish art criticism in "L'éveil d'une critique d'art juive et le recours au 'principe ethnique' dans une définition de l'art juif," *Archives Juives* 39(1) (2006), 7. Richard I. Cohen discusses both Schornstein's art criticism and his nonhistorical fiction in the context of the ghetto nostalgia phenomenon in "Nostalgia," 132.

69. Given that the journal lasted for only three years, the strategy cannot have been successful. By contrast, the two rival monthly newspapers, *Les Archives Israélites* and *L'Univers Israélite*, which were much less scholarly in tone, lasted from the 1840s until the 1940s.

70. Yerushalmi, *Zakhor*, 97. Rabbinic lineages constituted one major exception to this rule. And as Yerushalmi recounts, certain periods of extraordinary suffer-

ing, such as the expulsion from Spain, did spur medieval Jews to historiographic labor.

71. Schornstein seems to have adapted at least some of his stories from German models. Salomon Kohn, for example, published a story similar to Schornstein's with an identical title, "Der Kadisch vor Col-Nidre," in the *Sippurim* collection in Prague. See Krobb, "Between Exile and Assimilation," 47.

72. David Schornstein, "Deborah, la juive de Nuremberg," *La Vérité Israélite*, v. 4 (1861), 192. Subsequent references appear in the text.

73. "La légende du kabbaliste de Mayence" might at first seem an exception to Schornstein's hostility to religious study. The novella recounts how a young student comes to Mainz from Spain in the thirteenth century to study with a famous teacher who warns him against pursuing the esoteric knowledge contained in the Kabbalah. The end of the story, however, has him renounce his plan in order to study "the science of life" and marry the daughter of the rabbi.

74. Schornstein, "Les marannos, chronique espagnole," *La Vérité Israélite*, v. 6 (1862), 791.

75. Schornstein, "Les marannos," v. 5, 189.

76. In Balzac's novella *Adieu* (1830), on which this story seems partly based, a hero of the Napoleonic Wars attempts to cure his lover's madness by constructing an exact replica of the battlefield on which she lost her sanity. His therapy produces the desired effect, but the heroine dies moments after returning to reason. In *Adieu*, the madwoman can only say the word *adieu*, whereas in Schornstein's story, she can only utter her lover's name.

77. Joseph Cohen, "Profession de foi," *La Vérité Israélite*, v. 6 (1862), 481–486.

78. Schornstein, "Le Kaddisch avant Col-Nidré," *La Vérité Israélite*, v. 2 (1860), 336.

79. Widal, "Lettres sur les moeurs alsaciennes," 643–644.

80. Yerushalmi, *Zakhor*, 96.

Conclusion

1. *La Revue Blanche* was founded by the Natanson brothers in 1891.

2. Cited in Michel Trebitsch, "Les écrivains juifs français de l'affaire Dreyfus à la Seconde Guerre mondiale," in *Les juifs de France*, eds. Jean-Jacques Becker and Annette Wieviorka (Paris: Liana Lévi, 1998), 174.

3. Evelyne Bloch-Dano, *Madame Proust*, trans. Alice Kaplan (Chicago: University of Chicago Press, 2007), 35.

4. Pascal Ifri discusses Céline's antisemitic diatribes against Proust along with Proust's influence on Céline's writing in *Céline et Proust: Correspondances proustiennes dans l'oeuvre de L.-F. Céline* (Birmingham, AL: Summa, 1996). In one revealing letter to a friend, written during the Nazi occupation, Céline rants

about Proust, "That style? that bizarre construction? . . . From where? who? . . . that? what? Oh, it's very simple! TALMUDIC!—The Talmud is more or less constructed, conceived like the novels of Proust, tortuous, arabescoid, confused mosaic—the genre without tail or head. . . . Proustian poetry, conforming in style, in origins, to semitism!" Céline asserts that Proust's Jewish style cannot be understood by the "uninitiated," which is to say by non-Jews, and attributes Proust's lofty reputation to a cabal of Jews controlling the media. Letter to Lucien Combelle dated February 12, 1943, cited in Ifri (*Céline et Proust*, 11–12; my translation). Two excellent studies of the antisemitism of Céline and other French writers of the interwar period are Alice Yaeger Kaplan, *Reproductions of Banality: Fascism, Literature, and French Intellectual Life* (Minneapolis: University of Minnesota Press, 1986), and David Carroll, *French Literary Fascism: Nationalism, Antisemitism, and the Ideology of Culture* (Princeton, NJ: Princeton University Press, 1995).

   5. "Proust was himself (on his mother's side) half-Jewish; and for all his Parisian sophistication, there remains in him much of the capacity for apocalyptic moral indignation of the classical Jewish prophet. That tone of lamentation and complaint which resounds through his whole book, which, indeed, he scarcely ever drops save for the animated humor of the social scenes, themselves in their implications so bitter, is really very un-French and rather akin to Jewish literature." Edmund Wilson, *Axel's Castle: A Study in the Imaginative Literature of 1870–1930* (New York: Scribner's, 1969 [1931]), 144.

   6. Bloch-Dano notes that Proust arranged for a rabbi to officiate at her funeral (*Madame Proust*, 240).

   7. Cited in Jonathan Freedman, "Coming Out of the Jewish Closet with Marcel Proust," in *Queer Theory and the Jewish Question*, eds. Daniel Boyarin, Daniel Itzkovitz, and Ann Pellegrini (New York: Columbia University Press, 2003), 342. Freedman in turn cites Jean Recanati, *Profils juifs de Marcel Proust* (Paris: Buchet/Chaste, 1979), 68.

   8. Bloch-Dano, *Madame Proust*, 39–43.

   9. Hannah Arendt, *The Origins of Totalitarianism*, pt. 1, *Antisemitism* (New York: Harcourt Brace Jovanovich, 1968), 80.

   10. Bloch-Dano, *Madame Proust*, 199.

   11. "The Jews did not want it to be possible for anyone to believe that they defended Dreyfus because Dreyfus was Jewish. They did not want anyone to be able to ascribe their attitude to a distinction or to a racial solidarity." Léon Blum, *Souvenirs sur l'affaire* (Paris: Gallimard, 1935), 43.

   12. Cited in Freedman, "Coming Out," 343, and Bloch-Dano, *Madame Proust*, 193. The letter is translated by Ralph Mannheim in *Marcel Proust: Selected Letters, 1880–1903*, ed. Philip Kolb (London: Collins, 1983), 121.

   13. Freedman discuss the connection between homosexuality and Jewishness in Proust's novel at length, as does Elaine Marks in *Marrano as Metaphor: The*

Jewish Presence in French Writing (New York: Columbia University Press, 1996), 81–84.

14. Maurice Samuels, "Metaphors of Modernity: Prostitutes, Bankers, and Other Jews in Balzac's *Splendeurs et misères des courtisanes*," *Romanic Review* 97(2) (March 2006), 169–184.

15. Marcel Proust, *Remembrance of Things Past*, trans. C. K. Scott Moncrief and Terence Kilmartin (New York: Random House, 1981), v. 1, 620. I have elected to use this modified early translation because I think it is the one with which readers are most familiar. All subsequent references to Proust come from this translation, except when otherwise specified.

16. Lawrence Schehr provides an instructive reading of Rachel's ambiguous Jewishness in *Figures of Alterity: French Realism and Its Others* (Stanford, CA: Stanford University Press, 2003), 187.

17. One wonders if this fictional conversation is inspired by the conversation about Jews between Proust and Montesquiou that precipitated Proust's extremely tactful letter (see note 12).

18. Proust, *Remembrance of Things Past*, v. 2, 298. The following two references to this volume appear in the text.

19. Proust, *Remembrance of Things Past*, v. 1, 831.

20. The term *antisemitism* is usually thought to have been coined by the antisemitic German writer Wilhelm Marr in 1879.

21. Here I differ substantially from Alessandro Piperno, who in *Proust antijuif*, trans. Franchita Gonzalez Batlle (Paris: Liana Lévi, 2007), uses Proust's condemnation of Bloch to support his assertion of the author's "antisemitism": "Proust is not content to simply verify the differences between the races with an objective eye; he often goes into particulars, he judges—and most of the time denounces—Jewish behaviors. He deplores Bloch's chameleonism, considering it the very symbol of semitic snobbery" (65). I would argue, on the contrary, that his condemnation of Bloch is a rejection of Bloch's futile attempts at assimilation.

22. Elisabeth Ladenson analyzes the theme of homosexuality in the *Recherche* in *Proust's Lesbianism* (Ithaca, NY: Cornell University Press, 1999). On Proust as a philosopher, see Joshua Landy, *Philosophy as Fiction: Self, Deception, and Knowledge in Proust* (New York: Oxford University Press, 2004).

23. Arendt calls Proust the "greatest witness of dejudaized Judaism" (*Antisemitism*, 80).

24. In "The Rise and Fall of a Polish Tallith," Ben-Lévi traces the assimilation of a Parisian Jewish family through three generations, beginning in 1780. These generations approximate those of Swann's family: Swann's father, the stockbroker, a contemporary of the narrator's grandfather and thus born around 1800, would be about the same age as Jacoubé. Swann thus represents the next stage in the assimilating process after Jacoubé. In *Le cygne de Proust* (Paris: Gallimard, 1989), Henri Raczymow notes that the father of Charles Haas, the model for Swann,

was born in 1799 in Frankfurt and became an associate of the Rothschilds (73). On Swann's Jewishness, see also L. Scott Lerner, "The Genesis of Jewish Swann," *Romanic Review* 89(3) (1998), 345–365.

25. Proust, *Remembrance of Things Past*, v. 1, 16. Raczymow recounts how Haas boasted of being the first Jew, aside from Rothschild, to be admitted to the Jockey Club. He was admitted only on his fifth attempt, as a result of his war record in 1870 (*Le cygne de Proust*, 16–27).

26. Proust, *Remembrance of Things Past*, v. 1, 98.

27. "Moins il est juif, plus il est fin." The Englishness of Swann's name becomes, like the transformation of Jakob Rothschild into James, a sign (cygne?) of his remove from Jewishness and hence, paradoxically, of his Frenchness. Raczymow, *Le cygne de Proust*, 16.

28. Proust, *Remembrance of Things Past*, v. 2, 194.

29. Proust, *Remembrance of Things Past*, v. 3, 996.

30. Freedman comments on the resonance of the name Rozier ("Coming Out," 347), as does Seth Wolitz, *The Proustian Community* (New York: New York University Press, 1971), 205.

31. Proust, *Remembrance of Things Past*, v. 3, 1012.

32. Proust, *Remembrance of Things Past*, v. 2, 603. In *Marrano as Metaphor*, Marks identifies the crypto-Jew as a major topos in modern French literature.

33. In *Modernism, Nationalism, and the Novel* (Cambridge, U.K.: Cambridge University Press, 2000), Pericles Lewis likewise argues that Jewishness in Proust, whether biologically or socially constituted, represents an obstacle to national cohesion: "'Jewishness' turns out to be a form of theatricality, in which the Jew plays a role assigned to him by history and/or nature. This role, however, seems destined to conflict with the narrative of nationhood" (155). According to Lewis, though, the threat to national identity posed by Jews (or homosexuals) does not have the positive connotations in the *Recherche* that these other critics attribute to it.

34. Marks, *Marrano as Metaphor*, 81–84.

35. Julia Kristeva, *Time and Sense: Proust and the Experience of Literature*, trans. Ross Guberman (New York: Columbia University Press, 1996), 141–163; and Julia Kristeva, *Proust: Questions d'identité* (Oxford, U.K.: Legenda, 1998), 20–26.

36. Arthur de Gobineau, the founder of French racism, was the author of *Essai sur l'inégalité des races humaines* (1854).

37. Proust, *Remembrance of Things Past*, v. 2, 194.

38. Interestingly, this passage from the last volume of the *Recherche*, *Le temps retrouvé*, is omitted from the Moncrief and Kilmartin translation. It has been restored in a newer translation: Marcel Proust, *Finding Time Again*, trans. Ian Paterson (London: Penguin, 2003), v. 6, 246.

39. Proust, *Remembrance of Things Past*, v. 2, 715.

40. Lewis makes a similar point about race in Proust: "While it is possible to

see the narrator as a sort of stooge of gentile and heterosexual ideology and thus to discredit his observations, ultimately the author (by way of the plot he creates) seems to suggest that a kernel of biological heredity underlies the admittedly contingent constructions of homosexual or Jewish identity (Lewis, *Modernism*, 164).

41. This passage is also omitted from the Moncrief and Kilmartin translation but is restored in the Paterson translation: Proust, *Finding Time Again*, v. 6, 246.

42. Freedman, "Coming Out," 359.

43. Proust, *Remembrance of Things Past*, v. 2, 715–716.

44. "Tous les Israélites sont solidaires les uns des autres." The motto was shortened in 1887 to "Tous les Israélites sont solidaires." Lisa Moses Leff, *Sacred Bonds of Solidarity: The Rise of Jewish Internationalism in Nineteenth-Century France* (Stanford, CA: Stanford University Press, 2006), 172.

45. Proust, *Remembrance of Things Past*, v. 2, 723.

46. Proust, *Remembrance of Things Past*, v. 2, 604.

47. Proust, *Remembrance of Things Past*, v. 2, 603.

48. Proust, *Remembrance of Things Past*, v. 2, 605. Raczymow goes further: "The fact that Swann's 'Jewishness' comes to the surface at this point is not exactly a compliment on Proust's part. Swann regresses to a previous phase of development, inferior with respect to his own evolution/ascension, as well as to that of his parents. It represents a collapse" (*Le cygne de Proust*, 33). Raczymow argues that Swann's eventual illness, which the novel documents in humiliating detail, represents Proust's exorcism of his own purely social self, the part of him that he had to reject to become a writer (34).

49. Proust, *Remembrance of Things Past*, v. 1, 436. Raczymow glosses Proust's descriptions of the dying Swann as a kind of sadomasochistic exercise, in which Proust denigrates the parts within himself he both loves and despises, including his Judaism: "Proust reduces Swann to a pretentious and insignificant little Jew; what he shares with the prophets is constipation . . . here Proust besmirches what he loves most; what he venerates. He's Mlle. Vinteuil spitting on the photo of her father" (*Le cygne de Proust*, 36). Piperno, on the other hand, sees the desecration of Swann as a more basic gesture of self-hatred, a simple exorcism of Proust's Judaism: "We can see here, for example, the desire to destroy, in the only way he knows how, that part of his nature that he claims to be the cause of all his misfortune: the deep and distant place of this mother, the Jewish place, which has determined his difference in advance" (*Proust antijuif*, 124).

50. I am referring to the title of Piperno's *Proust antijuif*.

51. It is interesting that several of the artist figures in the novel are Jewish or are associated in some way with Jewishness. One thinks here of Rachel, an actress, and Bloch, a playwright, but also of the more noble figures of the actress Berma (not specifically named as Jewish but modeled on Sarah Bernhardt) and the writer Bergotte, the Schlemihl, modeled in part on Henri Bergson (Proust's cousin).

Index

The authorized representative in the EU for product safety and compliance is:
Mare Nostrum Group
B.V Doelen 72
4831 GR Breda
The Netherlands

www.ingramcontent.com/pod-product-compliance
Lightning Source LLC
Chambersburg PA
CBHW020405100426
42812CB00001B/213

* 9 7 8 0 8 0 4 7 6 3 8 4 4 *